CAMP FLOYD
AND THE MORMONS

CAMP FLOYD
AND THE
MORMONS

THE UTAH WAR

Donald R. Moorman
with Gene A. Sessions

THE UNIVERSITY OF UTAH PRESS
Salt Lake City

© 1992 by The University of Utah Press. All rights reserved.
Preface © 2005 by The University of Utah Press

 The Defiance House Man colophon is a registered trademark of the
University of Utah Press. It is based upon a four-foot-tall, Ancient
Puebloan pictograph (late PIII) near Glen Canyon, Utah.

09 08 07 06 05   1 2 3 4 5

Library of Congress Cataloging-in-Publication Data

Moorman, Donald R., 1931–1980.
    Camp Floyd and the Mormons: the Utah War / Donald R. Moorman
with Gene A. Sessions.
       p. cm. — (Utah centennial series ; v. 7)
    Includes bibliographical references and index.
    ISBN-13: 978-0-87480-845-2
    ISBN-10: 0-87480-845-6
    1. Utah—History. 2. Mormons—Utah—History—19th century.
I. Sessions, Gene Allred. II. Title. III. Series.
F826.M66   1992
979.2'02—dc20   91–51098
                                                       CIP

Printed on recycled paper with 50% post-consumer content.

To my three sons:
Chuck, Jim, and Bruce

Donald R. Moorman
(1931–1980)

CONTENTS

FOREWORD

Statehood, which the series this volume is part of celebrates, is both a cherished expression of localism and a practiced relationship of American nationalism. In one of America's great success stories, states evolved through varying periods and conditions of territorial apprenticeship. For the original thirteen the training was in the colonial system of Great Britain and the crucible of revolution. For Texas and California it was through dramatic and dynamic experiences in the Republic of Texas, in the Mexican War, and in the early boom of the Gold Rush. Powered by fortuitous political and economic circumstances, other territories moved quickly and smoothly to statehood, while the territorial sojourn of still others continued for decades. Utah, a territory from 1851 to 1896, was among the latter. Indeed, few territories experienced stormier apprenticeships than did Utah where problems related to the practice of polygamy and the appropriate relationship between church and state complicated the transition to statehood.

Few events in America's long experience with territories involved a more dramatic statement of national control over the territorial learning process than did the "Utah War," which Professors Donald Moorman and Gene Sessions examine in *Camp Floyd and the Mormons*. Moorman first came to the work nearly a third of a century ago, bringing to his research and early drafts interests in frontier conflict and narrative treatment then current among western historians. His efforts were terminated by his untimely death in 1980. With help from his colleague Jerry Bernstein, who also died, Gene Sessions carried the study through final preparation for publication. The work is offered here as volume VIII in the University of Utah Statehood Centennial Series.

Camp Floyd and the Mormons is a study in Americanizing processes, couched in the broad social relationships and evolving

dynamics of frontier federalism. The role of the Mormons, as first
on the scene, and of the Utah War, as the vehicle which brought
new people, federal influence, and an Americanizing diversity to
the territory, are central to the story Moorman and Sessions tell
and hence give the book its name.

Simply stated, theirs is the story of how a United States army
came to Utah, and how that event ended the isolated and uncon-
ventional Mormon Kingdom. More than the Gold Rush before
and the railroad a decade later, indeed more than anything except
the radical reconstruction of the legislative and judicial raids of
the 1880s, the Utah War and the presence of an occupying force
at Camp Floyd helped bring the Utah/Mormon territory into the
American system.

Many of the questions asked about colonialism by the Revolutionary War and by the combined experience of the early territories were reiterated during the struggle. Problems later carried
full scale in the Civil War were rehearsed in microcosm. Cultural
issues, economic systems, racial relations (involving Indians and
not Blacks in this case), and the tension between central authority
and homerule submitted the nature of the Union to a close examination that had it not been for its proximity to the overshadow-
ing centrality of the Civil War might well stand even more promi-
nently in the annals of American constitutional history.

The hard issue at hand, the relationship of the metropolis to
the frontier, was quite as fundamental to the character of American federalism as was slavery although the stakes were obviously
smaller. As the Utah War turned out—in a powerful but unde-
clared victory for conventional Americanism—it was the product
less of specific territorial policy and Mormon resistance than of
the contending forces of democracy in an evolving context. Meeting a crisis of definition and integrity, President James Buchanan,
General Albert Sidney Johnston, Church President/Territorial
Governor Brigham Young, new Governor Alfred Cumming, Judge
John Cradlebaugh, freighter suppliers Russell, Majors and Waddle,
Chief Pocatello, and even "destroying angel" William Hickman
often worked beyond the established institutions of empire; but
safeguards built into the system worked ultimately to forestall both
the efforts to expand the meaning of self-determination and the
tyranny of the majority as Utah moved slowly towards statehood.

Although the Utah War was pre-empted by the oncoming
Civil War and by Abraham Lincoln's election, the seeds of resolution were sown between 1857 and 1861. Conventional gender
relations were strengthened, church involvement in affairs of state

was modified, Indian relations entered new and increasingly tragic phases, the use of the military for what were essentially domestic purposes matured, and the administrative, legislative, and judicial branches worked towards the dual adjustments in a maturing federal system.

As handled by Moorman and Sessions, *Camp Floyd and the Mormons* deals sympathetically with the Mormons yet applies the standards of a narrative frontier interpretation to them as well as to constitutional issues. The book throws new light on the army's role in the territory, on the exploration that made Salt Lake City a literal crossroads, and on life at the interior West's premier military installation, Camp Floyd, and in the neighboring Fairfield and other towns. It also put many issues—including transportation, communication, and traffic in merchandize and cultural interaction—in perspective. Finally, it offers restatements of the Mountain Meadows Massacre and of the period's judicial and administrative struggles, as well as giving close attention to frontier accounts of Indian wars, and to reports of the violence and lawlessness that boiled out of the City of the Saints as they did at other frontier centers. In its sensitive response to the early record and its concern for the spirit of the actors involved it lets one sense the dynamics of America's colonial system working its way on the frontier.

—Charles S. Peterson

PREFACE TO THE
PAPERBACK EDITION

When this book appeared in 1992, the historiography of the Utah War usually came down to writers reporting that "the best work on the subject remains Norman Furniss, *The Mormon Conflict* (1960)." Don would be disappointed to learn that authors continue to repeat that clichéd phrase in their footnotes to this day, often without mentioning *Camp Floyd and the Mormons.* Whether Furniss's excellent book really is still the best work on the subject does not matter and is in many ways immaterial, because Moorman's volume is truly unique in that it does not attempt to repeat the work of Furniss or anyone else.

Don labored for nearly two decades with primary sources to describe the whole cloth of the Utah War episode, and I believe deeply that he succeeded in many profound ways that another careful reading of his book has ratified in every particular. With a remarkably panoramic view, Moorman saw clearly the powerful clash of cultures that the coming of Johnston's Army wrought, and he saw it with surprising insight from both sides. Eschewing the temptation to take sides or to cast blame, Don left all the axes to those who would grind them. In the best tradition of the historian's demanding craft, he wrote a balanced narrative that he painstakingly compiled from the documents he read. Perhaps the best and most cogent example of this is in Chapter 7, "The Tragedy of Mountain Meadows." Moorman's modest attempt at retelling the tale had some advantages that not even the great Juanita Brooks (1950) enjoyed—namely, an apparently full access to Massacre-related holdings in the LDS Church Archives. As I reread the book this last time, I reconstructed in my mind the numerous times Don described to me his adventures during the 1960s in the bowels of the old Church Administration Building, where Joseph Fielding Smith and A. Will Lund watched over the contents of its dusty archives like wide-eyed mother hens. Smith and Lund told him that every primary document the Church possessed relative to the event resided in two cardboard boxes, which Don remembered had scrawled labels reading "Mountain Meadows Massacre File." He looked at every document in both containers. Later, he worried that much of that material and other stuff he had seen in the old facility had been "lost" when the archive moved to the new Church Office Building in the early 1970s and underwent a professional cataloguing and a resultant reshuffling into papers collections, usually under someone's name. He doubted that much if any of it had been confiscated for hiding, but he lamented that never again would old-fashioned researchers such as himself be able to peruse those documents with such ease. As a consequence of this remarkable information, I have to believe that the Gentile historian from Joliet, Illinois, may have been the only scholar in the last century to examine freely everything the Church had at the time relative not only to the Mountain Meadows Massacre but to all of the other subjects Camp Floyd investigates.

Beyond the Meadows, however, where does *Camp Floyd and the Mormons* take the reader that perhaps no other book does? Literally hundreds of scholars and others have written about life in nineteenth-century Utah, and why not? There is no other time and place quite like it. "The Great Basin Kingdom" of the Latter-day Saints presents historians, novelists, anthropologists, and an assortment of other writers with a fertile field of investigation. From polygyny to theocracy and everything in between, nineteenth-century Utah could not be more intriguing, but rarely does a scholar get under the surface of it all to come to a down-and-dirty comprehension of what it was really like. Thoughtful readers of *Camp Floyd* who venture into the deep waters of its story get an immersion into the insalubrious realities of 1850s Utah, both for Mormons and *uitlanders* alike. Readers learn about life on the Utah frontier the same way they might learn about living in turn-of-the-century urban America from reading Doctorow's *Ragtime,* but without the fiction writer's embellishments. One might argue that Moorman's propensity for dramatic phraseology pushes his work toward that of the novelist, but his strict adherence to the historical method and his careful documentation prove that the reader has been as close to being there as one can get without the use of a time machine. The "purple prose" just makes the sensations more palpable.

During this last reading of the book, I marveled at the very big story Moorman told in a few pages about only a few years of Utah history. In the midst of all the misunderstanding that existed between Mormons and Gentiles, the sometimes poignant interaction of the two groups revealed so much about both. From the lonesome teenaged soldier at Camp Floyd who wrote home just before he died about the filth and dust, the heat and cold, and the boredom of life in Cedar Valley, to the poverty-stricken women of the surrounding Mormon farms who could not find enough rags to care for their sanitary needs, the characters of the book pull readers into a world few can imagine or even hope to understand today.

Due to yellow-ribboned John Wayne movies, Americans see the history of the army in the West as a glamorous pageant of righteous Indian wars and the inevitable march of white civilization into a rugged but spectacular landscape. Concomitantly, during pioneer sermons and testimony-bearing every July, Latter-day Saints think they comprehend life in early Utah, because it seems that it was only getting "across the Plains" that was a problem. Neither mythology gets close to the starkness of scenes Moorman has painted with his deft historian's brush. For example, the reader smells the rotgut of the saloons that lined the streets of Frogtown as those odors mingled with the pungent aroma of poorly placed latrines across the street at the fort. A young soldier's encounter with Mormons returning from the Move South provides a similarly powerful sense of verisimilitude: "They...were wretched-looking beings— men, women, boys and girls, ragged and dirty, though some of the young girls had endeavored to make as respectable an appearance as possible, by making garments out of corn sacks." These views are a long way from what one might get from a seat in a movie theater or a comfortable pew in a modern Mormon church. Most Latter-day Saints would be startled to know the extent of rampant sinfulness in Salt Lake City just a decade after its founding as the new Zion. By the end of the 1850s, it had become a decidedly unsaintly city (as Moorman labels it in Chapter 13) that would rival any on the frontier for murder, thievery, prostitution, gambling, and drunkenness.

There is the old saying about how military service consists of moments of sheer terror and days of agonizing boredom. General Johnston had little of the former to offer his men, as the Utah War ended anticlimactically, and he knew the dangers of the latter, so he sent the troops out on various expeditions to deal with the Indians and to reconnoiter the region for future overland travel. Indeed, he had selected the site of Camp Floyd specifically because he believed it would sit astride the main transcontinental wagon road to California. So the men of Camp Floyd stayed relatively busy. Moorman's book leaves the unmistakable impression that their wide-ranging activities exacerbated the Indian problem rather then helping to solve it. The work also vibrates with the constant danger of open conflict, inasmuch as soldiers, whether on duty or not, constantly crossed paths with suspicious Mormons as both sides viewed every movement of the other as prelude to unacceptable aggression. Where other studies of the Mormon conflict have focused largely on causes and effects of the actual crisis of 1857–58, Don dealt with the whole of the experience, from the beginnings of the Utah Expedition to Camp Floyd-now-Crittenden's last day in 1861 as an outpost of the federal government in the Far West. Some of his most impressive work is in the last two chapters where he deals first with the lasting impact of the Utah War on the Mormon economy and then with the fate of those who served at Camp Floyd.

All of this is to suggest that Don Moorman's eighteen-year sortie into the Utah War has paid healthy dividends to those of us interested in Utah/Mormon history and the history of the American West. This is, however, not to suggest that his book is flawless. As I read it now, I discover many details and interpretations that my own studies would suggest are inaccurate. For example, I doubt the very existence of the infamous "Missouri Wildcats" who play such a prominent role in Don's chapter on the Mountain Meadows affair. But that is what makes history so fascinating and so alive. Until we can find that Wellsian time machine, we will have to rely on great craftsmen of history like my friend Donald Moorman to provide such wondrous glimpses into times long past and places forever changed.

Gene A. Sessions   April 2005

PREFACE 1992

In the Spring of 1980, my colleague and friend Don Moorman indicated to me that after eighteen years of painstaking research, writing, and revision on his manuscript on Camp Floyd he felt fairly comfortable with its form and hoped to have it finally ready for publication by the end of the year. A few days later, a persistent fever caused him to miss his first day of class at Weber State College in those same eighteen years. Shortly thereafter, his physicians informed him that he was suffering from lymphoma, a cancer of the lymphatic system. Six months later, after a temporary recovery and more work on the Camp Floyd manuscript, Donald R. Moorman died in Ogden at the age of forty-nine.

A native of Joliet, Illinois, Don came to the West to study the region's history after service in the Navy. Fascinated with the drama and pageantry of the American frontier, he completed his doctorate in western and southwestern history at the University of New Mexico and accepted a position at Weber State College, an institution in the throes of rapid growth as it graduated from a junior to a four-year college. Arriving in Utah, he became immediately intrigued with the state's history, and in particular the early struggles of its Mormon inhabitants to build a separate kingdom of God in the midst of the burgeoning American empire.

Within a few days of his arrival in Ogden, Don undertook an exploratory research trip to Salt Lake City where he quickly gained the confidence of those in charge of the archives at LDS Church headquarters. Despite his status as a non-Mormon scholar, he became first-name friends with Church Historian and Apostle Joseph Fielding Smith as well as with A. Will Lund, a guardian of the archives famous for his unapproachable manner and tight control of its resources. Don soon became a regular fixture in the Church

Historian's Office, habitually spending every Thursday (later Friday) poring through materials on early Utah history. He dreamed of producing at last the definitive scholarly biography of Brigham Young, but to satisfy an earlier interest in frontier forts, he planned in the interim to write a history of Camp Floyd and its effects on early Utah society. As it turned out, that interim project consumed his considerable intellectual energies literally for the rest of his life.

After Don's death, his colleagues in the Department of History at Weber State determined in consultation with his family to bring the Camp Floyd manuscript to publication. In the ensuing decade, other individual projects seemed constantly to keep Don's book on the back burner, although it was always in some stage of progress toward completion. Our first task was to try to determine which of the many revisions Don had made was the best, if not the last. At least ten different manuscripts existed in his papers, all basically similar and yet each signifying a different stage in Don's thinking and demonstrating his constant dissatisfaction with what had become his life's work.

Perhaps his closest associate in the department was Jerome Bernstein, whose wife Barbara possessed excellent skills as a writer and editor. So we turned the many manuscripts over to her. She labored for several months to combine them all into one final draft. At that point Jerry and I began a slow and constantly interrupted process of going through the manuscript page by page in an attempt to catch errors and inconsistencies, check notes, and try to recreate what Don had intended. As this work proceeded, we agreed that despite our labors the book would remain Don's, that we would resist the temptation to redo it according to our own understandings and predilections. For example, we contemplated changing the title to *The Mormons, Camp Floyd, and the Overland, 1857–61,* in order to reflect more accurately the scope of the work, but we decided to remain with Don's choice of *Camp Floyd and the Mormons.*

We had finished that long and intermittent task by the fall of 1988 and had handed the manuscript to a typist for putting into a word processor. By that time, Jerry had begun to experience weakness in his limbs and was diagnosed to be suffering from Lou Gehrig's Disease. He died in January 1990, but not before we had readied Don's manuscript for submission to a publisher. Only Don himself deserves more credit for this book than does Jerry. It is a monument to both of them, devoted historians and great storytellers, an unbeatable combination in their chosen profession.

What follows is a great story, told more in the tradition of mainstream nineteenth-century historiography than that of the current age. The reader will notice immediately Don's propensity for colorful language and his desire to convey all the pungent flavors of frontier America. The temptation has been great during the completion process to make of his work something beyond what he apparently intended. Although we felt free to revise for clarity and accuracy, we chose not to add to or subtract from the narrative in any significant way. Consequently, we made no attempt to update his sources with scholarship that has emerged since his death, nor to add lengthy sections of analysis to his text.

While critics may argue that this has limited the importance of this work to something less than it might have been, we would suggest that any other course of action on our part was impossible. Don was an intensely proud scholar who would have been unhappy with any distortion of his work. Our loyalty to him served as a constant sentinel as we undertook the privilege of "finishing" his book. This is truly Don Moorman's book. It represents his thinking, his point of view, and his notion as to the scope and significance of his subject. To modify it beyond minor adjustment would have violated that principle. In the final analysis, we feel comfortable and secure in presenting to the reader this work in a form we believe Don would have approved. In any case, *Camp Floyd and the Mormons* is a posthumous publication, and we have not attempted to make it into anything else.

Perhaps the most impossible part of this task is making an attempt at acknowledgments. No one but Don could begin to list all of the people who assisted him along the way. Certainly the members of his family deserve great credit, sacrificing along with him the many hours he spent in pursuit of the Camp Floyd story. Staff members in the LDS Church Historian's Office, later to become the Church Historical Department, undoubtedly earned many thanks from Don over the years, as did employees in other repositories he visited as he searched for the threads of evidence that he would combine to weave his tale. A host of clerks in the Department of History at Weber State College (now University) endured Don's exacting demands in retyping and reassembling the manuscript countless times. Dorothy Draney, department secretary during the final stages of Don's career, worked closely with him and deserves special mention as does LaRee Keller, secretary of the Faculty Senate at Weber State, who used both her clerical skills and her experience as a trained historian to work through the manuscript as she typed it into a word processor. In the final phases of production, Dean Richard Sadler of the College of Social and Behavioral Sciences at Weber State gave generously to assist us in bringing the manuscript to final form. Marsha Steele and Lesli Pantone assisted in the final revision of the manuscript following the able copy-editing of Richard Firmage. Lesli also assisted in the preparation of the index. Stan Layton, Charles Peterson, and Floyd O'Neil were among the last scholars to read the manuscript and offer suggestions for its improvement; they deserve credit for significant although subtle contributions to the final version. All of Don's other friends and associates who helped him and suffered with him during the work on *Camp Floyd and the Mormons* know who they are, even if, regrettably, the rest of us do not. I trust they will forgive the omission

If there is blame for shortcomings in this book, Don would happily absorb it and probably even enjoy it in his peppery and defiant way. But having spent a summer preparing the final draft, I must accept some of that responsibility and hope readers can forgive us both for whatever imperfections they may find.

Gene A. Sessions   3 November 1991

CAMP FLOYD
AND THE MORMONS

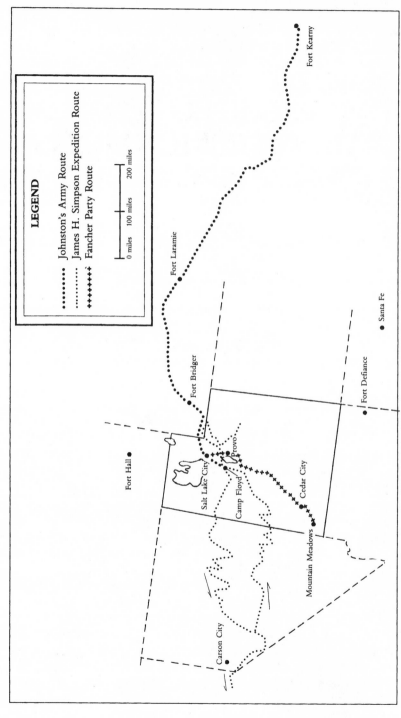

Map showing general route of Johnston's Army to Utah and site of Camp Floyd, as well as Fancher Party and Simpson Survey routes.

LEGEND

●●●●●●● Johnston's Army Route
·········· James H. Simpson Expedition Route
+++++++ Fancher Party Route

0 miles   100 miles   200 miles

Fort Kearny

Fort Laramie

Fort Bridger

Fort Hall

Salt Lake City

Provo

Camp Floyd

Cedar City

Mountain Meadows

Carson City

Santa Fe

Fort Defiance

CHAPTER ONE

THE GATHERING OF THUNDERCLOUDS IN THE EAST

The California mob came in today. The news is that the president of the U.S. is going to send on enough soldiers to kill all of the Mormons off.

—*Andrew J. Allen*[1]

A THOUSAND MILES from Fort Leavenworth, between the great granite fortress of the Rockies and the towering peaks of the Sierra Nevada, sprawls a distant and silent landscape torn by windswept mountains and parched wastelands—beautiful in its contortions and color, but always barren in its emptiness. This is Mormon country. After ten years in this distant desert (1847–1857), impoverished by drought, pestilence, and death, whether at the hands of the Indians or nature, the Mormons transformed the harshness of the frontier into an American saga. In this brooding solitude rose a religious community that maintained a balance between religious theocracy and paternal democracy, deeply embedded in its legendary sufferings and spiritual triumphs. In this same decade the mountain ranges swept the currents of history around the Mormons, and, except for the brief moment of the California gold rush in 1849, they went on taming the Great Basin wilderness, seemingly unaware of the great political events occurring across the continent.

But times changed. The bitter sectional differences that grew from the debates over the extension of slavery into the territories tore the nation apart in 1856 and could no longer be ignored; thus, with this accumulation of frustration, the slumbering "Mormon question" was drawn into sharp focus. Hysteria cast its false simplicity across the land, replacing the orderly constitutional process of democracy, and twisting national politics into strange and disturbing shapes. As the cry "free land and free soil" swept the remote western landscape, the long arm of fate stretched across the plains to bring relations between the federal government and the Saints to a breaking point. Considered by many to be alien in great part by birth, and entirely alien in religion, the Saints proved to be more foreign to many nineteenth-century Americans than were the inhabitants of the most remote continent. Eleven years after their exodus from Nauvoo, the time of isolation ran out for the Mormons.

The marked changes that neither Brigham Young nor most of his followers understood struck dramatically on the quiet morning of June 26, 1858, when a cavalcade of federal soldiers poured from the western slope of the mountains into the streets of Salt Lake City. With one broad sweep of its military fist, the federal government ended forever the Saints' dream of implanting a millennial society on the fringe of the frontier.

The bitter impasse that generated this unprecedented event had its roots in a uniquely American religion born in an age of hope; a religion that matured against a background of irrepressible conflicts, and that survived by placing a premium on obedience and loyalty to hard-visioned leadership. Driven successively from Ohio, Missouri, and Illinois, their ranks often divided against themselves, the Saints persevered in their dream of establishing a Utopian settlement apart from the mainstream of national society. Finding it impossible to realize these hopes along the frontier of the Mississippi Valley, they pursued their dreams westward in a new search for a promised homeland, ultimately settling in the Great Basin as a final haven against disaster.

The flight across the Great Plains, with its severe and sometimes fatal demands, united these zealots in a common bond of suffering that was capable of withstanding all but the most powerful of challenges. More than a thousand miles of wilderness trail, stretching from the Missouri River to the Great Salt Lake, was marked by graves belonging to this new breed of frontiersmen—monuments to Mormons seeking their New Jerusalem. From this suffering the mettle of Mormonism was fused. In the words of Wallace Stegner: "For every early Saint, crossing the Plains to Zion in the Valleys of the Mountains was not merely a journey but a rite of passage, the final, devoted, enduring act that brought one into the Kingdom."[2]

Upon the arid soil of the northern rim of the Mexican empire, they planted their first colony in 1847; and with the prophetic pronouncement of Brigham Young, "This is the Place," the new Zion was consecrated. Yet the appearance of the Saints in the Valley of the Great Salt Lake was only a part of the epic saga of western expansion, symbolized by the ringing watchword of Manifest Destiny—an "irresistible urge, inarticulate but almost instinctive, to occupy, develop, and make fruitful the empty lands beyond the frontier. . . ."[3]

Hidden deep in the Mormon conscience and in the mind of Brigham Young was the "Great Western Measure," a vague, undefined dream for developing the Kingdom of God in the vast retreat of the Rocky Mountains. Encouraged in this great adventure by the unexpected Mexican War that exploded on the Texas frontier, Brigham Young sent five hundred Mormon volunteers with the Army of the West under General Stephen Watts Kearny in the federal thrust across the Santa Fe Trail to San Diego to strengthen the Saints' claim to any territory that might fall in the conflict. The "Mormon Battalion" was to march through the upper provinces of Mexico where, in the words of Brigham Young, "they are to be disbanded at the expiration of one year from the day they leave Council Bluffs, receive the fit out pay of the regular soldier of the United States Army and equipment *GIVEN THEM* in addition that they may stay, look out the best location for themselves and friends and defend the country."[4]

Fully aware of the president's need for volunteer soldiers, Brigham Young hoped to take advantage of the situation. "The U.S. wants our friendship, the president wants us to do good and secure our confidence. The outfit of these 500 men cost us nothing and their pay will be sufficient to take their families over the mountains. There is war between Mexico and the United States to whom California must fall prey, and if we are the first settlers, the old citizens cannot have a Hancock or Missouri pretext to mob the Saints."[5] In a final stroke of diplomacy, Brigham Young bartered the Mormon volunteers for a federal government guarantee that the Saints would have the privilege of settling "anywhere they pleased" on unoccupied public domain.[6]

Although it was the ultimate judgment of history that the Mormon Battalion would have little influence on the outcome of the war, the dimensions of the difficult march to the western sea would be remembered by successive generations of Saints who would create a noteworthy dynasty of folk heroes from this military pilgrimage.

Mormon influence spilled into California in 1847 when the discharged members of the battalion elected to spend a season on the American River, near Sutter's Fort, until they were ordered to rejoin the main migration in their new home in Utah. Also, several small colonies of Saints radiated from Yerba Buena, having been delivered by the packet ship *Brooklyn* the previous summer and controlled by the colorful Samuel Brannan. Faced with a heavy immigration and a short harvest, Brigham Young advised destitute California Saints to winter on the Pacific shores, while the more financially able remainder were ordered to return immediately to the Great Basin to plant spring crops. A handful of Saints elected not to move eastward and lingered near the area where Sutter's superintendent, James Marshall, discovered gold. "This day some kind of mettle was found in the tail race that looks like goald," wrote Henry W. Bigler, a young battalion soldier.[7]

Seven hundred miles to the east, Brigham Young's vision of empire was no less dramatic than Sutter's. Yet he could hardly have failed to grasp the significance of the treaty of Guadalupe Hidalgo that ceded to the federal government all Mexican territory north of the Gila River, including the Great Basin. "It seems certain that when Brigham Young first stared at the sun-baked desolate valley," wrote one modern scholar, "his vision was not limited by its mountainous margins and great Dead Sea, but reached far beyond to an imagined encompassing empire of which the [Salt Lake Valley] would be but the nucleus."[8]

Unwilling to see what he considered the Mormons' religious birthright swept away by an accident of history, Brigham Young took advantage of congressional indecision over the fate of the Mexican Cession and gave notice that the Saints claimed the intermountain country as their own. By the spring of 1849, a convention was called to form the "State of Deseret," a name drawn from Mormon literature symbolizing the hard-working qualities of the ideal society. It was in one sense a natural creation, and the position of its capital at Fillmore, in the heart of the Great Basin, was symbolic of the Mormons' buoyant spirit of expansionism. The great inland desert empire was bordered on the north by the Columbia River, on the south by the Gila River, on the east by the Continental Divide, and on the west by the crest of the Sierra Nevada. To assure easy access to the western sea, a narrow corridor through El Cajon Pass was mapped to prevent the empire from being landlocked.

In theory, the territory's constitution provided a relatively stable and energetic government that guaranteed manhood suffrage, religious freedom, and free speech; yet in one important respect it differed from other provisional governments of the frontier. It established a Kingdom of God, a religious abstraction that fused temporal and spiritual powers in the hands of an intricately structured ecclesiastical organization over which Brigham Young exercised absolute power.[9] Critics of the Mormons, in fact, frequently charged that the new constitution left little room for popular rule and was nothing more than a calculated, secret political conspiracy to build a governmental structure around Brigham Young and the Council of the Twelve, a handpicked collection of the most important ecclesiastical men in the territory. Although Church leaders comprised only a small fraction of Utah's population, their detractors claimed that they controlled the major sources of wealth in the Great Basin—its virgin forests, grazing holdings, real estate, and Church spending. Without weighing this charge, it was nevertheless true that under Brigham Young's leadership the limited mercantile traffic was allowed to fall under the control of non-Mormons. A generation later the same fate would allow these Gentiles, as the Mormons called them, to monopolize the territory's mineral deposits of gold and silver.

The long struggle for statehood began in 1850 when Congress refused to ratify the constitution of the new State of Deseret as well as the vast areas claimed by its supporters. It was an ominous reminder to the Mormons that their political fortunes were to be darkened by the storm clouds that hung over the western territories. Overlooking the troublesome religious issue, President Fillmore signed into law the Omnibus Bill in the Compromise of 1850, reducing the State of Deseret to the status of a territory and stripping away its western corridor leading to California. Latent discords were present when Congress named the territory after the local Indians, much to the dismay of the Saints. No less forceful in its impact was the Mormon realization that the power to appoint territorial officials rested with the president of the United States, bringing the singularly menacing fear that Washington could transform the character of the territory's government with a single stroke of a pen. The Saints had reason for concern. Traditionally, territorial offices were a source of patronage, attracting men of limited political acumen who lacked specialized expertise or a seasoned understanding of the people they would govern. Consequently, they were quickly discouraged by low salaries, a hostile or indifferent population, and inadequate funding of territorial operations.

In Utah the tangled religious and political ideologies further threatened whatever harmony might have been anticipated between the government officials and the Mormons. Nevertheless, the creation of the new territory fell on the shoulders of President Millard Fillmore, who conciliated the Saints by naming Brigham Young as Governor and Superintendent of Indian Affairs; hence, "Deseret remained real for the Mormons even if unrecognized by the nation."[10] Counterbalancing this appointment, the president divided the remaining federal positions between Mormons and Gentiles, suggesting that patronage figured largely in the early organization of the territory and hinting that anti-Mormonism was strong in Washington. Consequently, the selections did not contribute to political stability in the territory, for the Saints' experiences in Missouri and Illinois left them basically suspicious of federal power and the officials responsible for its execution in Utah. As a result, when conflict broke out in 1850, neither side was prepared for what happened.

The appearance of the non-Mormon executive and judicial officers in the Great Basin sounded like an alarm in the night and revealed how deeply the seeds of dissension had penetrated the political soil of Utah. As a result, the careers of these federal officials followed a familiar pattern, beginning with an introductory phase of amicable relations with the Church that quickly degenerated into a period of acrimonious dispute. The Saints, antagonized and weary beyond measure by the federal officials' frank campaign to endow Mormonism with a secular social conscience, were not disposed to relinquish their control to the governmental partisans of Washington. Rightly or wrongly, the non-Mormons viewed the struggle as a powerful majority controlling a helpless minority. Enraged by what they then believed to be the lingering legacy of Brigham Young's authoritarianism, they left the territory armed with ominous complaints, each preparing the way for the destruction of Mormon sovereignty in the Great Basin. However, although the degree of prejudice to which these officials were subjected was somewhat exaggerated, there remains little doubt that had the Gentile officers been men of outstanding ability and discretion, which they were not, it is unlikely they would have received the full cooperation of the Saints. The situation was hardly better for sympathetic Gentiles, for they too soon ran afoul of the Church, setting the stage "for the first of many bitter battles between Mormon and federal appointees for control of Utah's government."[11] The verbal war between the federal judges and the Saints continued for seven years with no immediate victory for either side. During this drawn-out struggle two men were more reckless in their dislike of the Mormons than the rest—Perry E. Brocchus and William Wormer Drummond, both of whom entered the territory like armed gladiators.

From the very moment of his arrival in Utah, Perry Brocchus hardly fit the stereotype image of a stern hard-visaged territorial judge. In an age of dissolving political labels, Brocchus cultivated an expansive personality that appealed to the Saints, priding himself on his impeccable taste for vintage wine, fine food, and amiable companionship. A handsome and imposing man of fastidious habits, the associate judge suffered from partial deafness and, like others similarly afflicted, was inclined to hear only what he wished to hear. At times disarmingly charming, at other times bitterly sardonic, he possessed an abundance of energy. His face was marked by frequent brawls, for he often engaged his opponents with a quick resort to his fists.[12]

Thrust into political importance by Baltimore politics, Brocchus arrived in Utah during the summer of 1851 and watched the Mormon-Gentile struggles with mounting interest. Directing his own private investigation along a path well-trodden by anti-Mormons, Brocchus let himself believe that the territory was controlled by a tightly knit elite of wealthy churchmen through whom Brigham Young controlled the territorial legislature, as well as the municipal governments. After months of thought, he charged that the Mormon Church tenaciously asserted its sole right to pass upon a wide range of social legislation—censorship, marriage, birth control, and education—and showed no intention of relinquishing its grip. These and numerous other complaints found their way to Washington in a series of mischief-making letters addressed to the president.

Not content with fighting the Saints on secular matters, Brocchus waded into the troubled waters of religious reform. An opportunity presented itself the following fall when he requested the privilege of addressing the semiannual Church conference regarding a proposal to send a block of Utah marble as the territory's contribution to the building of the Washington Monument.[13] When the congregation assembled in the pavilion atmosphere of the Bowery, Brocchus drew the line tight for the coming battle, but neither he nor Brigham Young was prepared for what was to follow. With supreme arrogance and unmatched naiveté, the judge looked down his patrician nose at the women in the audience and launched a blistering attack against polygamy. "He spoke irreverently of that institution," wrote T. B. H. Stenhouse, a witness to the sermon, "going so far as to assure the ladies of its immorality, reproved the leaders for their desrespectful language concerning the Government and their consignment of President Zachary Taylor to the nether regions."[14]

No one who heard the judge's harangue doubted the meaning of his words—the Mormons were guilty of conspiracy, treason, and civil disobedience. The crowd looked shaken and anguished. Calming the audience, Brigham Young rose to answer the judge like a merciless avenging angel. Planting one hand on the podium and waving the other in threatening gestures, Young denounced the speech as an unmitigated piece of arrogance and demanded an apology. Hurrahs went out as he accused Brocchus of attempting to ride to political prominence at the expense of the Saints, a familiar theme that echoed around the careers of all Gentile officeholders. The judge turned away from the prophet and stormed out of the Bowery. After a heated exchange of letters with Brigham Young that accomplished little, Brocchus bade farewell to Zion. Other Gentile officeholders followed his example, leaving the Mormons and the federal courts decimated.[15]

Successors to these "runaway" officials, as the Mormons labeled them, fared no better in their attempts to secularize Utah; each returned to Washington with a welter of contradictory statements and fragments of evidence that charged the Saints with "lawlessness and seditious conduct." Throughout these recurring dramas, Washington remained unconvinced and refused to recognize the challenge of polygamy or other problems associated with the growing conflict. Yet, while these estranged officials accomplished little for themselves, they did draw public attention to the issue of polygamy and to what they regarded as Mormon disloyalty to the Constitution and the federal union.

The churning debate over federal control of Utah came to a head in 1855 with the ill-timed appointment of William Wormer Drummond to the territorial bench. No figure in the development of the Utah War proved to be more troublesome to the Saints than did this unknown midwestern attorney, and no man expended more effort working for Brigham Young's downfall. The most feared and in every respect the most awesome of the federal judges the Mormons faced, Drummond was born and educated in Virginia and moved to Illinois in 1838 where he received training in the law.[16] During this period he was regarded as a man of intrigue and controversy who could distinguish the reality of political power from its outward trappings. Ruthless, cold-blooded, and a clever gambler in political matters, he identified himself with the Democratic Party and was in a position to know the important men of his age, including Stephen A. Douglas, who secured his appointment to the Utah bench. But deeper and more difficult currents controlled the life of Judge Drummond. For all of his unquestioned abilities, he was tactless and overbearing, possessing a passion for serpentine cunning, liquor, harlots, and gambling—habits that eventually caused his undoing.

The worldly thirty-five-year-old federal judge arrived in Utah, after abandoning his wife and children in Chicago, sporting on his arm an attractive Washington prostitute, Ada Carrol. From the beginning, Judge Drummond's brief stay in Utah was a scandal. Indulging in excess at every opportunity, the incautious judge openly cavorted with his mistress in the territorial capital, even going so far as to permit her to share his judicial bench. One of the most revealing incidents in Drummond's life was told by Jules Remy, a French writer of note in Mormon history, who claimed that the judge boasted that money was his god and gambling his uncontrolled passion.[17] Unprincipled and devoid of honor, Drummond suspected that others were similarly inclined, and he offended the Mormons by his unsavory conduct behind the bench. Although the Saints denounced his unorthodox behavior, they tolerated his attacks and discriminatory taxes as long as he refrained from challenging the territory's laws governing local courts and polygamy.

Yet there was more than bacchanalian immorality that gave Drummond a prominent part in the Gentile-Mormon conflict in Utah. Standing firm, the federal judge challenged the political power of Brigham Young and the conservative territorial legislature. The fight between the combatants revolved around a number of issues, all closely related to the limits of the authority of probate courts, which had unlimited control over all matters relating to the administration of justice in the territory.

Although the conflict was sharpened by prejudice and inherited attitudes of distrust of both parties, Drummond viewed the struggle in simpler terms: Do the people of a territory have the right to establish inferior courts to circumvent the authority of the federal government as represented by its courts? The judge answered his own question by repudiating the Legislative Act of 1852 that granted Mormon-controlled probate courts original jurisdiction over both civil and criminal cases. Yet, not long before he had completed his term of office in the territory, Drummond realized that the prospect for breaking the judicial power of the Saints was bleak. Nevertheless, in a mood of political militancy, he "set aside all judgements rendered by probate judges, and annulled all their proceedings, except such as pertained to the usual and legitimate business of the probate courts."[18] The battle line was clear.

Aware of their inherent constitutional rights guaranteed them as American citizens, the Mormons pursued a scrupulous policy of refusing to bring federal cases before the Drummond court. In a new belligerent spirit, they accused the judge of adultery, of which there was no doubt, and claimed that he was using the probate court issue as a pretext to rupture relations between the Mormons and the federal government. Disregarding the real dangers inherent in his course, Drummond maintained his crusade against the probate courts until May of 1856. As the public clamor exploded around him, Drummond reluctantly journeyed to Carson Valley to convene the territorial court at the western edge of his district. After a brief and stormy court session, he continued to San Francisco where he launched his most severe attack against the Saints, filling the pages of newspapers with demands that they be brought up to the bar of judgment and condemned as traitors. After carefully considering his next step, the judge traveled to Los Angeles where he abandoned his mistress before embarking on a ship to New Orleans.[19]

During the voyage, Drummond painstakingly drew up his resignation, carefully cataloguing the events that had led him to abandon his territorial judgeship. His chief criticism centered on Brigham Young, not because Drummond had quarreled regularly with the religious leader, but because Young symbolized the monolithic structure of the Mormon Church. The federal courts were hopelessly inadequate, he warned, for the political regime permitted no open opposition. The federal judges could not carry out their duties without arousing suspicion, he continued, adding that secret groups of

destroying angels made life in Utah one long nightmare. In his zeal to
damage the reputation of Brigham Young, he recklessly charged the
Church leader with treason, with destroying numerous government
records, and with a series of ruthless acts against American citizens
that exhausted the tolerance of non-Mormons.[20] It was an extraordinary document, aimed at drawing the immediate attention of newspapers.[21] Drummond's message was intriguing and appealed to the prej-
udices of nineteenth-century Americans, easily aroused against the
moral evil of polygamy and its twin specter, slavery. Arriving in New
Orleans by mid-March, Drummond swelled arrogantly, publicly
advertising what he considered his major triumph over the Saints in
Utah. But the judge did not leave the matter there, for he saw new and
grander possibilities. Among the men with whom Drummond found
common cause was a reporter for the *New Orleans Courier* who interviewed the judge and subsequently published an account of their
meeting. The exiled judge spun his own version of his quarrel with the
Mormons. In part the story read:

> A leading characteristic of the followers of the Mahomet seems
> to be a settled and abiding hatred of all "Gentiles," as they are
> pleased to style all who do not subscribe to their dogmas and
> conform to their unique and revolting creed. Although they come
> mainly from the northern portion of this republic they look upon
> the United States with no other feeling than hatred. Patriotic love
> of the country which gave them birth, and which they disgrace,
> has no place in their bosoms. . . .
> Could a correct side of those horrible transactions be known
> throughout the country, a crusade would be preached against this
> foul horde that would soon put an end to their sway.[22]

With those words, Drummond left New Orleans; but before he
reached Chicago, he had learned a great deal more about the power of the
press. "I have stirred the waters of the Saints and shall keep up the war in
all time to come," he bluntly boasted to a friend. "A new Goverment and
Military aid will be sent to Utah now mark it, and Brigham will starve
from under the appointments of the Federal Government." Demonstrating a wistful yearning for public office, he continued, "I may go to Utah
as Governor if so look out for a merry time. I will take it with military
aid."[23]

Drummond's widely heralded statements struck the Mississippi Valley like a thunderbolt, exploding into print a barrage of journalistic insanity wherever they appeared. Support for his assessment of the Utah situation flooded the newspapers, an example of which follows:

> I was glad to see in this morning's issue, the letter of W.W.
> Drummond, late Chief Justice of Utah, and am glad to see you

taking the lead in calling on the present administration to put a stop to the hitherto unchecked career of crime and treachery so openly practiced in that God-forsaken country.

I crossed the plains on my way to California, in 1850, and spent several weeks in that Great Salt Lake City and had unusual opportunities to witness the in and outdoor life of the Mormons. I do not think that Mr. Drummond has told all. Polygamy was practiced at that time by every man in the valley, and I was personally acquainted with one who had a woman and four daughters, the youngest scarcely fifteen years of age, sealed to him, as they express it. They do indeed regard us of the States as their bitter foes, and he who hails from Missouri, Illinois, or Ohio, is sure to be reminded of Independence, Nauvoo, and Kirtland, and on that account refused the necessities of life. When I wished to purchase flour I could not get it because I hailed from Ohio, but had to get a Pennsylvanian to purchase for me. When Brigham Young heard how the emigrant from the three obnoxious States procured their flour and provisions he said in public speech "he would sooner see any Gentile from the States buried deep in hell before he would relieve him from starving; let them all die the death of dogs." My California friends who were in Salt Lake in July, 1849, will never forget that speech and the base passions it aroused against the emigrants.

To it I attribute the terrible suffering on the Humboldt River and the desert, which decimated the unfortunate sufferers. Although now surrounded by every comfort, I can never rest satisfied, until the ulcer of corruption called Salt Lake City is cut out of the bosom of North America, and [all] of it are obliterated. Every train started from Salt Lake unprepared to meet the terrible desert which separate it from the Sierra Nevada. Tongue can never tell, nor openly describe the terrible sufferings on that river of hell, as the Humboldt is aptly called, starting as it does near the Salt Lake, and sinking into subterranean salts on the desert. Many acquaintances remained over winter in Salt Lake, not able to procure provisions; their fate God only knows and many started for California to perish on the roadside rather than remain with the troops at Salt Lake. . . .[24]

The Mormons watched the spreading contagion with growing alarm. The reactions of others were often similar: "A stagecoach operator who had lost his mail contract to a more efficient Mormon contractor charged they were plotting to kill all Gentiles; an Indian agent on the Upper Platte hinted that the red-men were being armed to aid in the massacre."[25] Drummond's calculations bore fruit when the newspapers along the frontier closed ranks to charge that the Mormon-dominated territorial government was suffering from an incurable illness: "A festering mass of corruption," cried George W. Brown, editor of the Lawrence, Kansas, *Herald of Freedom*.[26]

Once more the devil was waving his scepter over the Republic, wrote Brigham Young to George Taylor and others:

> The North, the South, the East, the West, the Politicians, the Priests, the Editors, and the hireling scribblers all take up the cry for blood! blood! blood! Exterminate the Mormons, that is sweep them from the Earth, go to their mountain home, lay waste their cities, destroy their crops, drive off their stock, raze their dwelling to the ground, cause an innocent people to flee for safety and then return and gloat over the misery we have caused.[27]

Beneath the surface of Drummond's center-stage performance, other currents moved. Brigham Young viewed with mounting apprehension the unexpected popularity of the judge in the divided political circles of Washington.

> It seems that the press at least have been most effectually hum-bugged by the fellow Drummond and some two or three irre-sponsible and anonymous letter writers in this city. Were we not used to such things we might be surprised at the mass of rubbish that found its way here by the two mails. . . . I shall not notice them, but I confess that I feel amused the humbug offenses so complete, wonder if the press will acknowledge themselves duped when Drummond gets up where they can look at him. It proves that we were correct in our conclusions last winter when we regarded the non-resident officers as using all their influence to create a disturbance between us and the government, truly the press has sent its most efficient aid to accomplish this thankless task. We look, for a reaction, when they find that Mormon oppres-sion has pressed them out—the truth is they had made their false statements and expecting they might be published and fled for fear of the report which might come by the mail.
>
> They did not know which end of the gun they loaded would shoot the hardest; therefore, they left in time. Their humbug do not disturb me, their troops will find nothing to fight if they come, as is threatened. There has been no disturbance here, all is peace and quietness.
>
> We are fearful that the government is not willing to restore their favorite doctrine of popular sovereignty to Utah but are desirous of abandoning themselves of the present fervor all of which I need not tell you are foul and malignant falsehoods all for good of his Saints.[28]

As a catalytic agent, Drummond had a profound effect in determining the beginnings of the Utah War; yet the far-reaching conflict cannot be attributed to any single cause or explained by any simple formula. On the national scene, the cancerous issue of slavery no doubt helped to precipitate the disaster. The contest over the admission of Kansas into the Union divided the nation more than any other issue. Both militants and political moderates searched for alliances that would swing the balance of power in their direction; overnight the prairie territory became a neutral ground where the first blood of the Civil War was spilled. The shadow before this tragedy, the Kansas-Nebraska Act, gave direct impetus to the rise of the Republican Party, which in the election of 1856 committed itself to the abolition of the "twin relics of barbarism: slavery and polygamy." Flexing its political muscle in the election of 1854, the fledgling party had tried in vain to force military intervention in Kansas. During this troubled period of unceasing agitation over home rule in Kansas, the Democrats were torn apart by indecision, further fracturing the already splintered party.

In the struggle that preceded the election of 1856, Republicans shared a common hope—to discredit Buchanan for not openly denouncing plural marriage and to prevent the further extension of slavery in the territories. Brigham Young did not overestimate the importance of this issue:

> I might enumerate injuries by scores. And if these things are not so, why is it that Utah is so knotty a question? Why could Drummond and a lot of other mean scribblers palm their infamous slanders swallowed with such gusto? Was it not that by Administration, as their satellites, having planned our destruction, were eager to catch at anything to render specious their contemplations of blood; or in plain terms the Democrats advocated strongly popular sovereignty. The Republicans tell them if they join in maintaining inviolable the domestic institutions of the South, they must also swallow polygamy. The Democrats thought this would not do, as it would interfere with the religious scruples of many of their supporters, and they looked about for some means to dispose of the question. Mr. Buchanan, with Messrs. Douglas, Cass, Thompson and others, after failing to devise measures, put upon the expedient of an armed force against Utah, and thus thought, by a sacrifice of the Mormons, to untie the knotty questions. Yes, by destroying or killing a hundred thousand innocent American citizens, to satisfy the pious, humane and patriotic feeling of their constituents, take the wind out of the sails of the Republicans and gain to themselves immortal honors.[29]

The South, for its part, stood at the crossroads of indecision, its leadership badly split over the Mormon question. In the rapidly changing political climate, many Southern leaders believed that the theory of popular sovereignty should be applied to polygamy; and that the complicated moral question of plural marriage, like that of slavery, should be left to the people of the territories. In short, the South reasoned, the Mormons championed states' rights. On the other hand, a small but articulate minority of Southern congressmen supported federal military intervention to protect slavery in Kansas if necessary.[30]

Four months after the explosive campaign of 1856, the presidency passed from Franklin Pierce, a nominal friend of the Mormons, to James Buchanan. The Saints, as a group, saw nothing ominous in the rise of the new president. Quite to the contrary, they remembered him as a senator from Pennsylvania who had befriended Joseph Smith during the periods of recurring violence in Nauvoo.[31] But as the great restless question of slavery became more widespread and a subject of national articulation, a new man emerged from the figure of James Buchanan.

Inaugurated as the fifteenth president of the United States at age sixty-six, Buchanan was one of the oldest men to live in the White House. As a middle-of-the-road former farm boy from Mercersberg, Pennsylvania, Buchanan worked hard at being a Federalist but later moved into the Democratic Party after opposing Federalist protests to the War of 1812. Affable and confident, with a flair for identifying himself as a national rather than a sectional candidate, he was a gifted debater and learned in the law, talents that allowed him to rise rapidly in politics by understanding both sides of any issue without committing himself to either position. As a political moderate, he was an acceptable candidate to both the North and the South. Well-meaning, he was not the sort of man "who could personally attract a large following and was often the victim, rather than the mover of events."[32] Although no president came to office so eminently qualified by long years of public service, Buchanan was destined to follow the shooting star of slavery into political oblivion.

In the rising crisis, Buchanan, a strict Constitutionalist who believed that the peaceful abolition of slavery was impossible, tried in vain to stem the tide of secession by appealing to the distraught nation to support the Union, its courts, and federal laws. While spectacular events in Kansas pointed more and more to territorial anarchy and civil war, he expressed deep concern over both fire-eaters in the South and anti-slavery Republicans in the North, and he was determined to stop the growing infection of sectionalism. In a remarkable progression of logic, Buchanan proposed not to destroy slavery but to end all agitation over its extension—then, hopefully, the growing confrontation would pass.

In his inaugural address, Buchanan ignored the Mormon question, repeatedly pledging that he would remove the Kansas issue from politics; but the sweep of events carried the president into uncertain channels. Drummond's sudden and dramatic resignation came at a moment when the president suspected that a coalition of anti-Mormon adversaries, pro-slavery congressmen, and abolitionists would force the issue of armed intervention in the territories, especially Kansas and perhaps Utah. As an ugly symptom of his frustration, the president issued secret military orders directing General Winfield Scott to collect an army to march against the Mormons. Utah would serve as a testing ground to reassert federal control over a region claiming nominal independence from the Union. As a last threat to extremists in both parties, the president was prepared to use force to prevent the self-destruction of the Republic. At the same time, it is highly doubtful that Buchanan reached such a decision without first consulting close friends within the Democratic Party.

A glimpse at some of the advice he received is revealed in a letter from Robert Tyler, the son of the tenth president of the United States and a well-known friend and political ally of Buchanan. "The public mind is becoming greatly excited on the subject of Mormonism," wrote Tyler. "The popular idea is rapidly maturing that Mormonism (already felt slightly in our large Northern cities) should be put down and utterly extirpated." The debate over slavery in the territories could be superseded by the excitement of an anti-Mormon crusade, he added. "Certainly it is a subject which concerns all the religious bodies and reached every man's fireside with particular interest. Should you, with your accustomed grip, seize this question with a strong fearless and resolute hand, the country I am sure will rally to you with an earnest enthusiasm and the pipings of Abolitionism will hardly be heard amidst the thunders of the storm we shall raise." Neutrality, as far as the Mormon problem was concerned, was no longer feasible, for the followers of Brigham Young could not be defended by the laws of conscience, reason, or philosophy, the young Democrat pleaded. "The eyes and hearts of the Nation may be made to find so much interest in Utah as to forget Kansas." This letter, so outrageous in its attempt to pander to religious prejudice, cast deep shadows over the history of the Buchanan administration and the political destiny of the Saints in Utah.[33]

The first wave of rumors recounting Buchanan's actions reached the territory one month before the first soldiers gathered at Fort Leavenworth when William I. Appleby, editor of *The Mormon*, rushed a dispatch from New York to Brigham Young alerting him to the president's decision. "A few days since Gen. Scott, issued his orders directing General Harney to leave Florida where he is at present and move to Fort Leavenworth, and several other officers, with their companies some to proceed to Fort Kearny, others to Fort Laramie; while others were to move along the Platte River, with mules, horses, etc., there to receive their instructions the whole amounting to some 2500 men." The information was based on a conversation with James Gordon Bennet, the editor of the *New York Herald*, who was considered by friends of the president to be one of the "greatest knaves" who ever lived. The newspaper man guessed correctly that "it is the intention of the Government to send them to Utah and appoint a Governor to follow."[34] The statement warned that Buchanan had decided to settle the Mormon question by appointing not only a new governor, but also a complete slate of non-Mormon officials who were to be escorted into the territory by the army. "All hell appears to be wide awake, against us," wrote George A. Smith to Brigham Young, "the press is doing its wickedest, Drummond is one of the most popular men in the nation at present. . . ."[35]

With these words still echoing in his mind, Brigham Young weighed three possible courses of action—stand and fight, allow the army to occupy the territory, or abandon the territory to the army, leaving behind the labor of ten years. Once again the Mormons took their place at the crossroads of history, led by one of the most powerful and enigmatic figures in American history. In retrospect it is difficult not to admire Brigham Young, a towering legend in his own time who, like the vast majority of the Saints, had his mind wrapped around the roots of religious consciousness. In common with many folk heroes of his age, he was viewed with ambivalence by his friends and enemies alike, and stood in the center of the major controversies in the political, economic, and religious history of Utah during his lifetime and for a generation following his death in 1877. Resolute in a stubborn sort of way when he was sure he was right, Brigham Young had a cool, watchful temperament, a splendid memory, and a sharp political intelligence. He came to symbolize the most revered as well as disliked qualities of the Mormon temperament.

A cadenced yet charismatic speaker whose passionate words swelled and broke over his audience like a thunderclap, Brigham Young was keenly aware that history was focused on him, and never doubted his destiny as a star of the first magnitude in the West. Yet his beginning gave little hint of the brilliant career that was to follow. Born in Whitingham, Vermont, three months after the presidential inaugural of Thomas Jefferson sounded throughout the land, he followed the crowded dreams of a carpenter, cabinetmaker, and painter, during which time he learned the rudiments of grammar and a smattering of mathematics. But most important was religion, which found direction when he encountered the mind of Joseph Smith, Jr.—perhaps the most important single event in Brigham Young's life. The Mormon prophet infused into his followers a deep religious purpose that rested in part on principles that closely interwove theology and politics. A convert to Mormonism in 1832, Young became one of its strongest defenders. Traveling throughout England and the eastern part of the United States spreading his newfound gospel, the missionary returned to Nauvoo at the death of the prophet—a move that was to have far-reaching consequences. A man uncorrupted by power or wealth, Brigham Young was destined, as head of the Council of Twelve Apostles and by a series of uncontrolled events, to become second president of the Latter-day Saints, and to assume the role of a Mormon Moses chosen by God or fate to lead his people through the wilderness.

An eastern correspondent visiting Utah in 1856 described Brigham as a heavy-set man with an imposing figure: "He had a strong determined face, stood slightly under six feet tall, with light blue eyes, sandy hair, well perfumed and combed, a large stocky body weighing over two hundred pounds which grew more portly each year from want of physical activity."[36] At fifty-six he habitually wore a black suit, a white cravat, a fashionable black hat, black cotton gloves, and knee-length boots and sported a large gold-headed cane. Yet his manners and speech were always overlaid with frontier coarseness.

In a period of swirling currents that threatened to destroy men and their age, Brigham Young imparted to the Mormon Church an aura of solidarity, based on a great popular backing of his people that was unequaled in Utah history. His actions were dynamic and persuasive, his judgment of men penetrating, his mind keen, his courage immense; and, like other strong leaders, he had an expansive personality that appealed to the essentially parochial mind. Order was his passion, and work formed the backbone of his character. As the most brilliant American colonizer of the nineteenth century, he had the capacity to inspire limitless devotion or unspeakable contempt, a result of an unbending iron will that brooked little opposition from his followers, and even less from his enemies. In short, "he was a man who could both demand and receive unquestioning obedience and one whose performance inspired confidence."[37]

His long shadow was cast across thirty years of territorial history; he molded the Mormon people and their institutions as no other man save the founder and first prophet of the Mormon Church. "Feared with a stronger fear, venerated with a more national veneration, but not loved with the same clinging tenderness that the people still felt for Joseph Smith," wrote John Hyde, Jr., an apostate elder who had bolted the church in 1856, "Brigham swayed the Saints to his will." Friends and enemies alike "learned to dread his iron hand; and were daunted by his iron heart."[38] Yet to a marked degree, an extremely important element in Brigham Young's personality was his intense loyalty to his friends, whose reputations he staunchly defended although evidence at times suggested he should have done otherwise.[39] But there was another pivotal part of his makeup—he held in common with other frontiersmen a suspicion of doctors, lawyers, and government officials, crucial attitudes that helped shape the important events during the early months of 1857.

The long spring silence from Washington gave way to summer, and with it a bewildering flutter of reports from the frontier hid from Brigham Young the activities of the Utah Expedition stationed at or near Fort Leavenworth. Meanwhile, arrangements were in full swing for the Saints' celebration of their tenth anniversary in the Great Salt Lake Valley. Everything had been planned on a grand scale. Thus, as the long procession of celebrating Mormons moved into Big Cottonwood Canyon throughout the week that ended on July 24, 1857, Brigham Young and his trusted lieutenants put aside their thoughts of the impending crisis to join in the summer holiday.

Establishing camp on the shores of Silver Lake, the Mormons played that morning in much the same fashion as in the past, unaware that their fate was about to be drastically altered. It was in this setting that four horsemen galloped into camp, sending clouds of dust over small clusters of people huddled here and there. Moments later the travel-stained riders—Abraham O. Smoot, Mayor of Salt Lake City, Postmaster Judson Stoddard, Probate Judge Elias Smith, and Orrin Porter Rockwell—stopped beyond the reception tent where Brigham Young and a half-dozen citizens came up and greeted them.[40] Ushered into a small clearing, the four horsemen reported that somewhere between Fort Leavenworth and Fort Laramie twenty-five hundred troops were marching against the Saints.[41] Later that afternoon Brigham Young assembled the leading elders of the Church and calmly repeated the ominous message. Under these circumstances, Daniel H. Wells, Commander of the Nauvoo Legion (the territorial militia), announced to the gathered multitude the approach of the federal forces; but the Saints received the serious news of the crisis quietly. "They renewed their dancing in the boweries," remarked one spectator, " satisfied that the angels had charge concerning them."[42] The Mormons broke camp the following morning at daybreak to retrace quietly their steps through the canyon. As more bad news poured in, the leaders of the territorial militia closed ranks and returned to Salt Lake City to await further instructions from Brigham Young.

War was literally declared the following Sunday when the Saints filed into the Tabernacle to hear Brigham Young deliver the formal announcement of President Buchanan's decision. Understanding how deeply slavery had entered into all aspects of territorial politics, he claimed that Utah was being made a scapegoat for the disaster that was sweeping through Kansas: "James Buchanan has ordered this Expedition to appease the wrath of the angry hounds who are howling around him. But woe, woe to that man who comes here unlawfully to interfere with me and this people." To these words he added: "According to their version, I am guilty of the death of every man, woman, and child that had died between the Missouri River and the California gold mines; and they are coming here to chastise me. The idea makes me laugh; and when do you think they will get a chance? Catching is always before hanging."[43]

The dark events of Missouri and Illinois shadowed every word voiced by the prophet and other speakers who followed. Heber C. Kimball, Brigham's closest associate and counselor, recalled ten years of continuous persecution, the frenzy of slaughter at Haun's Mill, Missouri, and the smashed homes and belongings that were left in its wake: "I have been driven five times, been broken up and my goods robbed from me, and I have been afflicted almost to death," spoke the Apostle. "I feel to curse my enemies, and when God won't bless them I do not think he would ask me to bless them; if I did it would be to put the poor curses to death who have brought death and destruction on me and my brethren, upon my wives and my children that I buried on the road between the states and this place. . . ." Of the federal force, he warned, "God almighty helping me, I will fight until there is not a drop of blood in my veins."[44]

The Saints girded themselves for battle. In an emotionally charged directive to his district military commanders, General Daniel H. Wells made no secret whatever of his attitude toward the government and its federal army. "In such time, when anarchy takes the place of orderly government and mobocratic tyranny usurps the power of rulers, they, the Saints, have . . . the inalienable right to defend themselves against all aggression upon their constitutional privilege."[45]

With the Saints fully aroused, Brigham Young erected a human wall of soldier-settlers to bar the federal army from entering the territory; overnight the muster rolls of the Nauvoo Legion swelled from several hundred volunteers to a force of more than five thousand men.[46] Each city, village, and hamlet had its self-sufficient local militia, led by a junior officer who operated under the commander of the land forces. As a general rule, many of the men were without military experience while the officer corps was drawn from the ranks of the religiously important. Few of the volunteers were uniformed. Rather, the Mormon army dressed in the costume of the frontier with rough leather shoes or buffalo boots; rolled bedding was slung over their shoulders, and a wide assortment of hats completed their appearance. Rifles were carried in hand and pistols tucked in their belts or in homemade holsters, for both officers and men were expected to arm, equip, and feed themselves. Nevertheless, the needs of the Mormons were great, both in weapons and equipment. As the storms of winter gathered, two arsenals were established in Salt Lake City to produce rifles and pistols. A correspondent for the San Francisco *Herald* reported: "I visited the arsenal, found they had a fair display of artillery. I also visited their public and private workshops, saw them casting cannon-shot, and manufacturing grape and canister in great abundance, and some fifty men making Colt's dragoon-size revolvers."[47] Arms and ammunition were smuggled into Utah in a variety of ways or purchased from passing emigrants; nevertheless, an important weakness in the Legion was the lack of artillery. As a result, the battle for the territory was to be determined not by guns but by an efficient home military organization operating on terrain unfamiliar to the invaders.

Basically, Mormon strategy called for the defense of all heights overlooking the landward approaches funneling through Echo Canyon, a task that proved formidable even to the most optimistic observer. Between the Rockies and the Sierras, Utah lay exposed to attack from the north and

west, while to the south the Virgin River flank was vulnerable to a threatened invasion from California. Believing, however, that the federal army
would launch its attack only from the high plains, Brigham Young
ordered the colonies along the Sierras abandoned, and their settlers were
instructed to hurry east to prepare for the defense of Utah.

Meanwhile, a small but efficient band of Mormon rangers made its
way across the overland trail to determine the position of the advance
guard of the army. Approaching Pacific Springs, a short distance west
from South Pass, they located the federal forces carefully plodding their
way toward the Rockies. It was here they noted that the army formed a
line that stretched endlessly across the plains. Turning down an obvious
invitation to fight, the Mormons raced to Fort Bridger, advance headquarters of the Legion, where they reported the size, disposition, and
strength of the Utah Expedition.

Events were moving like a prairie fire. Brigham Young wrote to
George Q. Cannon, editor of the San Francisco *Standard*:

> The Government have at last hit upon the long sought-for plan
> to extinguish "Mormonism." What that plan is we can form no
> idea except from the effects growing out of it, which are these; one
> Mr. Cummings of St. Louis, Mo. is appointed Governor, a fellow
> by the name of Morrel is Post Master, besides the list contained a
> Secretary, Judges, U.S. Marshall, and Surveyor and Attorney Gen-
> erals, all of course from the ranks of our most bitter enemies. Then
> there are 2500 regulars coming with them as a body guard to
> execute their commands, to sustain them in their exalted posi-
> tions.[48]

The officers and men of the army were especially eager to hang several
dozen Mormon leaders, Brigham wrote in a letter of the same date to
Silas Smith, F. D. Richards, and Edward Partridge: "It is reported that
amongst the Officers; it is a query whether they will hang me with or
without a trial. The idea prevails generally amongst the editors that the
real object of the expedition is to kill Mormonism partly by hanging the
authorities here, and partly by working upon the fears of the masses."[49]

As Mormon fears intensified during the second week of September,
Captain Stewart Van Vliet, assistant quartermaster for the Utah Expedition, rode into Salt Lake City escorted by two Mormon rangers, Bryan
Stringham and Nathaniel V. Jones.[50] The scene was barely believable. And
it was likely that Van Vliet thought so too, for throughout his career the
captain had developed an unflagging sympathy for the Saints. Although
politics and duty pushed Van Vliet into this unwelcome assignment, he
understood the Mormon temperament and was considered by the people
as one of a dozen military men who avidly championed their cause within
the army. Months of idleness and living on subsistence rations made the

captain appear leaner than Brigham Young had remembered him at Winter Quarters: "Less than ten years ago, if I remember correctly, he was then officiating as Assistant Quartermaster; he is again in our midst in the capacity of Assistant Quartermaster," explained the prophet to his close advisors. "From the day of his visit to Winter Quarters many of this people have become personally acquainted with him." Reflecting on earlier times, the Church president found little that he did not like in Van Vliet's character. "He has invariably treated them [the Mormons] kindly, as he would a Baptist, a Methodist, or any other person, for that is his character. He has always been found to be free and frank, and to be a man who wished to do right and no doubt would deal out justice to all, if he has the power."[51]

As Brigham Young's office filled up with his deputies, the captain handed him a secret communication, dated July 28, 1857. The message stated that the government had reorganized its western districts by creating several new departments, including Utah, and planned to establish a military camp in the vicinity of Great Salt Lake City.[52] It was the captain's mission, the letter explained, to determine what supplies were available in the territory to feed and house the soldiers of the expedition. Under close questioning Van Vliet disclaimed in a ponderous but professional manner any knowledge that President Buchanan considered the Mormons to be in a state of rebellion. He was simply a soldier of the American government operating under the instructions of his superior officer.

The atmosphere grew tense as Brigham Young reduced his thoughts to the nondiplomatic language of a threatened warrior and overruled any cooperation with the government. The Saints would not furnish provisions; furthermore, if the army persisted in occupying the territory, the Mormons were prepared to destroy the army or be destroyed themselves. Then in a tone of deep emotion and bitterness, he added: "There shall not be one building, nor one foot of lumber, nor a stick, nor a tree, nor a particle of grass and hay that will burn, left in reach of our enemies."[53] Captain Van Vliet braced himself for further difficult negotiations; meanwhile, the Saints continued to pursue a collision course with the army.

While wild rumors circulated in the city about the talks, Brigham Young dispatched an express rider to Cache Cave, the Mormon command headquarters in Echo Canyon, with orders directing the Nauvoo Legion to bring pressure to bear on the army before it reached Fort Bridger. The plan was a simple one. "If the forces show a determination to come in after the Captain has passed them," Brigham Young wrote to his officers in the field, "pitch on to the animals whenever and wherever you can safely do so and not be seen by them, do the night work on them this we think will stop them for this fall and no blood shed, a collission [sic] is to be avoided."[54] The struggle for Utah thus began.

Returning to the conference table, Brigham Young prolonged negotiations with Van Vliet for six days. After an interlude of cat-and-mouse exchanges that ended in a hard standoff, Captain Van Vliet warned that it would be wise for Brigham Young to accept the government's pro-posal—mainly because the Saints could not hold back the army near Fort Bridger, nor the reinforcements that were sure to come. Brigham Young went silent. The Mormons would promise nothing except to throw their support to anyone who promised them peace. Everyone in Salt Lake breathed a sigh of relief when the captain retraced his steps east through the mountains accompanied by John M. Bernisel, Utah's delegate to Congress. Nathaniel V. Jones, Stephen Taylor, and two Mormon dra-goons were ordered to guide the captain and his men through Mormon lines to assure their safe passage to the army's encampment.

With his path now clearly before him, Brigham Young placed the territory under martial law. Raw and unfinished, like the temple founda-tion now buried under a mound of straw and dirt, the territory braced itself for the expected assault by federal warriors storming toward Zion.

CHAPTER TWO

MARCH TO THE RIVER JORDAN

Those who oppose the military expedition upon humanitarian grounds, in reality do the Mormons no service, for in Missouri, Kansas, and the States of the northwestern frontier there is a deep-seated feeling of exasperation towards the Saints, which will be likely to break out in a ward of extermination, unless the government should check and restrain the latter by the strong arm of civil law sustained and enforced, as alone it can be, by military power.
                                        —New York Times[1]

COLONEL EDMUND BROOKE ALEXANDER, a fifty-four-year-old regular army officer who would have preferred to serve out his enlistment in the warmth and comfort of garrison duty rather than as head of the Utah Expedition, had marched within two days of South Pass with elements of the Fifth and Tenth Infantries when his scouts reported the approach of Captain Van Vliet and John M. Bernhisel. The journey through the mountains had not been an exciting one for the captain. Van Vliet reported to Colonel Alexander that the Mormons were determined not to allow the army uncontested passage into the territory. Beyond immediate vision and scattered through the mountains, he warned, Brigham Young had rushed three thousand militiamen to guard the entrance to the territory. Any landward approach through Echo Canyon and the ill-defined battle zone between the expedition and the Nauvoo Legion would be difficult and perilous unless the army was supported by powerful batteries of artillery that could breach the Mormons' defenses. Furthermore, Brigham Young and his generals were adamant in their refusal to provide food or forage for the expedition.[2]

The two men talked for nearly an hour. Later the colonel discussed the situation with his staff officers who openly urged their commander to ignore Brigham Young's threats. Privately and individually they saw Alexander as a man lacking in courage. "He is," one of them wrote, "the most worthless old fogy in the world, frightened to death. He is in his dotage. . . ."[3] This harsh assessment was not entirely deserved, for instead of harkening to his fears and halting his army in a spirit of conciliation, Alexander directed his troops toward Ham's Fork, twenty miles northeast of Fort Bridger, to protect the supply wagons of the civilian contractors and to lay out a temporary campsite.

Marching without the protective cover of the dragoons, the army swarmed down the road leading to Fort Bridger, hoping the Mormons would withdraw from their mountain strongholds without a fight. At the narrowest part of the trail, Orrin Porter Rockwell, leading a small band of mounted horsemen, tried but failed to stampede the army's livestock near Pacific Springs.[4] A major blow came three days later, when a second attack against the expedition on the sage flats near Green River left two large supply trains containing several thousand pounds of provisions burning along the trail. But the army continued its westward advance.[5]

A brilliant tactician, Brigham Young avoided meeting the better-trained and well-equipped federal infantry in open country. Instead, he skillfully directed the Nauvoo Legion to withdraw into a kind of impenetrable Maginot line near Forts Bridger and Supply. In an effort to outlast rather than outfight the army, he ordered the two outposts destroyed and the Legion reconcentrated in Echo Canyon, where the war would be won or lost. To maximize his opponent's losses in livestock, all grass near and along the Oregon Trail between Ham's Fork and Fort Bridger was burned. The emergency measures also included launching two large-scale raids against the remaining army livestock and supply trains, a move calculated to leave the expedition completely immobilized.[6] One prime objective governed Brigham Young's strategy: by destroying the food and forage of the expedition, he hoped to bring about a swift recall of the army. However, in the superheated atmosphere any mistake might prove fatal.

The Mormon leader realized that he needed a smashing defeat of the federal army without glory or bloodshed. "Should a collision take place between the good people of Utah, and the detachment sent thither," Bernhisel had warned him, "the news of such an event would produce the most intense excitement throughout this vast confederacy, and the tide of public sentiment would set against us with tremendous force."[7] Fortunately, the army's own military folly was allowing Brigham Young to carry out his dangerous strategy. The expedition had started badly. The conservative pro-slavery antagonists, led by Buchanan's representatives in Kansas, were unanimous in their decision to hold back the major elements of the Second Dragoons that were originally intended to escort the supply trains of Russell, Majors and Waddell to Utah. Thus, it was not until September that they were released to rejoin the Utah Expedition.

Brigham Young struggled desperately against the odds, being upheld by his trusted general and member of the First Presidency, Daniel H. Wells. Like other born leaders, Wells set all experience aside and launched, with great vigor, a campaign to destroy the army's last source of supply. As September gave way to October, Mormon cavalry rode from the burned-out shell of Fort Bridger toward the Green and Big Sandy Rivers, at which point the long procession of army supply trains had come to a halt. After passing through the open country undetected, the Mormon rangers caught the federal troops and teamsters by complete surprise and without a fight destroyed several thousand pounds of equipment and supplies.[8] Other victories were achieved without a struggle, greatly distressing the expedition. After the incredible attacks, nobody in the army knew quite what to expect.

Baffled and perplexed by such unprovoked assaults, Colonel Alexander was thoroughly convinced that his beleaguered army could not penetrate the defenses at Echo Canyon; he shifted his strategy. Knowing that he must strike quickly to avoid being trapped in the open country by winter, he ordered the expedition's forces to move up to Ham's Fork, setting his course to the northwest along the Bear River. The strategy was to enter Mormon-held territory through the defenseless corridor of Malad Valley, feeding off the land to conserve the fast-disappearing rations. While the Mormons watched in confused astonishment, the army entered the primitive wilderness.[9] The movement along Ham's Fork proceeded erratically and slowly as the seven-mile-long column of infantrymen crossed into the unmapped country separating the Bear and Green Rivers. After three days of hard marching, its men and their animals drained of energy, the army found itself marooned a scant thirty-five miles from where they had started by the first harbinger of winter—a numbing, freezing sheet of snow that stopped the column in its tracks. Ahead lay the long mountain reaches that walled them from the Mormons.

Meanwhile, in his well-warmed quarters in Salt Lake City, Brigham Young ordered General Wells to withdraw his troops to the eastern canyon entrances of the territory; but the commander was instructed to post spies to observe the position and movements of the expedition. "As the enemy continue to keep baffling about on Ham's Fork, like a flock of geese without a leader, it is probably best to order all the men east of you to fall back and occupy comfortable localities on Echo Canyon. . . ."[10] At this point General Albert Sidney Johnston, the newly designated commander of the Utah Expedition, caught up with the war.

President Buchanan's hand-picked successor to General Harney found his new command hungry, weak, and rapidly becoming frost-bitten. After a hasty conference with his subordinates, Johnston dispatched a courier with a message ordering Alexander to retrace his steps to Ham's Fork where he was to rendezvous with the main element of dragoons that had escorted the general from Fort Leavenworth.[11] In a last painful scene, Alexander turned his troops once more down the river, marching in broken formation for seven days in mild winter weather until they made contact with eight companies of dragoons, at which point the colonel turned over his command to General Johnston.[12]

Surveying what was left of the expedition's animals and supplies, the new commander grew increasingly pessimistic. Although there was little immediate danger from the Mormons, Johnston faced the disintegration of his army. Campaign losses were incredibly high—three hundred thousand pounds of food had been put to the torch by Mormon marauders; eleven hundred animals had been captured or run off; and more than 3,000 head of livestock had perished from starvation or cold.

The problem of supplies was only the beginning of a series of difficulties for the general. Of more immediate concern were the falling temperature and blizzard conditions that dropped six or seven inches of snow on the ground. Since there were no natural defenses or protection in the open country, on November 6, Johnston began a desperate thirty-five-mile race to reach the sheltered valley near Fort Bridger. Painfully pushing south-by-west along the Mormon Trail, the expedition's hardships steadily increased, with tired and dejected soldiers swarming through the countryside in a radius of ten miles. Captain Jesse Gove, a highly reliable chronicler of the Utah Expedition, gave a vivid account of his men's exhausted, faint, and disheartened condition in a letter to his wife. "No fire except what we could make from the sage brush. It was awful. Never was men more exposed or had a harder tour of duty. Some of the men were frostbitten."[13] The animals had no corn "and the grass, what little there is," he continued, "is under the snow, and they come some 1100 miles, poor as can be, hundreds dropping down in the harness for want of strength to stand up. When all these things are taken into consideration you will come to the conclusion that we are having a hard time. We are."[14] Eleven days after it started, the main elements of the army arrived at Fort Bridger only to find the old trading post reduced to a burned-out hull of charred timbers and roofless stone walls.

Faced with a full list of difficulties, General Johnston's strategy was reduced to a single objective—collect his army and go into winter quarters. The plan was not easily accomplished. Meanwhile, one day's march from Fort Bridger, Colonel Philip St. George Cooke and his command of six companies of dragoons rode toward the main element of the Army of Utah. For two months, catastrophe had hovered over the courageous brigade. Few men had worse luck than Colonel Cooke. After a brief tour of duty in Kansas, Cooke's dragoons moved out of Fort Leavenworth in mid-September; but halfway to Fort Kearny seventy-five men were lost to desertion. Two days west of the frontier outpost, rain and snow bogged down the supply wagons, turning the march into a walk while buffeting the reinforcements with hailstones and hurricane winds. "Snow, Snow, Snow," wrote a young teamster. "Sage brushes looking like mounds of salt, mules and beef cattle dying, the ground so hard we broke our wooden tentpins, saddle-blankets freezing to the horses."[15]

After resting briefly at Fort Laramie, the dragoons struggled across a seemingly endless confusion of rolling hills, vanishing and reappearing through a wall of snow and sleet, until they grappled their way down the western slope of South Pass. Here the men continued to fight their way ahead through storms and across difficult terrain. "After that," one participant recalled, "the weather kept getting worse and worse. Three days, three nights, it snowed. Not a storm of falling flakes; no, but a blind, choking tempest of swirling powder spray." Mules "had squeezed themselves in close together, their tails to the wind, and their muzzles gray with frost. And their long eye-winkers got white, looked brittle, like glass; and it was pitiful to hear those animals, they cried so and moaned, shivering in the cold."[16]

In arctic temperatures that plunged to forty-four below zero, the column and its contingent of new territorial civil officers followed the emigrant trail south to Ham's Fork, then plodded southwest to Fort Bridger. All but thirteen of Cooke's hundred and forty horses were lost, some frozen grotesquely in their tracks. Miraculously, only one soldier died, a victim of lockjaw.[17] For Samuel Wragg Ferguson, a fresh-faced lieutenant with a West Point crease still in his uniform, the memory of that winter was forever frozen in his mind:

Between the summit of the mountains and Fort Bridger we encountered the carcasses of the animals of some of the belated supply trains, literally blocking the road. They lay just as they had fallen, even yoked together, often six or more pair, with log chain still attached. The wolves and ravens apparently had not attacked them—perhaps because they were frozen so hard, or, perhaps in the number of carcasses their depredations were not observed. At all events they remained until thawed out the next spring.[18]

With ingenuity that comes often from despair, General Johnston quickly pulled his command together, expanded the limits of winter quarters from the smoke-blackened ruins of Fort Bridger to the small sheltered valley cut by Black's Fork, and named the new campsite in honor of his aging commander, General Winfield Scott. Outside the limits of the encampment, the expedition's livestock were moved across the frozen land to protected grazing sites.

As a strong-willed, new force in the expedition, Johnston gave fresh life to his army, which drew the immediate attention of Brigham Young and General Wells, both of whom misinterpreted the westward march of the expedition as the beginning of an offensive. In less than a week, 1,250 reinforcements were ordered from various military districts to Echo Canyon to defend the eastern approach into the basin.[19] But the attack never came; the army's march stopped at Fort Bridger. Satisfied that an invasion could not be accomplished that winter, the Saints gradually withdrew from the remote wilderness, leaving only a handful of Legionnaires to guard the main roads leading into the territory, a duty that was largely one of reconnaissance. The menace of the army declined further in late December when the territory was sealed off from the east by a wall of snow, guaranteeing peace until the following spring. "Our enemies have gone into winter quarters near the ruins of Forts Supply and Bridger . . ." wrote Brigham Young to William Cox in San Bernardino, "and they have not even done any scouting in this direction, except a picket guard's occasionally riding out a few miles. The brethren by tomorrow evening will have come in, except a few at certain points, and there is every prospect of our enjoying a very quiet time during the winter."[20]

Whatever Brigham Young may have thought or feared about the Utah Expedition, he was not blind to the new dilemma he now faced. It was one thing to force a floundering army to suffer wintering on the high plains, and quite another to prevent a large, fully reinforced and resupplied army, commanded by a first-rate general, from entering the territory the following spring. After much discussion and prayer with Wells and others, Young reached a decision that non-military settlement to the crisis was imperative to avert a full-scale tragedy.

The first stage of this diplomacy culminated in an interview between Bernhisel and President Buchanan and his Secretary of War, John B. Floyd. But results of the Utah delegate's efforts were discouraging from the beginning. "I have been endeavoring to procure the appointment of a Commission to proceed to Utah and investigate the rumors and charges which have been preferred against the people of the Territory," he wrote to Brigham Young, "but I regret to say that the proposition has not been favorably received either by the President or members of Congress."[21]

War fever was dangerously high by the time Bernhisel drove up to the White House on January 16, 1857, for a second conference with the president. The talks had no sooner reconvened when the thorny question of mistreatment of Gentile office holders by the Saints came under discussion. "He said that all the officers had stated that they had been driven from there. He determined that the military shall force their way into the valley, though he says he does not wish any blood to be shed," the delegate wrote the following week in a letter to Brigham Young.[22] The president firmly reiterated "that he had no desire to interfere with the religion of the people of Utah and added that he did not wish to hurt a hair of their heads, but that the laws must be enforced." Continuing his account, Bernhisel reported that Buchanan "intimated that if the people submitted to the laws, the troops would be withdrawn after a short time, except a few companies to keep the line of travel to California, for it would be too expensive to keep troops there."[23]

The war was far from an end, for despite his reassuring words to the delegate, Buchanan was pursuing his own course with results far more ominous than Bernhisel could have imagined. Considering a major engagement with the Mormons altogether possible, the president requested Congress to authorize an additional four regiments of soldiers to be sent to Utah. While Congress debated the political as well as the financial problems associated with this requisition, Major General Winfield Scott, commander of the entire American Army, broke his sphinx-like silence to infuse the Utah Expedition with new strength. Ordered to be regarrisoned at Camp Scott were the First Cavalry Regiment, the Sixth and Seventh Regiments of Infantry, two companies of the Second Artillery, two companies of the Second Dragoons, and more than eight hundred recruits.[24]

As these reinforcements made their way toward South Pass, the Secretary of War carved from the Department of the West the military district of Utah to be commanded by General Persifor F. Smith; but following his death on May 17, 1858, the office fell to General William S. Harney.[25] Meanwhile, new contracts were let to Russell, Majors, and Waddell to transport twelve months of provisions (16,000,000 pounds of freight) to Utah.[26] To meet this demand, the freighting company bought 40,000 oxen and 1,000 mules, virtually pushing the price of livestock out of reach of emigrants moving west from Leavenworth. By the early spring of 1858, twenty-six hundred wagons, manned by more than one thousand teamsters, were on the trail to Camp Scott.[27]

Notice of the unexpected reinforcements reached Brigham Young when he received a copy of the president's annual message to Congress outlining these movements, words that he took seriously. "We consider the message decidedly hostile, however, lamentable it may appear for the President of a great nation to be influenced by falsehood and prejudice, and upon that basis exercise the power of the Government to crush out not only the liberty but the very existence of an innocent people, yet it is so." The Church leader pressed his claim that Buchanan had not taken the "proper steps to inform himself in regard to our affairs falling into the common prejudice of the people, thinking that to be the most popular course, and hence the easiest, saving the trouble of investigation and fear of being convinced of his mistake. He calls resistance to such foul and unhallowed oppression, rebellion[;] with us it is self defense."[28]

The sheer sweep of these dramatic events overshadowed a lone Mormon who rode into Salt Lake City from California with news that a traveler from Washington was making his way across the southern overland route toward the city. The weather turned bitterly cold the following day, February 24, when a second rider handed Brigham Young a carefully scrawled note: "I trust you will recognize my handwriting. The date of my letter will apprize you of my journey hither. That I have made it in six weeks from New York will persuade you that I am on no fool's errand, and have no want of confidence in my ability to convince you what is the true feeling of our people and the President toward yourself and the good citizens of Utah." The message, which was neither unrealistic nor encouraging, urged that Brigham Young "postpone any military movement of importance until we meet and have a serious interview. If you are unprepared to see the expedience for doing so, I entreat it as a favor in requital of the services which I rendered you people in less prosperous days."[29]

The mysterious stranger proved to be Colonel Thomas Leiper Kane, an old and trusted friend of the Mormons. As a multi-dimensional humanitarian given to great practical efforts for unpopular causes, Kane was one of the most imposing figures in Mormon history; but he was a political curiosity outside of Utah. Born to live in the shadow of his distinguished father, John K. Kane, and his brother, Elisha Kent Kane, the famous arctic explorer, he represented the conventional wisdom whose voices of restraint and compassion went largely unheard in the decade that preceded the Civil War. A heavily built, erect man slightly under six feet in height, with dark hair and dark eyes, Kane looked older than his thirty-five years of age, but was unmistakably handsome. In private conversation he spoke quietly with a voice that echoed his native Philadelphia. A political writer of note who was familiar with the French language, Kane began a brief diplomatic career at the American Embassy in Paris under Lewis Cass in 1836 and later served as a correspondent for *Le National*.[30]

Colonel Kane had followed from a distance with grave apprehension the progress of the Utah War. Finally, after months of inactivity, he embarked on a long diplomatic struggle to bring hostilities to an end. Disregarding the advice of his family and close associates who were pessimistic from the start regarding the success of such a mission, Kane appeared unannounced at the White House. President Buchanan reacted quickly and declined to endorse Kane's mission to open peace negotiations with the Mormons, warning that the trip was hazardous, if not impossible in winter. Furthermore, he cautioned that it was doubtful whether Kane could alter the course of the war. The president concluded his statements with a powerful combination of arguments that indicted the Saints for treason and open rebellion, adding that only a miracle could bring a bloodless solution to the Mormon problem. The decision of war or peace in the territory should be left to the belligerents, he declared. Kane disagreed.[31]

While trying to conceal from the president his personal commitment to the Saints, Kane vigorously pursued the argument that the use of troops in the western territory would plunge the nation into civil war. Since neither side was prepared to back away from their positions, he continued, only a third party could bring peace to the far-flung desert basin. Kane's seemingly cold-steel nerves impressed Buchanan, who reluctantly agreed to the mission. Officially, Buchanan would not endorse Kane as a government mediator; unofficially, he addressed two letters recommending the full cooperation and assistance of all federal officers whom he should meet during the course of his odyssey.[32]

For the next several days Kane's movements were a mystery, but troubles multiplied within the Kane family when the colonel's father strenuously opposed the action of his son. Putting his thoughts in a letter, John Kane wrote: "The Mormons can hardly have misconceived the honest and kindly aims and purposes of the President, and I do not believe you will be able to impress them with the feeling of our American people." The aging father, who was to die before his son reached Utah, touched briefly on the purpose of the war and included a warning that if the Mormons attacked the army their fate was sealed. "You know, and I know, how anxious Mr. Buchanan is to prove himself their friend and you know, or if you don't, I do, that if the Mormons once assail our troops, the sentiment of the country will never be satisfied while a Mormon community survives on this continent." The senior Kane refused to admit that his son could influence the course of the war, or that there was much hope for his mission to succeed: "Yet such is the judicial blindness, that seems to cover your friends in Utah gallant and clear sighted as I know many of them to be, and such too are the essential embarrassments, in which evil counsel and precipitate action have involved the question, that I have only faint hopes connected with your mission."[33] The letter was never mailed; instead, it was tucked away among the colonel's clothing to be found during his long journey to Utah.

Armed with a letter of introduction from the president, Kane resigned as clerk of the United States District Court in Pennsylvania and, on January 5, 1857, boarded a mail steamer bound for the Isthmus of Panama. Throughout the month of January he made his long and perilous voyage to California, traveling under the title Dr. Osborne, the surname of his servant, and reaching Los Angeles during the first part of February. The journey across California brought one disappointment after another, with citizens of the southern communities crying out for vengeance for the victims of the Mountain Meadows Massacre.[34]

At San Bernardino, the gateway to the Great Basin, Kane's true identity was discovered and his life threatened by unruly vigilantes who were determined to block his passage into the territory. Heading the unruly mob was a man identified as Pickett, who organized a mass meeting in front of the colonel's hotel to demand a full explanation of his mission. The Philadelphian, scanning the faces of the shouting men, somewhat unwittingly answered Pickett that he was an emissary of the president, secretly dispatched from Washington to prevent a general war with the Saints. The grievances on both sides were many, he added, but all aspects of the perilous situation had been personally weighed by the president; to achieve peace in the basin the Mormons would have to allow the army to enter the territory unmolested. It took some time before the vigilante committee dispersed, leaving the colonel to continue the second leg of his journey through El Cajon Pass. "The conduct of the gallant Doctor throughout has gained the applause of the respectable portion of this community," wrote Ebenezer Hanks, a witness to the stormy interview, "and Mr. Pickett, foreman of this committee, was fully satisfied with the integrity and uprightness of this Gentleman in the brief interview of an hour and a half and delivered his report to the meeting who were anxiously expecting the same and resulting in the unanimous voice of God Speed Him."[35]

After spending a restless night, Kane departed for Salt Lake City in the company of his black servant and three Mormons, John Mayfield, George Clark, and Joseph S. Tanner.[36] Entering the frontier on February 6, the party followed the hardest part of the old Spanish Trail to Williams or Cottonwood Camp, a short distance from the present city of Las Vegas.[37]

At the nearly deserted outpost they encountered Amasa Lyman, camped near an open fire. A confident of Brigham Young and an apostle in the Church, Lyman had been sent to the Colorado River to investigate reports that the federal government was about to launch an attack against the Saints from the southwest.[38] Now faced with a greater mission, Lyman resolved to escort Kane across the waterless lower reaches of the territory to Salt Lake City. After a brief delay caused by the deteriorating condition of Kane's health, the combined forces headed east to the Muddy River where they were overtaken by two Mormon missionaries, Thales Haskell and Ira Hatch, who had just negotiated a peace treaty with the Paiute Indians.[39] Within twenty-four hours of this meeting, the small company made its way through the remaining barriers of mountain ranges, past a network of Mormon communities, and reached Salt Lake City during the last week of February.

Once inside the city's disconnected walls, Kane was greeted by Wilford Woodruff and the principal councilors of the Church, and was driven past a sea of curious faces to the Staines mansion where he rested and waited for word from Brigham Young.[40] At dusk a short note was delivered by messenger: "I will not multiply words upon paper but I will be happy to wait upon you at my Beehive House at eight o'clock this evening. My carriage will be ready to receive you at your present lodgings at half past seven. I cannot express my joy and surprise at your arrival."[41] As events were to prove, the meeting was more than an informal gathering of friends. Showing no sign of tension, standing erect and poised, Kane addressed a joint conference of the First Presidency and the Council of Twelve.

Surprisingly, Kane's remarks were simple, almost casual, and strangely evasive. Admitting that he was authorized to lay before the Mormons the views of the president of the United States, the colonel stated that a way must be opened through which the federal government could support a compromise to end hostilities. It was soon apparent to all those present that Kane's thoughts were for Brigham Young alone. After thirty minutes the colonel ended his remarks and the two men adjourned to a secret meeting.

Although the proceedings began in an atmosphere of goodwill, what transpired during this and subsequent meetings is unclear. At least one contemporary claimed that Kane "impressed Brigham Young with the determination of the Government to subdue all opposition, and satisfied him that in the coming spring the troops would force a passage through the canyons, and would occupy the city if any resistance were offered to the installment of the new Territorial Governor and the Federal officers."[42] The only surviving record of that interview was recorded by Brigham Young's secretary on scrap paper. According to that note, Kane "admitted that the action of the Government in relation to the affairs of Utah has been so precipitate as to be legitimately open to misconception, and expressed his surprise at learning, as he said for the first time—that no adequate explanation has been before offered of the intentions of the Administration in ordering the army to Utah, that I had received no notification from the Government that my official conduct in any respect was open to censure or to misconstruction. . . ."[43]

Towering over all other issues was Young's refusal to allow the army to enter the territory, a major point over which the Buchanan administration was adamantly inflexible, and which position Kane made clear. Yet there was room for compromise. Not unexpectedly, Kane assured his old friend that the federal troops were sent to Utah to guarantee the installation of the new federal officials, to construct such necessary forts within the territory needed to control the Indians, and to regulate overland emigrant travel. The remarks had all of the overtones of an official report as Kane "told Brigham that, on the whole, he approved the Buchanan administration, and that he believed the differences between the Mormons and the administration could be worked out without bloodshed."[44]

From the beginning, the interview was marked by concessions from the Mormon prophet; but he did not accept in total the terms meted out by President Buchanan. Reluctantly, Brigham Young instructed Kane that he was prepared to meet the government demands halfway: he would receive the territorial officials but warned that under no circumstances would the Mormons agree to permit the federal troops to enter the Great Basin. Not totally willing to bind himself to this agreement, Kane prepared to leave the society of Saints and travel to the army encampment at Winter Quarters to present the compromise to the new governor, Alfred Cumming. Guided by a squad of Nauvoo Legionnaires, the party struck out through the mountains, fighting the deep snow through the passes, after which the Mormon horsemen turned back, leaving the peace envoy to enter the army lines alone. The journey consumed five days.

The sudden and unexpected appearance of Colonel Kane at Camp Scott on March 13 precipitated an extraordinary episode that quickly propelled him into the limelight at Winter Quarters. Guided by the belief that his mission was entirely civilian in nature, the colonel made only a token gesture at observing military protocol, at least if the army's version of his first meeting with General Johnston is to be believed. In his description of the event, Major Fitz-John Porter reported Kane's entrance as that of a shallow demagogue and denied him a shred of common sense.

> While in my tent (office) the Mr. Kane rode up to the colonel's tent with a very self satisfied air (playing the grand presence of a number of teamsters there about). The Colonel was informed by the servant that a gentleman wished to see him, and the gentleman was invited to enter. The Colonel stepped to the door, and the man said, "I left the States on the 5th of January, and am the bearer of dispatches to you and to Gov. Cumming." "Dismount and walk in Sir," said the Colonel—"With your permission Sir," looking around on what he supposed an admiring audience but one laughing at his conceit and self-efficiency—"I will see the Governor first." "Certainly Sir," Johnston replied. "Sergeant, lead me to the Governor." and was led—like an ass— Quite Theatrical—[45]

Unwilling to prolong the disturbing scene, the general allowed Kane full run of the camp, although his frequent absences from his tent increased suspicions that he was carrying on secret consultations with the Mormons. Soon after Kane began his tenuous negotiations with Governor Cumming, he wandered off by himself into the foothills surrounding

Camp Scott and became totally lost. After traveling in circles for several hours, he foolishly fired his revolver to signal his position, drawing the attention of a soldier who came running in the direction of the explosion. Making his way through the ebony blackness, the picket stumbled upon Kane and, without giving him an opportunity to identify himself, fired at the unidentified target.[46] Fortunately, the sentry's bullet passed harmlessly past the ear of its intended victim. "Pity they did not rid him of life," was the feeling of one officer. "It would have saved one fool from troubling us."[47] Still suffering from shock, Kane was arrested and returned to camp where he was placed under the protective custody of the governor. More determined than ever, he continued to press his mission. But Governor Cumming was not yet prepared to admit that peace would come easily to the territory. Instead, he encouraged Kane to continue his efforts on behalf of the Saints.

> The storm so long impending, is now ready to burst upon the deluded inhabitants of this Territory—Whilst it is my duty to enforce unconditional submission to the authority of the United States, yet in the performance of that duty, I would gladly temper justice with mercy, and prevent the unnecessary effusion of blood—Especially, I would shield women and children from the sufferings incident to civil war. I therefore earnestly desire that you will persevere in your mission of mercy—and give up for the present at least, your purpose of returning to Philadelphia.[48]

The peace negotiations caused an acute crisis at Camp Scott. Through trial and suffering, the fire-breathing troops had survived the winter with only one thought—the Saints would pay bitterly for the personal humiliation they all felt. A belief of invincibility permeated the ranks as the high-water mark approached. Few soldiers doubted that victory would come with spring, an attitude that was reflected by General Johnston in a conversation with the war correspondent of the *New York Times*, J.W. Symington. "The Mormons have declared, as fully as words and actions can manifest intentions, that they will not longer submit to this government, or to any government but their own," he claimed with obvious reference to the destruction of his supply trains by Mormon dragoons. "The people of the union must now submit a usurpation of their territory—to have a government erected in their midst, not loyal to, or rather not acknowledging any dependence upon, or allegiance to the Federal government," said the future Confederate leader, "and what is not less impolitic, and entirely incompatible with our institutions, to allow them to engraft their social organization upon ours and make it a part of our system or act with the vigor and force to compel them to submit." The contagion out of Utah must be stopped by blood, he added with increasing bitterness.[49]

Though impatient with what he considered the slow rate of progress of the peace negotiations, Kane found Cumming's faith in Johnston badly shaken, if not wholly destroyed. For five months Cumming had steadily moved away from the general's hard-line attitude to the territory's pressing political dilemma. In this internal power struggle the governor was joined by a handful of civilian officeholders who found common cause in Cumming's suspicion that the general's hatred of the Saints was a thinly disguised move to weaken civilian control of the territory, despite Johnston's protest to the contrary. Like Kane, Cumming resented Johnston's heavy-handed treatment of civilians at Camp Scott and insisted that his authority was superior to that of the military commander. The results were predictable.

Precisely what happened next is unclear, but shortly after a comparatively minor confrontation, Kane challenged the general to a duel. Only the interference of Chief Justice Delano Eckles prevented the match from taking a disastrous course. In an interview she gave during the waning years of her life, Kane's wife, Elizabeth, recalled this incident:

> It may seem as if it were an anticlimax that Colonel Kane, on what he felt to be a God given mission, should challenge Albert Sidney Johnston to fight a duel. But old-fashioned chivalry in that day still believed in dueling and Colonel Kane welcomed the chance given him by Johnston's blunder in arresting him on his arrival in camp to claim Governor Cumming's services as his second. The former Georgian's southern code of honor was fired by the insult offered to his guest, and he at once became willing to act as his second. . . .[50]

The real significance of the episode was the influence it had upon subsequent events, for it bonded the two men into an alliance against Johnston with both long- and short-range effects. The results more than answered Kane's growing expectations. The heaviest blow to the general's partisan cause came on the afternoon of April 2, 1858, when the governor informed Johnston that he was prepared to leave for Salt Lake City to assume the duties of chief executive of the territory. "I have decided to go in person to Salt Lake City, for reasons of state," he informed the expedition's commander, "and wish to obtain assistance in transportation and that I may not be dependent upon the Mormons for supplies. I call to procure some additional quantity from the commissary."[51]

In that last meeting, Governor Cumming was sanguine about the long-range ameliorative effects his visit would have in establishing peace. "I wish to go to Salt Lake City to meet B.Y.—next week a conference or convention of the people will be held . . . from what I have understood the matter of peace or war will be determined." The pronouncement certainly fell hard on Johnston, but the governor continued uninterrupted. "I wish to go as far at least as Echo Canyon, where I will meet with either no opposition, indicating a peaceful tendency, or a force to repel one, and which it would be useless to oppose."

"Governor," the commander asked, "am I to understand that you are expected: that there is some invitation or impression made to you that your presence is desired. As without some such understanding, I should be inclined to enter my protest."

But Cumming had already made up his mind and brushed aside Johnston's objections. "Yes, Sir, there is such an understanding—I am expected—and I think it would be beneficial for the country that I go—as for my person I have nothing to fear, unless from some of those fanatics, who are opposed to a peace and would be glad to see a collision with the Government. . . ."[52] The governor's answer was clear and unquestionable—the tiresome affair had to be ended.

The stiff-necked army man demonstrated a clear lack of diplomacy. In addition, his politics and personality drew the governor's fire. The general insisted that Cumming was no match for the Mormons and cautioned that to leave for Salt Lake City without an army escort would compromise the honor of the country and the dignity of his long-suffering troops.[53] But in the end Johnston was powerless to stay the governor's decision.

When the spring weather cleared, Cumming, Kane, and two teamsters set out on the road alone to Salt Lake City. Contact with Mormon lines came as a mounted patrol rode out from the foothills to guide the federal officer through the first leg of his journey.[54] Hours later, Porter Rockwell joined the caravan and headed it along the old emigrant route to the entrance of the territory. After several days on the trail, the party struggled down the labyrinthine road of Echo Canyon, along a passage that meandered mazelike between high, battlemented, red stone walls. The horses' footsteps echoed with a ghostlike cadence as the caravan slipped through the canyon all day without a hint of danger. But the second night on the trail saw an end to the serene passage. Suddenly the mountains were illuminated by great fires of juniper and pine, reflecting on the sheer walls like a giant kaleidoscope. As if to print indelibly these ghostly scenes on the governor's mind, sentries leaped from the gathering mist along the trail to demand in rasping, imperious tones, signs and counter-signs before they allowed the chief executive to proceed. As Cumming approached other points along the trail, officers led him through lines of tents drawn up like a barricade along the road, past troops of Legionnaires who saluted him as governor. At least on one occasion Cumming was allowed to review well-dressed and equipped soldiers.[55]

The deceptive drama contributed to Cumming's growing belief that the Saints could field an enormous army capable of destroying the expedition, and it appears to have motivated, in part, his excessive cooperation with the Mormons during the ensuing peace negotiations. With his touch of paranoia, Cumming would never be capable of asserting the power and authority of the federal government; rather, he was to be easily accessible to the Church hierarchy, to the exclusion of critical Gentiles and the army command. As the governor passed through the Wasatch Range, he overhauled hundreds of Mormon settlers fleeing south to escape the anticipated ravages of the Utah Expedition. Unknown to the governor, the move was but another masterful strategic maneuver on the part of Brigham Young.

Having received intelligence from his rangers along the overland that General Harney was advancing toward Utah with several thousand troops, Young schemed to win public support for the recall of the reinforcements. The Saints, showing remarkable confidence in the prophet's judgment, abandoned all settlements north of Provo, each family taking only what one wagon could carry.[56] With heartfelt grief, they left their remaining possessions behind under a mantle of straw and wood to be burned by the Mormon rear guard if the army decided to occupy the northern towns and villages. Those who had not suffered exile in Missouri or Illinois were ordered to leave first, the rest when transportation and quarters become available.[57]

When the weary governor came riding into Salt Lake City with his escort, the streets were crowded with people on foot and in wagons moving in a steady stream of traffic toward the Jordan River. After making his way through the long passage of fleeing pioneers, Cumming penned his impressions of the mass migration to his superior in Washington with strained pathos.

> The people, including the inhabitants of this city, are moving from every settlement in the northern part of the Territory. The roads are everywhere filled with wagons loaded with provisions and household furniture, the women and children of ten without shoes or hats, driving their flocks they know not where. They seem not only resigned but cheerful. "It is the will of the Lord," and they rejoice to exchange the comforts of home for the trials of the wilderness. Their ultimate destination is not, I presumed, definitely fixed upon. "Going South" seems sufficiently definite for most of them, but many believe their ultimate destination is Sonora.[58]

Viewing these same events with a sympathetic eye, a correspondent for the *New York Tribune* found the streets screened with clouds of dust as hundreds of wagons and herds of livestock moved through the wide corridors of the city. "So extraordinary a migration is hardly paralleled in history. The depopulation of Acadia, a hundred years ago—strong political reasons as there were for it—has not left a very fragrant odor behind it."[59]

Having been ceremoniously greeted as a territorial governor by the mayor, aldermen, and members of the city council of Salt Lake City near Hot Springs, Cumming was escorted to the Staines mansion to await the arrival of Brigham Young. The Church president, who had lately been in Provo supervising the "Move South," arrived in the city the following day to greet his replacement. Four years senior to Brigham Young, Governor Cumming was somewhat on the heavy side of two hundred pounds, of average height, with a head topped with gray hair streaked with black and supported by a bull-like neck. Those inclined toward theatrical outburst claimed he was "tub build," or on the hard and ungraceful lines of a work ox. After delivering another speech of welcome in which he congratulated the governor on his latest appointment, Brigham Young advised Cumming that the territorial seal and records were at his disposal whenever he chose to receive them.[60]

The governor's open diplomacy with the Mormons dragged on into May with both parties moving slowly toward a settlement; but there were several areas of agreement between Alfred Cumming and Brigham Young. The Saints prepared to accept the authority of the governor and all federal representatives, provided that the federal army was kept out of the territory. Clearly mistaken in his thinking that the peace negotiations would turn the army into an obedient servant of civilian authority, Cumming promised Young that Johnston would not be permitted to march on the city without his permission. The prophet accepted Cumming's statement with some reservations. As a result of these negotiations, the territorial executive departed for Camp Scott, again under the watchful eyes of Porter Rockwell and a handful of mounted dragoons. A week of difficult travel brought him once more to the army bivouac at Camp Scott. His reception by the army was anything but friendly.

For five days the governor avoided a face-to-face confrontation with Johnston. Finally, on May 21, he informed the commander: "After a careful investigation I am gratified in being able to inform you that I believe there is at present no organized armed force of its inhabitants in any part of this Territory, with the exception of a small party subject to my orders in or near Echo Canyon."[61]

General Johnston was chagrined, angered, and unconvinced. The commander left little doubt that he would not abdicate his military responsibilities as spelled out by the Secretary of War and renewed his preparations to march on Utah. Notwithstanding this impasse that left Cumming dolefully predicting a bloody collision between the army and the Mormons, the decision of war and peace passed from their hands. Unaware of the course of events in the mountains, President Buchanan dispatched a peace commission to Utah in early April to bring the embarrassing Mormon War to an end. Bending to the Republican bloc in Congress that accused the Democratic administration of using the Mormon question to divert national attention from the more burning question of slavery in the territories, the president placed the decision of war squarely on the shoulders of Brigham Young. If the Saints refused to accept a lenient pardon and pledge obedience to the nation's laws, Buchanan reasoned, the Mormons would be stigmatized by their treacherous behavior, further justifying the mustering of the Utah Expedition.

The climax came on June 7, 1858, when the peace commissioners—Lazarus W. Powell and Ben McCulloch—appeared in Salt Lake City. Although the negotiations extended across two more weeks, Brigham Young finally settled the issue—peace would return to Utah.

CHAPTER THREE

THE DAWN OF CARPETBAG RULE

To commence with the latest news, let me say that the blackest hour of Utah's difficulties is seemingly the present. I honestly confess I do much fear trouble from Uncle Sam's representatives on their way to Great Salt Lake City. The ultimate issue of any treachery, foolishness or madness on their part never troubles me; but that they mean mischief if they can, is doubted by none.

—T.B.H. Stenhouse[1]

THE YEAR 1858 was long to be remembered in the history of the Saints. It was a gray, drizzling spring morning when Buchanan's peace commissioners set out for Salt Lake City from Winter Quarters to present the president's proposals to the Saints. After making it over the emigrant road in five days, Powell, McCulloch, and Jacob Forney, Superintendent of Indian Affairs, arrived at their destination as the first week of June ended; but they found Brigham Young absent from the city.[2]

The commissioners waited, passing their time wandering through empty streets, moving up and down unpaved bypaths and through Temple Square. On the third day, the Church president arrived from Provo.[3] At best they faced a touchy business. Surrounding himself with the important religious and military leaders of the territory, Brigham Young received the delegation with confidence that the meetings would quell the political agitation which had grown so alarmingly.

Although he wished for the impossible, Young realized that neither war nor peace would stop the threat of federal control of Utah. But the scene would have to be played out. With the die already cast, the Mormons and the peace commissioners drew up an agreement they hoped would end the unrest that flickered across the territory.

After a series of public meetings in the city, Powell and McCulloch returned east and informed Johnston that all difficulties between the Mormons and the federal government had been settled. The Saints had accepted the presidential proclamation of amnesty, the commissioners reported to the commander, and had agreed to exchange their promise of loyalty for a guarantee that their lives and property would be protected by the army.

Publicly the general welcomed the end of the expedition's tortured history with a deep sense of gratitude; privately, however, he agreed with Captain Jesse Gove and other officers in his command, who complained bitterly that the army had been deprived of an opportunity to revenge itself against the Saints. "The Mormons have accepted the pardon but it is no more in earnest than the wind; they are as impudent and villainous as ever. The problems of the conquered territory would not be resolved." Irrational desires for revenge seemed paramount in their assessment of the situation. "We have got to give them a sound whipping, hang about 100 of them, and then the rest will submit. They have accepted only to gain time. The President has damned himself and the country."[4] Damned or not, the army could do nothing but accept the verdict of the president.

Life in the high plains wilderness came to an abrupt end on the morning of June 13, when the rasping, clear, and unmistakable bugle call summoned the Army of Utah to muster for the last time. Amidst the grumbling, coughing, sometimes cursing sounds of men awakened from a restless sleep, the army prepared for the last leg of its journey to Salt Lake City. With a detachment of Second Dragoons leading the way, the troops impatiently filed across the plains and made their way to Outpost Butte where they looked back across the shadowed valley toward Camp Scott for the last time.[5] From a distance, Winter Quarters resembled a helpless hostage in a vast foreign land. Silhouetted against the skyline, chimney-stacks, roof poles, and abandoned equipage stood ghostlike on the empty landscape. With a flagging sense of relief, the army put behind its bitter struggles and followed the emigrant road westward toward the gateway of the Wasatch Mountains. Snaking through the vast and increasingly rolling terrain, they passed over sparsely populated Indian country. For the better part of two weeks the soldiers tramped on toward the red-bluffed ramparts of Echo Canyon, now deserted by the Saints. Marching in six separate columns, the expedition moved on under clear skies that turned into gloomy clouds with raw gale-like winds that rattled against the mountain wall and turned the trail into a blinding dust storm. "In the ranks the men rode with chins tucked low, a bandanna or other oddment of cloth secured to shield their nostrils, making them resemble a gang of highwaymen."[6] Then, however, spring returned with temperate rains that drenched the soldiers to the skin, lathering mules and oxen in steam, "as if heated by an inner fire," according to one participant.[7]

The ordeal of the trail ended on the morning of June 26, 1858, when the long column emerged from the mountains and spilled out onto a broad plateau. Directly below the ancient sea-washed bench, nestled against the foothills and barricaded by a shimmering lake, Salt Lake City glistened in the warmth of summer and seemed to encompass the genius of Mormondom. From the crest of the plateau, the valley loomed before them like a vast chess board of small farms and adobe houses, geometrically divided by chalk-colored avenues that rolled and dipped to the Jordan River. Beneath the vast open skies, a trackless desert stretched endlessly to the horizon, a contrast to the bleached silver wheat fields resting under the bright sun. It was the first sign of civilization the army had seen since leaving Fort Leavenworth and it strongly suggested the heat and stillness of rich-foliaged bottomlands of the Missouri River.

After repeated delays, the regiments moved forward unopposed. But as the advance screen of dragoons appeared before the city, unfamiliar horsemen mounted on silver-ornamented saddles circled the column, then disappeared into the settlement.[8] The federal dragoons, immovable in their saddles, could do nothing except curse the Mormon cavalry as it passed and remember their year of difficult experiences. "They were thinking of the many cold, sleepless nights they had spent on guard in the snow, all to no purpose," a young lieutenant who witnessed the scene wrote, "for they had dreamed all the while that they would exact reparation for their trials; and now, on the very eve of the fulfillment of their anticipations, had come from Washington a committee . . . to arrange terms of peace with the Mormons; who thus went unwhipped by justice."[9]

Sunrise found the exhausted column at the gateway of the city, now naked before its attackers and wrapped in the foreboding silence of a graveyard. Before entering the settlement the soldiers nervously reshaped and brushed their tattered uniforms, dusted their rifles, and brightened their bayonets, and then stood silently waiting for the command to begin the most imposing military pageant ever to pass through the streets of Salt Lake City. When the march was completed, the course of Utah history would never be the same, for the Mormons could no longer claim exclusive control of Utah and they knew it. The army would uphold the power of the federal officials sent to run the territory and would pose a constant threat to the Saints' suzerainty in the Great Basin.[10]

The war drums rolled again. With the regimental colors rippling smartly in the wind, the army was ordered forward, marching to the cadence of "One Eyed Riley," a bawdy soldier's ballad of uncertain origin that was selected to show the army's complete contempt for the Saints:

> As I was strolling round and round
> A-huntin' fun in every quarter,
> I stopped meself at a little Dutch inn
> And ordered me up Gin and Water.
> One Eye Riley, Two Eye Riley,
> Ho! for the lad with one eye, Riley[11]

The huge column surged through the city down Brigham Young Street, past Temple Square in the direction of the William Staines mansion, already occupied by Governor Cumming and his wife.

With the exception of a handful of Mormons who watched the army through cracks in boarded windows, Salt Lake City had been abandoned to its fate—as fragile and forlorn as a medieval city depopulated by a great plague. "In the place of the usual crowd to gather and gaze at or hang upon the heels of the troops," recorded Captain Albert Tracy, of the Tenth Infantry, "no single living soul, beyond the lounging vagabonds . . . appeared—and only those by twos and threes, at corners, with clubs in their hands, and pistols ready slung at their belts."[12] Unknown to the army, Colonel Robert T. Burton, commander of the Nauvoo Legion contingent in Salt Lake City, watched the passing parade from the Beehive House, ready to fire the city if the army set up their quarters in the settlement.[13] The order was never delivered. Nevertheless, John R. Young, the grandson of the second prophet of the Church, was left with a life-long impression of that memorable day:

> I sat with the guards in the upper room of the Lion House, and saw that army in death-like silence march through the deserted streets of the dead city, a few of the officers with uncovered heads, as if attending a funeral. To us western mountain boys, the solemnity of the march was oppressive; and glad relief came to our strained feelings, when we saw the soldiers camp fires kindled on the other side of the Jordan.[14]

Leading the cortege was perhaps the most promising general of the pre-Civil War army, Albert Sidney Johnston, a tall, angular man, standing well more than six feet in height, weighing close to two hundred pounds, with brows that arched thickly over bright, searching eyes that rendered his appearance unmistakably military. According to one, he had an "open, pleasant countenance, full of amiability and manliness, (with) 'an eye like Jove's,' to threaten and command. . . ."[15] Among the rank- and-file Johnston was without question the most respected officer in the Utah Expedition, wrote an unidentified dragoon.

The men love him as a father, especially those who passed through the campaign of last winter at Camp Scott, and declare that no other man, save "old Scott," who always is an exception in matters of praise, could have conducted the affair so well as he did. "When we," they say, "had eight ounces of flour per day, General Johnston had the same; when an attack was apprehended, and we camped in the snow, General Johnston shared the same cold comfort. In short, when we suffered, he suffered; and such a man is worthy of honor and steem." That he deserves the highest praise and honor is undeniable, and the Government will ever find the old Texan patriot one of its bravest defenders, so long as liberty, integrity and justice are its watchwords, and their sustenance its greatest aim and object.[16]

Born into a modest and conservative landowning family of Washington, Kentucky, Johnston graduated from West Point in 1826, and entered federal service to spend eight disappointing years without distinction at various military installations. He was ambitious, and to improve his fortunes he resigned his commission and turned west to Texas where he offered his services to the fledgling republic. There he passed through various ranks of the frontier army before being appointed Secretary of War of Texas. However, the lure of the rich bottomlands led him to abandon temporarily his military associations. But the daily routine of civilian life overwhelmed him with a restless longing for life in the barracks. With the outbreak of the Mexican War he rejoined the Texas army as a colonel, and participated in the battle for Monterrey, Mexico. Shortly thereafter he was appointed paymaster in the federal army with the rank of major. He was fifty-five years old when a new chapter of his life started with the expedition, and his selection as commander of the Department of Utah "was a measure of his rising prestige in the army."[17]

But if Johnston held the eyes of the nation, Colonel Philip St. George Cooke, riding on the general's right flank, was the only soldier genuinely popular with the Mormons. The commander of the six companies of dragoons assigned to the expedition was born of colonial stock and, while he did not belong to the tidewater aristocracy, he was a Virginian in the most exaggerated sense of the term. Tall and imposing, with a heavy, blackspade beard slightly tinged with the snow of age, Cooke possessed an aquiline profile that exaggerated his clear, penetrating eyes and made men feel uneasy in his presence, often leading to complaints by his followers that he was a strict disciplinarian, if not a martinet. Unsoured by long years on the frontier, he was profoundly loyal to the army. With the successful ending of his formal education at West Point, he was commissioned into the infantry, and two years later he turned to the task of reconnoitering the Santa Fe Trail as a junior officer under the command of Colonel John James Abert.[18] As a young, promising major during the

Mexican War he led the Mormon Battalion across the southern desert to California with the iron determination of a conqueror and triumphed over all difficulties in the face of many dangers. As a final compliment to the Saints, he memorialized Congress with a message commending the Mormon foot soldier for his unselfish valor.

Riding along with the general's staff were two peace commissioners, Lieutenant Colonel Charles Ferguson Smith, and Jim Bridger, the famous mountaineer whose career spanned the history of the Rocky Mountain fur trade. Few events in Bridger's life were more sublime than this triumphant ride through the heart of Salt Lake City, culminating a chain of mistakes and failures that left him no impartial judge of Mormon character. His anger and resentment of the Saints boiled over after he was driven out of his trading post by a posse of Saints led by the self-confessed "Destroying Angel," Bill Hickman, after a bitterly contested struggle over control of the Green River country.[19] Exhausted and discouraged, he viewed the military occupation of the territory as the entering wedge to recapture his claims to Fort Bridger. Nevertheless, the Utah War had been a strange conflict when gauged by the standards of the western wilderness. Words replaced bullets. The offensive army became an army of surveillance, scorned by those it was directed against. The ways of prophets and politicians were beyond his reasoning.[20]

The fate of the Mormons also greatly concerned Colonel Charles F. Smith, an infantry officer with an excellent bearing and implicit sense of duty whose career spanned three decades of federal service. The physical portrait of Smith conformed to West Point standards, though no single feature revealed a man who attracted attention. At the outbreak of the Mexican War, Smith was classed among the most promising men in the federal army and went on to serve as instructor, adjutant, and commander of West Point.[21] Whatever he may have thought of the army's arduous journey to Utah, one thing was certain—he had a profound dislike of things Mormon, as events would demonstrate. No one was more aware of this attitude than Johnston, and this, in part, made the colonel an ideal candidate to serve as commander of any post that might be established in the Great Basin.[22] Through the developing stages of the fort, the relationship between the two men was amicable, although Smith's policies were completely submerged by Johnston's single-mindedness, which allowed the colonel only limited direction over territorial events.

Against a background of a thousand thoughts and aspirations, the march continued to the Staines Mansion where it halted. With a squad of dragoons leading the way, General Johnston, his staff, and the peace commissioners dismounted to discuss the terms dictated by Washington. A short time later the national ensign was raised, signaling the federal government's control and occupation of the territory. Although the meeting went smoothly, lulling the governor into believing that his bitter feud with the army was over, nothing could have prepared Cumming for the events that were to follow.

Viewing the polite diplomatic exchange, the soldiers were incensed that their government had abandoned all charges of treason against the Saints, an unmistakable sign that the day was rapidly approaching when the "Rogue's March" would be the marching song of the territory. Angered beyond measure, one officer remembered in his journal: "The soldiers hold a bitter feeling against the Mormons; everything which has transpired since the starting of this expedition from Fort Leavenworth up to the present time has tended to excite the rancor of the former against the latter."[23] Peace was the worst enemy, for without firing a shot each soldier believed he had lost a personal war. "The Mormons compelled the soldiers to undertake this arduous campaign across the sand plains," the officer continued, "destroyed so much of their supplies as to force them to live more than six months on short rations, caused them to winter in the bleak, desolate Rocky Mountains, insulted them to act, when from want of instructions they dare not punish it; belied them, defamed them, and prostituted their honor publicly. . . ."[24] A young lieutenant compared Buchanan's unwelcome decision to "that king of France who marched up the hill and then marched down again. . . . We marched the hill for the honor of our country . . . our country orders us down."[25]

Johnston came away from the governor's meeting profoundly depressed and in an unguarded moment was overheard saying to his close friend Major Fitz-John Porter that "he would give his plantation for a chance to bombard the city for fifteen minutes. . . ."[26] Whatever the general's true feelings might have been, he gave the order for the army to resume its march.

Led by Colonel Alexander, the tightly knit fighting unit of Tenth Infantrymen filed through the city. The unseasonably warm weather began to tell on the soldiers as men fell from the ranks from exhaustion and the spellbinding heat that reduced the column to silence. A light battery of the Fourth Artillery lumbered by, its men, hungry, weary, and footsore, the end of the first of three divisions of the expedition.[27] Moments later, Colonel Carlos Waite trudged through the city leading elements of the Fifth and Seventh Infantry. Only a short time elapsed before the twenty-four howitzers of the Third Artillery pounded the road into a nightmare of dust that filtered the sun from the moving lines of grenadiers and horsemen who followed the heavy caissons.

Even before the dust clouds came to rest on the men and animals, 250 mounted riflemen temporarily detached from the Department of New Mexico, a mixed regiment collected from elements of the First Cavalry, and the Third and Sixth Infantries, all led by Colonel William W. Loring, edged to the center of the settlement. A phalanx of volunteers headed by Captain Bernard Bee, composed of four companies of teamsters, herders, and laborers, largely recruited to guard the supply trains, marked the end of the expedition.

As the leading regiments emerged from the end of the avenue of full-foliaged young trees, the army passed over the Jordan Bridge and went into camp along the barren flatland bordering the river. After the march, with all its privations and hardships, the Mormon settlement had left an indelible impression on the soldiers who passed it. "Such a queer, quiet town!" wrote a member of the Second Dragoons. "Not a breath of smoke from a single chimney. Late in the afternoon the dust raised by column after column of the army was like a red vapor. It bloodshotted the sun, and the houses stood silent and solemn and stared at us, with their little windows that had no glass in them." Wrapped in a cloud of dust, the city was a microcosm of the world that the soldiers had left behind. "Here and there, in the dooryards, behind the palings or high fences, the fruit trees were all splattered over and bleeding with ripe cherries. And we were hungry for them, our mouths watered for them, but not one of them was touched. Nothing was touched not a house molested."[28]

Looking back at the broad valley sweeping in front of the mountain chain of the Wasatch, the soldiers were more and more impressed with the size, the magnificence, and the orderliness of the Mormon community. On both sides of a broad, straight avenue, adobe cottages, half-hidden behind rows of poplar and maple trees, were cast like a toy village, upright and tight. "They were set well apart," wrote Captain Albert Tracy of the Tenth Infantry, "nearly each by itself, and within the enclosures about them one saw that which one so longs to see from long familiarity with these deserts—perfectly bright green and luxuriant trees and shrubbery. The streets, as we viewed them from our height, are straight and wide, crossing each other generally at right angles. Beyond the city the Jordan River, running north and south. Beyond this the gray of the eternal desert, hemmed remotely by picturesque peaks and mountains."[29]

The mood of the military adventure heightened shortly before sundown when the last of the 600 heavy army wagons came clacking through the empty streets, trailing a herd of livestock that stretched from the gates of the city to the entrance of Emigration Canyon.[30] When General Johnston returned to his troops that same evening, he looked on as the soldiers washed off the dust of the campaign in the cooling waters of the Jordan.[31] Nothing the Mormons feared had come to pass. The army had slipped through the city without disturbing a single piece of property save an occasional cherry spoiling to be picked. To isolate his troops from the Saints and the horde of camp followers that trailed the army, a double guard was posted on the Jordan Bridge that spanned the waters.

Despite the stunning beauty of the surrounding mountains, the salt-trimmed land was overspread with gravel and prehistoric lake deposits of sand that readily became airborne and caked on men and animals alike. Two of the mainstays of an army in the field, grass and timber, were lacking; consequently, when the men ran short of fuel, they dismantled wooden windbreaks and fence lines to get firewood. Psychologically, the terrain gave the weary soldiers a sense of sadness, withdrawal and depression, and when they dipped their canteens into the brackish stream, they complained that the water was bitter as gall and undrinkable.[32] Johnston agreed. But there was also a silent fear that a temporary bivouac could not be constructed within gunshot of Salt Lake City without an eruption of blood and passion that would certainly jeopardize the army's mission among the Saints.

The Mormons were more than willing to offer their own solution. Early the following day, a delegation of Mormons, headed by Seth Blair, appeared at the Jordan Bridge and requested a meeting with General Johnston, who soon appeared before the Saints and escorted the visitors to a field tent occupied by Colonel C. F. Smith, Captain Jesse Reno, Major Fitz-John Porter, and Peace Commissioner Powell. After introducing Blair to his staff, the general turned the proceedings over to Smith and departed.[33]

The visit was brief. Although the Mormons' position had been weakened measurably by the close proximity of the military, Blair instructed the commander that the needs of the army would be better served in Cache Valley or some other point at a distance from Salt Lake City. The unsettled calm exploded, for Colonel Smith interpreted the statement as a request for a negotiated withdrawal of the expedition from the territory. His mind clouded by despair and exhaustion, the colonel warned Blair that the Mormons were in no position to bargain; furthermore, as far as the army was concerned, it "would like to see every damned Mormon hung by the neck."[34] Sensing something dangerous in the wind, Blair lost no time in leaving the conference to report the incident to Brigham Young. Old scores would be settled later.

At that moment officers jammed the road leading into Salt Lake City to explore the abandoned settlement, their curiosity driven by the confused model of Mormonism that they brought with them. "We were agreeably surprised," wrote Captain Gove, a self-appointed, free-lance reporter for the New York *Herald*, "to find the American banner attached to the top of several flag-staffs in different parts of the city, though from want of wind drooped gloomily by the side of their supporting staffs." The captain, always contemptuous of Mormon patriotism, added: "The language and deeds of the past, however, are not forgotten. Some of the flags had bees upon them instead of stars."[35] The officers observed the many-gabled Beehive residence of Brigham Young, the gothic-styled Assembly Hall, numerous dwellings of Church officials and boarded storehouses scattered throughout the city. When darkness put an end to their sightseeing, they finished their day at the Globe, the only inn Young permitted to remain open.[36]

Life turned pleasant as officers ate their first home-cooked meal in more than a year. In the following hours they were also entertained by the piping and drumming of a Mormon band, which for some unexplained reason appeared before the Globe to serenade the soldiers. But as the evening ebbed away, polygamy slipped into the officers' conversation, for nothing about that institution escaped their notice. After listening to the barracks-style impressions of Mormon women individually, and polygamy in general, the innkeeper exploded in anger. The host charged that the army had brought into the country a cauldron of unsavory men who were determined to seduce or rape every woman in the territory. As the lecture wore on, the innkeeper became more terse and accused the army of disregarding the well-being of the people of the territory while at the same time he condemned their irreverent attitude towards the many tragedies that had drenched the lives of a generation of Mormons.[37]

When the innkeeper finished, Captain Randolph Barnes Marcy rose to answer his host. Impaling his adversary with a mocking rebuttal, he asked proudly that if Brigham Young "should invite me to stay over night, what would you advise me to do?" Pointing to the Beehive House, he continued: "I am afraid after being so long virtuous to trust myself among so many pretty women, as many of them must necessarily be in suffering condition and it would be a severe tax upon my virtue if any of them should make an attack upon it. I think therefore upon reflection that I should decline the invitation."[38] In the half-light of the evening the officers walked somewhat happily away from the Globe and retraced their steps across the Jordan, their suspicions of future conflicts with the Mormons more than justified.

Under different circumstances, General Johnston and his staff were welcomed by Governor Cumming with a banquet of roasted venison and fresh strawberries, washed down with vintage Catawba that had been carefully transported across the plains. Although pitted against each other as natural enemies, both men agreed that a fort near Salt Lake City invited disaster; so when the general informed the governor that he intended to march his troops away from the city the following morning, tensions relaxed. Cumming showed no sign of concern when Johnston guessed that he would locate his force either in Rush or Cedar Valley. Meanwhile, he continued, the expedition would concentrate its forces ten or fifteen miles south of the city and await the return of the pioneers from the southern settlements. The always nervous Cumming received the intelligence with a sense of relief.[39]

Having made these commitments, Johnston made a sincere effort to establish closer relations with the governor by extending an invitation to

Cumming to accompany the army south, but the governor refused. At this point the intimacies of personal diplomacy ceased. In the future the two antagonists would fight their battles at long range and with deadly results. It was in this atmosphere of alienation that the commander left the city, never to return. Nor was he ever to meet Brigham Young or exchange correspondence with his implacable foe.

The army started south up the Jordan River on the morning of June 28, but without its commander. Accompanied by Ben McCulloch, Indian Agent Garland Hurt, and members of his staff, Johnston traveled westward to reconnoiter central Utah in search of a permanent camp. The trip took the advance party past the inhospitable southern shores of the Great Salt Lake, and across the rolling terrain that flanked the snow-capped Oquirrh Mountains to Rush Valley, at which point they plotted their course due south.[40]

Trooping through the long valley that was walled in on two sides by a series of continuous mountain ranges, the detachment arrived at the military reserve that had been set aside by Lieutenant Colonel Edward Genner Steptoe in 1855. A quick visual inspection of the site found the land less than adequate for the needs of the army and, having mentally sketched in detail these observations, General Johnston crossed the southern edge of the Oquirrh Mountains and continued on to the level floor of Cedar Valley.

Searching the horizon to the east he saw the naked peaks of the Lake Mountains silhouetted against an enormous sky; to the west the promontories of the Oquirrhs furnished an unforgettable landmark that stood guard over a broad circular basin. At the higher elevations the mountains were forested with stands of black pine and juniper, while at the lower elevations the semi-desert was covered with greasewood, sagebrush, and bleached-out wild grasses. Through a small cloud of dust the general could see a ribbon of cloudy water threading its way across the valley floor before disappearing into burning sands. From a distance the Wasatch Range loomed against the clouds in a series of dark curves, forming a great wall of stone that exaggerated the valley's isolation. In the central and northwestern part of the flat plain, two Mormon farming communities were located a short distance from each other, sustained by a few acres of agricultural land. Here and there, scattered livestock browsed on wild hay under the lazy summer sun. Cedar Valley would suit the needs of the army.

Stark tactical considerations also came into play, for Johnston's immediate concern was the security of the settlements that dotted the Mormon corridor from Brigham City in the north to Cedar City in the south. The army was impressed particularly by the thought that the valley was within a short march of the largest Mormon cities and within striking distance of the territorial capital at Fillmore, close enough to crush any insurrection against the federal government.[41] Moreover, it was strategically located to enable the army to guard the many segments of the overland routes leading to California, thus assuring a degree of safety to western migration.

The exploring party crossed Cedar Valley and rode north, passing through a funneled gap separating the Traverse Range from the Lake Mountains where they rendezvoused with the expedition's rear guard. Under the command of Colonel Alexander, the army had already struck its tents and marched southward upriver for a distance of sixteen miles, pitching camp at West Creek on June 30.[42] During the first week of July, Johnston held his men on the dry flats that separated the Jordan River from the eastern slope of the Oquirrh Mountains in anticipation of the return migration of the Saints; but they were slow in coming.[43]

As the dull routine of camp life dragged on, the thunder of Phelps's light artillery—"Brigham Young and his Twelve Apostles" as the officers christened them—opened the military celebration of Independence Day. Faced with sagging morale, Johnston allowed his men to drink freely, unrestrained by regimental whiskey rations. At noon, a special meal of fresh mutton, dried fish and fresh vegetables, purchased from Mormon farmers, was washed down by a pint ration of the "best nineteen cent whiskey" the commissary could command.[44] When the soldiers wandered from the camp they returned with locally distilled "Valley Tan," a raw liquor known to bring about a complete change in the personality of drinkers, having the same salubrious properties as novocaine. As the liquor flowed freely, intoxication festered, bloomed, and ended with the jailing of several officers and men. The arrests led to a quick estrangement between Colonel Cooke and his subordinates, for the Dragoon commander was not prone to overlook breaches in military conduct. "The patriotic fervor of said Cooke does not appear to lead him to the recognition of too much noise," wrote Captain Tracy, "even upon this, our nation's holiday. Why not, oh Cooke, the wind itself arrest, for it is upon a most royal blow-out and roaring at the top of its voice?"[45]

Across Utah Lake the Mormon settlers passed the day quietly, almost unnoticed by the army. Several days earlier, Brigham Young had disconsolately weighed the decision whether or not to end the Mormon Exodus, a decision that hinged on the recall of reinforcements marching toward Utah under General Harney. "We do not consider it advisable to return to our homes at present," he wrote to the adjutant general of the Nauvoo Legion, James Ferguson, "but when we receive information that reinforcements are actually ordered back and witness still further the peaceable disposal of the army here then we can return with assurance that the President is sincere and intends to carry out his pledges made through his Commissioners."[46] Two days later, June 29, the eagerly awaited word reached Provo: Harney's reinforcements had halted. With the exception of three columns ordered to continue on to Camp Floyd, the remaining elements of the army were redirected to other territories.[47]

With pretended indifference to the army's presence, Brigham Young ordered the Saints to return to the northern settlements. "All who wish to return to their homes in Salt Lake City are at liberty to do so," he was reported to have said.[48] As the prophet spoke, he was well aware that the Saints had reached the end of their endurance and "it seemed wise . . . to announce the official end of the exodus before his people began to abandon it of their own free will."[49] The great push north was set in motion on the first day of July, with Brigham Young at its head, followed by the members of the First Presidency and a trickle of Nauvoo Legionnaires. Thirty thousand Saints eventually followed, but a large number of Mormons "who had exhausted their resources were not able to leave immediately, and some remained permanently where their flight had landed them."[50]

Meanwhile, the Utah Expedition again set its course toward Cedar Valley. The marching orders came none too soon, for the soldiers had suffered in silence the powdered inferno caused by thousands of unyoked livestock wandering near and around the camp. The correspondent for the *New York Times*, one of the half-dozen journalists to march with the army, described the site as "intolerably dusty, and the high winds to which we were exposed aggravated the nuisance; the water was scant also, and we below were either forced to drink a mixture of mud and water, of the consistence of molasses, or send some two miles into the mountains for a clear specimen of the protoxice." The same writer suggested that the departure might have been hastened a little by the collapse of the general's tent and the good dusting he received during one of the violent blows. "I cannot say with certainty, but it was rumored immediately after the accident alluded to, that a move would be made the next day. As the majority were eager to leave, we might remark that the wind blew somebody good, even if it did bring down the general's ranch."[51]

Strung out in long parallel columns, the army staggered in a zigzag pattern in search of grass and water, much to the astonishment of passing Saints. At times the army found itself entangled in the lines of returning settlers who swarmed over the dugway on foot, on horseback, or in wagons. For Private Henry S. Hamilton, and every member of the expedition who passed the Mormon caravans, the suffering of the Saints was visibly apparent: "They numbered more than a thousand, and were wretched-looking beings—men, women, boys and girls, ragged and dirty, though some of the young girls had endeavored to make as respectable an appearance as possible, by making garments out of corn sacks. They were driving a number of animals, consisting of cows, sheep, and pigs."[52] Another witness wrote,

The refugees returning from the southern settlements continue to line the road with their trains of wagons, herds and flocks. Some of these trains present scenes by no means pleasant to the eye. Here we see a young girl of eighteen, with bare feet and half-clad form, driving a yoke of oxen, and there a tender little girl of scarcely 8 years of age, whipping up two or three obstreperous pigs, dragging her little feet wearily and painfully over the sharp gravel road.[53]

"The wagons are usually piled up with the coarsest and commonest furniture, with a chicken coup and its crackling [*sic*] occupants strapped upon the rear," wrote another. "Sometimes the pig occupies this post, and the chickens are packed inside the vehicles with the children. But everywhere, poverty—poverty—squalid poverty, meets us, turn as we will."[54]

The noise and motion of the caravans frequently brought the two forces in contact with each other, the men and their wives receiving special attention from soldiers: "Say, old boy, can't you spare one of those women?" "Say, don't they whip you sometimes?" "Do you all sleep in one bed?"[55]

One incident followed another until the Saints could no longer suffer in silence. As the day wore away a Mormon caravan attempted to cross in front of the advancing regiments, only to be halted by a coarse, wide-shouldered sergeant. At that moment a man came out of the wagon and stepped in front of the soldier, his hand resting on a brace of pistols. There was quiet for many seconds before the Mormon ordered the wagons to advance through the army lines. "I have helped to build this road and I will travel it," would be the only words spoken.[56] The lines of hatred were firmly drawn.

Moving as quickly as trail conditions would permit, Johnston marched his troops away from the main road, skirted west around the Lake Mountains and encamped with his army along a small creek flowing into the northern end of Cedar Valley. It required two days to complete the extraordinary task of collecting the enormous quantities of supplies and draft animals, and soldiers met their old enemy—grey, billowing, alkali dust. "It becomes as powdered as the wagons pass over it on our march," wrote Captain Gove, "so that, with perspiration on the face, we get as black as though we were painted. Dust so thick that you cannot see a foot before you for most of the day."[57]

As the army carried out the routine of military life among these natural discomforts, Lieutenant Colonel Daniel Ruggles laid out a permanent post, and two days later the first ground was broken. In fact, construction had begun before General Johnston received the necessary authorization from the War Department.[58]

Throughout the fall and early winter, Camp Floyd moved rapidly towards completion, aided by an army of Mormon laborers and mechanics who flocked to Cedar Valley to offer their services at three dollars a day.[59] Several hundred discharged teamsters were also given short-term contracts by the Quartermaster Department to quarry native stone from nearby bluffs, which masons turned into walls for the stockades and arsenals. Soon other men, recruited to haul black pine from the Oquirrh Mountains, joined the great drifting mass of workers who labored under trying conditions in a mad race against the approach of winter. A mix of rain and dust plagued man and beast alike, reported an eastern newspaper correspondent.

> The ground all over a space of several square miles had been ploughed by a thousand teams, until the dust lay six or eight inches deep. The steady rains at the beginning of this week have changed it into a gigantic mud pudding, and the appearance of the camp yesterday was suggestive of the town of Eden, commemorated in *Martin Chuzzlewit*. Military water-gods, in soaked blue overcoats and cowhide boots, were wading disconsolately around the *adobes*, some of which, from lack of roofs, were beginning to melt under the patter of the rain.[60]

Under fair skies or graying clouds, Mormon adobe makers worked around the clock to manufacture 1,600,000 earthen bricks, receiving thirty thousand dollars in gold for their efforts. Through their agents, Brigham Young and Heber C. Kimball sold $70,000 worth of finished lumber that was used to roof the barracks.[61]

During the first month of construction, workers were forced to improvise their own tools, since most of the army's implements had been destroyed in the disastrous fall campaign of 1857. Working in concert, Mexicans roofed the pueblo-styled structures with pine poles over which brush and dirt were thrown, while Mormon handicraftsmen pounded the clay floors into a glossy hardness under the quartermaster's supervision. Over the dirt floors layers of canvas and other coverings gave an almost luxurious insulation against the winter cold. Plunging into the activity, teamsters reshaped rough lumber for framing and army blacksmiths hammered wrought iron straps and hinges to bind timbers into doors and window shutters.

The prodigious feat of erecting three hundred buildings was accomplished in the incredibly short space of four months. With an eye more toward utility than beauty, the soldiers' living quarters were one-storied buildings, divided into rooms twelve or fifteen feet square, with comfortable fireplaces. Because of the high cost of glass, windows were disproportionately small. During the first year in the camp's history, however, the Seventh Infantry preferred to build circular or elliptical walls of adobes, four or five feet high, roofed by Sibley or wall tents.[62]

From a distance, the camp appeared as an unwalled rectangular fortress. Fronting on Cedar Creek was a half-mile-long row of infantry barracks divided from the officers' quarters by a street fifty feet wide. Phelps's and Reynolds's artillery batteries were anchored on the eastern end of this line.[63] Locking the western edge of the post from Cedar Creek south, an unbroken expanse of fourteen buildings that headquartered General Johnston and his staff crowded the valley floor. Across the camp's southern perimeter the warehouses, workshops, and outbuildings of the Quartermaster Department took form, and to the east were the corrals and stables of the Second Dragoons. Behind these structures a mountain of firewood was stored and "acres of wagons clustered in masses . . . with their tongues in air like bristling mighty lances of olden time."[64] The eastern flank was open, giving spectators a view of eight or nine avenues that ended at departmental headquarters. Scattered within this area were living quarters for civilian employees and army officers, as well as four hospitals, five guardhouses, numerous bowling alleys, canteens, sutler's stores and scores of utility buildings. "We have to provide storage for two years of provisions, quartermasters, ordinance and medical stores," Johnston wrote to his son. "These require 2,000 wagons to have them, each carrying about 5,000 lbs.—these buildings alone 12 or 14 about 600 feet long will be a heavy work to complete."[65]

But less than two months later, on November 9, the new fort was ready for occupancy and was dedicated in honor of the Secretary of War, John Buchanan Floyd. A thousand miles or more from his home, Captain Albert Tracy carefully noted in his diary the beginning of the fort's history. "In the presence of the whole force, under arms, and with the national salvo from Phelps' guns, the flag of our country is today raised at Camp Floyd. A whiskey ration is further-more enjoyed by the men, and at headquarters, punch and lunch by the officers."[66]

The year ended with a howling blizzard—a portent of events to follow.

CHAPTER FOUR

THE SCOURGE OF GOLD: FAIRFIELD

Great is the town of Frog,
Where reigneth Barley-corn;
Where we barter cares at night;
For the head-ache of the morn;
Where hushed in grim repose,
The Tiger waits his prey—
And the prey steals in—but Frog, oh Frog
The joys may never pay!

—Valley Tan[1]

ALMOST FROM THE DAWN OF CIVILIZATION every army had its Fairfield. The Mormons called it Sodom and Gomorrah of the Great Basin; soldiers, the most fearless of whom quaked at prospects of passing through its streets, named it Frog or "Dobe-Town." Like a malignant cancer, it sapped the life from Camp Floyd, and in this respect resembled a number of western boom towns which through an illegitimate birth existed to serve the army's need for dissipation. In short, Fairfield was an anomaly in Utah politics, a government within a government, the relative independence of which posed a genuine threat to the Saintly Kingdom. Yet unlike its historic counterparts, the early beginning of Fairfield was marked by events typical of thousands of settlements that sprang up along the western frontier.

During the spring of 1854, almost seven years after the Saints reached the territory, Mormon pioneers rode into Cedar Valley, led by John Carson, his four brothers, and Amos Fielding. Through suffering, uncertainty, and persistent danger, they followed the well-established pattern installed by Brigham Young for colonies located at distant points in the western desert. A thick-walled fortress was built

59

with primitive materials near the north bank of Cedar Creek, strategically anchored to control Indian movements through central Utah. Though the outpost offered very little in the way of man-made beauty, it rose abruptly above the sage-strewn valley floor to enclose four square rods of living space, including a stone food warehouse, eight deep adobe apartments that butted against the interior walls, and a circular cistern that stored water carried from the nearby stream. Within the grey fieldstone walls of Fort Fairfield, a shooting platform formed part of the common roof and sloped from the top of the rampart to an interior courtyard which opened to the east with a heavy planked gate, ten feet wide. Partly because the fort was intended to serve as a fortification rather than a permanent outpost, dugouts were burrowed into the earth to house the remaining families, close enough to the fort to provide protection against a surprise attack by the Indians moving between the settlements of central Utah.[2]

But the earthen mortar had scarcely hardened in the fort's walls when the isolated settlement was attacked by a Paiute war party from Rush Valley. In an early dawn strike George Carson and John Barrow were cut down when they attempted to collect a herd of loose cattle a short distance from the fort. With the entire western valley suddenly aflame, the survivors abandoned any idea of further settlement, evacuated the stockade, and moved the settlement to Cedar Fort, a few miles northeast of the outpost. When the bloodletting was finally over in the spring of 1857, the Saints returned to Fairfield, only to abandon their fields once more with the advance of the federal army into Cedar Valley. But Johnston's Army proved to be but part of the Mormons' problem, for in the turbulent times that followed, Fairfield seemed to the Saints like a demon materializing out of the muck of the Cedar Creek marshes—a symbol of the depravity of man and the triumph of evil.

Advancing like locusts freshly hatched by the summer sun, a swarm of bullwhackers, mule skinners, gamblers, and other unruly characters drifted into Fairfield to open a new chapter in the village's history. Simultaneously, General Johnston called a meeting of the most respected men of the community and warned them of the immediate disorders and moral decay that were soon to come. The general's forebodings, not without bias since he was not a newcomer to the West, were addressed to John Carson: "Mr. Carson, I have felt since I have been here that you feel like me and my men may harm you or your people. I want to tell you we do not intend to molest you or your people at all, but I do want to say this—whether you know it or not, there is always a rough element that follows any army and they are coming here now."[3] After a brief pause the commander continued: "I can handle them on my side of the creek. It may be with a few police you have you may not be able to keep order. That is why I asked you to come here. If that time ever comes and you need some help, let me know and I will be glad to help you, Mr. Carson—Good Day."[4] The general's warning proved well-founded: he foretold the death of the Mormon village.

A dark and evil-laden world came to Fairfield two days later when a swelling mass of "blacklegs" swarmed into Cedar Valley, breaking the orderly mold of the Mormon community. Under the wary eyes of the army and a handful of Indians, the camp followers took possession of the abandoned fort, homes, and private dwellings, and proceeded with their plans to establish their own capital within the shadow of Camp Floyd.

That tragic day dawned when Carson returned to Fairfield to find a tall, willowy man standing against a corral, smoking a cigarette; but when the Mormon approached closer, the curious figure of a gambler stepped forward like a man bent on revenging some unforgivable injury. At the same moment, Carson noticed that someone had laid claim to his buildings and constructed a rectangular pigsty along the river. Just as suddenly, the Saint developed a sharp awareness that danger threatened. Hidden in a belt under the other man's waistcoat, Carson caught sight of a bowie knife and a cannon-like revolver. A doubled-barreled shotgun was carelessly held diagonally across the gambler's chest.

Acting out his bluff, Carson insisted on knowing who erected the corrals, where the person was who gave such authorization, and if the gambler was prepared to explain his presence on Carson's property. The questions were answered with the menacing click of a shotgun being readied for firing. Pointing with his weapon in the direction of the stream, the blackleg warned: "I am putting that [pigsty] there, in spite of Brigham Young, General Johnston, or God Almighty."[5] Carson nodded his head in disapproval, turned his back on the gambler, and returned to Cedar Fort to remap his strategy. The following day he confronted the outlaw for the second time. Again the conversation was cut short by the gambler, who dropped his wiry hand to his pistol and warned Carson that if he again set foot on the north side of Cedar Creek he would be a dead man.[6] For one of the few times in his life, John Carson knew terror and turned his eyes to Camp Floyd.

Still smarting from his humiliating experience, he penned a courtly note to General Johnston explaining what had transpired and requesting the army's support in moving the gambler from his property. The Mormon did not have to wait long for an answer, for the general was visibly annoyed by the contents of the dispatch. Arming himself with a brace of pistols, Johnston led a procession of dragoons along the long rows of partially constructed barracks, through the parade ground, past soldiers and horses in parade lines north to the Mormon settlement. Crossing the narrow planked bridge into Frogtown, he stopped the detachment short of the gambler's living quarters. After conferring with Carson, the general ordered the dragoons to enter the house, and moments later the gambler stood facing the general. With the fate of Fairfield hanging in the balance, Johnston informed the gambler that under normal circumstances he would not consider the blackleg's activities worthy of a second thought, but since the animal pens were endangering the health of the army, as well as the citizens of Fairfield, he could not remain indifferent. As he spoke, the general looked directly into the gambler's eyes, causing them to cow and twitch.

Having brought the charlatan under his influence, the commander read aloud Carson's dispatch, then asked the cardsharp to repeat the remark in his presence. The blackleg, gazing back with panic-stricken eyes, answered uncomfortably: "I am putting that there, that there, and that there, in spite of Brigham Young or God Almighty."[7] This time he carefully omitted mentioning Johnston's name.

The general exploded, and with a harsh voice warned the blackleg "that unless those things were away from there in thirty-six hours he would be moved at the point of a bayonet." The gambler's heated protest had little effect; the commander's face remained cold as iron. Barely a day later the gambler abandoned his holdings. However, before very much time had passed, he opened a brothel and gaming house east of the city and became one of the celebrated men in the wasteland of Fairfield.[8] The incident was one of a series of events that tested Johnston's cautious approach to Mormonism; but to the Saints' chagrin, the general's actions were to fluctuate dramatically with time and proximity.[9]

Sheltered under the protective arm of three thousand federal troops, the indefatigable Carson dismantled the Fairfield fort and, using the salvaged materials, expanded his modest home into a long, pleasant two-story wayside inn. The building's walls were constructed of adobe bricks, its roof supported by hand-sawn pine that grew in the nearby Oquirrh Mountains. The architecture of the Stagecoach Inn, as it was later called, was in keeping with the primitive country, and stood like a greying sentinel standing guard in an otherwise hostile land. The ground floor of the inn consisted of several connected rooms, the walls garnished with the clutter typical of the frontier. The largest and most attractive room was the downstairs parlor, which served as the center of entertainment, dimly lighted by an oil lamp hanging from the ceiling. Normal decorations, such as a wooden clock, family and church portraits, as well as rough furniture, complemented the simple surroundings of the countryside.

Doubling as a dining hall, where the innkeeper presided at meals and led the conversations, the sitting room was the center of the inn's social life. The bread was freshly baked, the food always abundant, well-cooked, and consumed rapidly and silently. The upper level was entered by a small door at the left of the living room, and after ascending a twisting, narrow flight of stairs, guests found themselves facing bedrooms that varied only in size. Bedding was usually plentiful and clean. Customers washed from a common porcelain basin inevariably flanked by a bar of yellow soap, and were expected, when weather permitted, to immerse themselves in the nearby stream or not bathe at all.

For five hundred miles west of Fairfield no accommodations matched the Stagecoach Inn, which seemed opulent in comparison to the verminous way stations that dotted the Great Basin. The social life at the inn attracted a large number of traveling showmen and prominent personalities who passed an otherwise idle hour in safe comfort. The lighthearted officers of Camp Floyd found the quiet life of the hotel a welcome sanctuary from their congested living quarters or the disease-ridden hovels of Frogtown. History destined the inn to become a major stopover for the Overland Stage and the Pony Express, and for a decade following the completion of the transcontinental railroad, it offered the last stage service between the Wasatch Mountains and the Nevada border.[10]

In contrast to the serene atmosphere of the way station, the dusty, smoky streets of Fairfield became, in the eyes of many spokesmen, a refuge for all of society's outcasts and criminals. Situated astride Cedar Creek, Front Street was lined with a dense network of connected gambling dens, dance halls, brothels, and other second-rate establishments that reflected the lawless character of the village. The picture was enlarged somewhat in 1859 when an additional wave of gamblers and saloon keepers swarmed into a second district, a half-mile row of one-story frame buildings that began at the Fairfield bridge and extended north until it topped out abruptly in the desert. The outskirts of Fairfield were dotted with canvas-covered shacks, wagon-box huts and dugouts pitched among the chaparral—all marked by ingenious advertisements that spelled out the specialty of the house. Scattered through the heavily frequented streets, 10,000 inhabitants moved ankle-deep in mud after heavy rains or suffocated in the talcum dust in summer, seldom escaping the pungent odors of uncollected human and animal waste.

In these troubled times life in Frogtown was dominated by gambling, and one did not wander far without running into this social phenomenon. Gaming was carried on privately and publicly and, though forbidden by territorial statute, it became the consuming pastime of the idle, the indolent, and the professional gambler, all of whom seemed to be addicted to crimes of violence. The debris of a displaced society was drawn to the basin from the far reaches of the continent—cardsharps fresh from the goldfields of California, Mexicans muffled in their serapes who could lose a fortune without moving a muscle, smartly dressed Monte dealers from the river trade whose good or ill luck was not betrayed by a change in facial expression, and discharged soldiers and teamsters. In its time, the gambling halls of Fairfield became legend, being more numerous and notorious than those in any other frontier town of equivalent size. But to the Saints, the town was a den of vipers.

At the height of the Fairfield boom, Charles Bailey, a prospering Mormon merchant, described a marathon card game he had witnessed: "During the winter," he wrote in his journal, "I in company with some others went up in the gambling room and seen more Gold stacked up in the center of the table than I ever seen before or since." He noted the variety of expressions on the faces of the two shadowy men who sat at a square table under a heavy tobacco haze, a coal oil lamp sputtering a cloud of black smoke. The raw-boned, cadaverous-appearing gamblers were "betting and dealing cards and the other two exchanging the checks according to the winning and losing. The money was not touched, it remained there as a bank. It was said 32,000 dollar was the hand. They played for about two days and nights when one of them lost." The young observer, who could not resist his own fascination for the game, looked over the backs of the gamblers and saw each man armed with a revolver which rested on the table next to his free hand. "I thought that looked terrible because I see the waiter of the house keep bringing up four little glasses of liquor and I would wonder what would be their outcome but all came out all right one made happy and the other miserable."[11]

At the time these words were written, another military spectator, Henry S. Hamilton, described his impressions of one of the Fairfield gambling dens. "At one part of the room would sit an ugly-looking individual with a pile of gold, a wheel, a deck of cards and in his hands a revolver, waiting for a victim."[12]

Few visitors to Frogtown failed to find a game to their liking, though the favorite game in Utah was three-handed Monte, an uncomplicated exercise in cards that offered a reasonable chance of winning and limited opportunity for cheating. Nevertheless, cheating was present wherever gambling was found. Lured by the temptations of easy riches and extravagant living, gamblers devised ingenious systems of cheating, ranging from elementary exercises in switching decks, palming, or dealing off the bottom of the deck to trimming, marking, or edging the cards. Mirrors, secret drawers, signals, and a wide range of devices were kept in reserve to move the odds still further in the professionals' favor. When the stakes were high, roulette was played to the advantage of the house, but more characteristically Lady Luck was nudged along by braking devices operated with a slight movement of the gambler's knee. Men lost their fortunes with the turn of a card or the roll of a wheel. In the confusion and emotional turbulence of amateurish attempts to match the gamblers at their trade, seasoned sergeants who waged a private war on green felt tables from Monterey to Camp Floyd, young lieutenants fresh from penny-ante games of the West Point barracks, and officers from Virginia who were schooled in Southern gaming all lost to the professionals. Nevertheless, it was an exciting time that sharpened the instincts for self-preservation for adventurers accustomed to a life of ceaseless danger.

From the beginning, Fairfield was plagued by frequent outbreaks of violence, and no man felt safe without a weapon close at hand. Border-ruffians walked the streets by day, always ready for an argument, or prowled by night, robbing and murdering unsuspecting victims.[13] Those fortunate enough to live through their ordeal at Frogtown, such as John Young Nelson, never forgot their experiences. From the pages of his memoirs one gains some idea of the explosive temperament of the time, along with the repeated catastrophes that dogged life in the raw frontier community.

Long before the national standard had unfurled over Camp Floyd, Nelson had participated in a full range of frontier experiences in the changing West, joining the Utah Expedition at Fort Leavenworth as a wagonmaster in the spring of 1857. Arriving in the territory, he continued on the federal payroll and during the next year helped in the construction of Camp Floyd. With the arrival of the first federal gold from California during the spring of 1859, Nelson left government service with eighteen months back pay in his pockets, preferring the gay and certain profits of the saloon trade to freighting. At this point he formed a partnership with another young fortune hunter named Lewis, and opened a freewheeling tavern in the heart of Frogtown. "There were plenty of cut-throats, gamblers, and thieves there who supported us," he later wrote in his autobiography, "and as the troops also favored us with their patronage, we saw before long we were in for a very good thing."[14] But Nelson's fortunes were beginning a reversal.

During the first months of his stay in Fairfield, when Cedar Valley sweltered under the blazing desert sun, Nelson walked out of his saloon to test his luck at the gambling tables of his competitors. However, as he passed one of the saloons, he saw the curtains pummeled aside and, driven by curiosity, he stopped and almost mechanically glanced through the window. Suddenly he became apprehensive. "I just peeped through the window to see how they were getting on. There I saw two men with their bowie-knives drawn, standing over a man who was stretched out on the floor," he related. "I thought to myself, 'hello, there's a murder. I am better off out of this,' and I walked away quickly."[15]

About this time a large, grizzly bear of a gambler charged out of the saloon cursing in unprintable language, and demanded to know what the teamster was doing. Nelson's reaction to this outburst was to reply that he meant no harm, he "was looking for a friend." Angered by the answer he received, the gambler lurched forward and drew from his scabbard a sharp broad-knife, already stained with the blood of one victim. Nelson stared in horror, immobilized by fear. "He then called me all the names he could think of, and said he would teach me better manners," the teamster remembered, "winding up by making straight at me with his knife, and expressing a determination to have my heart's blood."[16]

At that moment the murderer lunged forward, his weapon swinging in a wide arc; but Nelson stepped to one side and avoided the strike. As the gambler struggled to regain his footing, Nelson ran along Main Street, only to realize that the killer was sticking hard on his trail. There was no escape. Suddenly, Nelson stopped, drew his pistol, and waited. "He would not listen," Nelson continued, "and made a dart forward, but I slipped out of his way and fired a shot in the air to let him know I was capable of defending myself. This seemed to enrage him the more, for he now came at me with his knife like a bull at a gate." Drawing a deep breath, Nelson fired. The gambler "threw up his hands and fell backwards with a groan."[17]

After he recovered his composure, Nelson leaned over the wounded gambler and saw a deep cavity torn in the man's stomach. Kneeling over the wounded man, Nelson spoke to his victim: "I told him I was not to blame; that he would have killed me if I had not protected myself. . . ." As a crowd gathered, Nelson lifted himself to his feet and returned to his saloon. As news of the shooting reached every backroom gambling hall, he bade farewell to his friends and started east on foot toward Provo. Under the circumstances, the decision to leave Fairfield was unavoidable. "In those days the settlement of those matters was usually decided by the majority. I did not know what friends he had, but a glance told me that one or two in my place at the time would be of no assistance to me. I therefore thought discretion the better part of valor. . . ."[18]

After a thirty-mile trek, he arrived in Provo, exhausted by the terrifying experience. Shortly afterwards, he learned that the killing had been judged self-defense; but the news did little to reassure him.

Without thinking twice, Nelson remarked, "If I returned I should probably have to kill some of his friends, who would try to avenge his death, or should get killed myself." Having received his baptism by fire into the roughnecked fraternity of frontiersmen, he added, "the law of six-shooters was the only one then in existence, and revolvers were called into requisition to settle all matters in dispute."[19]

The prevalence of lawlessness paralleled the introduction of prostitution. The shortage of marriageable women precluded enforcement of the territorial laws that prohibited such traffic, so houses of ill-fame that met every taste and purse flourished openly. Such places occupied street corners as well as some of the blocks in between where travelers reported that harem-type brothels rivaled each other seeking to draw the attention of susceptible customers. One of the most popular houses on Front Street, a gaudy, two-story building resembling a small-town hotel, lured men to rumpled beds with a crimson and yellow marquee that read: "Love House."[20]

Though adroit operations were cosmopolitan in their recruiting, Fairfield brothels were never comparable to the tenderloins of San Francisco; yet the lack of sybaritic surroundings was scarcely noticed by most of the single men and a substantial number of married men who spent a large part of their time and money in these establishments. In the uncomplicated logic of the frontier, every female was a delectable paragon of love, given enough time. Half-naked harlots charged exorbitant sums for their services. Sometimes neurotic, more often passive from long years of abuse, prostitutes obeyed codes not of their making and enjoyed neither happiness nor financial security. Preferring the noisy friendships of the Fairfield saloons to the harsh home life of frontier women, they were exploited mercilessly by their "owners," who bought and sold them for one hundred dollars apiece.

Representing every nation of the globe, masquerading under deceptive euphemisms were such feminine personages as "Gentle Annie," "Dobie Mary," or "Pretty Polly." They were experts in liquor, gambling, and backroom violence. Hoping to capitalize on the shortage of women, the "Soiled Doves of the Wasatch" used a variety of approaches to lure men to bed, depending on the willingness and experience of the customer. Regulars were sold five-minute dances for a dollar and then promenaded to one of their cribs for further pleasures. Life in the bawdy houses was primitive, but for the young, inexperienced plainsmen several preliminaries often were added before going to bed. "The girl was usually prepared for this and was well coached. So while the gambling stopped—the other girls giggled—the boys at the bar whooped, he and 'Sweetheart,' stripped naked as they danced. No cover charge."[21]

Far more dramatic was the whiplash violence created by a class of border ruffians generally called teamsters.[22] There were countless descriptions abounding in Fairfield that attested to the characters of these men. One bitter chronicler, Captain Phelps, saw them as "young, half savage men who looked as if they had not washed their persons or dress since leaving the Missouri," easily provoked to violence, brazenly quarrelsome, and universally expert in use of vulgar language, the mildest form of which could sear prairie grass for a distance of fifty yards.[23]

Among those whose eyes turned westward to the Utah frontier was Richard Thomas Ackley, an extraordinary observer of the flood of events that inundated the territory. In a series of vivid sketches that would remain forever a part of the history of the Mormon people, Ackley left his impressions of this special breed of westerner. John Lainhart was a Missouri swaggerer who "would do what he was bid, from killing a man to anything else that could be mentioned." Inspired by Ackley's trust, Lainhart confessed to killing two men before he had joined the wagon train headed for the territory.[24] Becoming familiar with the bloody diversions of the restless frontier, Lainhart took

> charge of one of the trains that came out from the River and sold considerable goods to Traders on the road, and he collected a great deal of money on the trip. The men in the train were aware of this, and they plotted a scheme by which they expected to kill John, and take possession of the train, and go across the country to Mexico. So one fine morning they made an attempt, by the leader of the party coming up while the train was in motion and catching John's mule by the head, made a demand for him to turn over to him all the money he had. Of course, he was well armed. John very calmly remarked, "Just let me have time to get down," and as he got off on the opposite side he cocked his double-barrel shotgun and let the fellow have one barrel in his head. He never spoke, was killed instantly; of course this created some little commotion. The rest of the party soon surrendered.[25]

One of Ackley's protagonists was John Scudder or "Black John," the son of a frontiersman and native to St. Louis. "Black John" was often unscrupulous, quick to anger, ruthless in his dealings, and lived a raucous, fast life as clerk on a steamboat on the Mississippi and Missouri Rivers. But like many others who drifted to the West, he settled down to gambling and an occasional murder that gave him considerable notoriety. "John was good company, but would get on a spree once in awhile."[26]

Another example of a teamster who possessed no small degree of courage was George Hewitt, better known as George Harney, who was born in Washington and was a nephew of General "Squawkiller" Harney. A dapper bandit and a notorious street fighter who was impossible to mistake, George Harney gave the impression of a man anxious to kill somebody. "He wore a large pair of horse pistols for months, that were given to him by Hart, a noted gambler, that was in the country at the time. Harney always wore pistols sticking out in front, and was a little too fond of pulling them out and cocking them on any person, that would give him cause."[27]

In an effort to outlive his companions of the high plains, the twenty-seven-year-old Ackley abandoned the unrestrained life of a teamster to operate a mercantile house owned by Captain Andrew B. Miller of the firm of Miller, Russell Company. One of the most celebrated men in Utah in 1859, Miller was born in Pennsylvania, though he lived most of his adult life in the West.[28] In little more than a decade, Miller had recast his career from a cook on a Mississippi keel boat to that of "captain" of one of the many gothic steamboats plying the river trade—a title by which he was addressed the rest of his life. To his enemies he was a clever faro dealer, hot-tempered and quick to react violently to any affront. In 1855 he traveled to Fort Leavenworth, where he multiplied his wealth by a series of successful commercial investments; but for Miller these were violent days, for the merciless warfare of the Kansas bloodbath haunted him for decades. Embroiled in this struggle, he raised a company of pro-slavery volunteers who became the "terror of the U.S. troops operating against him as his men were of the most desperate character."[29]

The movements of the Utah Expedition from its base in Kansas drew Miller into freighting and merchandising, leading to his partnership with William H. Russell. The partner was taken into the firm when William B. Waddell was asked to help furnish the firm with goods and credit.[30] When Johnston's Army settled into Camp Scott, Miller opened a sutler store and remained in winter quarters until the expedition marched into the territory. Such was the mentor of Richard Thomas Ackley.

While in Fairfield, Ackley witnessed the deep-running currents of lawlessness sweep past his door, a grinding drama of bloody ambushes and midnight assassinations. Soon after his arrival in Fairfield, a young Kentuckian, Oliver H. Rucker, entered the trading house and walked unhurriedly to the rear office of A. B. Miller. The shop appeared deserted with the exception of John Lainhart and George Harney, who were sitting on the counter smoking, when a second man, Langford M. Peale, stepped up briskly to the cashier's cage and asked for the store's owner. Ackley glanced up from his work and avoided a direct answer by pointing to the back room. As Peale reached the rear door he confronted Rucker coming out of the office. Well-armed and ready to fight, Peale drew his dragoon-model pistol and shouted, "I have come to kill you."

"What do you want to kill me for?" Rucker said grimly, looking around the room for help.

"Because you have been cheating me," came the unwavering answer.

Rucker snapped back a reply, "Well, if you want to kill me you had better do it now."

Instantly the room seemed to fill with the acrid smell of exploding gunpowder, Ackley later recalled. "Rucker, who always was quick as lightning, after receiving this death shot, drew his pistol and fired at the man, the ball passing through his thigh. I jumped of course to try and prevent more shooting, but to no good purpose. Rucker lay on the floor and this other person laid by the door with his head resting on a sack. They were about 12 paces apart and kept on firing."[31]

With a single-minded intent, both men emptied their pistols at each other. Rucker's first shot struck Peale in the jaw. The remaining bullets splattered against the wall near the assassin's head. Peale's return fire struck the floor three feet from Rucker, but two shots glanced off the timbers, severing Rucker's middle and index fingers before smashing through the front window. Another one of Peale's bullets struck Rucker in the chest, a second four inches above the heart.

The battle raged fiercely for only a minute and when it was over, Ackley rushed to the fallen bodies. "I was the first one to be by their sides. I picked up the empty pistols. Rucker says to me, 'I am a dead man.' The other fellow says, 'Tell her I died game.' "[32] Teamsters were a tough lot.

The history of Fairfield reflected little credit on the federal government, itself a knowing contributor to lawlessness by recklessly exploiting the labor of teamsters only to abandon them to the misfortunes of unemployment. The problem started shortly before the completion of Camp Floyd. The conflict grew in intensity when the Secretary of War ordered the discharge of nine hundred teamsters from federal service to reduce operational costs of the Department of Utah, thereby silencing congressional criticism of the heavy expenditures of the Utah War.[33] In his headquarters deep in Cedar Valley, General Johnston was ordered to examine the army payroll thoroughly to find additional ways to reduce military spending in the territory, a decision that was both unwise and poorly timed. Apparently lacking rudimentary geographic knowledge of the West, Washington failed to take into account that the lateness of the season made it impossible for the ill-equipped and inadequately clothed teamsters to reach California or Missouri without meeting extreme hardship or death. As the dark winter months came to Cedar Valley, there seemed little hope that the teamsters could survive without suffering extreme hardships.

Governor Cumming bitterly assailed the federal directive, the results of which were hardly lost on the sensitive executive. In a message that failed in diplomacy, the unhappy governor sharply criticized the ruinous policies of his superiors, and instructed Johnston that it was the army's responsibility to prevent any impulsive reaction on the teamsters' part that would lead to the loss or destruction of Mormon property.[34] In response, the general played down the terrible specter that haunted the Mormons, assuring the governor: "I do not think that there should exist any apprehension of a great disturbance of the peace. The men now discharged by the Government almost without exception appear to be orderly and well disposed, and I hear nothing to the contrary. . . ." Of the low character of the teamsters, Johnston wrote: "Among such a number of transient persons there are always some disposed to give trouble." He assured the governor that "there was a little doubt in his mind that the civil police force now employed will find it quite within their power to restrain all such."[35] The general underestimated the tense and bitter atmosphere that hung over the valley.

In the early part of November 1858, the first winter storm swooped down from the Oquirrh Mountains. Crowded into their improvised dwellings, the unemployed teamsters' anger reached the boiling point. The new truculent attitude among the teamsters led to a representation from a self-appointed committee demanding that the army guarantee either employment or transportation out of the territory.[36] Already operating Camp Floyd on a skeletal appropriation, Colonel C. F. Smith rejected the demands, leaving the men no other choice but to wait out the winter in suffering. The following April an angry mob marched to Johnston's headquarters to pour out its grievances. On receiving the delegation, Johnston merely read the proclamation from the War Department, explaining the intentions of Washington as he went along; he then denied their request for transportation out of the territory. He softened his refusal by offering to let them supply firewood to the camp at fifty cents a cord, half the price the army paid its soldiers per cord.[37] By granting this privilege, Johnston deprived his soldiers of one of their few sources of extra income, which would cause frequent quarrels between them and hungry teamsters.

Johnston tried to pass the problem back to the territorial governor. Under pressure from the Mormons to get rid of transients, Cumming dismissed any suggestion of public assistance to the teamsters on the grounds of insufficient funds. Any new liability would bankrupt his administration, the governor warned.[38] More correspondence passed between the two men during the following months, but in the end both washed their hands of the matter—a decision filled with hazards. Left to their own resources, the discharged teamsters flooded the labor market, depressing the cost of services while simultaneously enlarging the rolls of unemployed among the Saints. One by one the jobless teamsters turned to crime for a solution to their economic sufferings. As a result, the crime rate in the area took a sudden jump, particularly with regard to the common frontier offense of cattle rustling.

As winter set in and law enforcement broke down, an epidemic of rustling broke over Utah. More than a thousand head of unattended livestock owned by Russell, Majors, and Waddell, plus twice this number of cattle grazed by the army in the valleys paralleling Camp Floyd, turned Fairfield into a rustler's paradise. Horses also became fair game for stock thieves. "We have been informed that horse stealing is being practised to a considerable extent in the vicinity of Camp Floyd. Now the thieves have become so brave as to run the horses off in bands," complained the *Valley Tan* to its readers.[39]

In this new episode of Frogtown's history, local outlets for stolen livestock were few; however, the well-traveled roads to California were choked with the dust of the contraband cattle being driven to the boom towns of the Pacific coast. Despite its many disadvantages, the southern route through rugged, arid country gained favor with bandits transporting their snorting beasts to market. As illicit trade increased, the army quickened its interest in the region, but the very nature of the country precluded any real success in stopping the traffic from reaching its destination. Though the army deployed its soldiers at various check points along the trail and threatened quick punishment to thieves, its efforts were not equal to those of the rustlers who brazenly drove herds of government cattle past the gates of Camp Floyd in broad daylight.[40] Reports of stolen cattle and horses served as a constant source of irritation to both military and civilian authorities—a symbol of the uncompromising hostilities in the new land.

This point came fully home when Governor Cumming's matched team of white horses was stolen in front of his mansion, causing consternation and embarrassment at Camp Floyd.[41] In Fairfield no horse was ignored, and when the prized mount of William A. Hickman was stolen, the act raised the eyebrows of even the most brazen rustlers. Hickman, himself the center and mainspring of several bands of outlaws and better known by his enemies as the "Destroying Angel," suffered the loss within a few feet of the saloon where he sat drinking whiskey.[42] No unattended horse was safe. Orson Hyde was stunned by the sudden disappearance of a circus horse during the middle of a Provo performance. "The thief got the horse," he reported with a touch of amusement, "but not the swiftest one. A Mormon posse overtook him just at the edge of the Provo bench. He refused to stop when requested and was fired at three times; he then dismounted and the horse was taken back to the circus."[43] To protect his livestock and personal property, every able-bodied man in Frogtown became a walking arsenal, whether he was skilled in the use of weapons or not.

The close relationship between the number of weapons in the territory and those in Fairfield undoubtedly contributed to the ferocity that swept Cedar Valley, for every man considered himself naked without a firearm of some kind. The exact number of weapons brought into the territory by the army and related personnel is unknown; nevertheless, hundreds of pistols, carbines, and muskets made their way into the open markets.[44] With public apathy on the wane, the innocent fell with the guilty. Among the first to fall victim was a teamster identified only by the regal sounding title of Prince.

Aside from the circumstances that surrounded his death, Prince was no different in appearance from any one of a thousand nondescript individuals who blended unnoticed into the fabric of the noisy, backcountry community. And, like others caught up in the surging tide of violence, he could not help dealing with it in one manner or another. Disappointed by his failures in government service, the teamster opened a cabaret on Front Street, ultimately growing wealthy in the troubled world common to gambling. It was an exhilarating life that developed bad habits with monotonous regularity. Prince was a familiar figure in the town's gambling saloons, where he mentally noted the systematic fleecing of gullible customers. It was a harmless habit as long as he kept his observations to himself. By the middle of the spring of 1859, however, rumors and hints of his activities multiplied throughout the underworld, and as the deadening summer's heat shimmered over the town, Prince's fortune turned drastically toward the worse.

At the height of the controversy Prince walked into a ramshackle cabaret and took his accustomed place near the card tables, unaware that his movements were being carefully monitored. Amid the rumble of masculine voices in a smoke-filled room, he watched expressionlessly the exchange of gold coins across the gaming tables. Suddenly, a dim lamp illuminated the presence of a dark man walking toward him with a revolver in hand. Recognizing the man as a gambler with a notorious disposition, Prince raised himself from his chair and walked slowly around the tables toward the open door, only to find his escape blocked by six gunmen. Observing that he could go neither around nor through the crowd, Prince ran for the back door but was stopped by John J. Rice, one of the gamblers accused by rumor of cheating. The sight of Prince infuriated Rice, who accused the teamster of spreading lies about him throughout the community. Still quaking from his experience moments before, Prince pleaded in a quiet voice that he knew nothing of the accusation, neither its source nor origin. His words further ignited the anger of Rice, who moved back several paces and fired his revolver twice. The first shot struck Prince high in the chest, the second embedded in his skull, killing him instantly. In the confusion that followed, Rice moved through the surging crowd and escaped to Salt Lake City where he took sanctuary with other fugitives from the law. Murder was a safe gamble in Frogtown.[45]

There was no escape from the terror that engulfed Fairfield, and during the town's boom period, the sight of unburied bodies littering the streets became increasingly common. Each dawn seemed to reveal the remains of gunshot victims, recorded Richard Wilds Jones. "When we went to breakfast (Sy and I) there lay a gambler deade, shot in a drunken gamble by another gambler at daylight." Concluding that death at the end of a rope, by gunfire at some grim rendezvous, or by a slashing knife in an unlighted alley, was a certain reward for remaining in the village, he resigned himself to all.[46]

Enlisted men from Camp Floyd frequently fell victim to the bandits and malefactors who swarmed through the city, wrote Captain Phelps. "Two or three soldiers have been shot and wounded recently in the settlement across the creek by the provost sergeants. The heat, dust, whiskey and the discomforts of our position almost drive a man mad. . . ."[47] On rare occasions Mormon diarists recorded that no man was safe within the shadows of Frogtown: "This day many of the soldiers was so drunk and there were some fifty fights and knock downs. Some carried off in blankets. Camp Floyd here it appeared as though hell was boiling over."[48] Gentiles and Mormons both agreed on that.

The tide of lawlessness, meanwhile, had caused serious repercussions among peace officers of Cedar Valley, and night patrols in Fairfield seldom proved uneventful. Among the staunchest supporters of the theory that given enough room, the criminal element would destroy itself, Sheriff William B. Coates dealt with the problem in a piecemeal fashion. The peace officer's plan misfired during the closing days of April 1859, when Coates entered one of the more infamous gaming houses, attracted by a violent quarrel between several gamblers. There the sheriff saw "Happy Jack" Wilson standing over a card table angrily waving his fist and charging his playing partners with cheating. With the appearance of the sheriff the shouting stopped abruptly and "Happy Jack" left the saloon.

Viewing the gambler's actions with suspicion, the sheriff followed the gambler into the shadows of Front Street. As Coates passed an unlighted alley, he caught the faint sound of someone moving, but before he could draw his weapon, "Happy Jack" sprang from the darkness, knocking the sheriff to the ground with the butt end of his pistol. Incredibly, the force of the blow caused Wilson's weapon to fall harmlessly to the bottom of an empty rain barrel. The sheriff managed to draw his hunting knife to defend himself. The assailant drew back, pulled a razor-edged stiletto from his boot, and shouted at the sheriff a series of unintelligible sentences, the tone of which left little doubt of his intentions. In one furious movement the gambler lunged at the sheriff. Reacting to the charge, Coates stepped aside and tripped "Happy Jack," simultaneously driving his weapon deep into the gambler's stomach. The blow was fatal. Wilson reeled, clutched his wound with his hands and collapsed on the sidewalk. A short time later Coates recovered from his mauling and resigned from office, leaving Frogtown without a peace officer for several months.[49]

Writing from within the safe confines of Camp Floyd, Judge Eckles described his impressions of life in Fairfield to President Buchanan in a letter dated August 17, 1859.

Murders have been very frequent of late in different parts of the territory and crime since my return here in June seems to be much on the increase. There is said to be in this district alone one hundred and sixty persons murdered for which no one has been brought to punishment. Larcenies are of daily occurance. Indeed Sir, they have ceased to occasion surprise. All the persons arrested for either offence have been permitted by Mormon Sheriffs to escape and report says these escapes, have been *voluntary*. Indeed Sir, the officers are powerless.[50]

The grisly aspects of Fairfield were given added dimension by the large volume of liquor that was consumed by its inhabitants, the most popular of which was "Valley Tan." This singularly destructive intoxicant, manufactured by the Saints under territorial license, was also known as "Tiger Sweat" or "Tarantula Juice." Horace Greeley, the famous *New York Tribune* journalist who visited the territory in 1859, described "Valley Tan" as "compounded of spirits of turpentine, agua fortes, and steeped tobacco," adding, "its looks alone condemn it—soapy, ropy, turbid, it is within bounds to say that every pint contains as much poison as a gallon of whiskey." In the course of a conversation with the noted newspaperman, a Weber County tavern keeper replied: "There ain't nothing bad about this whisky; the only fault is, it isn't good."[51]

Three generations later, Irwin S. Cobb described a brew which might well have been the peculiar liquor of Utah territory: "It smells like gangrene starting in a mildewed silo, it tastes like the wrath to come, and when you absorb a deep swig of it you have all the sensation of having swallowed a lighted kerosene lamp. A sudden, violent jolt of it has been known to stop the victim's watch, snap his suspenders and crack his glass eye right across."[52] The ancestry of the liquor could be traced in bottles labeled "Moon's Best," "Howard's Superior," "Pure Dew from the Moon," "Mountain Dew," "Cincinnati Rectified," "St. Louis Rectified," and "Double Rectified" sold only with the guarantee that it improved with each glass.[53] Its cost was ten dollars a gallon, twice its price at the Missouri River.

As in most frontier settlements, hard liquor was the bane of Indians and soldiers alike. Few people took the time to examine the long train of events that created the problem of unrestrained drinking. An exception to this was Ebenezer Crouch, the very bright, teenaged son of a Mormon merchant who recalled the liquor-washed streets of Fairfield.

The business part of Dobie Town was made up of saloons, gambling houses and every kind of business that goes to make up a rough place. There were always Indians camped close around and what with the Indians and soldiers there was always something rough going on. The Indians would get crazy drunk and go riding through the town on their ponies whooping and yelling until they came in contact with drunken soldiers and then there would be some gun play.[54]

Crouch's encounter with life in Fairfield was not a happy one:

Every store used to sell liquor and the one Father kept was no exception. Across one end of the store was a row of forty gallon barrels containing liquor of different kinds. The store was often filled with soldiers buying and drinking liquor. They were the worst lot of petty thieves I ever saw. They would steal anything in the store they could lay their hands on and then turn around and trade it to Father for drinks as he would be busy serving them he could not watch them all. He used to stand me upon the counter where I could see them all and I would give him the alarm if they stole anything.[55]

In the light of the desperate struggles that whirled around him daily, the young man believed that life in Fairfield was a self-pronounced death sentence: "I have often thought of those rough times and wondered how Father escaped bodily injury but he seemed to have a way with him that commanded their respect and he could calm them down when it seemed they were about to tear him to pieces."[56]

The young Saint recorded dispassionately the frequent undisguised acts of violence between soldiers and young warriors:

One day when there were plenty of Indians in town, a drunken soldier seized one by the hair of the head and pulled him off his horse. Seeing this, Sanpitch, chief of the band, drew his six shooter and leveled it upon the soldier. The soldier dodged behind a gambler for protection and the gambler found himself looking into the mussel [sic] of a drunken Indian chief's gun. He never flinched but calmly told him to put that damned thing down before he did some mischief.[57]

The situation changed for the soldiers overnight when the general placed Fairfield off limits to all military personnel, except officers, under penalty of twenty days hard labor and a fine of five dollars.[58] To assure compliance with the order, troops patrolled along the south bank of the Cedar Creek while armed squads were posted at the main entrance at Fairfield bridge. No one was allowed to enter the fort without a pass or written permission. Yet since Camp Floyd was an open fort, too extensive and too strong to need a stockade wall, the measure failed to bring about the desired results. Tradition claims many soldiers were shot while attempting to wade Cedar Creek to reenter the fort, an apparent exaggeration since there is no evidence to substantiate this widely circulated belief. Still, the regimental guardhouses did not suffer from want of inmates.

The Mormons found Fairfield no less a problem than did the army. There can be no doubt that Brigham Young found the town a source of mounting dissatisfaction, and a threat of his control over the well-ordered Mormon commonwealth. "The influx of camp followers," he wrote to Colonel Kane, "of whose character you are somewhat acquainted, consisting of Government speculators, traders, gamblers, rowdies, and bullies, is perfectly outstanding. It appears as though it was their object to flood us under, and can scarcely keep believing that this is part of the program enacting against us. I would not mention it but it is a thousand times more dreaded than the Army. . . ."[59]

During this unsettled period, wrote one Mormon diarist, the flood of prosperity bent the will of even zealous Saints with alarming consequences. "Camp Floyd Fairfield was full of rotteness and evil of every description and I'm sorry to say our people of both sexes mixed up with them largely and of how bad it did look to see young ladies whose parents were faithful."[60] New alliances were formed for a fistful of dollars: "What difference in less than a year with some of our people. Lots of those men that were full of faith and would do anything, gave way and you could not tell the difference of them and the Gentiles. Of course this was only a small portion but far too many."[61] As this tide continued, Charles L. Walker lamented: "Some of our women are at the camp of the U. S. troops playing the harlot."[62]

Commercial affairs followed the disorders of everyday life, frequently with unusual consequences. One story records a settler unloading a wagonload of produce to a Frogtown merchant, after which he walked forward to the cashier's counter to be paid. Upon inventorying the bill, the accounting clerk proceeded to pay the farmer, shouting out the count as he dropped the money into the hands of the settler, exceeding the payment with a twenty-dollar gold piece. The farmer picked up the gold coin and prudently slid it across the counter to the clerk, reminding the man of his error. To the Saint's astonishment, the employee flipped the coin back: "We never rectify mistakes here," he shouted.[63]

The Saints delighted in telling the tale of the nervous counting-house teller who found the responsibility of handling large amounts of money a thoroughly frightening experience. One version of the story claimed that when the clerk counted out a stack of gold coins to meet a large demand of a Frogtown merchant, he inadvertently dropped a gold coin to the floor. But before the coin could be retrieved from the sawdust, a heavy teamster's boot was firmly planted over it. Without waiting for an explanation, the "cashier handed out another coin and promptly forgot the incident."[64]

The widely advertised wealth of Fairfield brought the county tax assessor to the town. When he appeared, pandemonium followed. To no one's surprise, the merchants of Frogtown refused to pay the levies and were in unanimous agreement to tar and feather the county agent, James Rodeback, if he set foot inside their stores. Their arguments had a familiar ring: the territory had not rendered any tangible services to the town; moreover, Fairfield's tax revenues might be used to strengthen the Church's political control over the territory. In either case, they were determined not to be a party to the process.[65]

On the other side of the valley, Rodeback received a hand-carried message from an unidentified source, instructing him to "appoint a deputy there and let him be such a man as would not be bluffed off." Only one qualification was necessary: "If need required would shoot."[66] Less than two weeks later, the stagecoach from Salt Lake City rattled its way along Front Street and pulled up at the Carson Inn, discharging a visitor almost as distinguished as Billy Hickman. The new tax collector proved to be Richard Keith Johnston, alias Joaquin Johnston, a California swag with a head full of get-rich-quick schemes. In the midst of other troubles and harassments associated with horse stealing, Johnston completed his tax collections before the spring thaw, then looked across Cedar Creek to Camp Floyd for new sources of revenue. However, his enthusiasm was matched by the reticence of General Johnston, who refused to permit him to enter Camp Floyd.[67] This failure in no sense minimized his unsavory reputation among the camp followers of Fairfield; quite the contrary, Johnston's vigorous method of collecting taxes earned him the respect of the townspeople who elected him sheriff of Fairfield.[68]

The final battle between the newcomers of Fairfield and the Mormons was waged at the ballot box, where Gentiles could hardly hope for success. Obviously laboring under a complete misunderstanding of Mormon voting patterns that were forged by the calamitous events of their history, the Gentiles were hardly worthy opponents for the unified Saints.[69] Gathering at Fairfield and Salt Lake City during the late summer of 1859, they launched their first serious offensive with the formation of the Union Ticket.[70]

The Gentile drive for political independence started with a mass meeting held in Fairfield in July, 1859, at which time a slate of candidates was selected: Delegate to Congress—Dr. Garland Hurt; Territorial Councilmen—William H. Lent and James Bigler; Representatives—S. C. Mills, J. M. Wallace, and C. W. Crocker. The party platform denounced the Saints for their blinding theological solidarity and, amidst loud choruses of cheers, listed specific grievances:

> By legislative enactments, they have granted to church officials the exclusive privilege of establishing ferries and bridges over the

principal rivers, and a large percentum of the enormous tolls exacted from emigrants, goes to their emigration fund.

They confiscate to the same use stray property found within the territory.

They have granted large and valuable tracts of public lands to church officials to the exclusion of all others.

They have created a corporation by chartering their church, investing it with powers destructive of the best interests, and dangerous to the liberties of its inhabitants.

They have imprisoned American citizens, for no other cause than that of refusing to attach themselves to their revolting institution.

They have murdered, and then robbed whole trains of emigrants not sparing defenseless women and children, whose cries for mercy found no "ear to hear, no heart to feel, and no arm to bring deliverance."

They have debauched, and then murdered, helpless women.

They have taken the lives of American citizens by order of their priesthood.

They have made eunuchs under church authority, and they still claim the right to continue the diabolical practice.

They have incited the merciless savages to rob and murder unprotected people.

They have prevented the execution of the law by conferring criminal jurisdiction upon courts of their own creation in violation of the organic act.

They have refused to provide jails, or other means, for the safe keeping of prisoners.

They steadily refused to provide money, to enable the federal courts to try and punish offenders.

They have in nearly every instance prevented the arrest of criminals, and when a few were arrested, their officers have permitted them to escape.

They have inspired witnesses and jurors with fear, by threats of terrible meaning.[71]

When the polling stations closed their doors on Monday, August 1, the Union Party predicted victory. "Where the lion of the Lord has been accustomed to proclaim his *ipse dixit*, and rule the nominations, and the supremacy of his wishes secure the election of his favorites, a small band of the spirit of '76 have maintained their privileges and voted their choice." Despite feverish pressure from the Saints, the Gentiles had managed a heavy turnout: "The returns are not yet in, but sufficient is known to alarm the Saints, and make the negligent repent the disinterestedness," wrote a spectator for an eastern newspaper.[72]

The specter of the army's entrance into the county race increased the

Saints' fears "that the transients in the service of the army and the freighting companies would for the immediate future, at least, comprise a
significant portion of the territorial population."[73] But before the vote was
taken, a bill was introduced in both houses limiting voting rights to those
living in the territory at least six months prior to the election. No soldier,
however long his tenure at Camp Floyd, could "act as jurors, voter, nor
hold office unless they were residents prior to entering service."[74] A final
discriminatory provision of the law specified that non-taxpaying residents were disfranchised. The decree affected one-fourth of Utah's population, nearly all of whom were connected with the military occupation.

What could not be won legally was taken outside the law, wrote
Nathaniel V. Jones, an unofficial poll watcher appointed by Brigham
Young to oversee the election.

> I was in Fairfield, on yesterday, the day of our general elections.
> About 9 a.m. Judge Eckles superceded the acting justice of the
> precinct, I will not attempt to explain unless the importance of the
> soldier's [sic] votes required the interference of his honor. After the
> polls were opened Judge Eckles announced that they were ready to
> receive votes and that the United States Soldiers could vote at the
> election. In a short time Fairfield and the polls were taken as by
> assault, and in less than an hour the town was filled with officers
> and soldiers, very many of them breathing out invectives against
> the nominations by the "Old Citizens." I saw soldiers pass
> through files of the guard where they received tickets ready folded,
> and after depositing them go through a side door to a saloon
> where liquor was being freely dispensed, probably the price of
> their votes.[75]

The political weakness of the Gentile efforts to gain control of Cedar
Valley became clear when Probate Judge Zerubabbel Snow ruled the
Fairfield election void on the grounds that the soldiers had fraudulently
declared themselves residents of the territory. As it turned out, the one-
sided decision could well have been written by Brigham Young; the judge
declared the "Old Citizens," or Mormon candidates, elected. Not unexpectedly, Snow argued that "most of the 768 votes cast were illegal as the
voters were soldiers, teamsters, and other non-tax paying residents of
Fairfield."[76] The constitutionality of this decision was affirmed by Governor Cumming, ending all hope that the powerful authority of Brigham
Young would be seriously challenged—at least during the existence of
Camp Floyd.

Fairfield continued to be a source of Mormon displeasure until 1861,
when it settled down to a slow decline typical of western boom towns.
The tide of the Civil War would sweep the army from the valley, leaving
Frogtown a sleepy little supply center resting uneasily on the desert flats,
for the "hell roaring Fairfield blew out as suddenly as it had blown in."[77]

CHAPTER FIVE

LIFE AT CAMP FLOYD

*Capt. Tracy says that life in this camp gives the feeling of convicts
in prison for life clamoring to be let out and hung by way of relief.*
—Captain John W. Phelps[1]

CAMP FLOYD was no ordinary fort. Like an unsheathed sword
piercing the very heart of Mormonism, it was an acknowledged
symbol of federal authority in the Great Basin and reflected the enigmatic attitude of the American people towards the Mormons.

The lonely outpost dominated the Mormon frontier for three
years, acquiring a personality of its own, unique and varied as the lives
of the soldiers who manned its defenses. To a great degree it was the
dramatic upheaval of the Industrial Revolution that was responsible
for the Europeanization of the American army. Once on the American
shore, the new citizens entered federal service for a variety of reasons—grinding unemployment, illusions of high adventure, flight
from the drudgery and loneliness of the farm, and a few, only a few,
because they loved the "damned army."

With each tide of overseas migration to the eastern shore, the eth-
nic composition of the American army changed; but at mid-century
the enlisted ranks were composed mainly of Irish and German enlistees, new to all things American. In addition, the presence of Mexicans, Italians, Scandinavians, and a handful of blacks gave the army at
Camp Floyd the appearance of a foreign legion.[2] The tension, pathos,
and despair that beset discontented soldiers were frequently reflected
in morale problems, for during no period in the army's history were
its ranks composed of soldiers with such varied ideologies. In barracks discussions at Camp Floyd, fire-eating abolitionists denounced
slavery, southern autocrats within the officer ranks damned the
Republicans and their black allies in the northern cities, freewheeling
advocates of temperance proclaimed themselves saviors of the hard-

81

drinking Irish Catholics, who in turn cursed all Baptists and the way they viewed Catholicism as the "Great and Abominable Church." But for most soldiers, frontier life was already too difficult to allow quick-spoken words to destroy comradery within the ranks. The men preferred to spend their tours of duty gambling, swearing, and joking a great deal, but mainly drinking.

Although liquor had been forbidden in the barracks since 1832, most frontier soldiers regarded heavy drinking as an absolute necessity. The dreariness and isolation of military life exacerbated a habit which for many soldiers had originated in childhood. Still, the soldiers at Camp Floyd were not much more intemperate than the civilian population of nineteenth-century America, whose pleasures in liquor gushed wide and deep.

The army permitted officers to consume alcoholic beverages in their quarters, and frequently allowed whiskey to be served to enlisted personnel on holidays and special occasions. Beer or lager was sold at the post exchanges, and later several beer halls were built at Camp Floyd. General Johnston did not tolerate alcohol in the barracks, for he believed that soldiers under its influence were intractable and incapable of carrying out their duties, as well as less inclined to obey their superiors. Persistent drunkenness was the greatest infraction for which soldiers were punished. Drunk and disorderly soldiers served short sentences at hard labor in the rock quarries of the Oquirrh Mountains.

As in most frontier posts, discipline was always the first casualty of holiday celebrations, a time when noncommissioned officers were inclined to wink at violations of post regulations. The celebration of St. Patrick's Day filled the regimental guardhouses with fighting, "damn-your-eyes" Irishmen who used the holiday to express their pride in their particular regiment. At Camp Floyd, as elsewhere, punishment failed to stop drunkenness.

The widespread disappearance of whiskey from under the eyes of guards at the quartermaster's storehouse galled the fort's three-man Board of Survey, who found it difficult to explain large shortages of spirits that amounted to 100 gallons of liquor for every 700 gallons stored.[3] Leakage and evaporation could not account for it all. Outright theft was committed by commissary sergeants who relied on liquor to uplift their men's sagging morale. Soldiers bartered clothing and stolen equipment for whiskey, although the punishment for stealing was harsher than that for possessing liquor.[4] Stolen goods were fenced by sutlers, who frequently discounted the value of the stolen goods and marked up the price of whiskey by 50 percent.[5] One of the opportunistic Mormon suppliers of hard spirits was John Lowe Butler, who claimed that he exchanged liquor "for clothes, pistols and one thing and other. . . . The Mormons would get a good overcoat for about $2.00 worth of whiskey and they could get a gold revolver about the same."[6] The Saints did not scruple to sell whiskey, since they suffered from a chronic shortage of clothes and weapons. Mormon profits from the liquor trade encouraged them to cling to their monopoly of the distilleries in the eastern half of the territory.

The resourcefulness of the human spirit was more than an even match for the army, wrote a self-styled "Bold Dragoon" who added a touch of humor to the old craft of bootlegging. "If you should ever get patriotic and turn soldier, I will tell you how to fool them . . . provided they is disposed to be vigilant, which don't often happen." The soldier went on to detail patiently his instructions:

> You must gilt a tin coffee pot, and stop up the holes which can be got from the company's quartermaster's clerk, for a small consideration, which is not worth while to mention; then fill up the spout with milk and the main vessel with whiskey, and the chances is you will get her through without any trouble.[7]

A half-breed dragoon bugler called "Black Jack" found Camp Floyd's "aridity" unbearable and developed his own system to circumvent military regulations. "Black Jack" sat "deliberately on his sharp spur, allowing the rowels to penetrate his trousers and epidermis until it bled; he then ran for the hospital tent, declaring that he was bitten by a Rattlesnake." The army surgeon treated the wound by administering a quart of liquor to the victim, the result of which left the dragoon gloriously drunk. Notwithstanding his success, "Jack thought it was a joke to fool the doctor and boasted about it, so a Court Martial made his short drunk cost him one month's pay—and one month in the Guard House where he could ponder over the old saying, that 'Silence is Golden.' "[8]

The temperance movement even found its way to Camp Floyd, led by the Anti-saloon League that labored for "the moral and social regeneration of the many unfortunates addicted to the use of spiritous liquor."[9] During the crusade, the temperance leagues extracted 200 pledges of abstinence, but the tradition of heavy drinking combined with long spells of unbearable idleness soon undermined their efforts. In the last analysis, the vast majority of the soldiers remained unpersuaded, and uncertain payrolls and meager wages were the only things that ever kept them sober.

With the nearest federal treasury no nearer than St. Louis or San Francisco, soldiers were paid twice a year—spring and fall. Between times, soldiers who squandered their money were forced to pledge part of their future earnings to regimental sutlers in exchange for overpriced common necessities of post life. The sutler held a rank equivalent to warrant officer. Although his position was secured through political patronage, two things distinguished his position from Gentile and Mormon merchants who were also allowed to sell to the quartermaster department:

> His rank was higher than enlisted men and below the commissioned personnel, but in the social circles he and his wife stood with the officers and their wives. He was subject to a general court-martial for capital offenses and could be dismissed by garrison or regimental court-martial.[10]

Although financial records of the sutlers are incomplete or almost nonexistent, the system plainly increased the cost of goods for soldiers, bringing complaints to General Johnston that having sutlers was not in the best interest of the army. The first step toward regulating the advancement of credit came from the War Department, instructing department commanders that enlisted men's indebtedness could not exceed one-third of their monthly wage—which was the price of one bottle of bootleg whiskey.[11] Additional obligations could be contracted by enlisted men with written permission from their company commanders, but under no condition was the total amount of indebtedness to exceed one-half the soldier's monthly earnings. A second regulation required regimental sutlers to present to company commanders an account of the money owed by soldiers three days before the end of each month. When an account was in dispute, sutlers were required to produce the original affidavit, and the company commander would pass judgment on the debt's validity. Following verification, sutlers could accompany the paymaster to collect their debt. The army retained first claim against the soldiers' wages, followed in turn by the laundress, and the sutlers' claims came third.[12]

Sutlers set exorbitant prices for their poor goods and frequently attempted to evade their statutory head tax of ten cents a month for each man served. Theoretically, the cost of all commodities sold at Camp Floyd was closely regulated; in reality, noncommissioned officers siphoned off bribes and allowed goods to be sold at whatever price the market would permit. The responsibility of preventing such underhanded activities fell to the Board of Survey, a three-man committee that met once a quarter to establish the retail value of merchandise, subject to the post commander's approval.[13] Nevertheless, soldiers found themselves at the mercy of the vagaries of the market, and complained that while their wages remained unchanged, prices at Camp Floyd continued to rise, sometimes to double the retail costs at the Missouri.

Matters grew worse when the army failed to meet its first payroll, effectively drying up the chief source of hard currency in the territory. As the soldiers suffered, Kirk Anderson humorously reviewed their plight:

> An enterprising officer, by some means, to use a legal phrase, "was siezed" of a ten dollar gold piece which he had deposited in a glass case, hired a small "Dobie" building and was exhibiting the afore-

said "full Eagle" as a curiosity at the rate of two bits a sight, pay-able when the specie train arrived. In the last account he was realiz-ing a fortune—in prospective.[14]

After such interludes, the spring arrival of the heavily guarded army specie train brought a mad scramble for federal gold and was hailed by the *Deseret News* as "The Good Times Coming."[15] Across the river, Frogtown's lawless outcasts waited—confident, buoyant, optimistic— knowing from experience that the army payroll would come their way one way or another.

As fall deepened into winter, life at the outpost crept along in a mean-ingless monotony. Away from the pleasures of society, every activity assumed a new sense of importance, whether it was writing letters, mending equipment and clothing, or swapping stories around the fire-places. In order to meet the demands of his daily journal, Captain Phelps carefully noted the ordinary activities of ants and ground squirrels bur-rowing their way in and out of the dirt floor of his quarters. His greatest apparent joy, however, was a one-sided love affair of the spirit with Queen Victoria.[16]

While the enlisted personnel found it difficult to escape from the deep gloom that hung over life in the barracks, officers made determined efforts to re-establish patterns of life with which they were long familiar. Exploring the rolling countryside on horseback, General Johnston found his amusements chasing jackrabbits, stopping frequently to satisfy his scientific curiosity about animal and plant life in the Basin. He frequently sent botanical samples to far-off museums.[17] Accompanied by their stag hounds, a cluster of officers and their orderlies tracked coyotes that were drawn to the slaughter pens of the quartermaster department.[18] Animals not killed in the hunt were brought back to the barracks for regimental pets: a fox was mascot for the Fifth Infantry; the heavy battery of artillery was represented by a coyote; the Tenth Regiment raised a grizzly bear, a bald eagle, and a Great Dane.[19] But the pets felt no different about life at Camp Floyd than did their masters, remembered a young enlisted regular:

> The bear we obtained while young, and kept him until from the men annoying him so much, he became so cross and ugly that we had to kill him. Our American eagle suddenly disappeared, dis-gusted without doubt, with Mormonism; while our dog, Jack, whom we obtained from the Mormons, could not be prevailed upon to leave the Saints.[20]

During the soldiers' first troubled winter in the territory, some dis-covered the pleasures of rural Mormon society. This refreshing insight came to Private Henry Hamilton and five members of a quadrille band who traveled to Battle Creek to celebrate the Christmas holidays. "We were kindly welcomed upon our arrival," he wrote several years after his visit, "and quartered in a comfortable hotel, kept by an Englishman. On Christmas Eve we serenaded the principal men of the town, and at its close received a cordial invitation to take Christmas dinner with the councilor."[21] In the country, at least, he found the Saints content and even happy, although the shortcomings of rural life were embarrassingly present. "Their houses were small, one-story buildings, with thick, thatched roofs and while eating dinner, which was served in a graceful and cheerful manner by his five better halves, a young mouse apparently just born, fell from the straw roof directly upon my plate." In an effort to ease his host out of his dilemma, Hamilton immediately ran his fork through the mouse and, holding it up for all to see, informed the Mormon patriarch that he was not quite ready for dessert. "The councilor smiled and replied that such occurrences were frequent, and that it was utterly impossible to keep the mice out of the roofs." The holiday passed swiftly and in his dimly lighted quarters Hamilton looked back at his experience with fond memories. "Although the credit of the Mormons did not stand very high in the estimation of the Gentiles, I can truthfully say that I never enjoyed a week better in my life. The people of Battle Creek were kind and hospitable, and strived to make it pleasant and enjoyable for us."[22]

During other brief periods of inactivity soldiers prospected for precious metals, and at least one officer, Captain Phelps, discovered traces of silver, gold, and lead near the present site of Bingham.[23] The report of silver-bearing ore spread rapidly to Salt Lake City where Kirk Anderson gave the discovery exaggerated importance: "It is a very pure specimen and discoverer of this new Silver Eldorado asserts that the precious metal can be obtained in large quantities. The locality is at present, a secret, but we are informed that it is within two or three hours' ride of Camp Floyd."[24] As the editor of the *Valley Tan* developed the story, he recognized the possibility of fusing silver with politics. "We may yet (and it will be no difficult job) throw Pike's Peak entirely in the shade. These Wasatch range of mountains may yet develop resources that will create a revolution in this valley. . . ."[25] Pondering these printed words, a local charlatan and station master along the overland route to California, "Dugout Joe," greatly simplified the digging of his new well near Simpson Springs. At the propitious moment, he carefully circulated rumors at Camp Floyd that he had discovered gold.

When the first reports reached the post, a horde of soldiers drifted to the diggings to watch the excavation. When asked about his activities, "Dugout Joe" answered that he was searching for water. This explanation, however, did not satisfy the soldiers. Remaining strangely uncooperative and uncommunicative for several days, "Dugout Joe" clandestinely salted the well with shavings from a brass candleholder and shortly thereafter announced his discovery to the bystanders. "I can never hope to hide the discovery of gold from the bad element," Joe claimed, "so if you are willing to keep my secret and help develop my find, I'll reward you handsomely."[26]

As the haggling over the disposition of the gold concluded, the soldiers agreed to dig the proposed mining shaft for equal shares in the claim. Not surprisingly, the station keeper consented to the mutually acceptable settlement and the work began. But the soldiers' optimism was dampened when the shaft reached a depth of ten feet without any sign of the mother lode. Finding no trace of gold, a doubting private took the small leather bag of the earthen samples to Salt Lake to be analyzed. The following day he returned to Simpson Springs to report to his comrades that they had been duped. In the end neither gold nor water was found—at best a pyrrhic victory for the embarrassed soldiers.[27]

To boost the morale of his men, General Johnston encouraged wholesome pastimes such as "The Military Dramatic Association," organized by the Fifth Infantry in November 1858. A carnival atmosphere surrounded opening night, undeterred by the theater's dark atmosphere that smelled of coal oil intermixed with stale tobacco and damp clothes. Visitors could not help noticing the building's dirt floor, four earthen walls, and unvaulted ceiling supported by logs, although the place was furnished with broad slab benches, and long rows of smooth-shaved benches for field officers and their guests. On hand for the first performance were six hundred officers and men who paid an admission charge ranging from fifty cents to a dollar.[28]

Resourceful regimental promoters offered a variety of performances ranging from two-act farces to classical English dramas. As a rule, the Dramatic Association avoided performances that brooded over the tensions between men in faraway places, considering them depressing, and psychologically too close to home. "All that the writer will have to do," wrote one reporter, "will be to combine and relate actual occurrences in order to form tragedies more appalling and horrid than any in Macbeth, Hamlet or Othello."[29] Moved by the intrigues and instability of the society surrounding the fort, another soldier claimed that plots for such performances were not lacking: "The Mountain Meadow Massacre, the murder of the Parrishes, and Young Jones and his mother . . . all furnish the material and ground work for tragedies of most 'thrilling and exciting' interest," claimed another critic of the *Valley Tan*.[30]

Satires on Mormon society played to packed houses, and few Church leaders escaped the barbs and lampoons of "gutter satirists." The comedy team of Crawford and Willis proved so popular that to satisfy the growing demand for tickets for their performances the act was moved to the newly constructed pavilion of the Soldiers Circus, where it was performed three times a week to an enthusiastic audience.[31] Kirk Anderson, that indefatigable military boaster and herald of everything Gentile, strongly endorsed the act for its "simplicity, clarity, and fruitful style."

Their tricks and witticism invariably brought down the audience in roars of applause; but the capping of the climax was in the burlesque on Mormon emigration, which was rendered to the satisfaction of all who were present.

Willis' personification of the Mormon Bishop was rendered so well that it afforded material for laughter for days afterward; and Crawford was at home in the taking of the character of a Mr. Johnny Bull, just arrived from Hold Hengland, at Echo Kanyon, or some other point of reception, by the Mormons, who, on finding out his poverty, respectfully sent him to another settlement where his poverty will be better appreciated. They have gained a name among the soldiers for comicality and "side spliting laughter" that will always ensure them a good house.

It is the only place of amusement in Camp Floyd worth going to.[32]

Flagrantly disturbing to the Saints was a long string of caustic anti-Mormon satires that victimized Church leaders and proved immensely popular—notably "The Battle of Echo Kanyon," "Dobie Town Militia," and "Salt Lake Scene." Most soldiers judged the Mormon themes in good taste; the exceptions, sneered one observer, were "those whose love for Mormon crinoline was greater than their love for their country."[33]

As dusk deepened into night during the winter season, several regimental theaters gave the soldiers a great variety of entertainment, with vaudeville attractions intermixed with plays of several acts. At best, the humdrum performances combined low standards and high zeal, being characterized by missed cues, forgotten lines, and poorly timed stage entrances; but help was not far away. Sergeant Richard C. White, instigator of the theater at Camp Floyd, recruited a number of Mormon women for the garrison theater. The first performer to be pirated was Mercy Westwood Tuckett, bred in the genteel and anemic tradition of the Social Hall Theater. She imposed restraint, conformity, morality—even priggishness—on the garrison theater.[34]

Mercy Tuckett's frequent appearance at the theater, entering unobtrusively on the arm of one or more blue-coated officers, was a tonic to the soldiers' jaded spirits. Excesses of ribaldry were usually softened by her presence, but on the night of January 15, 1859, she was subjected to the humiliation of an obscene ballad called "Root Hog or Die." Soldiers whistled and stamped their approval, shouting bravos. She left the theater alone, settled her financial affairs with the stage manager and returned to Salt Lake City to rejoin her polygamous husband. Within a week, Mrs. Tuckett was followed by the remaining Mormon actresses.[35] When criticism over the affair became widespread, Kirk Anderson, arbiter of the

Gentile community, expressed his regret over the incident in the *Valley Tan*:

THE REASONS FOR THEIR LEAVING
The Solons of the green room considered it was better to have some low parody on "Root Hog or Die," sung and insult the feelings of these ladies, than retain their services.

LET THE PUBLIC JUDGE
We must honor the ladies for the position they have taken, they are right and let them stand by it, they will be more thought of when they again appear and show the "Pacha with fifteen tailes" the meaning of the word "Principle."[36]

The apology settled the incident. Several days later the female troupers returned to Camp Floyd to receive uncounted apologies.

Having made her final decision to remain at Camp Floyd, Mrs. Tuckett abandoned her polygamous husband and four children in order to share the fortunes of Sergeant Richard White, who left the army to pursue his stage career in Virginia City. The young couple moved to Folsom, California, where Mercy Tuckett-White was unexpectedly taken by death. Four years later, in 1867, Richard White returned to Utah to act in the Salt Lake Theater. He married another Mormon woman and eventually drifted to San Francisco where he managed the Tivoli.[37]

A score of different forms of entertainment ranging from minstrel singing to variety shows competed with the legitimate theater; the former proved popular enough to have a separate building constructed to house the activities.[38] The Mormon itinerant "Bartholomew's Green Pioneer Circus" emerged full-blown during the second summer of the army stay in the territory, later merging with the "Soldier's Circus."[39] For those favoring classical music, a symphonic orchestra drawn together from corps musicians presented public performances.[40] Paralleling these developments, the "Germanic Singing Club" held bilingual audiences spellbound and later sponsored the first grand opera in the territory.[41] But the fare could be heavy for those not familiar with the language, General Johnston wrote to his daughter:

> The colloquy in German was I suppose in content well sustained, but not knowing the language I can only judge from the apparently thorough acquaintance they seem to have of their parts—and the amusement they afforded to the German part of the audience in which the American portion heartily participated whenever the comic parts were comprehended which was not infrequent.[42]

The craze for horse racing attracted an enthusiastic open-pursed following from the barracks and the surrounding countryside, for almost everyone in Cedar Valley looked forward to a few pleasant hours away from their isolated farms and villages or the dictates of their leaders.[43] A half-mile racetrack was laid out near the fort with the finish line near the departmental headquarters. Behind the box seat reserved for General Johnston and his staff, bleacher seats were crowded with staff officers, civilian guests, and well-dressed ladies. Four military judges flanked the finish line on two sides. Important races usually emptied officers' quarters and barracks, bringing military activity to a standstill.[44]

Soldiers gambled heavily in much the same spirit as ancient Greek warriors who tossed dice during the Trojan War. The urge seemed overpowering and usually resulted in heavy losses, for soldiers learned their lessons only through brutal experience. A familiar figure among the horseplayers pushing into the grandstands was the wily Joaquin Johnston, who developed a remarkable ingenuity for bilking the unsuspecting. In a classical con game, the renowned brawler, gunfighter, and all-around troublemaker habitually raced a swaybacked sorrel, betting heavily that the horse would finish the race in front of military mounts or other favorite entries.[45]

In the fall of 1859, a blustering lieutenant, John Sappington Marmaduke, staked the wages of the Second Dragoons in a race between his horse Brownie and Johnston's mongrel entry. The dragoons had every reason to be optimistic over the prospects of the race, for carefully leaked rumors claimed that the gambler's horse had never won a race, while Brownie was "the fastest horse in the territory." Moreover, Johnston's entry was a slow starter, plunged and reared dangerously, and, as a colt, had sustained a serious leg injury. The morning after the race, the *Valley Tan* reported to its readers: "It became apparent to the most verdant that it was a disgraceful sell." The sorrel won easily.[46] Johnston, however, was not the only one holding a few tricks in reserve.

Next to Joaquin Johnston, a gambler named Madison attracted the most attention at the Camp Floyd races. Their rivalry eventually pitted them in one of the most infamous horse races in Utah. In that contest Madison's thoroughbred outdistanced Johnston's horse by several lengths, and when the loser's rage subsided, he was several thousand dollars poorer. To the gambler this was an intolerable affront, and a few minutes later the winning jockey was dead. Several days after the incident the *Valley Tan* reported:

> A young man residing in Fairfield named Faust winning jockey alleged unfairness in the manner in which Johnston's horse was put upon the track; an altercation ensued, of which the result was the death of Faust . . . by a knife in the hands of a boy whose common name was Jack who acted as a champion for Johnston.[47]

Although "Jack" claimed self-defense, he was immediately arrested for murder and escorted to the Fairfield jail to await trial. The debate over the suspect's guilt or innocence dragged on through the night; meanwhile, Johnston walked into the city jail and demanded the release of the prisoner. With two dragoon pistols pointing at his forehead, the jailer offered no resistance and unlocked the cell. No further attempt was made to arrest the jockey.[48]

Hundreds of people poured into Camp Floyd on appointed days to witness military sharpshooters test their marksmanship against all takers with stakes adjusted to attract the range of talent.

NOTICE

Be it known to all persons that "G" a resident at Camp Floyd, sends forth on this 10th day of May, 1859, this challenge to any person in the Territory of Utah.

That "G" will load and fire "TWO SIX SHOOTERS" (Army or Navy style) on horseback, and at a gallop, in LESS TIME than any other man in Utah.

The revolvers to be loaded with cartridges similar to those used by the U.S. Dragoons.

On this I am willing and ready at any time to stake any sum of money from $50.00 to $200.00.

For further information apply at Messrs. Livingston, Kinkhead, & Co., Camp Floyd.[49]

Religious believers found little satisfaction at Camp Floyd, where theism often sank under the dangers and uncertainties attending life on the frontier. Fighting men were more inclined to place their faith in their rifles than in their maker and were unlikely to participate in crusades against gambling, alcohol, theaters, or dancing. In the absence of ordained clergy, church services were conducted by laymen, chiefly for the benefit of a handful of officers and a dozen families that lived on the post. Enlistees usually attended the interdenominational services for the dead, and donated generously to charitable causes,[50] yet a lingering worry persisted in the military command over the absence of church discipline in the barracks. Eventually a search was launched for ordained clergy to fill these needs.

A partial resolution to the dilemma was reached near the end of January, 1859, when the Post Council of Administration addressed a letter to the Archbishop of Baltimore, Francis Patrick Kenrick, requesting a "native born" Catholic priest for chaplain duty in Utah.[51] While the War Department searched for an American-born shepherd for its flock of Catholic fighting men in Utah, the Lord in His mysterious way was routing them a wandering priest from Bavaria.[52]

Like Escalante and Dominguez who preceded him to Utah almost a century earlier, Leonard Keller was a European. Born in Unterweigtshofen during the reign of Max Joseph, he arrived in the United States after a decade of unspectacular scholastic studies in Rome.[53] Father Bonaventure, as Keller was called after his ordination, eventually reached California in 1859, after spending seven stormy and controversial years in various parishes in Texas, New York, Ohio, and Pennsylvania. There are many missing pieces in the story of Keller's arrival in Utah. According to one account, he joined the Camp Floyd paymaster in Benicia the winter before his arrival, and, following a lengthy trip overland through the southern desert corridor, reached Salt Lake City sick and empty-pocketed. Eschewing any missionary work among the Mormons, he traveled to Camp Floyd on a scorching day in July and was welcomed by a number of Catholic soldiers, who gave him their devotion and support. General Johnston offered Father Bonaventure-Keller a temporary chaplaincy at an unspecified monthly salary, along with the right to draw subsistence rations, and the Franciscan thought that his religious odyssey was at an end.[54] Unfortunately, less than two months after his arrival, Father Keller came under attack from Nativist officers, who demanded his resignation because he was not born on American soil.

A curious synthesis of nineteenth-century Protestantism, Nativism played on people's fears that "hordes of foreign 'scum' would outbreed, outvote, and overwhelm the old 'native' stock."[55] Camp Floyd Nativists blocked Father Keller's appointment as post chaplain. A significant number of officers shared Captain John Phelps's nightmare that implacable Jesuits and Franciscans would carry the gold and white banner of the papacy into Camp Floyd. "By making allowances for the peculiarities of foreigners," Phelps argued bitterly, "we are adapting our ideas to their notions, rather than assimilating their notions in our ideas."[56] His diary's rhetorical excesses reflected the provincialism that was so common in the pre-Civil War army. "The robes of the Catholic Priest are for the first time seen in our halls of Congress, and an American army selects a Catholic for its chaplain,"[57] Phelps complained, voicing the bigotry that simmered in the camp. Father Bonaventure decided not to make a painful situation worse, and he left the territory the following October. The search for an American-born chaplain continued, and several priests succeeded one another in his place until the gradual deactivation of Camp Floyd made their presence unnecessary.[58]

In the midst of the Nativist furor, the Episcopal chaplain of Fort Laramie entered Salt Lake City unannounced but in much higher style than Father Bonaventure-Keller. William Vaux arrived on the doorstep of the Lion House, Brigham Young's official residence, escorted by Superintendent of Indian Affairs Jacob Forney and Territorial Secretary John Hartnett, and bearded the lion in his house.[59] After a short talk, Brigham Young invited Vaux to preach in the Tabernacle because, although he walked a different religious path, he had convinced the Mormon prophet that they both moved towards the same enlightenment. The clergyman was struck by the poise and dignity of the Mormon leader, whose image in the press was that of a dissipated, evil man. With high hopes, William Vaux returned to Salt Lake House to prepare his sermon. The following morning he awoke to the sight of Saints busily placarding the city with printed announcements of his scheduled Tabernacle address the following Sunday.[60]

On the appointed day, the Tabernacle was packed to capacity, and Vaux informed his audience: "I came not to battle your peculiar opinions, or to interfere with your worship, but as a humble minister of Jesus Christ, I wish to preach a plain, doctrinal discourse."[61] Charles Walker viewed the whole performance as a doomed attempt to rekindle the smoldering ashes of Protestantism: "There was no life in his preaching and I think I never heard the name of the Deity used as often and needless as this man did while preaching."[62] After the clergyman finished speaking, he spent the remaining part of the day with Brigham Young, who entertained him at a late evening dinner.[63]

Leaving Salt Lake City the following morning, the chaplain visited Camp Floyd, where he paid his respects to General Johnston and officiated at the marriage of the daughter of Major Isaac Lynde. The young bride, half unconscious from a severe case of mountain fever, was carried into the theater and placed in a soft chair facing the chaplain. The ceremony could not await her recovery, for at the frontier outpost, a wedding had to coincide with the arrival of a clergyman, and was seldom at the convenience of the bride: "A dozen officers present, Mr. Vaux . . . in his robes. Her mother the only lady in camp, gave her away, the father being absent on duty."[64]

For many soldiers, membership in the "Rocky Mountain Lodge" of Masons provided a refreshing diversion, although controversy over its secret meetings and signs rocked the military outpost almost to its foundation. "There is an effort being made to get up a secret society among the soldiers and officers," wrote Captain Phelps. "One of the privates of my company is, I understand, an important member of a lodge to which officers belong. The soldier should have his head shaved and be drummed out of service and the officer be cashiered."[65]

When the charter reached Camp Floyd from St. Louis in April, 1859, construction of a temple began.[66] Despite the opposition of a large Catholic majority within the enlisted ranks, 162 members were secretly sworn in to the Lodge. After successfully riding out a storm of "high criticism," the Lodge channeled a great deal of its members' energy into providing supplies for destitute emigrants passing through the territory on their way to California, a philanthropic activity that continued until the abandonment of Camp Floyd.[67]

For all of their preoccupation with entertainment, politics, and philosophical controversies, soldiers functioned within prescribed routines that varied only slightly from season to season. Much of their time was taken up with the endless task of repairing and improving the buildings of the fort, or in constructing such necessary projects as a conduit system to supply fresh water to the barracks. "As Spring opened," recalled Richard T. Ackley, "the men were busy building and rearranging the garrison. Captain Turnley, the Quartermaster of the post, was very efficient in his duties. A very large spring of water started close by and the Captain had it nicely cleaned out and walled up."[68] A mile below the spring, Cedar Creek was dammed and a grist mill constructed to prepare feed for the dragoons' horses.[69] The enterprising soldiers stocked the small lagoon behind the dam with fish brought in from Utah Lake. Soldiers also found time to plant a forty-acre garden within the treeless limits of the fort. Though there was little water to spare for irrigation, potatoes and vegetables were planted in irrigated rows. Their experiment in agriculture proved encouraging, and the harvest was divided among the regiments that took turns irrigating, weeding, and otherwise tending the garden.[70]

Harvesting wood for fuel, shelter, and fencing became an increasingly common activity as the army's needs for wood expanded. The post commander kept fatigue parties in the mountains for seven days at a time cutting firewood, frequently at a terrible cost in human suffering. In summer, warm winds rushed over the flat valley from the southwest desert, picking up speed at the foot of the Oquirrh Mountains to swirl clouds of dust across the middle of the fort or open encampments. The sky would fill with clothes, boxes, tents—anything that was not tied down. "There is neither nook, cranny, or crevice, impervious to dust particles," wrote Captain Tracy, "which will find their way into even books closed up, and fast locked and strapped down in our trunks."[71]

Within a matter of hours, Indian summer could vanish into winter, accompanied by sleet, thunder, hail, and arctic winds. Bundled in their bulky wool coats and heavy buffalo boots, men on mules and on foot tramped out trails to the mountains, often wetting the snow with their blood. Hands and feet froze from the effects of wind–driven particles of hail; tearing northern gales swelled and closed soldiers' eyes, and their faces were lost under a thick coating of frost. Snow–blinded and maddened mules floundered in white powder, their hides bleeding from the constant prodding necessary to keep them moving through the rolling sea of snow.

Laboring in five-hour shifts through cloudbursts, hailstorms, strong gales, or thirst and parching heat, work parties leveled the sparse stands of pine and juniper and hauled the wood down to the base of the mountains where it was periodically removed to Camp Floyd. Because of the great amount of firewood necessary to meet the needs of cookhouses, barracks, and officers' quarters, the wood-cutting operations continued the year around.[72]

In this spartan setting most of the soldiers enjoyed good health, probably because of the abundance of food and water, the excellent medical
attention, and the absence of swamps and marshes in Cedar Valley. However, mountain fever was a real danger to frontier soldiers, and one patient
died of it for every eighty-six cases treated during the three-year medical
record history of the fort. For the most part, however, the frontier regulars suffered only occasional discomfort from fevers, digestive ailments,
respiratory problems, muscular degeneration, venereal diseases, and a
wide range of personal injuries and campaign wounds. Camp Floyd had a
lower mean mortality rate than any other department of the army, except
West Point, averaging only slightly more than eight deaths per thousand
men, so at least the soldiers met the rigors of their lives in good health.[73]

At least 100 men stood daily watch over the fort, and every junior
officer and enlisted man kept either a nightly vigil in two-hour shifts, or a
four-hour double daylight watch. With monotonous regularity the rasping voice of the Officer of the Day could be heard shouting, challenging
the alertness of sentries who were expected to recite the general orders of
the day from memory.[74]

Stormy, starless skies made the ocean of sagebrush appear as lonely as
a graveyard and tested the sentries' nerves. Officers passing beyond the
fort to check outlying guard posts were chilled by mournful echoes of
coyotes howling in the nearby flats, attracted by the viscera and trim-
mings of butchered animals left exposed near the slaughter pens. Their
nightly dolorous serenade, wrote one officer, "sounded as if the devils of
the pit had broken loose for a holiday."[75] However, the men's fears were
groundless. Like many of their western contemporaries they failed to
distinguish between the docile coyote of Utah and the more aggressive
timber wolf of the eastern forest. Nevertheless, the ear-splitting howl,
sounding as if the devil were coming for his own, was a never-to-be-
forgotten experience, wrote Captain Tracy:

> Northwesterly and between camp and the point where the guard
> is stationed lies the usual stretch of sage. . . . Over the ground . . .
> wolves are wont at night to traverse in packs. . . . These animals
> appeared particularly on the alert tonight, and, with my orderly—
> both of us on foot—I had proceeded near half way . . . when at the
> front and somewhat to the right, there arose a long drawn deep
> howl. . . .[76]

The men took a brief respite before continuing toward the sentry.

> Presently from the neighborhood of the lower camp, there came
> the answer, then another, deeper and wilder of note, and finally the
> chorus of the troup under full head, in one direction. I did not
> linger for the advance, and if I did not run, I imitated the Kentuck-

ian in some rapid walking. Nearer and nearer the pack came on, till I fancied I could hear the sagebrush crash beneath them.[77]

The captain pushed his way through the undergrowth and came out into a small clearing, glowing with the protective fire of the sentry outpost. It was not difficult to persuade Captain Tracy to return with an additional escort, his orderly noted: "There wasn't an officer in camp who could beat Captain Tracy walking."[78]

Guard duty was not confined to Camp Floyd. During the first part of every month, twice a month in winter, patrols of infantrymen and dragoons marched to Rush, Steptoe, Skull, and adjoining valleys to protect the government herds that grazed on the public domain. Once in the field, the majority of the troops preferred to live in the easily transported and erected Sibley tents. "When going on these expeditions," reported one soldier, "we take our tents with us, clear away the snow, which is generally about two feet deep on the mountains, pitch our tents, and with ample supply of buffalo robes, make ourselves comfortable as the exigencies of the case will permit."[79] When winter could not be faced in tents, soldiers bivouacked in stone-walled shelters covered with canvas, or accustomed themselves to living in earthen dugouts.

In camp, soldiers faced other unpleasant duties, ranging from cleaning stables to entertaining visiting Indian dignitaries. However, standing parade inspection during winter months outraged officers and enlisted men alike. Driven into the parade grounds by early reveille, soldiers stood at rigid attention in arctic temperatures, studying the leaden sky that moved angrily toward Cedar Valley "like a monster," commented one observer. On one occasion, as darkness fell over the troops, a cold blast of wind "swept through the ranks; freezing the exposed parts of the soldiers' faces and numbed hands and feet with arctic temperatures."[80] Ominous clouds thickened rapidly, the air sharpened, and a powdery sheet of snow began to sift through the ranks. "By the time . . . Colonel Charles F. Smith had gotten into place, with his staff as reviewing office, the great cloud launched itself over the peak towards us, and the snow was seen advancing in a thick white wall." The full fury of the blizzard continued with raw gusts of stinging sleet softened by snow that surrounded the men in mists. "Guidons, or even the line of the companies at front were scarcely discernable, except at their shoulders, or tops kepis or pompons, and we only guessed at points of wheeling, following as we might in the track of our predecessors—for the guidons were alike invisible."[81] Although darkness had fallen, obscuring the camp commander and his staff, regimental officers saluted scarecrow figures with their sabers before stumbling off the grounds with their men to the warmth of their barracks. To soothe over the wretched ordeal, Colonel Smith ordered one gill of whiskey to be distributed to his men, leading one officer to comment,

"There is no other man in this army who could have done all this with impunity."[82]

Against this background, soldiers saw their military fervor disintegrate and disappear, remembered private C. E. Gould in a letter to his brother: "In the first place it is as bad a place as you can find for morals," he warned, and as for work, "if they think a soldier's life is a lazy one they will find themselves much mistaken . . . out here . . . at least . . . I find exactly the opposite."[83] He cussed about having to rise before dawn in the summer, and complained bitterly over being awakened in winter at five in the morning to the nerve-shattering sounds of reveille. There were, according to Gould, endless work details that dragged on until six in the evening:

> When not at work we have drill six hours a day, then you mount guard every fourth night or so and you cannot turn out with an old rifle or belts and shoes have to be blackened till they shine like patten [sic] leather and your rifle not the least bit of dust on it so that it would not soil the whitest handkerchief ever was.[84]

The letter ended with the advice: "*Frederick never enlist.*"

Despite momentary recognition accorded outstanding deeds of heroism, promotions were slow or nonexistent in the peacetime army, which weakened enthusiasm for military service. Every soldier hoped to retire on a government pension, but trouble often multiplied like dragon's teeth and frequently led to dismissal from the service. In a world governed by detailed written regulations, discipline at Camp Floyd was severe. Isolated from the public eye by geography or by public indifference, enlisted men were often subjected to arbitrary punishment not prescribed by the military code, a violation that was increasingly accepted though not publicly admitted by the army.

The journal of Private J. E. Farmer revealed that these practices had penetrated the soldiers' lives at Camp Floyd. With a possible handful of exceptions, officers often subjected enlisted offenders to "bucking and gagging, carrying large timbers before the guard house, knocking them down with their muskets, maiming them by saber cuts and in some instances shooting them." Flogging was frequent, he wrote as he continued to pen his impressions: "At this period and for many years I knew the wording of the charge, the specifications and the penalty and could go through the former without a hitch as I listened to the reading so often."[85]

Even stiff-necked dragoons deplored such severity. An unidentified sergeant who had often seen cruelty firsthand was shocked by the army's handling of military criminals.

> In the foregoing, I have made use of the term "bucked and gagged," which perhaps will need explanation to some of your readers. It is a punishment never resorted to except in aggravated

cases, and this is, I understand the first case that has occurred in Captain Anderson's company since he entered the army. To "buck" a man, his wrists are first firmly bound together as close as possible. He is then placed in a sitting posture, and his knees are forced between his arms. A stick is then introduced between the bend of his legs and the bend of his arms; and he is unable to move without grumbling over on his back, which, from his helpless condition, is no pleasant feat to perform. Gagging is simply introducing a stick between his teeth and fastening it with strings that was drawn so tight as to cut the corners of their mouths, and cause the blood to flow down on their coat collars, but this is too severe, and few officers resort to it except to silence a man who otherwise cannot be induced to keep quiet.[86]

The harder they looked, the more convinced soldiers were that the punishment inflicted by officers was an intolerable tyranny, a mockery of freedom; and all that could be said was that there was no alternative but to bear it without complaint. Some victims cowered abjectly; others bore the punishment with fortitude.

At the same court-martial, an artilleryman, whose name I have forgotten, was tried for desertion, and was sentenced to forfeit all pay and allowances due him at the time he deserted, to receive "fifty lashes on the bare back, well laid on with a raw hide," to serve the remainder of his time (three years and nine months) at hard labor in charge of the guard, wearing a ball weighing twenty-five pounds attached by a chain three feet in length to his leg, to forfeit in the interim all his pay except fifty cents a month, and at the expiration of his time of service to be drummed out of the army. Pretty rough usage that, and telling very poorly for the merciful disposition of our military men. But it's all right, I suppose.[87]

Theoretically at least, corporal punishment was considered a deterrent to crime, but the evidence from the army's own records strongly points to the conclusion that the results did not serve the ends of justice. The whole issue came into the open when Colonel Charles F. Smith charged that punishment was always stamped with the mark of its executioner. The commander complained that while some soldiers were beaten within an inch of their lives, others were scarcely touched by the whip. He argued, not without some justification, that corporal sentences were in conflict with the Constitution, which forbade the use of cruel and unusual punishment; yet these acts continued unabated during his entire tour of duty at Camp Floyd.[88] General Johnston's role in punishments is unknown in the history of the fort.

Convictions for theft, desertion, or other breaches of the military code brought the prisoners marching in double-time to the parade grounds, escorted by armed infantrymen. In full view of their regiments, prisoners' uniforms were stripped of all marks and insignia, the men undressed to the waist, and their hands tied over their heads to the flagstaff. Scourgings were frequently executed by field musicians, who took turns at administering the beatings "well laid on."[89] Standing to one side of the victim, the post or regimental surgeon held the power of life and death over prisoners, and he ordered the punishment to proceed or stop, depending on the severity of the beating. Spectators fell from the ranks "pale as sheet" at the sight of these mutilations, or agonized in tears over the torments suffered by their luckless comrades.[90] A veteran of Camp Floyd recounted that no incident in his life brought greater sorrow than when he was forced to carry out the flogging sentence of a military court. "I was ordered by the quartermaster to take a rope and rawhide and proceed to the square where the flogging was to be executed," Henry S. Hamilton remembered. "After reading the sentence, the man was told to remove his shirt, after which the officer of the day ordered me to tie him to the wheel of the cannon." The private stood for a moment, erect and poised, but tears poured down his face. "I was dumbfounded and did not wish to do it, but was told that I must, and to lay it on well, or he would have me court-martialed for disobedience of orders, so I had no alternative but to execute the order." The prisoner was strangely calm, showing no sign of tension. The quartermaster handed the musician the whip and ordered the sentence executed.

> He began by saying "one" in a loud tone, and at that I raised the rawhide and commenced the brutal work; but instead of following him, he had to follow me, and very quickly, too, for I seemed to lose all presence of mind, and knew nothing and saw nothing until he seized me by the arm and I was about giving the man one blow more than his sentence demanded. Throughout this punishment my sufferings, mentally, were equal to those of the culprit. It was a great shock to me, and I felt both ashamed, disgusted, and sad at the spectacle before me.[91]

When at last the punishment was completed, prisoners were carried to the stockade where their wounds were treated by the departmental physician. Once confined, very few prisoners escaped from the military prison, though several inmates tried to tunnel under the fortress-like stone walls. Judged by any standard, the suffering of prisoners was extreme in many ways. Inmates confined to hard labor were assigned to stone quarries a few miles distant from the fort, or toiled daily ten to twelve hours haying or cutting timber in the mountains. Discontent and sorrow showed openly when prisoners were marched single file to their cells, holding twenty-pound balls chained to their legs.[92] Even the Board of Administration for Camp Floyd recoiled in disgust when they found prisoners' quarters so "small and so badly ventilated that they were unfit for even cages for wild beasts. . . .''[93] Kept alive on a scanty diet of hard bread, dried beef, beans, and water, convicts were chained to the prison walls at night and exercised in the morning with large logs or burlap sacks of sand strapped to their backs.[94] Yet for all these abominations, there is no evidence that capital punishment was carried out at Camp Floyd, or that prisoners died from such inhumane treatment.

Soldiers charged with drunkenness were spread-eagled, gagged with bars of lye soap and left to "sweat off their liquor" until they were overcome by nausea or dehydration. Those unfortunate enough to be arrested with whiskey in their possession were sentenced to "bury the bottle," a singularly repugnant task of digging, burying, and refilling a grave-like trench. Still others were ordered "on the chimes," a sentence that forced prisoners to balance themselves on the rim of a whiskey barrel for eight hours.

Approaching the end of their confinement, prisoners were branded with the initial of their crime as part of their punishment,—e.g., "D" for desertion, "T" for theft—which also made them more recognizable. After all traces of facial hair were removed, the ball and chain was removed, and, while drums and bugles played "The Rogues March," they were escorted out of the fort to end their careers in disgrace.[95] The army was now satisfied that the criminal could not go and sin elsewhere.

Yet the frontier regulars at Camp Floyd accepted punishment as part of the hazard of their enlistment; they adjusted to the rhythm of the life around them, finished their tours of duty, and disappeared from the federal muster rolls. Commenting on life in the Utah frontier, one dragoon humorously remarked: "Let our friends at home be assured of the fact that we are progressing and that, to use the classic language of some filibusterers, like the slow but intrepid steps of a mule toward a pack of oats."[96] For those readers equipped to appreciate it, another soldier wrote: "Should the readers of your Journal in the States see these communications, they will understand that notwithstanding we are serving in the most God-forsaken country in the habitable globe; yet with the 'Soldier's Circus,' with Willis as clown, the 'Military Dramatic Company,' and the Valley Tan to drink and the *Valley Tan* to read, we are all right."[97]

General Johnston remembered his tour in Cedar Valley as "worse than any imagined horrors of a Siberian exile. . . ." The general's passion for privacy was gradually reduced to an endless longing to return to his family and lifelong friends.

> The scenery of the Utah Mountains which is sublime and magnificent preserved its novelty to me for a long time but after one year in the territory, the novelty of the sublime magnificence of the valley was gone and it has resolved itself into a huge prison wall, a

barrier to cut me off from all those I love. . . . For a long time I have tried to believe that I was an exception and backed up [with] pseudo philosophy I have fancied myself sometimes content. . . . But in the midst of this monotony my philosophy has been thrown overboard and I find myself no more content . . . than the rest of mankind.[98]

CHAPTER SIX

"ONE-EYED JEFFERY": THE ODYSSEY OF JUDGE JOHN C. CRADLEBAUGH

This attempt of the Mormons to interfere with the administration of the law, and control the courts, has been one of the chief causes of difficulty between the judges, sent by the Federal Government to Utah, and the Mormon people.

—*John C. Cradlebaugh*[1]

JUDICIAL CONFRONTATIONS between Mormon and Gentile litigants weakened the status of the federal courts in the Utah territory. In the standoff between the Saints on one hand, and the army and the anti–Mormon judges on the other, old fears and hatreds were reborn.

The "Great Conspiracy," as the Gentiles were soon to label it, burst into the open in 1852, when the territorial legislature enlarged the powers of the probate courts, extending their jurisdiction to "practically all the legal business, except a few cases in which the United States was a party. . . ."[2] Rivaling the federal system of courts, these local judicial districts roughly corresponded to the Mormon ecclesiastical organization, with each judge holding tenure at the discretion of Brigham Young and the Church hierarchy. Susceptible to religious pressures and demands, the probate judicial bodies gave rise to popular Gentile dissatisfaction, especially among federal judges who complained that the probate courts exercised original jurisdiction in both civil and criminal actions, thereby effectively undermining federal authority in the territory.

Although Utah was not the only region to make broad use of

probate jurisdiction, the charge persisted that the local courts gave the Mormon Church extraordinary influence in civic affairs in the territory, and thus added to the general turbulence of territorial politics. With the Saints' policy hardening around the exclusive use of the non-federal courts, Gentiles were quick to note "that while the probate judge was an elected officer, he was usually a Mormon bishop or held some other important Church position, and thus was influenced strongly by Church ideology and practice."[3] Here the controversy balanced precariously until 1857, when the powerful post of Chief Justice of the Utah Territory was given to Delano R. Eckles, while the associate judgeships fell to Charles E. Sinclair and John Cradlebaugh, all non-Mormons.

The establishment of the carpetbag government under the watchful eye of the federal army accentuated the obvious division between Gentiles who believed it necessary to eliminate the lower courts in order to destroy Mormon authority, and those less extreme men who, in order to heal the wounds opened by the Utah War, resisted the army's attempt to reform territorial justice. By far the most active in the former camp was Chief Justice Eckles, a fifty-two-year-old native of Greencastle, Indiana, who epitomized anti-Mormonism. In physical appearance he was a stoutly built man of medium height, weighing perhaps just under 200 pounds, outwardly resembling the Charles Dickens prototype of a ruthless, hard-fisted merchant of industrial England.

Eckles stumbled onto the territorial judgeship because of his long and faithful service to the Democratic party; and although his credentials colored him as an honest, able, discreet man of some education, he was a fire-breathing nationalist who could accommodate no beliefs or actions but those that supported the position of the federal government. Whatever his past experiences with Mormonism might have been, he came into the territory with an intense dislike for Brigham Young, and his "intransigent attitude toward the Saints prolonged the tension between Utah and the nation."[4] Within a month of his arrival in Salt Lake City, he collected a folio of confidential confessions that led him to believe that the Mormon people were in secret if not open rebellion against the United States and "firm in their determination of resist *even to a bloody issue*, the due execution of the law."[5]

In Eckles the Saints found a dangerous adversary. The pattern of his political power was a familiar one, based on his personal friendship with the Secretary of State, Lewis Cass, through whose voice in Washington he hoped to purge the territory of real and imaginary evils. The Saints' response to Eckles was immediate and explosive. They bitterly denounced him as a chronic drunk who had been brought to the territory to embarrass the Mormons, and they thun-

dered a lengthy list of accusations against him. Brigham Young effectively neutralized Eckles by pitting the friendly federal attorney, General Alexander Wilson, against Eckles's court. Nevertheless, the judge
remained a source of continuing discomfort to the Mormons.

While Eckles represented the old-line political appointee common
to western territories, Charles C. Sinclair became the Gentiles'
unchallenged hero. Among his contemporaries, the restless, head-
strong twenty-eight-year-old "baby" judge was regarded as the finest
mind in the territory.[6] Modest and restrained in his personal manner,
he was assigned the Third Judicial District, headquartered in Salt Lake
City, where he lived outside the mainstream of Mormon life. Among
the staunchest supporters of federal authority, Sinclair favored the
overthrow of Brigham Young and the implementation of a harsh
peace settlement. His strategy was to assert that the growing danger
of Mormonism made it necessary to put the country in the hands of
the federal judiciary.

Neither Sinclair nor Eckles provided any immediate relief for the
Saints when the territorial courts were reorganized in 1858 at the
remote capital of Fillmore. The southern march of the judges under
escort of eighty dragoons for protection against the Indians was
uneventful except for the sight of charred remains along the route that
gave mute testimony of violence and depredations.[7] Respect and
goodwill were absent during a month-long reorganization of the federal courts. "Their very appearance," George A. Smith wrote coolly
of the judges, "under an escort of dragoons, served to inspire in the
breast of every citizen a sense of deep contempt."[8] This statement was
influenced by an earlier report that the jurists had planned to arrest
participants in the Mountain Meadows Massacre. It was a cruel falsehood that originated from unidentified sources. Matters worsened in
Salt Lake City with the return of Judge Sinclair, resulting in a head-on
collision between the federal judiciary and the Saints, and further
multiplying tensions.

Sinclair reopened his court by charging the Saints with treason as
well as other offenses ranging from violations of postal laws to
obstruction of justice.[9] The judge's indignation burned uncontrolled
when the federal district attorney, Alexander Wilson, a Gentile from
Iowa, refused to prosecute, arguing that President Buchanan had pardoned the Mormons for all treasonable acts:

> Treason is a crime against the laws of our country, and the pardon
> of the President was for this crime against the laws of this country.
> Now, a pardon, by law, to be valid, must be delivered and
> accepted, and it must also be specifically pleaded in bar of punish-
> ment for a crime committed. If there has been no crime committed

the pardon cannot be accepted. If the pardon is accepted it must be for a crime committed.[10]

Without Wilson's cooperation, the judge could do nothing but note for the newspapers:

Notwithstanding all this; notwithstanding the Mormons have treated, and do treat, the pardon with contempt yet Mr. Wilson takes upon himself the responsibility of forcing it down their throats, and thus gives them the opportunity of crying out to posterity, "persecution, persecution!" and denying the fact that they ever committed treason, although they now enjoy the immunities and privileges conferred upon them by a pardon for this treason.[11]

There was also at this time a legal assault on James Ferguson, a Mormon lawyer and adjutant general of the Nauvoo Legion, who was charged with slandering Judge George P. Stiles, a former member of the federal judiciary.[12] The conduct of the grand jury investigation was no worse than the Mormons might have expected, but when Brigham Young was called as a material witness, intrigue heightened. After three unsuccessful attempts by Marshal Peter Dotson to subpoena the Mormon patriarch, Sinclair received a note from Young pledging his full cooperation, a message that ended with the statement that he would obey the process of the court. On the following day, December 3, he appeared before the grand jury that convened in the basement of the Social Hall.[13] But the Mormon leader refused to be dominated by the court or be panicked by the threat of a full-scale investigation of his public or private life. The hall was packed with a nervous assembly of several hundred of his followers, well-armed and eager to assure the safety of the Lion of the Lord.[14]

Although the hearings monopolized the headlines during the first week of December 1858, accentuating the air of crisis in the city, Brigham Young appeared at the courthouse in fighting spirits. However, in a letter to the *New York Times* after the meeting, a correspondent described the scene in another vein: "The court was crowded to its utmost capacity. In the bar, by the side of Mr. Ferguson, was seated the live prophet himself, Brigham Young . . . dressed plainly in a neat suit of black, and during the sitting of the Court sat with his hat off, but with a silk handkerchief tied about his head. During the greater portion of the time he rested his head upon his hand, and his countenance wore a careworn, melancholy expression."[15] This was his first appearance in public since the entrance of the army into the valley. Sharing the same bench with Young were Heber C. Kimball, Daniel H. Wells, George A. Smith, several of Young's sons, and a score of other dignitaries of the Church. "Immediately in front of the judge sat Governor Cumming . . . and ranged round in the bar opposite

Brigham were the 'Gentile' attorneys. Among the crowd which filled the hall in the rear we noticed several persons notorious as members of the 'Danite band,' and also several of the 'starred' police of the city."[16]

Although feelings were high, the contest ended abruptly. The grand jury refused to bring forward any indictment, essentially arguing that even if all of the evidence were true, no action could be taken that conflicted with the letter and spirit of the presidential proclamation of amnesty.[17] Inglorious or not, the decision caused a minor explosion of criticism as well as approval.[18] The Saints' elation was short-lived, however, for Sinclair did not accept the defeat with good grace. The angered magistrate enlarged the ranks of civilian attorneys by admitting to the bar a legion of anti–Mormon lawyers, including Kirk Anderson, editor of the newly established periodical, the *Valley Tan*. The summation of Sinclair's sins found expression in the *Deseret News*, whose editor reacted sharply:

> Individuals of no legal knowledge whatever, officers of the army, merchants, merchant's clerks, loafers, gamblers, doctors, transient traders of all kinds, etc. etc., have been admitted to practice in the District Courts and in the Supreme Courts of the United States for this Territory, some of them not knowing the difference between a *capias ad respondendum* and a *demurrer*, not the difference between either of these and a plea to the jurisdiction of a court.[19]

Despite this reaction, Sinclair was beaten, observed Brigham Young, for "there had not been a judge in Utah that had been so completely taken up and set down in the mud as Judge Sinclair has been."[20] But, the following spring another hornet's nest, even more dangerous, was stirred up.

Into this highly charged atmosphere stepped John C. Cradlebaugh, the last member of the federal judiciary to appear in the territory. For reasons largely unexplained, he arrived in Utah during the late evening of November 4, 1858, after having been driven in a carriage to the mountain cabin of Ephraim Hanks by an unidentified woman. There is no evidence connecting Cradlebaugh in any illicit way to the mysterious companion, who was apparently returning home at the time of the incident and volunteered to transport the judge into the territory.

Once under shelter, John Cradlebaugh introduced himself to Hanks as the long-absent territorial judge. After a spartan meal, the two men sat across from each other near the fireside, exchanging ideas on the Drummond conflict and tales of Mormon hardships at Nauvoo and Missouri. Hanks listened to Cradlebaugh's observations of Eckles and Sinclair, whose opinions, he gathered, were so colored by emotion and propaganda as to make justice difficult to attain for the Mormons. While Hanks doctored Cradlebaugh's frostbitten fingers with a poultice of scraped turnips, the judge criticized the press's misrepresentation of the Mormons. This bewildered Hanks, who was accustomed to expect the worst from federal judges. The brow of the Mormon again contracted when Cradlebaugh asked for an interview with Brigham Young. Although the statements of the jurist were mildly assuring, Hanks looked at him doubtfully, mentally observing "the judge possessed but one eye and that is a very good one."[21]

Before the sun appeared on Little Mountain the following morning, Cradlebaugh departed unexpectedly on foot across the lonely expanse of the canyon. Trying to overtake his guest, Hanks hurried his horses up the trail, only to be hailed by Surveyor-General David H. Burr, a prominent leader of the anti-Mormon faction in the territory. One of the most knowledgeable and cynical of all the Gentiles in Salt Lake City, Burr had come to escort Cradlebaugh into the territory, and he asked Hanks if he had seen the missing jurist. The surprised look on the Mormon's face told Burr that he had passed the judge minutes before, riding away on the tailgate of a wood wagon. Burr turned his carriage and headed back down the canyon, followed closely by Hanks. Each man hoped to reach Cradlebaugh before the other.

Traveling in a light carriage, Hanks had little trouble overtaking the wood wagon and ordered the driver to halt. Cradlebaugh jumped down from the rear of the wagon, wholly taken aback by Hanks's reappearance. The Mormon explained his unusual conduct, claiming he wished to assure the judge's safe passage to Salt Lake City. Moreover, he would furnish Cradlebaugh with an introduction to Brigham Young or any other authority the judge wished to interview. He hoped, Hanks added, that the conferences would be helpful to Cradlebaugh's understanding of territorial conditions. Cradlebaugh's reaction failed to mask his obvious irritation, and, not surprisingly, he did not entertain much respect for Hanks's interference. "I do not want any of these airs, I have come here to do my duty."[22] It was still morning when Cradlebaugh scrambled down from the lumber wagon and lost himself in the crowded streets of the city, and Hanks sped a message to Brigham Young, ahead of him, outlining the events that had transpired.

Cradlebaugh's career in the territory was astonishing. Relatively few men could match his intolerance toward his intellectual inferiors, and he was a much more complex barrister than either Sinclair or Eckles. Yet he took a broad view of the problems facing the territory and the frictions that separated Utah into two hostile camps. In the beginning, he shared the Mormons' belief that the army should actively promote the general welfare of the citizens of the territory, a point of view that swayed George A. Smith to remark, "It is refreshing to hear a man speak who knows so much, and has so much pluck in him. Individually Sinclair knows nothing but Cradlebaugh knows it all. . . ."[23] Yet within six months Cradlebaugh was the strongest and most outspoken foe of the Saints, and signs of his power would scar the territory for a generation. In the end, the one-eyed jurist fulfilled most of the Gentiles' expectations, for "no Gentile caused Brigham Young more trouble than did this tall, lean, middle-aged lawyer from Ohio and the work of his court . . . threatened to reopen conflict between Mormons and Gentiles."[24]

The drama began to unfold with a series of clandestine midnight interviews and private investigations from which Cradlebaugh pieced together the Mormon puzzle, eventually leading him to an "understanding of the forces which worked against judicial stability in the territory."[25] However, the most serious battle in the courts was not fought out in Salt Lake City, but in Provo, forty miles to the south. Operating from his makeshift courtroom at Camp Floyd, Cradlebaugh launched a second examination into a series of murders committed near Springville, accumulating a mass of evidence from all parts of the territory. In an account to Congress several years later, Cradlebaugh outlined his charges:

> Springville is a village of several hundred inhabitants. There was one young man whom it was intended to kill. He ran to his uncle's and was followed to his uncle's house. Here are three persons killed, and the criminal goes unpunished.
>
> There can be no doubt but by the testimony of young Parrish that you will be able to identify those persons who were connected with it. He can tell you who was engaged in it, and who followed him to the house of his uncle. Here are three persons who were butchered in a most inhuman manner, and the offenders have not been brought to justice. This is sufficient to show that there has been an effort to cover up instead of to bring to light and punish.[26]

There were other murders equally deserving of attention.

> At the same place there was another person killed, Henry Fobbs, who came in from California and was going to the States, but got in here when the difficulties arose between this community and the general Government, and was detained. When Henry Fobbs was here he made his home at Partial Terry's, stayed there a few weeks; during what time his horse and revolver were stolen; he made his escape, tried to get to Bridger, was caught, brought back, and murdered; and that is the last of Henry Fobbs. No investigation has been made; his body has been removed several times, so that now, perhaps, it could not be found.[27]

In the weeks that followed, Cradlebaugh retired to Judge Eckles's quarters at the army post, privately confessing that he would return to Washington in the spring if he could not guarantee a return of justice to the territory.[28] Results followed quickly. Cradlebaugh requested General Johnston to furnish a military escort for his court, assuring the commander that troops were necessary to uphold the authority of the federal government in the territory. In this way the court could guarantee the safety of its witnesses while at the same time strengthening security arrangements around buildings used to house the legal proceedings. With his philosophy, patience, and ingenuity strained to their limits, and his personal hostility toward the Mormons in no way allayed, Johnston approved the request. Early on March 7, a detachment of the Tenth Infantry with twenty-day rations and seventy rounds of ammunition marched out of Camp Floyd for Provo, escorting the judge, the Territorial Marshal, Pete Dotson, and a half-dozen material witnesses for the prosecution.[29]

After an uneventful march, Captain Henry Heth turned over his charges to the custody of the court, then established temporary quarters near the outskirts of the town. With the Sinclair debacle still fresh in the public mind, rumors spread throughout Provo that the *posse commitatus* had come to the village to arrest all of the leading elders of the Church. In the night, an unidentified visitor warned Cradlebaugh that violence awaited him unless he would cease his investigation, so Cradlebaugh requested the troops to move into the center of the town. With all of the federal forces now in the city, Captain Heth ordered his men to take up positions near the Seminary, a modest religious edifice that the judge had leased for a federal courthouse. A corral of army wagons, called Camp Ridgely, sealed off the building from the rest of the community and succeeded in further aggravating the suspicions of the Saints.[30]

Mormons denounced the judge as a tyrant, claiming "Cradlebaugh would use this force to round up and execute Mayor B. K. Bullock and other dignitaries without regard to evidence of their implication in any crime."[31] The judge and his military commander publicly ignored the town's protest.

The opening session of the Second District Court only succeeded in increasing these fears. No single person in the territory served the army's short-term interest as well as did the one-eyed judge, nor was there a Gentile more immune to changing currents than John C. Cradlebaugh. Conflict increased when the irascible jurist presented the findings of his investigation to the grand jury. For the better part of an hour the jurist reviewed the rise and fall of the federal court system in Utah and pointed an accusing finger at those who thwarted or ignored his efforts to bring criminals to justice: "No person has been brought to punishment for some two years; and from what I have learned I am satisfied that crime after crime has been committed." Therefore, the judge charged, "if you desire innocent and unoffending persons to be protected, that you vigilantly and diligently prosecute all persons who are violators of the law." Justice had been crippled by the excess of ecclesiastical power, he continued, with a reference to the doctrine of blood atonement, and "no person can commit crimes and say they are authorized by a higher authority. . . ."[32]

The magistrate appeared as a "Methodist extoller" ordained for the purpose of saving the Mormons from themselves, wrote George A. Smith, sent to Provo by the Church to witness the court proceedings. "It is the first time, we people have had a religious tirade forced down our throats by Bayonets, which are bristling all around the Seminary."[33] The charge recalled another dark moment in Mormon history. "One would almost have imagined himself, hearing a lecture from a Sectarian Priest against Joseph Smith and the Mormons, some twenty years ago, with the single exception of the U.S. Bayonets forcing the dogma of this new preacher (a more potent weapon than simple tar and feathers, fir and fire brands of the former times)." Most frightening of all, Cradlebaugh summoned the principal civil and Church leaders of Provo to appear before his court, only to jail them without bond when they voluntarily came forward.[34] The action was received with much heat and bitterness and turned the court proceedings into near bedlam.

The people of Provo reacted to the arrest of their leaders by issuing a memorial to Cradlebaugh protesting the use of military force. The judge, further displaying his bias, rejected the address and issued additional subpoenas for the arrest of a dozen citizens in Springville, Nephi, Spanish Fork, and Battle Creek. The Saints, again denouncing Cradlebaugh's action, addressed a second plea to Governor Cumming, requesting the removal of the army from Provo. "The lives and liberties of all persons accused are jeopardized by the examination of witnesses and the action of jurors under the influence of a military intimidation and espionage," the petition read. "Should such an order of things continue, we have reason to fear that the time is not far distant when witnesses will be sworn at the point of the bayonet, and the law executed by the sword."[35]

Cradlebaugh responded by producing petitions of his own, a list of Springville citizens who requested the protection of the army against "despotic ecclesiastical law."[36] The judge went even further, producing apostate and Gentile memorials praising the conduct of the army. These documents supported the jurist's own finding that the Saints were guilty of the twin crimes of subverting justice and conspiring to undermine federal authority in the territory.

Then Cradlebaugh overextended himself. During the pre-dawn light of March 18, the citizens of Provo awoke to reports of the arrest of Isaac Bullock, the town's mayor, and citizens Henry Hamilton Kearns and Alexander F. McDonald, all charged with complicity in the Parrish-Potter murders. Also named in the warrant was Aaron Johnson, who had escaped arrest by fleeing to the mountains. The rumor spread through every level of society that the mayor's arrest was the signal for an open purge of the Church. An angry mob of citizens poured in from the surrounding countryside to protect their leaders from the temporal powers of the court.

The worst example of hysteria came when the army retaliated by ordering the military guards to shoot any person caught stoning the field camp. If it were impossible to determine who was responsible for the misconduct, soldiers were ordered to fire in the general direction of the mob. If the fire was returned, Heth ordered his men to "fire and retreat behind the wagons, loading and firing as fast as they can."[37] In this situation, the army steered a dangerous course.

The potentially dangerous situation lessened somewhat with the arrival of the Marshal of Provo, William M. Wall, who investigated the army's complaints of harassment. The marshal warned the army that the Saints would not be blindly led to the slaughter, for they did not trust either Cradlebaugh's or Johnston's intentions. Wall proposed that the army severely punish soldiers guilty of misconduct against the Saints, assuring the captain that this action alone would restore order in the besieged city. His transparent maneuver satisfied neither side.

Episodes of violence spilled over with nearly disastrous results. "One of the soldiers who was thrown in a wrestling match with John Hoopes," wrote one witness, "became very angry and made a rush for Hoopes who caught him as he came with the 'Hip Lock,' threw him violently some distance to the ground, and then the fun began and soon a hand to hand fight ensued."[38] The soldiers ran for their guns. For a few minutes there was a Mexican standoff, but trouble was averted when Captain Heth and Marshal Wall stepped between the combatants and ordered their men to return to their quarters.

Rumors of guerrillas in and near the town added to the army's problem. Marshal Wall embellished these fanciful rumors, undermining the posse's exposed position near the courthouse, already weakened by sagging morale. The army's suspicions turned to fear. At one point Lieutenant North Americus Manning Dudley warned that if the Saints attempted to rescue the wards of the court, the prisoners would be summarily executed.[39] The marshal answered the army by enlisting two hundred Saints as special deputies, which forced Captain Heth to request additional soldiers from Camp Floyd.[40] While the unrest continued, Heth gathered his forces around the courthouse to shield Cradlebaugh against the phantom army of Mormon militiamen. For the most part, however, the excitement created by Mayor Bullock's arrest proved to be premature. After reviewing the evidence against the innocent mayor, Judge Cradlebaugh dismissed Bullock, who was ushered out of the courtroom with unbecoming haste.[41] Beneath the surface, the unrest continued.

Unaware of the new change in events, General Johnston responded to Heth's communique. Several days later, the department commander ordered Major Gabriel R. Paul to the vicinity of Battle Creek, marching at the head of a column of three companies of the Tenth Infantry, four companies of the Seventh Infantry, a squadron of the Second Dragoons, and a reduced element of Phelps's light artillery. The general warned Paul that his sole mission was to prevent the escape of prisoners by "unknown forces"; therefore, under no conditions were his soldiers to participate in any action "except in self defense." The defense of Heth's command came first; all else must wait. In keeping with the spirit of this order, Major Paul was ordered not to enter Provo; instead he was to keep his command in readiness within a few minutes' march of the city limits.[42]

With eight hundred men, the major struck out eastward on the morning of March 20, arriving at the gates of Lehi a few hours past noon. The first stage of the outward trek ended with the army encamped near the adobe walls at the settlement. The expedition again took up its march to Battle Creek the following morning, but lack of forage forced the detachment to bypass the settlement and push on to Timpanogos Canyon near the site of the proposed Gentile settlement of Brown City.[43]

The column reached its destination before sundown, engulfed by heavy snows and sub-zero temperatures. The troops' hardships steadily increased, wrote Captain Albert Tracy, a member of the party who vividly described the column's exposed positions:

> The coming up of the wagons also being now much delayed, we were well-nigh literally frozen before we could get up tents or start in our sheet iron stoves, fire to cheer our blood withal. A gallon of good whiskey at my tent became very popular, for the time, and after a jorum to Corporal Davis and the "Captain's detail," who put up my tent blue in the face—dispensed the liquor to all comers.[44]

In a deep mood of depression he described the condition of the encampment: "But a more disordered and disconsolate looking camp than ours for the time being, by the mouth of the Timpanogos Canyon, and in the snow-storm—so long as it lasted—I have rarely seen, in the course of my experience."[45]

The bitter cold carried by arctic gales continued into the night and turned into a full-blown blizzard that had men burrowing under blankets and tent covers, which brought some relief from the biting temperatures. Morning broke with a flawless sunrise. The soldiers dug themselves out of the snow and fell back to routine military duties.

In the half-light of morning the men of the expedition moved their camp near the mouth of the canyon overlooking the valley and pitched their tents. But Camp Timpanogos proved to be in the neck of a funnel that caught the full brunt of the mountain winds, spoiling its value as a permanent camp. Hours later the army moved over the ice-crusted landscape to within two miles of Provo and rested on the heights overlooking Springville and Provo.

Before sundown soldiers pitched their tents and roped off a few acres for their horses and mules, then busied themselves with routine duties that followed them into the field. Roving patrols of infantrymen improved their marksmanship by firing at random targets, notifying the Saints of their presence. In an effort to create a crisis of nerves, Phelps's battery, commonly known as "Brigham Young and the Twelve Apostles," fired across Utah Valley, and the echoes were heard as far west as Camp Floyd. During one such exercise, a shell exploded in the muzzle of one of the howitzers. "A number of us including Dr. Moore," wrote Captain Tracy, "were standing within a few feet at the time, to watch the effect of the firing, and the ring and vibration of the metal with the explosion, was something to nearly deafen us. The piece, however, stood the shock with no damage done whatever."[46]

The end of March brought a change in activity. Under a cloak of secrecy, a force of 150 infantrymen and 50 dragoons descended into the valley to rendezvous with the federal marshal, Peter K. Dotson, to arrest Aaron Johnson, bishop of Springville. Shortly before midnight on the evening of April 2, the column halted a few miles south of the village, where its commander admonished his men "to break step upon the road, that their tramp might not be detected and the Dragoons to lash down their scabbards, that there might be no jingling thereof to alarm the enemy."[47] The soldiers lit no cigars or pipes.

Penetrating the walls of Springville under cover of darkness, the marshal, surrounded by a bodyguard of federal troops, forced an entrance into the bishop's house, only to stumble into the bedroom of Aaron Johnson's nine wives. If one soldier's account of the incident is to be believed, the troopers' entrance was met by the women with a torrent of unprintable insults. The uninhibited soldiers stacked their arms and staged an Indian war dance around the night pot, ignoring the fiery rage of their audience, who fought a rearguard action with pillows and blankets. Such diversions did not interrupt the progress of the search but, in the end, Mormon vigilance once again rebuffed the army. However, it was not because of the lack of effort, wrote one observer. The Saints "were fully apprised in advance of everything that transpired, or was expected to transpire—barring perhaps the war dance."[48] The Saints simply waited for the judicial blizzard to blow itself out.

Cradlebaugh and his marshal were discouraged but unwilling to give up the chase. Shortly after this setback, the judge deputized a dozen new peace officers to search the villages of Manti, American Creek, San Pete, and Goshen as well as the surrounding countryside for suspects wanted for questioning by the court. His plans were thwarted by a string of emergency outposts established along the face of the Wasatch Mountains, perched high on the ridges to oversee any movements of the army at Camp Floyd. Large enough to hide several hundred men for three weeks at a time, they were within a few hours' ride of the principal settlements of central Utah: the "Mountains of Hepsedam" served Provo; "Colob" hid Bishop Johnson and a hundred men of Lehi, American Fork, and Springville; "Castle Valle guard," the largest of the outposts, served Nephi, Manti, and the adjacent countryside.[49]

It was a difficult winter for the spiritual community and, as the ominous news of the army's activity filtered into Salt Lake City, General Daniel H. Wells mobilized the Nauvoo Legion to control the access roads leading from Camp Floyd.[50] The army interpreted Wells's action as a signal that the Mormons were collecting sizable military forces in central Utah to move against isolated patrols and outposts.[51] The judicial question dangled unanswered, and in the end it would not be force that would decide the issue, but the territorial governor.

In this struggle, Governor Cumming gained access to the inner circles of Mormon leadership and acted upon his bitter hatred of the army. Judge Cradlebaugh's activities in Provo reached Salt Lake City like battle reports and flooded the columns of the *Deseret News* with stories that damaged the public image of the federal courts. While the newspaper spread fear among the Saints, petitions from Brigham Young had their effect on Governor Cumming. In that same month of March, Wells delivered a message signed by Young to the governor's new residence, the Almon Babbitt Mansion. The petition attacked the actions of the army and the federal courts, reminded Cumming that the Mormon people had a genuine liking for him, and added that if he would not protect them, the Mormons would fight rather than submit to a repetition of the "Carthage Massacre." On the other hand, if the governor stepped forward to help the Saints "preserve peace he might depend upon being supported by the people."[52] Perhaps fostering future political ambitions, Cumming cast his lot with the Saints.

He drafted a sharp note to Captain Heth, ordering him to remove the federal troops from Provo. The captain refused, saying that he was under orders from General Johnston; therefore all communication must be addressed to him. Cumming wrote a second letter, this time addressed to General Johnston. After repeating his demands for the removal of troops from Mormon settlements, Cumming said that the army had no right to call into being a *posse commitatus*; only he had such authority. The general's answer was full and bitter and sustained the army's action: "To prevent any misunderstanding hereafter, I desire to say to your Excellency that I am under no obligation whatever to conform to your suggestions with regard to the military disposition of the troops of this Department except, only when it may be expedient to employ them in their civil capacity as a posse. . . ."[53]

Having gained little from the exchange, the governor sought out the leaders among the Mormons, and together they drafted a proclamation protesting the presence of the army in Provo.[54] But neither Young nor Wells was able to force Cumming to make any commitment to direct executive action. When the manifesto reached the streets it confirmed what the Saints had already guessed—Cumming was in no position to act in Provo, even if he had wished.[55] Nor were Young's actions any more decisive. He continued his self-imposed exile in the Lion House, behind hand-picked bodyguards.

The problems faced by the governor were few when compared to those confronted by the far more assertive Cradlebaugh. Hampered by a reluctant Mormon grand jury, the magistrate had changed his attitude toward the Saints. When the judge addressed the grand jury for the last time, he outlined the costly court impasse and angrily accused the territorial jurymen of defrauding justice. Believing that he had done all he could to avert injustice, Cradlebaugh labored over his remarks:

> The court took the usual course of calling your attention to particular crimes—the horrible massacre of Mountain Meadows. It told you of the murder of Young Jones and his mother, and of pulling down their house down over them and making that their tomb; it told you of the murder of the Parrishes and Potter, and Forbes almost within sight of this court house. It took occasion to call names for the purpose of calling particular attention to those crimes; the fact that they have been committed is notorious.[56]

The charge continued with an acrimonious history of his court, read from prepared notes.

In a final gesture of defiance, Cradlebaugh dismissed four prisoners indicted by the grand jury for rape and two Gentiles confined for theft. It was, the judge confessed frankly, wholly unreasonable to expect "that this court is to be used by this community as a means of protecting it against the peccadilloes of Gentiles and Indians; unless this community will punish its own murders, such expectation will not be realized. It will not be used for no such purpose." Cradlebaugh scarcely glanced at the jury as he continued: "When the people come to their reason, and manifest a disposition to punish their own high offenders it will then be time to enforce the laws also for their protection. If this court cannot bring you to proper sense of your duty, it can at least turn the savages in custody loose on you."[57] Steeled by his own words, the judge returned to his quarters that afternoon to prepare the second phase of his investigation.

Early on the morning of April 2, Cradlebaugh, after issuing bench warrants for the arrest of the participants in the Mountain Meadows Massacre, bound over to the army two Mormon prisoners to stand trial for murder.[58] "This Judge Cradlebaugh is quite a curiousity in his way," wrote John Jacques, a Mormon, "not content with his own functions of a marshal, gaoler, the Counsel, the jury; and if his impatience had given chance for any capital conviction, he would probably have aspired to the dignity of Jack Ketch! Cradlebaugh has attained the title here of one eyed Jefferies."[59]

Captain Heth requested Major Paul to bring up his troops to the center of the town. The column reached the outskirts of Provo the following day and poured through the center of the town, marching to the tune of "Doo Dah" while adding their own burlesque stanzas to the old song. South of the road bordering the Seminary, the army received its prisoners. Judge Cradlebaugh, Marshal Dotson, and Heth's command fell into position behind the reinforcements. When the Mormons saw the soldiers winding their way through Provo, they gathered along both sides of the streets, contenting themselves with minor shows of displeasure. After slow progress to American Fork, the soldiers were taunted by partisans who jostled each other for a better view of the army. As Captain Tracy remembered,

> There were cat-calls, groans and whistles, and one ambitious party went so far as to maneuver at our flanks after the fashion of artillery, with a long beer cask mounted on a pair of cart wheels. The train—a couple of Mormon boys, kicked and pranced and whinnied, and came into battery in a style quite ferocious, whilst following upon every imaginary discharge; an old splint broom was thrust into the beer-barrel by an assistant and the piece sponged. My sense of humor was decidedly struck with this latter performance, and there were numbers upon whom it did not appear wholly lost.[60]

The column hurried through the town and struck the road to Lehi.

For the better part of the day, Major Paul bivouacked his forces near the outskirts of the farming village where Judge Cradlebaugh, searching for evidence, questioned Alfred Bell about the hatchet murder of Joseph Lance. The exact motive for the murder was never accurately determined, but according to the coroner's testimony Joseph Lance fled to the territory to escape trial for the murder of his father. Some time later he took up residence at American Fork where he was charged with the rape of a Danish woman; however, before a verdict could be rendered, she revenged herself by axing him to death while he slept.[61] The fact that he was under heavy guard at the time of his murder led Cradlebaugh to believe that Lance had fallen victim to blood atonement.

No new evidence was uncovered, despite a house-to-house search of Lehi. Nor was a single witness found who was willing to shed light on the case. After exploring the town thoroughly and finding nothing that merited a longer stay, the entourage turned westward along the road to Camp Floyd. However, Cradlebaugh's investigation had already taken on a new and dangerous dimension.

The hounding of suspects by the court brought renewed reports of Mormon guerrilla activities to Camp Floyd. After a long delay, the army learned from a military herder stationed in Tooele Valley that a group of Mormon sentinels had been captured at Black Rock, a short distance west of Salt Lake City. Promised amnesty, the prisoners confessed that the Nauvoo Legion commander had ordered them to watch federal troop movements out of Cedar Valley, particularly those moving towards the major populated settlements to the east. The army employee added: "That as soon as they saw an established signal at the upper end of Tuille Valley they were to set fire to a large pile of wood, which was placed near them on the summit of the Rock, and that smoke made by day, fire by night, would be the signal to the people in the city and in the northern settlements that the troops were marching upon Salt Lake City."[62]

New evidence was brought to light when unidentified militiamen intercepted an Indian trader, James Garnmell, and attempted to purchase his complete stock of powder and lead, an offer that was refused.[63] Several evenings later two California merchants, passing through Utah for the Pacific coast, claimed they were stopped near Summit Creek by a party of twenty-five Mormon dragoons who ordered them to surrender their animals. The travelers recounted how they resisted these demands and that the Mormon posse withdrew after an apologetic explanation that "they had been ordered by Governor to hold themselves in readiness to fight, if his policy was not sustained at Washington."[64] Leaving the trail, the caravan stopped overnight at an inn in the heart of the village of Goshen. Here they were told that the Nauvoo Legion was ready to march against the army. By sundown they saw "armed men coming continually in and out of the house, together with a great deal of 'whispering and buzzing.'" The extended story charged that several mules were stolen during the night, an act which they attributed to the Mormons.[65]

Other isolated incidents of suspicious activity were reported to the army. Garland Hurt, Indian agent at Spanish Fork, claimed that guerrilla bands numbering up to 100 men had been dispatched to the mountains four nights in succession, and that a fifth party was preparing to move out while he sat composing the communique.[66] This letter was followed by still another report from the bandit Joaquin Johnston that a group of armed men had left for Goshen to investigate an accident and had been absent three days before returning to the city.[67]

From the northern settlements came word that the Saints were arming and awaiting orders from the commander of the Nauvoo Legion to march south at a moment's notice.[68] Through the crucial month of May every Mormon settlement appeared to be in open revolt. The dimensions of the uprising became clearer when Captain Daniel Ruggles, charged with guarding the army mule herds in San Pete Valley, learned that the citizens of Moroni, Fort Ephraim, Manti, and other nearby towns had recruited 1,000 soldiers, and were openly equipping them with rifles. Furthermore, three or four mountain howitzers were being reconditioned at Manti. Reading these signs, he warned: "If ordered, the greater part would turn out to fight against the United States—most of them would go without objection—some few are afraid to refuse."[69] Unknown to the army, however, the tide of events had already taken a turn, easing the pressures for war.

During the closing hours of April 24, 1859, Brigham Young, Daniel H. Wells, and George A. Smith paid an unscheduled visit to Governor Cumming. The call caught the governor by surprise. Partly conciliatory, Young told the governor that the army had made preparations to march on Salt Lake City, and that officers at Camp Floyd were surveying the high ground above his residence for gun placements. The governor assured the Mormon leader that the "gentlemen in stripes" were part of the Simpson Expedition who were mapping the longitude of the city before exploring a new all-weather road to California.[70]

Partially satisfied by the reply, Young reviewed his own futile efforts to bring peace to his people, secluded in the wilderness: "When we were driven here it was said to me thousands of times on the way, over the long and dreary sage plains and desert hills when we made the road into this country, will they ever follow us here? Can it be possible we shall not be permitted to live in this desert country in peace?" Then he returned again to the subject of the army: "This army has been sent all the way here purposely to destroy the leaders of this people. Were it not for one thing, I should be let alone and respected like other men and that is Mormonism, which is the work of God and it is true. There is a spirit that stirs men up to destroy the Priesthood or those who hold it."[71]

The perceptive governor did not lose sight of the real issue at hand. Cumming argued that the army would accept Young's challenge, if not welcome it, "and in a defiant spirit they would rush over it."[72]

Brigham Young, however, pressed his point that military intrigue and agitation had fanned the smoldering discontent into open rebellion. "You have acquired an honorable name by your firm course in administering in your executive capacity among this people," he replied, "but if you suffer that army to tread down the civil power and walk all over you, it will be the cause of you losing your influence, and, Governor, you will yet learn that the Lord gives nations, communities, and individuals character and influence and takes them away at his pleasure." Only the governor controlled the territory, he added. "The army will obey you, if you step forward and require them to keep still which is what the law requires of you as Chief Executive of this Territory, even if you were to exceed your powers in preserving peace you would be sustained in it, but I do not want you to do a thing only what the law and your instructions will sustain you in and clearly authorize you to carry out and nothing more is necessary at the present time."[73]

Neither Brigham Young nor his two companions had any way of knowing that the governor had just finished his final draft of a message to the Secretary of State, a document that testified to the good order and peaceful disposition of the Saints. Now quoting from that letter, Cumming read his charges against the army and an account of the conflict that endangered the peace of the territory. Also, the governor had come to an important decision—in the meantime all action would be postponed until he received further instructions from Washington.[74]

Looking across the room, narrowing his eyes to concentrate his anger, Young decried the governor's decision. The army, he warned, "is driving hundreds of men into the mountains and was laying a foundation for famine. . . ." Ten years of peace and prosperity had vanished with their presence. "We raised next to nothing last year that thousands of acres would lie idle because of the interference of the military with the people in seed time, but I do not know but it is the design to prevent the people from raising grain so as to favor contractors in freighting it here for the use of the army." Caught up in his own drama, Brigham Young declared:

> I care nothing about my character in this world. I do not care what men say about me. I want my character to stand fair in the eyes of my heavenly father. My religion is true and I am determined to obey its precepts, while I live. Were I to renounce my religion, I could go to Camp Floyd and be honored. I could go abroad in the world and be respected. . . .[75]

He warned that neither he nor his people would be consigned to the limbo of history by the federal government or its military satellite at Camp Floyd: "I will not be nosed about by the military and I will not go into their camp alive. It is in your power to put a stop to this difficulty, and if you do not do it, an action of the people will have to do it. My faith and our determination are that we will avoid a collision; at any rate we will do it if possible."[76]

When Young finished, Cumming answered that "he did not know what to do or to advise under the circumstances, and added that the troublesome ambiguity of Washington's instructions were at the heart of the serious conflict that followed."[77]

Young interrupted Cumming and, rehearsing all his complaints against the army, urged the governor to stay the hand of General Johnston. But as for advice, he continued, "with all due respect to your Excellency, I do not wish any. I do not calculate to take the advice of any man that lives, in relation to my affairs, I shall follow the counsels of my heavenly father, and I have faith to follow it, and risk the consequences." The governor was left alone to ponder his decision.[78]

It was in this state of mind that the governor issued his long-awaited proclamation to the people of Utah, a carefully written document that ordered all bands of guerrillas to disperse under penalty of arrest.[79] At the same time the governor asked the Mormons to be restrained and patient in their actions. If their rights were infringed upon, he said, the answer did not rest in violence, but rather in law and order. Operating under separate instructions from his superiors in Washington, he alone held executive jurisdiction to call out the army to protect the courts. Nevertheless, no matter how cautious and deliberate Cumming and Johnston might have been, they placed their personal jealousies and hatreds before their responsibilities to the people of the territory.

In this new atmosphere a record number of communiques passed between General Johnston and the Secretary of War, John B. Floyd, on one hand, and Governor Cumming and the Secretary of State, Lewis Cass, on the other. These position papers revealed that the judicial impasse was due in great part to the conflicting orders received from Washington. In his original instructions from the War Department, General Johnston had been ordered to provide a *posse commitatus* upon request of the governor, marshal, or any member of the federal judiciary of the territory.

Convinced "that a test of strength was required to settle whether federal authority or local autonomy was supreme in Utah," Johnston was prepared to back the federal courts with whatever force the situation demanded.[80] While admitting that the Mormon theocracy violated no provision of the federal or territorial constitution, the general believed it was incumbent on the federal government to obstruct any system that attempted to perjure or warp the administration of justice. Scorning Governor Cumming's policy of reconciliation, Johnston maintained that republican institutions could not survive in the territory without the surveillance of the army, arguing that without force it would be impossible for the courts to bring the "culprits to trial."[81]

On the other hand, no matter how accurately Governor Cumming might have interpreted his instructions from the Secretary of State, he was too easily convinced by his own findings and too willing to accept Mormon claims against the army. His earliest Provo proclamation served no other purpose than to stimulate civil disobedience and open hostility to legally constituted authority. As the judicial stalemate dragged on, and the demands for intervention mounted, a more prudent governor might have resolved the impasse without playing upon partisan feelings, avoiding the dismembering of federal authority in the territory. Nevertheless, during the bloodless duel, it appeared to the governor that by using a federal posse without his consent, Johnston was not only guilty of injudicious action but was using Cradlebaugh's appeal for arms as an excuse to settle longstanding accounts with the Mormons.

The conflict proved to be relatively brief, for President Buchanan soon moved to check his military and political mavericks in the territory. Disappointed as they were by their own failures, neither Cradlebaugh nor his willing military advocate, General Johnston, was prepared for what followed. Acting under the president's orders, the United States Attorney General, Jeremiah S. Black, instructed the territorial judge that only the governor had the power to issue a requisition for troops; furthermore, since peace had been restored in Utah, the judiciary no longer needed military assistance.[82] The Attorney General's dual-edged message charged that Cradlebaugh's actions endangered political stability in the territory. Henceforth it would be the responsibility of the federal marshal, not the judge, to requisition a military posse, and only after the officer had obtained written permission of the governor.[83] President Buchanan, in common with other men in his administration, found it difficult to sift the truth from an avalanche of conflicting reports emanating from his subordinates in the territory. Buchanan was unwilling to risk the use of force again, and "avoided provoking hostilities by shunning coercions of the Mormons."[84] The courts were now rendered helpless.

Buchanan's policy simply postponed the crisis. Instead of grappling with the difficulty, he vacillated, hoping to pass the problem on to his successor, wrote the editor of the *Valley Tan*.

> We have no hope that he will adopt bold measures now. The keynote of his policy is to be found in his weakness of character. To glide over or evade difficulties, instead of grappling with them boldly and subduing them, has been the governing role of his action.
>
> We presume the cost of the expedition to Utah and its maintenance up to this time amounts to not less than fifteen or twenty millions of dollars. In return for it the government has not even acquired moral force or influence. The cost of peaceful victories of Mr. Buchanan, as his organs call them, are dear luxuries. A few more of them would dry up the source of supplies. Their peculiarity is, that even in material outlay they are as expensive as war. His domestic as well as his foreign policy is equally extravagant in cost, and inconclusive in results.[85]

The charge that the president was unwilling to stand up against popular opinion in the territory oversimplified the dilemma Buchanan faced. Whatever his weaknesses and shortcomings, the president faced a divided Congress, openly critical of his indecisive handling of the Utah War and the Panic of 1857, two events that found ominous expressions in the congressional elections of 1858. As signs of a coming conflict multiplied, the president's thoughts were never far from the fledgling Republican Party, which demanded an investigation into the excessive expenditures incurred by his administration during the Utah Expedition.[86] Unwilling to risk playing into the hands of Republican firebrands, Buchanan contemplated removing Johnston to smooth over the conflict, but abandoned this course when he realized that neither the transfer of Johnston nor the recall of Cumming would rescue his territorial policies. In other words, "to relieve General Johnston, under the circumstances, might have the semblance of condemning him for obedience to orders; to appoint another Governor would look like an intent to pursue a decisive policy instead of the laissez faire course represented by Governor Cumming."[87]

Just as it was to be on the eve of the Civil War, no decision was considered a good decision.

CHAPTER SEVEN

THE TRAGEDY OF MOUNTAIN MEADOWS

"This act has set the Church back twenty-five years!"
—John C. Chatterley[1]

OVERWORKED AND disillusioned, haunted by his continuing chain of failures, Judge Cradlebaugh focused his eye on the tragedy of the Mountain Meadows Massacre. In the weeks that followed the Provo debacle, the judge conducted the first of a long series of federal investigations into the mystery that surrounded the drama that had preceded the army's entrance into the territory. The massacre of more than 100 emigrants near Cedar City had blotted the pages of the territory's history with cruelty perhaps unequaled in the history of the West.

As Juanita Brooks has written: "Mass murder, even in the name of war, is a highly complex act, requiring the creation of a mass mind and powerful psychic contagion of great intensity."[2] The roots of the Mountain Meadows tragedy sink deeply in the soil of Mormon history, but the Reformation of 1856 helped shape the course of events to follow, and its immediate results remained unknown to all but the few who took part in them.

In its broadest sense, the Reformation was a concerted effort to purge the Church of all subversive elements, a fanatical spiritualism that burned across the Basin with religious fury. Believers were subjected to a program of revivalism designed to counter the swift-flowing tide of secularism and neo-religious thought. The first generation of pioneers criticized the laxity of their children who rejected the superior wisdom of their leaders. The line separating modernism and democracy from spiritualism and theocracy had grown thin by the fall

123

of 1856 when Brigham Young fell under the mystic influence of his counselor Jedediah Morgan Grant. Persuasive, brilliant, and dogmatic, Grant set the tone of the religious crusade to shore up the framework of the Spiritual Kingdom of God and to prevent secularism from affecting Mormon life any further.[3]

As the movement got under way, Brigham Young expressed his enthusiasm for this new religious mission:

> There is quite a reformation springing up in many of the settlements, which we trust will increase and extend throughout the territory. A general desire to renew their covenants and live nearer to the Lord, to serve Him more perfectly and to be more circumspect and alive to the interests of Zion and her prosperity.[4]

As Young came to agree with Grant's strategy to reinvigorate the devotion of the Saints, he became convinced that a unity of religious belief was indispensable to social order and peace.

> It is too universally the case that when the Elders come home they throw off their armours and the people too frequently follow their example. This produces a coldness or rather deadness to spiritual things which leads into darkness and in the end, apostasy, but now that much of the shell of the winters thrashing floor has been floated off by the summer breezes, we trust that the Saints who are really such will awake from their lethargy and lay hold with an increased faith and energy, and not only obtain but retain the Holy Ghost in their bosoms, sufficient to enable them to walk humbly before the Lord of Hosts, and render more effective service in his cause.[5]

The winds of good fortune too frequently made the Saints unmindful of their duties to their religion and fellow churchmen and saw them pouring into their secular lives the energies that had been diverted from the building of Zion. "The people have generally been too unmindful of the blessings which the Lord has been so profusely pouring out upon them, they have not sufficiently appreciated his kindness and mercy." But by reason and human kindness, "they are now beginning to see it and are seeking by a reformation and a renewal of their covenants, to redeem themselves from these and many other evils which they have fostered untill [sic] the enemy of their souls had well nigh obtained the mastery over them. . . ." Taking his remarks as seriously as he took his religion, the prophet concluded, "thanks be to him who sitteth upon the throne that he has inspired his missionaries to go forth in the strength of Israel's God & put a timely check to this great and growing evil."[6]

Though these passionate polemics were meant to bring gradual reform rather than a turbulent revolution in the manners and mores of the people, neither Young nor his closest advisors were completely prepared for the results. Religious zealots transformed the character of the territory. The new ministers of reform were generally men of good morals and character, learned in Mormon theology, and devoted to the task of restoring fundamental Christianity among the people, wrote John Ward Christian. "They . . . taught that if any wronged another they must go to them and make proper restitution and in obedience to this teaching there were many articles that had been missing for months returned under the cover of night and many offenses were atoned for." Communicants were urged to "obey the commands that came through the heads of the Church, ask no questions but do as directed."[7]

The situation was complicated by the renewed development of the doctrine of blood atonement, also a favorite notion of Jedediah Grant injected into the new religious consciousness, stirring new hope that God would avenge the martyrdom of Joseph and Hyrum Smith. This concept, only a thread in the complicated tapestry of the Reformation, arose from the needs and fears of simple people who waited impatiently for divine intervention that would smite the army marching against the Mormon fortress of the Great Basin. Although the notion of blood atonement spread fear throughout the territory, the doctrine was never given the Church's official approval, and Brigham Young and his contemporaries denied its existence. Nevertheless, there is strong evidence for it, especially in southern Utah where living on the cutting edge of survival gave the doctrine more appeal. Referring to blood atonement, John Ward Christian claimed, "if men were found who were murderers and thieves and beyond the control of society and law it would be better if they were disposed of."[8] In Cedar City, John C. Chatterley reported on hidden persuaders:

> There were a number of individuals that formed a secret committee, called "Danites," or "destroying angels" one of their members came to me in the expectation of getting me to go on the road; to find out who trailed [to California] and their circumstances was a good [illegible] act as if I was about half baked I gave him a rough answer and told him, "I would see the whole crowd in Hell and damned first." A few days after this two of their crowd came to me, and told me "to look out for myself, as I was doomed," as it was concluded by a majority in one of their meeting that I must be *freat* out of the way, as I knew too much, and was much opposed to their hellish murderous conduct.
>
> From that time on, I dare not go out at night, or go alone far from town, when spring of 1858 came around, myself, with many others had to take our oxen into the hills for feed, I would make up a good fire, eat my supper, and go off a quarter of a mile, often more than that, and lay down in some little ravine, where I *thot* they could

not find me. Not a very pleasant life to lead, yet I can truthfully say, I did not feel afraid, I was cautious in my general conduct.[9]

In the midst of this turning point in territorial history, returning missionaries reported the murder of Parley P. Pratt near Fort Smith, Arkansas, by Hector McLean, a Unitarian minister. The first detailed information of the apostle's death filtered into the southern settlements during the closing days of July 1857, inspiring sworn pledges to avenge his death as well as the deaths of other Saints in Illinois and Missouri.

Arkansas accounts of Pratt's death alleged that "a Mormon missionary converted a married woman, seduced her into becoming his polygamous wife, assisted her in kidnapping her children, and was justly shot to death by a wronged husband."[10] Although his first concern was to strengthen his army and to balance his forces against an approaching unfriendly army, Young took time to denounce these statements as lies: Mrs. McLean had been estranged from her husband since 1854, when she converted to Mormonism while visiting San Francisco with her first husband. As for the husband, Young noted that he was a Unitarian minister who resented his wife's conversion to the new and unpopular faith and transferred his enmity toward Mormonism to Pratt.[11]

One of the most brilliant products of nineteenth-century Mormonism, Parley P. Pratt represented the best of the intellectual tradition of the territory, and the account of his death was not forgotten in the excitement of the impending federal invasion. An early and aggressive convert to Mormonism, Pratt was among the first Saints to traverse the Great Plains to the Rockies. His intensive exploration of the southern rim of the Great Basin helped change Mormon colonization patterns. He combined a quiet privacy with a desire to become sensitive to the needs of his people, his genius finding expression in religious thought and writing. What happened to Pratt in Arkansas affected many Mormons personally.[12]

His death brought a shudder of horror throughout the territory, kindled fires of resentment, and produced an atmosphere of fear in which reason was the first casualty. Every village produced at least one individual who reasoned that McLean was an "enemy of the Mormons, and every Mormon was the enemy of McLean; McLean was protected in Arkansas therefore every man from Arkansas was an enemy of the Mormons—and ought to be cut off. . . ."[13]

Frustrated in seeking peace, bankrupting themselves to gather stores and ammunition, and struggling to re-establish uncompromising faith among themselves, the Saints observed the advance of the Utah Expedition. "Fire and sword, tar and feathers are the only arguments that can be used against Mormonism," wrote a Parowan resident in response to the news of the approach of the federal army. Nor did Brigham Young discount the rumor that "Squaw Killer" Harney's army was operating under orders to exterminate the Saints. "The War-Hawks are abroad again and it becomes to us to prepare accordingly! Fix your guns for shooting if they are not already in that condition," the Church president instructed his lieutenants.[14]

Strong and confusing currents ran through southern Utah, wrote an unknown clerk of the Parowan religious stake of Zion. "The United States are sending 2500 infantry, besides Col. Sumner's dragoons, which are to rendezvous in Great Salt Lake City this winter, 100 teamsters, the worst description of men, picked up on the frontiers, which are more to be dreaded than the soldiers. They are making great calculations for 'Booty and Beauty.' "[15]

Unaware of the critical events stirring in the western territory, the Fancher party departed for California from Stiffler Spring, Arkansas, early on the morning of May 1, 1857.[16] Much in the manner of hundreds of other emigrant trains that would pass over the overland, the caravan was a fusion of various families drawn from the rich farmlands of the Mississippi Valley, assembled as a traveling company for mutual protection against the hazards of the trail.[17] As the train maneuvered across central Arkansas, it grew to more than forty wagons, including several hundred blooded horses and a thousand head of cattle; the total wealth of the caravan represented $70,000, by far one of the richest to cross the continent that year.[18] The man on whom the fate of the overlanders depended was Alexander "Piney Alex" Fancher, a tall, angular, rusty-complexioned farmer who had made two previous trips to the West, the last in 1855 when he had negotiated the purchase of a large tract of land in central California.[19] Second in command was John T. Baker of Crooked Creek.[20]

Before the slowly moving caravan reached St. Joseph, Missouri, two incidents occurred that would have both immediate and long-range effects on the destiny of the Fancher party. Sometime during the first week on the road, a band of self-styled "Missouri Wildcats" joined the original caravan, forcing several Arkansas families to leave the original party and continue the journey to California alone. While the Fancher party plodded northwestward, going deeper and deeper into the smoky green country of Missouri, the Wildcats poisoned several springs along the trail. Nothing was done to stop the unfortunate conduct of the Missourians, and "Piney Alex" maintained a grave-like silence over the acts of violence.[21]

With a strength variously estimated at from 100 to 200 men, women, and children, the Fancher train struck the Oregon trail, moving westward toward the great mountain wall of the Rockies. As the caravan approached O'Fallon's Bluff it made a brief halt to allow the advance guard of the Utah Expedition to pass its line of march. When in a reminiscent mood years later, Dr. Charles Brewer, an army surgeon, described the train: "There seemed to be forty heads of families, many women, some unmarried, and many children. They had three carriages; one very fine, in which ladies rode and to which he made several visits as he journeyed with them. There was something peculiar in the construction of the carriages, its ornaments, the blazoned stag's head upon the panels. . . ."[22]

Traveling in two sections, the train weathered the journey across the plains and gave every indication that it intended to pursue the snow-free southern route to California. In every respect the conduct of the Fancher party was exemplary: "They were as moral in language and conduct, and united regularly in morning and evening prayers."[23] But the Missourians proved to be a steady source of discomfort and difficulty. The frightened farmers could not sleep comfortably or feel safe in the company of the "Wildcats"; consequently, Captain Fancher ordered his train to encamp at a safe distance from the Missourians, a procedure they followed all the way to Mountain Meadows. Rumors of the Missourians' hatred for the Mormons spread quickly, wrote Eli B. Kelsey, a Saint who joined the party on the last leg of its journey to Salt Lake City. To his horror he found the "Wildcats" in an unusually disagreeable mood, swearing vengeance against the Saints and generally making a nuisance out of themselves. The insults never stopped. Fearing serious trouble, Kelsey warned Captain Fancher "that it was easy to provoke a difficulty; the whole country was excited over the news of the invading army. . . ."[24] The wagonmaster ignored the warning, though the indignation and excitement did not quickly subside, and the party continued that stage of the trying trip in a state of uneasiness. The Fancher party passed through Emigration Canyon and into Salt Lake City and encamped on Emigration Square. The Church Historian's clerk recorded the exact date of their entrance into the city: "August 5, an Arkansas train a passing through the city."[25]

The caravan marched to the west bank of the Jordan River and rested, probably after purchasing the remaining supplies of Livingston & Bell, run by a Gentile merchant soon to depart from the territory. An event of great importance to the emigrants occurred a few hours later when Charles C. Rich arrived at the river camp to warn the caravan not to travel the southern road to California. Captain Fancher politely declined the advice.

After laying in such supplies as they could buy, the train left the river and passed through Provo, where a lone straggler, William Aden, was added to the company. With the Missourians leading the way, the train proceeded through Springville, Payson, and smaller settlements without attracting attention until it arrived in Fillmore. At the territorial capital, Captain Fancher found the Mormons unwilling to sell supplies, except for a few perishable foods. But they would sell no grain for the animals. Other problems developed rapidly. The Missourians, greatly incensed by the Saints' refusal to trade, challenged the Mormons to stand their ground and fight "at the same time damning the 'Mormons' in a wicked manner connecting the name of Deity with all their oaths." According to the Mormon version of the incident, the "Wildcats" repeatedly expressed pleasure "that the government had sent troops to kill every Gdamned Mormon in Utah—they hoped they could do so and that they would like to help them to do the job."[26] After leaving Fillmore, the party had little trouble with the Saints for several days, although casual contacts were made with a stream of Mormon traffic moving in both directions.

At Meadow Creek they met more opposition from settlers who refused to sell them food or supplies, forcing them to continue to Corn Creek, the last watering place in Pahvant Valley for travelers going south. Here the Fancher train stopped within sight of a band of Indians under Chief Kanosh. A few hours later the column slipped quietly out of the reservation after buying a small quantity of government grain from the Indians, which was contrary to federal law.[27]

Among the Mormons at Beaver, a teamster boasted that he had partic- ipated in the Hauns Mill Massacre in Missouri, an atrocity in which a mob wiped out a Mormon settlement. Another frontiersman claimed to be carrying the gun that killed Joseph Smith, and another proudly claimed that he was personally responsible for the death of Parley Pratt. The Mormons were further outraged by the sight of cattle tramping through their grain fields, teamsters popping the heads off their chickens with long bullwhips, and other acts of aggression against their farming settlements. To crown their insults, teamsters rudely called their lead oxen Joseph Smith, Brigham Young, and Heber C. Kimball after Mormon dignitaries.[28] One "Wildcat" openly boasted that he would "cut a swarth through the country killing all [the Mormons] before him. . . ."[29] The Fancher party tarried in Beaver to repair their equipment, but were hur- ried on their way by gunfire of unknown origin.[30]

At Parowan, which took its name from an Indian term meaning evil water, the emigrants found the gates of the fort slammed shut against them. According to an old legend, a wave from Little Salt Lake had swamped a camp there, drowning several Indians. Waterspouts had also appeared on the lake. The Indians thought that evil spirits had troubled the waters, so they named the lake Pah-O-An. The Fancher party would add another stormy chapter to the area's history. The reluctance of local officials to sell them supplies revealed that word of the Missourians' con- duct had preceded them.[31]

As the emigrants camped in the shadow of the town's walls, they drew the attention of William Leany, a village elder who had not taken seri- ously his instruction not to sell supplies to wayfarers. Leany met the train near the outskirts of Parowan and was introduced to William Aden, a young artist with six months of frontier experience behind him. Less than a decade earlier, Leany had been saved from a mob by Aden's father while on a Church mission north of Paris, Tennessee. But the frontier reunion of these two friends had its beginnings in the early spring of 1857.[32]

The problem Aden faced when he left Henry County, Tennessee, might have overwhelmed one far stronger than the talented artist. Working his way across the plains sketching landscapes for passing emigrants, he arrived at Green River ferry, where a Mormon elder told him he could find work in the territory. In Provo he spent several months painting backdrop scenery for the local theater, but with the mobilization of the Nauvoo Legion he elected to continue his journey to the Pacific coast with the Fanchers. The only surviving description of him, written by his mother to Brigham Young two years after the Mountain Meadow Massacre, described Aden as "about twenty-one years of age, well grown quite uprightly, a good sign painter, writes poetry and some prose pretty well, makes a good speech—picks the Banjoe tolerably well—pretty good looking and is regarded as one of the most ingenious men of his age."[33]

After a reunion that must have touched both men deeply, Aden followed Leany to his home, where they shared their experiences of the past years. At the end of the visit, Leany gave the young artist a supply of food and wished him a safe journey to California. But the poignant reunion angered the local authorities; three days later Leany was called out of his house and severely beaten "by one of the local police on the charge that he had rendered 'aid and comfort to the enemy.' He was left for dead and indeed never did recover fully from the blow."[34]

The caravan's movement toward Cedar City proceeded smoothly and rapidly. On September 4, 1857, the combined train reached the village of fewer than 900 residents, located some 300 miles from Salt Lake City. In the autumn of that momentous year this last large outpost of the Great Basin was in the process of a slow physical transformation, with the citizens moving from the original fort to the present city, a task that was only half accomplished when the Fancher train rolled in.[35]

As was to be expected, there was a furor in the village when the train was again refused provisions. Thwarted, the Missourians abandoned all pretext of friendliness and rode into the heart of the town, fired indiscriminately at citizens at close quarters, and wounded several residents. After a series of incidents with the local authorities, buildings, including the town's storehouse of grain, were broken open and robbed. As the caravan neared the outskirts of the village, an emigrant swung a pistol above his head and swore the weapon had killed "Joe Smith and had one bullet left for 'Old Brigham.' "[36] Unprovoked and indiscriminate harassment multiplied throughout the night. At the emigrant bivouac three miles from the settlement, the travelers tore down fences and burned them for firewood, allowing five or six hundred animals to graze on unharvested crops.

The Cedar City police were incensed over the emigrants' lawlessness, and the frightened townspeople demanded that the military arrest the Missourians and bring them back to account for their crimes. All of this profoundly affected the High Council conference that convened in the local meetinghouse on Sunday, September 6, shortly before noon, to determine what action was to be taken against the Missourians. The council considered several resolutions: first, to treat the party as enemies of war and deal with them accordingly; second, to allow the train to proceed to California unmolested; third, to lay the case before Brigham Young and await his decision.[37] "Some of the more radical members present, suggest harsh measures (none, however, favoring any wholesale killing) and others were in favor of letting the thing pass off and not bother the company. During the conversation, Elias Morris, although the youngest member present, suggested the idea of laying so important a matter before Brigham Young, and not take any action until his judgment had been obtained in the matter."[38] In the end, the council appeared reconciled to Morris's suggestion, and the next day John James Haslem started for Salt Lake City.[39] Yet it was speedily apparent that something had to be done to stop the emigrants from leaving their camp at Mountain Meadows.

To carry out the High Council's strategy a messenger arrived in Harmony to summon John D. Lee to appear before Isaac Haight, president of the Parowan Stake of Zion and second in command of the Iron County militia. Colonel Haight gave Lee a long review of the events that had erupted within the community and declared that the Fancher party must be prevented from continuing to California. The militia commander paid special tribute to Lee for his work among the Indians and as a government farmer, adding that these services were now needed to further the cause of the Kingdom of Zion. Speaking in anger, Haight ordered Lee to persuade some Paiute warriors to surround the Fancher train and maintain a siege until a new course of action was received from Salt Lake City.

If Lee was innocently drawn into the impending disaster as he later claimed, he appears nevertheless to have been surprisingly unshaken by the colonel's order, and carried it out with initiative and elan. Many years later, recounting this significant episode of Lee's career, Elias Morris wrote: "Lee seemed very determined that the company should be made to suffer severely for their impudence and lawlessness, and said he had Indians enough around him to wipe the whole of them out of existence."[40]

Shortly after Lee's briefing, Nephi Johnson, soon to be another leading participant in the massacre, drifted into the settlement. As he later described it:

When I arrived at Cedar, Isaac Haight saddled his horse and rode with me to the Indian camp. He told me that John D. Lee had been up from Harmony the day before and had proposed to him to gather up the Indians and destroy the train of emigrants who had passed through Cedar two days before and said he had told him to go ahead and do so, but Haight said he had sent a man to President Young to know what to do about it.[41]

Johnson recalled the remaining conversation: "He asked me what I thought about it. I said to him it would be a fearful responsibility for a man to take upon himself to destroy that train of emigrants and that I would wait until I received word from President Young. He replied that Lee had already gone to raise the Indians."[42]

Lee returned to Harmony to collect a small Indian army for the assault against the Fancher train. An eyewitness account of this scene by John C. Chatterley claimed that John D. Lee played up his own role in this drama. "John D. Lee fixed up as much like a military officer as he could with the clothes he had, a red sash around his waist and a sword in his right hand, marched round the inside of the fort [Harmony], at the head of about 40 or 50 Indians, he called out 'All that wish success to Israel say Amen.'" Chatterley added, "Two or three responded with Amens, but too few spoke the word, so John D. called for a better response, which he got, but in very faint voice."[43]

From his headquarters in Cedar City, Colonel Haight dispatched Samuel Knight and Dudley Leavitt to Santa Clara, where they were to raise as many Indians as possible to join in the attack against the Fancher train.[44] Others drawn into the final tragedy were John M. Higbee, Jesse N. Smith, Philip Klingensmith, and lesser officers of the Iron County militia. Thirty-five years after the disaster, Mary Campbell, who lived in Cedar City in 1857, remembered seeing five men visit an Indian encampment near a grove of cottonwoods a short distance from her home. She told a Church scribe that "Jesse N. Smith, Klingensmith, John M. Higbee, John D. Lee passed by the end of her home to the Cottonwoods below where the Indian squaws came into the post and the bucks left for the Meadows: the squaws said the Indians were going to kill the 'Mericats' [Americans]. The Indians started at once."[45]

The Fancher party was astonished to find the Indians openly hostile near Hamilton Fort, a small settlement six miles south of Cedar City and seven miles north of Kanarra. Breaking the secrecy surrounding the affair, an eyewitness claimed: "Some of the Indians were also camped at the bottoms some came to the camp and conversed with Samuel J. White, who could talk the Indian tongue. Indians wanted to know why the Mormons did not kill the company, as had been talked of in Cedar, but White tried to pacify them by telling them the brethren in Cedar meant soldiers, not women and children in the company."[46] When he reported the incident to Colonel Haight, White was told "he should not have interfered with the Indians."[47] White, a man whose name was not associated with the tragedy, reported that after the massacre he recognized a horse he had traded to the Fancher party among the Indian mounts.[48]

The caravan arrived at Mountain Meadows late Monday evening, after a dismal march from Parowan. Men and animals were suffering from inadequate food, water, and forage, as well as from the intense September heat of the desert. Worse, the Arkansas party was left without the services and protection of the Missouri frontiersmen who, growing tired of slow travel, slipped quietly out of the Meadows, taking with them at least one Iowa emigrant, Zebulon Pike Fawcett.[49] But the train settled into the valley to take a much-needed rest. The Meadows were in an open valley abounding with spring water and a thick growth of grass. The place was a landmark and rendezvous for sojourners preparing to cross the wilderness beyond to California. After culling the weakest animals from the herd for food, Captain Fancher ordered the remaining livestock to be set free to roam the Meadows, attended by a few armed herdsmen. The travelers momentarily forgot the hardships of the trail in the stillness of evening campfires, but less than a hundred yards from the emigrant camp, hidden by the hills that cupped the valley, painted figures bobbed in and out of the shadows.

In the pre-dawn blackness of September 8, the Indians slipped quietly from their positions and charged down from the surrounding slopes toward the emigrant camp, led by Paiute chieftains Tat-se-gobbits, Nou-cop-in, Mo-quee-tus, Chick-eroo, Young-quick, and Jackson.[50] Though the Indians' fire was wild and uncoordinated, the scattered herdsmen were cut down before they could offer any resistance. Taking advantage of the element of surprise, a war party of Paiutes moved down a small ravine and mortally wounded more than ten emigrants before they could reach the safety of their wagons. For a time John D. Lee joined the Indians, disguised as one of the war party, but the tide of battle turned abruptly and unexpectedly. Responding to the Indians' frontal and flank assaults, Captain Fancher ordered the wagons into a hollow square with all of the surviving animals inside. The emigrants heaped a wall of earth and rock between and under their wagons to stop the Paiute bullets and arrows. Meanwhile, a battle of attrition continued. When Lee tried to lead his warriors closer to the Fancher position, bullets ripped through his hat and shirt; miraculously he escaped without serious injury.[51] Towards noon the Indians retreated into the hills, carrying their dead and wounded, and refused to continue the attack without reinforcements.

Lee left the Meadows to search for Sam Knight and Dudley Leavitt and their Indian reinforcements from Santa Clara. He met them ten miles from the Meadows, riding alone. The Santa Clara Indians had refused to join in the fight. Lee was noticeably "disappointed at not seeing Indians with Knight and Leavitt for he had expected a force with which to even the attack the next morning."[52] Through the night the emigrants tightened their defenses. They had chained the large prairie wagons together and dug a rifle pit large enough to protect the women and children against the Indians who had a full view of the meadow. The collapse of the Indian attack allowed the emigrants to nurse their wounded and dying.

While the assault stalled during the next two days, events took an ominous turn in Cedar City. Lee warned Haight by courier that he feared the Indians would turn against the Saints if the Fancher party's resistance was not soon broken. Isaac Haight hesitated. Perceiving the dilemma in military terms, Haight ordered the Iron County militia to muster near the old fort, and he requested Elias Morris to drive him to Parowan, where he met with Colonel William Dame, the district military commander of the Nauvoo Legion.[53] It was past midnight, September 10, when the ranking officers of the Iron County militia soberly reviewed the events of the past forty-eight hours. Colonel Dame tried to take control of the situation, despite conflicting advice on how to deal with the Indians and emigrants. Several contemporary accounts claim that the meeting reached a general understanding that would have allowed the emigrants to continue their journey in peace, providing the Indians were allowed to take all the live-stock.[54]

A short time later a firebrand re-ignited the powder keg. According to William Barton, who was present at the Parowan meeting, there was a second conference shortly after the council adjourned. Years later Barton signed his name to a document, written by a close friend, that concluded:

> The council then dismissed but later with some occasion a consul-tation of three consisting of I. C. Haight, Wm. H. Dame, and another man was held by the east gate of the Parowan fort wall. The three sat upon a pile of bark hence known in certain circles as the "Tan Bark Council." Right there and then the whole program was changed and it was decided to destroy the whole company. Bro. Barton saw the three in consultation himself but heard not what we said, but Isaac C. Haight afterward told Barton that that was the decision and Haight said to Barton afterward "There is when we did wrong and I would give a world if I had it, if we had abided by the decision of the council, but alas it is too late."[55]

Meanwhile, inside the wagon stockade at Mountain Meadows, the survivors debated what to do, for near the end of the third day their supply of fresh water was running dangerously low.[56] No word had been received from a three-man party that had left the earthen fortifications to enlist the aid of the Mormons at Cedar City. Unknown to Captain Fancher, the party had been attacked at Leach Springs when it stumbled into the camp of a squad of Iron County militiamen. One member, William

Aden, was mortally wounded; the other two escaped into the darkness with minor flesh wounds. The two riders had "turned toward California on the Spanish Trail, evidently feeling that their chance for survival would be better on the road than at the camp."[57] Escape was to be denied, however. They were hunted down in the desert, and their remains were discovered by passing emigrants.[58]

In Cedar City the crisis deepened. Haight called a war council inside the rustic fort and ordered the Iron County militia, drawn from Cedar, Kanarra, Harmony, Washington, and Santa Clara, to destroy the Arkansas party. Afterward, a resident of Cedar City wrote, events moved swiftly: "This council resulted in a company starting for the Meadows, numbering about 20 or 25 men."[59] Heading this company was Major John M. Higbee, first counselor to Isaac Haight, and Philip Klingensmith, a bishop from Cedar City. The column grew in strength as it rendezvoused with volunteers along the trail, reaching a total strength of fifty men before it took up positions around the Meadows and waited for daybreak.

The drama played to its conclusion on the morning of September 11, when a lone white man, William Bateman, appeared before the Fancher train in a small clearing, unarmed and carrying a white flag. Captain Fancher signaled the flagman to approach, but before he reached the wagons he was joined by J. Hamilton and escorted past the interior pickets into the center of the camp. Bateman told Fancher that the Mormons feared the Indians, adding that the Nauvoo Legion was prepared to escort the emigrants through the warriors' lines. The emigrants would have to leave behind all of their goods and surrender all their arms and ammunition to the Mormon militia. Captain Fancher dispatched a message to Major Higbee promising that he would seriously consider the proposition. Late that same afternoon, John D. Lee walked across the Meadows under a flag of truce, accompanied by his aide-de-camp, Dan McFarland, to accept the emigrants' surrender.[60]

Looking back in 1877 shortly before his execution for his part in the massacre, Lee remembered seeing the dead and wounded stretched out on the ground inside the wagon circle:

> I sat down on the ground in the corral, near where some young men were engaged in paying the last respects to some person who had just died of a wound. A large, fleshy old lady came to me twice and talked while I sat there. She related their troubles—said that seven of their number were killed and forty-six wounded on the first attack; that several had died since. She asked me if I was an Indian Agent. I said, "In a sense I am, as the Government has appointed me Farmer to the Indians."[61]

Lee reviewed for Captain Fancher the dual dangers faced by the Arkansas company: death by starvation and thirst or a bloody massacre and certain death at the hands of the Paiutes. The party would have to give up their arms and obey all the instructions of the Nauvoo Legion if they were to escape from the Meadows alive. Too worn down to see the danger of his decision, Captain Fancher surrendered his company to Lee and his lieutenants.

A short time after the conference, Captain Fancher led the first contingent of emigrants out of the corral, followed by two wagons driven by Samuel McMurdy and Samuel Knight. The first was loaded with eighteen children under the age of ten, along with clothing, equipment, and the weapons. The second was driven by Knight and contained one woman and a number of wounded men.

John D. Lee motioned the emigrants to proceed across the Meadows and assemble in two groups. Knowing that trouble was more likely from the men, the Iron County militia separated them from the women and older children, who formed a column immediately behind the wagons. The men brought up the rear of the party, each escorted by an armed militiaman. They marched northeast on a badly worn road, past a small knoll, where the first wagon containing the children disappeared from view. About 100 yards to the south, Major Higbee ordered the militia to halt and open fire on the emigrants. When the shooting started, the Indians joined the slaughter, killing women, children, and wounded men.

When nothing remained of the emigrant party but unburied bodies, the militia took their clothing, bedding, guns, equipment, and anything else of value. The plundered goods were loaded aboard the emigrant wagons and taken to Cedar City. The final disposition of the Fancher party's property has never been determined with accuracy, but it is recorded that a third of the cattle were brought back to the Mormon settlement. The Indians drove off most of the rest of the emigrants' stock, but scattered remnants of the herd drifted into the Bull Valley Mountains. Later, when a bounty of five dollars a head was placed upon them, the livestock were rounded up by cowboys and sold at public auction. The proceeds went into the Washington County school fund.[62]

The Mormons farmed-out the surviving emigrant children to households throughout southern Utah. A burial detail gathered at the battle site the following Saturday to bury the dead. In an atmosphere full of the smell of decaying bodies, Colonel Dame inspected the massacre site. He ordered the bodies of the dead men to be buried in the emigrants' shallow rifle-pit and the bodies of the women and children to be placed in a steep wash and covered over with a thin layer of dirt and rocks. He swore the men in the burial detail to secrecy. Later that night the road through the meadow was closed and barricaded to all who traveled by daylight. Among those who passed the Meadows shortly after the tragedy, none was more terrified by what he heard than was Marion Lyman, assigned to escort California Saints safely back to Utah: "We crossed the Meadow in the night and the remnant of the cattle from the [massacred emigrants] came rushing around our wagons, making the night hideous with their bawling, and that, mingling with the unearthly stench from the decaying bodies of the human beings, made it the most terrific night of my life."[63]

The aftermath of the massacre was marked by two occurrences: the first was the long-expected appearance of instructions from the Church authorities in Salt Lake City. The wording of the communique was clear and unmistakable:

> In regard to emigration trains passing through our settlements we must not interfere with them until they are first notified to keep away, you must not meddle with them. The Indians we expect will do as they please, but you should try and preserve good feelings with them. There are no other trains going south that I know of. If those who are there will leave, just let them go in peace.[64]

The other direct result was the singling out of John D. Lee to explain the tragedy in person to Brigham Young. So closely was the secret guarded that no written summary was made of Lee's explanation, probably because possession of such a document would have been a death sentence.

It was not until the closing days of September that Lee made the hard journey north, first stopping at Fillmore, where he met Jacob Hamblin, a respected farmer who owned a small ranch at the northern edge of Mountain Meadows. Several weeks previously, Hamblin had met the Fancher party going south and extended to them an invitation to camp on the southern rim of the valley. His roots deep in the soil of southern Utah, Hamblin was the most important Mormon missionary to the Indians, having just escorted a half-dozen warrior chieftains to Salt Lake City to talk with Brigham Young.

Hamblin listened in bewilderment as Lee related the events at Mountain Meadows. Recalling Young's reaction to the message, Hamblin quoted him as saying: "They have a perfect right to pass, when I want Martial Law proclaimed, I will let you know (or you will know it)."[65] Sensing the worst, Hamblin asked Lee the fate of the emigrant train, only to be stunned by the reply. "He told me that the afore mentioned emigrants were all wiped out excepting a few children, and that the brethren help [sic] to do it, I asked—what was that for? He said they were enemies to us and that this was the beginning of great and important events."[66] After the meeting was over, Hamblin continued south to Parowan where he searched out Colonel Dame.

The Legion commander showed a remarkable willingness to clear the air surrounding the multiple murders. After denying starting the affair, he charged that "Lee and the Indians commenced it (a bad job) and it had to be done (or disposed of) for if it should come to the ears of President Buchanan, it would endanger the lives of the Brethren. . . ."[67]

This answer stunned Hamblin and prompted the reply, "I had rather that James Buchanan and all his cabinet would know the Indians had killed and wounded a few men, than for the Lord Almighty to know that I had consented to the death of women and children." Not daring to utter those terrible thoughts that resulted from his own part in the massacre, the colonel answered, "But I tell you it had to be did to save the lives of the brethren."[68]

Several days after Hamblin and Dame's conversation, Lee reported the massacre to Young. His words echoed in the audience-room, remembered an unidentified office clerk who witnessed the meeting. Recording Brigham Young's own reaction, the clerk said the prophet did not appear to want Lee's explanation of the massacre.

> Lee called at my office and had much to say with regard to the Indians, their being stirred up to anger, threatening the settlements of the whites; and then commenced an account of the massacre; I told him to stop as from what was given I had already learned by rumor I did not wish any feelings harrowed up with a recital of details.[69]

Nevertheless, the Church president did not underestimate the gravity of the massacre or its possible consequences on the political struggles of the Mormons. Critics of the Mormons had often wrongly accused the Saints, but the massacre might justify the mustering of the Utah Expedition and cause a rush of reinforcements to the territorial border. Brigham Young attempted to isolate the tragedy from the rest of the world by blaming the massacre on the Indians. Captain Van Vliet appeared in Salt Lake City during the events at the Meadows, but Brigham Young tried to conceal the tragedy from the army and the nation in order to shield his people from the inevitable popular clamor. By this indirection he incriminated himself in the disaster, a liability he willingly assumed. But if Young's public statements concerning the affair were misleading, it was only to appease the federal government and prevent the dismemberment of Zion. Yet the Mountain Meadows Massacre was not going to be ignored, as he had hoped. "Occasionally I perceive, from papers East and West," he wrote to Colonel Kane, "that the massacre of the Mountain Meadows still elicits more or less notice and comment, a good share of which is not very creditable either to candor or veracity." The prophets of disaster were wide of their mark, he continued:

> Neither yourself, nor anyone acquainted with me, will require my assurance, that had I been apprized of the intended onslaught at the meadows, I should have used such efforts for its prevention as the time, distance, and my influence and facilities would have permitted. The horrifying event transpired without my knowledge,

except from after report, and the thought of it ever causes shudder in my feelings.[70]

Still the drama echoed unpleasantly in his mind. "The facts of the massacre of men, women and children are so shocking and crucifying to my feelings, that I have not suffered myself to hear any more about them than the circumstance of conversation compelled."[71] Nevertheless, Young's hesitant handling of the massacre brought mixed results, and all attempts to hide Mormon participation in the tragedy were doomed.

While all eyes were fixed on Mormon sorties against the Utah Expedition, a Mormon cattle merchant from Payson, George Hancock, arrived at the Spanish Fork Indian reservation to purchase surplus livestock advertised for public sale. In the course of the transaction he voluntarily informed Garland Hurt "that the California emigrants on the southern route had got themselves into a very serious difficulty with the Piedes, who had given them to understand that they could not pass through their country, and on attempting to disregard this injunction found themselves surrounded by the Indians and compelled to seek shelter behind their wagons." Hancock assured Hurt that an expressman had been sent to Salt Lake City to ask Brigham Young what should be done about the Americans. "The expressman had been allowed one hundred consecutive hours in which to perform the trip of nearly three hundred miles, and return," Hurt wrote, "which Mr. H. felt confident he would do."[72]

Amid these speculations, a Ute Indian returned from a pine-nut harvest west of Sevier Lake to report that a band of Piedes had told him that the Mormons had killed all of the emigrants. Three days later a second Ute, named Spods, returned to the government farm after traveling all night and confirmed the reported difficulties between the Piedes and the emigrants.[73]

At first Hurt reacted with pained surprise. But as the accumulated storm of information burst over his agency, he sent his Indian servant, Ute Pete, to Cedar City to learn firsthand the fate of the Fancher party. Six days later the servant returned, having visited Chief Ammon's village in Beaver County, where he met a band of Piedes returning from the massacre. The Indian claimed:

> They [the Piedes] acknowledged having participated in the massacre of the emigrants, but said that the Mormons persuaded them into it. They said that about ten or eleven sleeps ago John D. Lee came to their village and told them that Americans were very bad people and always made a rule to kill Indians whenever they had a chance. He said also, that they had often killed the Mormons, who were friends to the Indians. He then prevailed on them to attack the emigrants, who were then passing through the country, (about one hundred in number) and promised them that if they were not strong enough to whip them, the Mormons would help them. The

Piedes made the attack, but were repulsed on three different occasions, when Lee and the bishop of Cedar City, with a number of Mormons, approached the camp of the emigrants under pretext of trying to settle the difficulty, and with lying, seductive overtures, succeeded in inducing the emigrants to lay down their weapons of defense and admit them and their savage allies inside of their breast works, when the work of destruction began, and, in the language of the unsophisticated boy, they cut all of their throats but a few that started to run off, and the Piedes shot them.[74]

The first news of the tragedy reached California less than two weeks after the massacre and transformed Los Angeles into an armed camp. The most radical members in that city called a mass meeting to investigate the mass murder on the Salt Lake road. Chaired by George W. Whitman, the committee heard the testimony of George Powers, a Little Rock, Arkansas, resident who had followed the Fancher train through Utah in a California-bound Mormon caravan, captained by William Mathews and Sidney Tanner. Arriving at Cedar City the day after the massacre, Powers met William Dame, Isaac Haight, and twenty Indian warriors returning from the scene of the slaughter.[75] Powers's report, read by William A. Wallace, claimed:

> Mr. Dame said that he had been out to see to the burying of the dead; but the dead were not buried. From what I heard, I believe the bodies were left lying naked upon the ground, having been stripped of their clothing by the Indians. These Indians had a two-horse wagon, filled with something I could not see, as blankets were carefully spread over the top. The wagon was driven by a white man, and beside him, there were two or three Indians in it. Many of them had shawls, and bundles of women's clothing were tied to their saddles. They were also supplied with guns or pistols besides bows and arrows. The hind most Indians were driving several head of the emigrants' cattle, Mr. Dame and Mr. Haight, and their men, seemed to be on the best of terms with the Indians, and they were in high spirits, as if they were mutually pleased with the accomplishment of some desired object. They thronged around us, and greeted us with noisy cordiality. We did not learn much from them.[76]

When the train neared the Muddy River, Powers met Ira Hatch, traveling with two horse thieves, the Young brothers, who had escaped justice in San Bernardino. According to the affidavit, Hatch found the Young brothers in the company of one of the emigrants who had escaped the massacre.

> On his arrival there was not an Indian in sight, and that he has to give the whoop to call them from concealment. He said in

continuation, without appearing to notice the discrepancy, that on his arrival he found the Indians hotly pursuing the three men; and that they jumped upon the emigrants, and killed him before his eyes, before he could interfere to prevent it. He said that he threw himself between the boys and Indians and had great difficulty in saving them. The Indians were in a great excitement, as he said, but that as Mathews and Tanner were Mormons, they could pass without danger.[77]

Upon reaching San Bernardino, Powers attended a Mormon Sunday service and heard a particularly distressing sermon delivered by Jefferson Hunt. "He said that the hand of the Lord was in it! Whether it was done by white or red skins, it was right!" Powers reported. "The prophecies concerning Missouri were being fulfilled, and they would all be accomplished. Mr. Mathews said the work had just begun, and it should be carried on until Uncle Sam and all his boys that were left should come to Zion and beg for bread."[78]

The following day the extreme faction of the Los Angeles gathering passed a series of resolutions condemning the Mormons for the massacre, and a document to that effect was forwarded to Washington.[79]

The tragedy had its effects in San Francisco, where the editor of the *Daily Evening Bulletin* wrote: "The blood of American citizens cries for vengeance, virtue, Christianity and decency require that the blood of incestuous miscreants who have perpetrated this atrocity be broken and dispersed." The Saints should be confined to the fires of hell, he continued: "Once the general detestation and hatred pervading the whole country is given legal countenance and direction, a crusade will start against Utah which will crush out this beastly heresy forever." If the government was incapable of handling the Mormon question, he charged, "from this state alone, thousands of volunteers could be drawn, who would ask no better employment than the extermination of the Mormons at the call of the government."[80]

This widespread attitude crossed the backbone of the continent to the nation's capital and forced Congress to look into the incident. Denunciations from Arkansas demanded that the federal government inflict immediate reprisals against the Mormons: "From all accounts the President has not made a call [of troops] sufficient to subdue [the Mormons]," wrote William C. Mitchell, a father who lost two sons in the affair. "The four regiments together with what regulars can be spared is too small a force to whip the Mormons, and Indians, for rest assured that all the wild tribes will fight for Brigham Young. I am anxious to be in the crowd—I feel that I must have satisfaction for the inhuman manner in which they have slain my children together with two brothers-in-law and seventeen of their children."[81] Yet despite this appeal, reference to the massacre was strangely absent during the peace negotiations that ended the Utah War, offering some hope to the Mormons that the affair was covered by President Buchanan's blanket amnesty.

The Mormons themselves were "stricken and shuddered with horror at the thought of the barbarous crime and recital of the bloody work was as harrowing as it is today," wrote T. B. H. Stenhouse.[82] A cloak of secrecy was thrown over southern Utah. "After the massacre the teachers were sent around enjoining upon the people to keep their mouths closed," wrote Mary L. Campbell. "Example: If you see a dead man laying on your wood pile, you must not tell but go about your business. The people of Cedar are aware of the whites being guilty and hence cautioned to be silent from the first."[83]

Less than four months after the calamity, a mass exodus from Cedar City began, reducing its population to slightly more than twenty families in 1859.[84] Fear and suspicion had taken a heavy toll. "It was thought a pall of darkness lay over the community. Brethren passed each other on the street without looking up or speaking, neighbors avoided each other, wives who had the constant reminder of an extra child remained home from church."[85] Important civil and Church leaders scattered to the winds: Isaac C. Haight moved with one of his families to Toquerville; Philip Klingensmith departed for the Virgin River; Nephi Johnson went into hiding in the broken country that is now Zion National Park, while others melted into the urban population of Salt Lake City to escape notice.[86]

With the military occupation of Utah during the summer of 1858, there was a brooding feeling that pressured for full investigation of the massacre, but it was not until the following winter that Judge Cradlebaugh launched the first official inquiry into the mass murder. Yet long before that jurist gained any insight into the matter, Kirk Anderson denounced the participants in the act as leprous criminals who should be hauled before the bar of justice:

> Who did this damnable deed—the Indians? A strong suspicion rests upon the popular mind that white men, or at least those who claim to be white, were interested in it, and if not actual participants, encouraged the massacre. This wholesale murder must come to light, and we are glad to see that the Federal officers are moving in the matter, and that there is at least some probability that the parties, whether Indians or their adjuncts, Mormons, will be brought to justice.[87]

Despite such editorials, Cradlebaugh launched his investigation secretly, based on the testimony of two willing witnesses—Henry Higgins and Richard Cook. Higgins, who sought asylum at Camp Floyd, confessed to the federal attorney general "that there were other persons engaged in the massacre besides Indians, and these other persons, it was alleged, were Mormons inhabiting that section of the country."[88]

In the midst of the investigation, Superintendent Jacob Forney was ordered to Cedar City to collect the survivors of Mountain Meadows. To throw off Mormon suspicions, Jacob Hamblin and others were hired to locate the Fancher children, all of whom, the Saints maintained, had to be reclaimed from the Indians. In the midst of all this, rumors circulated throughout Cedar City connecting the Church with the affair. As Alexander Wilson wrote to Washington:

> Dr. Forney, in the course of his official duties, will visit, in a few days, the region of the country and place at which the massacre occurred, and he will make every effort in his power to ascertain the real facts in the case. As yet, his inquiries as well as those of the Governor, have been conducted with secrecy, as this is thought to be the best and only method of securing reliable information, or at least a sufficient starting point for public investigation. A mystery seems to shroud this wholesale butchery, but I entertain the hope that an avenging God will speedily bring to light the perpetrators.[89]

Operating under special instructions, Jacob Forney slipped quietly out of Salt Lake City in late March of 1859, traveling south to Provo in the company of his Mormon guide, Ira Hatch, and Deputy Marshal William Rogers. There he tarried seven days conferring with the attorney general; but when the Cradlebaugh court came to a standstill, the party continued on to the territorial capital.[90] South of Fillmore bad roads, rain, and minor accidents almost made him abort his trip. Reporting the journey stoically, Forney concluded: "Occasionally my mules would stray away; and always at a place from ten to twenty miles from any place. Patience would have been a great help, under such circumstances, but, never having any in my previous life, [I] had occasion to very carefully cultivate this quality."[91]

Riding long hours for the better part of a week, the slow-moving procession finally crossed into Mountain Meadows and marched to the southern edge of the valley during the afternoon of April 14. As they rested, they saw three burial sites, torn open by predators, exposing the mutilated bodies to the weather. Later, Forney described his impressions to the editor of the *Deseret News*: "I walked over the ground where it is supposed they were killed—the evidence of this being unmistakable from skulls, and other bones and hair laying scattered over the ground. There they are buried, as near as I can ascertain, 106 persons, men women and children; and from one to two miles further down the valley, two or three who, in attempting to escape, were killed, partly up the hill, north side of the valley, and there buried, and three who got near the Vegas or Muddy in all 115."[92] However, the meadow gave up few other secrets to the superintendent.

Leaving the valley with the first light of dawn, Forney followed the California Trail south to the settlement of Santa Clara, where the party camped in the village square. A day-long search for evidence failed to turn up a single witness or any new information for the investigation. It was apparent to Forney that the settlers were solidly opposed to the unraveling of the mysterious circumstances surrounding the catastrophe.[93] The superintendent retraced his march through the mountains to Jacob Hamblin's ranch, where he received sixteen surviving children and assumed personal responsibility for their safety. Shortly afterwards, Forney and Hamblin left for Harmony to collect the last child, Charley Fancher, who was in the custody of John D. Lee.

Forney told Lee that the federal government intended to conduct a thorough investigation into the massacre, probing for some hint of Mormon participation. Lee hotly denied any knowledge of the affair or of the whereabouts of the emigrants' possessions. He placed the entire blame for the massacre on the Indians.[94] Forney listened patiently to Lee, who added that the settlements were a proverbial powder keg, with disease, starvation, and death stalking the impoverished southland. He denounced the "mobbings and drivings which the Mormons had endured, accusing the President of sending an armed mob to Utah, and praising Brigham for permitting them to enter. The Saints had committed no offenses for which they needed pardon, he insisted; if the President had been sincere in issuing the amnesty, why did he send officers with soldiers at their heels?"[95] Unwilling to prolong this disturbing scene, the superintendent left Harmony with his charges to continue his inquiry at Cedar City.

When Forney appeared in the city, he was unpleasantly impressed by the lack of cooperation from the Saints and by their categorical refusal to shed new light on the massacre. After a two-day investigation, he returned to Salt Lake City where preparations were already under way to return the children to Arkansas.

During the agent's extended absence, Congress had appropriated ten thousand dollars to defray the expense of returning the survivors to their nearest relatives. The great western freighting company of Russell, Majors and Waddell offered to carry the children to Fort Leavenworth free of charge.[96] But neither General Johnston nor Forney wished to expose the children to a six-week plains crossing by ox caravan, so they graciously declined the firm's offer. After six weeks of preparation, the army provided three spring carriages, three matrons, three camp assistants, a baggage wagon and a military escort of three companies of dragoons for the journey to Missouri. The column slipped quietly out of Salt Lake City under the command of Captain Richard Herron Anderson on the morning of June 26, 1859, and escorted fifteen children to Fort Leavenworth; and from there William C. Mitchell transported them to Carrolltown, Arkansas.[97] Two boys were held back to serve as material witnesses in the anticipated trial to be conducted by Judge Cradlebaugh; with the demise of his inquiry, the children were returned to their families, escorted by Jacob Forney, who left Salt Lake City on October 6, 1859.[98] Two or possibly three children were never returned to Arkansas, but were raised by Mormon families and reached maturity as members of the Church: George C. Williams,[99] Nancy Cameron,[100] and Louise Linton.[101]

Mormon fears of Forney's investigation were realized when he delivered his findings to the attorney general in Utah in a report that was published in territorial newspapers. "I have made diligent inquiry," he reported to his reading audience, "got the written statements of persons living in the neighborhood, and finally visited the Southern country; and now . . . I deem it to be my imperative duty to say that the Indians had material aid and assistance from the whites; and in my opinion, the Paiute Indians could not have perpetrated the terrible massacre without such aid and assistance."[102]

The reaction of the territorial attorney general was peculiar. Alexander Wilson refused to prosecute the case, notwithstanding the heavy weight of evidence collected by Judge Cradlebaugh and the Indian superintendent. "To commence the examination of a case of so much magnitude and importance," he argued, "without evidence to thoroughly investigate and conclude it, would have been prejudicial to a successful issue." With the spectacle of the Provo grand jury impasse still fresh on his mind, Wilson was dilatory in communicating his intentions to Judge Cradlebaugh. He continually put off his investigation for reasons that were difficult to justify. One of his excuses was that the judicial examination should take place at the scene of the crime, but since funds were not available for such an extensive study, an inquiry would be impossible.[103] At this point United States Attorney General Jeremiah S. Black stepped in.[104]

In an open letter published simultaneously in the Washington *Constitution* and the *Deseret News*, Black informed Wilson that it was his duty to bring to light every crime committed in the territory regardless of who was responsible. "I need not say that you are to make no distinction between Gentile and Mormon, or between Indian and white man. You will prosecute the rich and the poor, the influential and the humble with equal vigor, and thus entitle yourself to the confidence of all."[105] Referring specifically to the Mountain Meadows Massacre, he continued:

> This crime, by whomsoever committed, was one of the most atrocious that has ever blackened the character of the human race. The Mormons blame it upon the Indians, and the accusation receives

some color from the fact that all the children who survived the massacre were found in the possession of Indians; others, among them a judge of the territory, declared their unhesitating belief that the Mormons themselves committed this foul murder. All the circumstances seem, from the correspondence, to be enveloped in mystery.[106]

The exasperated attorney general questioned Wilson's lax attitude in supplying information to the justice department.

In your letter the manner of the murder is described showing that the emigrants agreed to surrender their arms upon the promise that their lives should be spared, and after doing so were all of them treacherously butchered. Why does the information stop there? If that much be known how is it that we know no more? Who were the parties that received this surrender and how is it proved? Cannot the Superintendent of Indian Affairs or someone connected with that department of the public service trace back the children from the Indians in whose possession they were found to the corral, where their parents were slain.

It is said that some of the Mormon inhabitants of Utah have property of the emigrants in their possession. If this is true, will it not furnish a thread which, properly followed, would lead back to the scene of the crime?[107]

Black dismissed any thought of delaying the investigation, promising Wilson that Washington would absorb any reasonable expense to bring the matter to a conclusion.[108]

More vigorous action was taken by the Secretary of War in the spring of 1859, when John B. Floyd ordered his departmental commander of the Pacific and Utah to launch a joint investigation into the massacre with the aid of Judge Cradlebaugh. Major Henry Prince, paymaster for the Department of Utah, was dispatched to San Francisco and Los Angeles with a detachment of two noncommissioned officers and eight privates, headed by Lieutenant John Sappinton Maraduke.[109] During his stay in Los Angeles, Prince learned from General A. S. Clark, commander of the Department of the Pacific, that Major James H. Carleton would escort Prince's bullion train to the Santa Clara River and help investigate the Mountain Meadows Massacre.[110]

In May, 1859, the road heading to El Cajon Pass was crowded with dragoons and wagons plodding northeast toward Utah. Earlier, Camp Floyd was a scene of feverish activity as a detachment of troops prepared to march toward Mountain Meadows to meet the California column.[111]

The morning of April 21, Captain Reuben P. Campbell and a mixed expedition of dragoons and infantrymen marched out of the fort, moving south along the Mormon Corridor.[112] Traveling with them were Judge Cradlebaugh and various officers and witnesses of the court, the latter hidden in a covered wagon. The Saints viewed Cradlebaugh's movements with fear and alarm. "To strike the Barbarian Mormons with a proper idea of his dignity, he has secured the attendance of a squadron of U. S. Dragoons," wrote John Jacques to Brigham Young. "This pompous parading of soldiers around the Territory recalls to one's mind youthful visions and dreams of theatrical representations of royal cavalcades, fairy tales and the processional manners and customs of oriental princes, and appears more in harmony with such scenes than with the sober travelings of an American Judiciary in the latter half of the nineteenth century."[113]

Delayed by a wretched interior road system, the detachment arrived at Cedar City after a two-week march; but Captain Campbell found the inhabitants unwilling to furnish any new information concerning the massacre. Leaving the village after a short rest, the column maneuvered its way through the broken country to Mountain Meadows, hoping for a breathing spell from the dust of the trail. But nothing could have prepared them for the horrible spectacle that unfolded before their eyes. "In places the bones of small children were lying side by side with those of grown persons, as if the parent and child had met death at the same instant and with the same stroke," one soldier was quoted in the *Valley Tan*. "Small bonnets and dresses, and scraps of female apparel were also to be seen in places on the ground there; like the bones of those who wore them, bleached from long exposure, but their shape was, in many instances, entire."[114] Near the burial sites and in the ravine by the side of the road, the soldiers found that "a large number of leg and arm bones, also of skulls, could be seen sticking above the surface, as if they had been buried there, by the action of the water, and digging of the wolves had again exposed them to sight. The entire scene was too horrible and sickening for language to describe."[115]

In the hours immediately following the expedition's arrival, the grisly task of collecting and re-interring the remains of the Fancher party began.[116] The air became stifling; soldiers broke under the strain and appeared to go mad, which threw a sudden fright into the column, according to a teamster assigned to Judge Cradlebaugh. The enormity of the crime made "many brave men shed tears as they stopped to pick up all that remained of their fellow creatures."[117] The burial detail was ordered to a halt when a rider reached Campbell and informed him that the California column was nearing Santa Clara.

The detachment reached the assembly point without delay, pitched camp, and waited. At the sight of the army, the Paiute Indians rushed to the bivouac to proclaim their loyalty, virtually tearing the camp apart in search for food and supplies. Since Campbell's limited supplies could not keep pace with the Indians' needs, the officer instructed the warriors to leave the camp and gather downstream at the site of Chief Jackson's wickiup.[118]

But when Chief Jackson and a small war party appeared at the peace council, it was Judge Cradlebaugh, not the army, who had the most questions about the tribe's activities at Mountain Meadows. The chief acknowledged raids against emigrants who had mistreated members of his band, but he denied that his tribe had anything to do with the destruction of the Fancher train.[119] It was a deliberate lie, and Cradlebaugh knew it. Leading his witness, Cradlebaugh examined and reexamined every scrap of evidence that incriminated Brigham Young, and Jackson responded by giving the judge the answers he wanted. Not all the blame should be placed on the Indians, the Paiute chief claimed, because orders for the attack were received from the "big captains" who had ordered him "to go and help whip the emigrants."[120] Cradlebaugh determined that the weight of evidence against the Mormons was conclusive and incontrovertible.

Having completed his investigation near the river, Cradlebaugh hastened north with Campbell's troops to Mountain Meadows, reaching it on May 16, 1859. Here he greeted the California column near the spring where the Fancher party had camped.[121]

With all of the federal troops safely rendezvoused, Major Prince mapped the site and helped collect the dismembered skeletons of the slaughtered emigrants. Two days later he started toward Camp Floyd to deliver the long-awaited payroll.[122] The officers and men remaining at Mountain Meadows cleared a mass grave and raised a cairn of stones at the site. Major Carleton wrote:

> Around and above this grave, I caused to be built of loose granite stones hauled from the neighboring hills, a rude monument, conical in form and 50 feet in circumference at the base and 12 feet in height. This is surmounted by a cross hewn from red cedar wood. From the ground to the top of the cross is 24 feet. On the transverse part of the cross, facing toward the north is an inscription carved deeply in wood: "Vengeance is mine; I will repay, said the Lord." [On the base in granite] "Here 120 men, women, and children were massacred in cold blood early in September, 1857. They were from Arkansas."[123]

Carleton's investigation had come to an end.

The two detachments parted, moving in opposite directions. Captain Campbell struck out for Cedar City, where the impetuous Judge Cradlebaugh threw himself headlong into the task of ferreting out and arresting persons for the massacre. Two years later he would write of those days that he was plagued by unwilling witnesses "for none knew anything for a certainty, and if they did, they would not betray their brethren into the hands of the enemies of the church."[124]

Cedar City resembled a ghost town. "The village was deserted by the men, who fled not caring to settle scores with us," recalled a teamster who journeyed west with Cradlebaugh to the frontier settlements.[125] The magistrate rented an abandoned house to accommodate his court, issuing warrants and subpoenas for the arrest of a dozen settlers he believed were hiding around the old fort. Cradlebaugh also received clandestine night callers. As the breach widened between the court and the residents of the town, one unidentified informant confessed that he had participated in the tragedy and would reveal the names of the twenty-five or thirty men living near Cedar City who had assisted in the destruction of the Fancher train. "All those that called thus," wrote Marshal Dotson, "stated that it would be at the risk of their lives if it became known they communicated anything to him, and they requested the Judge if he met them in daytime, not to recognize them as persons that he had seen before."[126]

A house-to-house search was conducted for Lee, Haight, and their fellow confederates by a dozen deputy marshals working in conjunction with Pete Dotson. The federal agents uncovered several fine carriages and horses "quite out of keeping with the surroundings," believed to belong to the Fancher train.[127] The clothing of several women excited the suspicions of the peace officers, although the women denied any link between their apparel and the massacre. "The women that we saw were all dressed in silks and satins, and wearing their garments as every day clothing."[128] Mormon accounts detail similar observations. The mother of Elijah Everett reported that "after moving to Washington Utah Ma became acquainted with some of the wives of men that was in that affair and she thinks, or did think it was done for robbery. John D. Lee's wives and those of Hate [Haight] had silk dresses and fine carpets and bedding for years after the crime was done."[129]

While Cradlebaugh scrutinized this and other evidence, Captain Campbell was ordered to return his entire command to Camp Floyd. Dark political clouds settled over the investigation, then burst with a series of communiques from Washington. It had become critically important to President Buchanan to bypass the Mountain Meadows incident and all other legal questions that might stand in the way of peace in Utah.[130] No longer would the court be permitted to use the army as an extension of its jurisdiction; therefore, Cradlebaugh realized that he could not sustain his court in the field nor effectively carry out the duties of his office there. Yielding to the inevitable, he reluctantly prepared to return to Camp Floyd along with some witnesses who were under the court's protective custody.

Captain Campbell marched his troops back to the fort by way of the Sevier Bridge and Juab Valley. Between dawn and sunrise several days later, the captain sent scouts forward to arrest some horse rustlers reported hiding a short distance from the road, but a thorough inspection of the rough terrain revealed nothing. When the column swept away down the road again, fugitives Isaac Haight, J. M. Higbee, and M. D. Hambleton watched them from the high mountain fortress of Balleguard, a well-concealed Mormon campsite that overlooked the small settlement. As the detachment disappeared from view, the three men came off the mountain and turned south in the direction of Cedar City.

The Saints' luck momentarily ran out, however. As darkness fell, Captain Campbell divided his command into two squads—a diversionary move that screened a company of dragoons several hours in the rear. When the Mormon fugitives neared the Sevier River they were arrested by the rear guard, shackled, and ushered north to the main army camp. Kept at a distance from the open camp fires, the prisoners were forced to wait out the night with military sentinels crouched watchfully beside them. Whatever their inner thoughts and emotions might have been, the Saints were surprised to find that the army was interested only in their animals. "After daylight they examined our horses and found them all right, and let us go on our way, and right glad we were to get away from them, as some of our bitterest enemies were in camp, among which was Judge Cradlebaugh," wrote Isaac Haight.[131]

After an absence of nearly a month, the patrol returned to Camp Floyd, bringing with them nothing but some bleached bones and other human debris taken from the Meadows. Captain John W. Phelps wrote:

> Our government appears desirous of giving some strange political value to this Utah affair which renders their skulls perfectly unimpressive and unmeaningful. Instead of breaking up this nest of things our government seems to be cherishing them, and thus the death, of so many emigrants brought to light exposed under much saddening circumstances produces little or nothing of that effect which some of events ought to produce in any well regulated mind or community.[132]

Under cover of a stormy night, Judge Cradlebaugh left Camp Floyd for Carson City, where he arrived on June 4 to open the second session of his court.[133] All attempts to investigate the Mountain Meadows Massacre were now abandoned. Almost two decades would pass before a single suspect would be tried and executed for the mass murder; however, the tragedy festered in the Mormon conscience for at least a generation. In the meantime, the army concentrated its efforts on more pressing issues.

CHAPTER EIGHT

THE MARCH INTO
THE WILDERNESS

What were they like, the travelers on this
road, who gave it meaning, changing its being
with every footsteps and hoofbeat . . . to what
purpose did they journey?

—*Hodding Carter*[1]

T HE DAYS OF JUDICIAL CRUSADING, the days of Cradlebaugh, Sinclair, and Eckles, were followed by a burst of wagon
road activity that converged on the territory from three sides.

Marooned by geography, the Saints had long advocated federal
support for improved roads between Salt Lake City and the Mississippi Valley. However, their plans for a road and mail system over the
Oregon and Mormon trails were pushed aside by Congress as being
either too impractical or too ambitious. In their eagerness to increase
their influence along the Pacific Coast, the Mormons developed their
own network of roads with private and Church capital, first concen-
trating their efforts on blazing an all-weather route to California by
way of the Spanish Trail, and later initiating refinements of the Humboldt Trail. The Mormons maintained a general interest in a central
road to the Pacific for a decade.

The army's disastrous operations in the field during the Utah War
focused Washington's attention on the staggering logistical problems
of linking its far-flung forces with supply centers on the Missouri
River. Having lost a measure of pride and prestige at the hands of
Mormon guerrillas during the summer of 1857, General Johnston
that year ordered Captain Randolph Barnes Marcy south to Fort Massachusetts in New Mexico at the head of a party of sixty-four men to
get supplies and new mounts for the stranded army at Camp Scott
near what is now Fort Bridger, Wyoming.[2] Included in the expedition

151

were Tim Goodale, Jim Baker and Manuel Aleno, alias Mariana or Mary Ann, a Mexican mule driver who had been driven into Camp Scott by Mormons.[3]

Traveling by horseback and mule, the expedition departed from Camp Scott on November 27, 1857, and headed into the Uinta Mountains by way of Henry's Fork, marching in arctic temperatures along the Green River. Goodale and Baker turned the party to the southwest, around the Roan Cliffs of the Colorado Plateau. Although six inches or more of snow was already on the ground, the mountain men claimed the journey could be accomplished in fifteen to twenty days. Accordingly, the expedition took with it only forty days' provisions, believing this supply ample for the march to New Mexico. The clear mountain air must have made everything look closer to them.

Instead of the little snow they predicted, the soldiers were forced to travel 200 miles through drifts two to ten feet deep. To make matters worse, the men were forced to break a track over the plateau for their animals.[4] Eating mule meat when their provisions gave out, the party continued through the tortuous landscape, just trying to stay alive. Unknown to the captain, Private James Sweeney and three enlisted men had stolen a hundred pounds of flour, ten pounds of sugar, and six pounds of coffee from a sutler at Camp Scott. Wrote the young enlisted man, "The four of us who had the flour, sugar and coffee were called on more often than the rest and we were better nourished and stronger than the other men excepting Corporal McLeod of the 10th Inf., who was a very powerful man and had a wonderful endurance."[5]

When Sergeant William H. Morton of the Tenth Infantry died from exposure and fatigue, Sweeney reported to the commander his small cache of provisions. "One night soon after we got out of the snow we were camped by a small stream," remembered Sweeney, "and it was very cold. . . . Captain Marcy was standing by a camp fire shivering when I went up and told him if he could come over to our camp fire he would be more comfortable. He did so, and when he got there, I gave him a cup of coffee and a biscuit. He asked where I got it and I told him that I had stolen it from one of the wagons and that was the reason we were stronger than the rest. He laughed, but after that every morning and night he got his coffee and biscuit."[6]

Matters worsened when Mariana began to insist that Baker and Goodale were hopelessly lost. Instead of crossing the Rockies, he warned, they were paralleling the range and were caught in a web of trails that prevented them from entering Cochetopa Pass. The nature of the country forced the caravan to march in a great lateral movement, on the verge of total collapse. Guideless, the party struggled southward for several days until it reached a small stream where the Mexican mule driver informed Marcy that he thought he knew their approximate location. The company camped next to the river while Mariana worked his way upstream to locate an aspen grove that he had not seen for twenty years. "When he returned," wrote a member of the party, "he said he was all right, that we were one hundred and twenty miles from Ft. Garland, New Mexico. The Captain then told him to take his, the Captain's mare, and go to Ft. Garland or as far as the mare would carry him, then remove the saddle, turn the mare loose and proceed on foot."[7]

The slow, painful advance began again, winding through Cochetopa Pass. After crossing the summit, the famished soldiers forced their way down the eastern slope of the range to rendezvous with Mariana, but no sign of life was to be found. Tracing Mariana's trail, the expedition came out of the mountains and penetrated the San Luis Valley where their guide appeared escorting two ambulances, a doctor, and a small herd of mules. Carried away by what appeared to be a miraculous rendezvous, Marcy watched the soldiers' spirits soar: "Some of the men laughed, danced and screamed with delight, while others (and I must confess I was not one of the former) cried like children."[8] Many of Marcy's men were so exhausted that they had to be fed with a spoon. Camping on the frontier of New Mexico, the expedition rested for two days before setting its course for the Rio Grande. The column forded the stream at the first place they found a shallow spot and were intercepted by a relief train from Fort Garland, a short distance downstream from the Rio Grande's headwaters.

During his stay at Fort Garland, Marcy concentrated on buying all the available sheep, horses, mules, and draft animals in northern New Mexico for the stranded Utah Expedition back at Camp Scott. When northern New Mexico was depleted, the quartermaster of Fort Union dispatched scouting expeditions downstream to buy all of the available livestock in the Rio Grande settlements. In all, 160 horses, 1,000 mules, and several thousand head of sheep were purchased and driven north to Camp Scott.[9]

Once the assemblage of animals, wagons, and men was completed, Captain Marcy and his little army pushed out of Fort Union on March 17, 1857. Crossing Raton Pass, a short distance south of the territorial border, the army journeyed northward at the dragging pace set by the supply train and ranging livestock. In less than five days the column forded the Arkansas River at Old Pueblo, formerly a Mexican trading station, traveling to Fountaine Qui Boille where they remained for thirty days awaiting reinforcements from New Mexico.[10] The appearance of Colonel William Wing Loring with 200 mounted riflemen and infantrymen came on the heels of a rumor that the Mormons were expected to attack Marcy's re-supply column before it reached Fort Bridger.

The combined force hastened due north along the base of the Rocky Mountains, toward the divide of the Arkansas and Platte rivers, where it was struck by a blizzard. Thirty-six inches of snow covered the ground, forcing the troopers to hand-feed the livestock. The storm swept away uncounted sheep and 300 mules, but when the sky cleared, a rescue party located the animals fifty miles south, near the Arkansas River.[11] Beyond this point, three teamsters were found frozen to death, a scene that was later described by Captain Gove in his dispatch to the *New York Herald:* "Some of the Mexican herders started with them (the mules): of the two who kept on, one was found this side of the Arkansas dead, the other was found near the mules, crawling around on his hands and knees in a state of temporary insanity, nearly starved to death, and would have probably died in a few hours if he had not been found and taken into camp and well treated."[12] The second man perished within 200 yards of the camp, within a few steps of his companion's tent. The bones of a teamster were found where there had been a fire, with all the flesh burned off. "The poor man, doubtless suffering from the cold, had fallen into the fire and been burned up, all save his bones."[13]

After gathering all but five of the stray mules, the expedition waited out the storm, then continued its march to the South Platte River. At Cherry Creek they overtook John H. Gregory, along with forty other miners, searching through a sea of snow to unlock the treasures of the mountains. The disillusioned men had found nothing except misfortune and hardship. Marcy furnished the miners with two months' supply of provisions, and then he marched to the southern tributary of the Platte River.[14] To cross the wild, rumbling water, soldiers constructed a pontoon bridge from wagon boxes and walked the livestock to the opposite bank.[15] Aside from his normal trail duties along Bryan's road, Marcy left the trail to map new approaches to Fort Bridger. He claimed he had cut the distance from Camp Scott to the Mississippi by a hundred miles—which was not the case—but "his journey demonstrated the necessity of further explorations for supply routes into the Great Basin."[16]

Back at Camp Scott, Marcy learned that a second expedition had returned. The Flathead Expedition had been captained by Benjamin F. Ficklin, a former surveyor for William M. F. Magraw's wagon-road company.[17] Ficklin had been signed-on to head the army's probe to the Salmon River because he knew the country northwards to the headwaters of the Missouri and he was the only one who could speak the language of the Bannocks and the Nez Perce. The Ficklin company of eleven men pulled out of Fort Bridger on December 9, 1857, carrying thirty days' rations and four gallons of whiskey, to search the north country near the Beaver Head Mountains for beef cattle and horses to buy from trappers and Indians.

Their line of march took them over one of the oldest trails in the West to the Snake River, where Ficklin received reports of hostile Indians downstream. The last three days of the year were spent attempting to cross the mountains in a snowstorm. A thirty-mile forced march finally took them off the mountain. When their provisions gave out, they killed some of their animals to keep themselves fed until they could reach a white settlement.[18] Unable to discover a new passage through the high country, the expedition followed a well-traveled trace along the Salmon River to Fort Lemhi, the northernmost colony of the Mormons. Outside the settlement they were stopped by a sizable band of Indian warriors who said that they intended to destroy the fort because the Mormons had armed the Nez Perce, the enemy of the Bannocks and Snakes.

On the grassy meadow surrounding the fort, Ficklin warned the Saints that, although the Indians appeared peaceful, their dissatisfaction with the inroads of Mormon colonization jeopardized the settlement's safety. Believing Ficklin to be an advance guard of the army, the Saints discounted his warning of approaching trouble with the Indians.

Ficklin subsequently led his men across the divide of the Beaverhead Mountains, then slowly continued northeast along a series of rivers and ranges to the Bitterroot Valley, near the headwaters of the Missouri River. At the St. Ignatius Mission, the expedition learned from Father Hoken that 250 Bannock and Shoshoni Indians had attacked the Mormon settlement at Fort Lemhi, killing two men and wounding five others.[19] With the Flathead country in turmoil, the ill-starred army collected a herd of forty half-starved Indian ponies before it beat a hasty retreat to Winter Quarters. When the party rendezvoused with the army five weeks later, Ficklin reported to General Johnston that no new route to the Oregon country had been located.[20] The Flathead Expedition did, however, provide important knowledge of the relatively unexplored passages through the country that bordered the Bitterroot Valley and focused the army's attention on a new wagon road between Camp Floyd and Fort Dalles.

During the summer campaign of 1857, the great bulk of materials and supplies used to maintain men and animals was carried from the Missouri, which painfully exposed the military necessity for alternative routes into the territory. The value these roads would have was no longer questioned after the Secretary of War launched a series of ambitious road surveys to link the isolated Department of Utah to the military districts of California, Oregon, and New Mexico. The first probe issued from the southwest.

Captain John N. MaComb combined elements of the Eighth Infantry under Lieutenant Milton Cogswell to search for a military road into Utah from Santa Fe. Traveling with the mounted company were a handful of civilians, the most prominent of whom was Dr. John Strong Newberry, a member of the Ives Expedition of 1857, two years before. Albert H. Pfeiffer, a Ute agent, acted as guide and interpreter.

After its departure from Santa Fe on July 12, 1859, the expedition struck the Spanish Trail west of the Rio Grande and stopped briefly to rest its animals at the pueblo of San Juan and the village of Abiquiu. In extreme northern New Mexico, MaComb struck the Rio Chama and followed its erratic course for forty-five miles. Moving across the Continental Divide, separating the watersheds of the Gulf of Mexico and the Gulf of California, the men of the expedition rode through some of the most starkly beautiful country they had seen, a preview of the geologic majesty of the high plateau country. Three days later, their livestock grazed on the deep grass bordering the splashing waters of the San Juan. Crossing the headwaters of that river, the train traversed a well-worn Indian trail for seventy miles, pressing deep into the present state of Colorado. Not far from the southern edge of the Sierra de la Plata, the contingent discovered the ruins of several ancient Indian villages hidden in the barrens of the mountains—the site of the present Mesa Verde National Park.

The hardship of the trail began to show when the survey party emerged from the mountains onto the Colorado Plateau. Ahead of them hundreds of square miles of jumbled rock and monoliths rose above a desert thinly covered with mesquite and creosote brush. "Could anyone be elevated to a sufficient height over the center of the region and be gifted with superhuman powers of vision," wrote Dr. Newberry, "he would see beneath him what appeared to be a great plain, bounded on each side by mountain ranges, and here and there dotted by isolated mountain masses, rising like islands above its surface." Pointing to the southwest, he marked the plateau's extreme border. "He would see, too, the profound chasm of the Colorado Canyon scoring with tortuous and diagonal course, the plain, throughout the entire length of its greater diameter for nearly five hundred miles, the stream flowing 3,000 to 6,000 feet below the general level, and at all points bordered by abrupt, frequently perpendicular crags and precipices."[21]

At this stage the captain led his men into Canyon Pintado where they spent several hours digging the bones of a dinosaur, half-immersed in the gypsum remains of an ancient sea. Later the prehistoric remains were shipped across the continent to Joseph Leidy, one of the early scholars of vertebrate paleontology.

Breaking camp the following morning, MaComb marched to Ojo Verde, or Green Springs, where he left the Spanish Trail. After establishing a base supply depot on a grassy meadow, MaComb, Cogswell, Newberry, two technical assistants, and three porters left the main expedition and crossed the open country to the west, toward the junction of the Green and Grand Rivers. The small party labored for two days through the difficult landscape before reaching the end of the plateau. The sight that awaited them at the end of the plateau exceeded anything they could have imagined. Newberry later reconstructed his thoughts in print: "Everywhere deeply cut by a tangled maze of canyons, and thickly set with towers, castles, and spires of the most varied and striking forms; the most wonderful monuments of erosion which our eyes, already experienced in objects of this kind, had ever beheld."[22] The five men descended Labyrinth Canyon and scaled an isolated butte, despite the oppressive heat, hoping to locate a passage through the broken country before them.

The captain and his companions, torn between failure and the bewitching beauty of the canyonlands, stared in open disbelief at the resistant strata before them. As Newberry described it: "A great basin or sunken plain lay stretched before us as on a map. Not a particle of vegetation was anywhere discernible; nothing but bare and barren rocks of rich and varied colors shimmering in the sunlight." The geologist noted a horizon blocked out for a hundred miles by "fantastically formed buttes . . . pyramids, domes, towers, columns, spires of every conceivable form and size. . . . In every direction they ran and ramified deep, dark, and ragged, impassable to everything but the winged bird."[23]

As early as the light would permit the following morning, MaComb and his party retraced their steps to Oso Oho to take a well-deserved rest. Weary, disappointed, and increasingly anxious to return to the Rio Grande, the exhausted party moved with the greatest difficulty over the broken country of the Colorado Plateau to the San Juan River. Following the flow of the stream for six days, they turned south around a spur of the Nacimiento Mountains where the trail dropped noticeably. Farther east Captain MaComb and his troops camped near the pueblo of Jemez, a short march from the territorial capital. MaComb detailed the progress of his exploration to Washington from his quarters in Santa Fe.

The report concluded that a northwest passage from New Mexico to Camp Floyd was not to be found by way of the San Juan Basin; consequently, General Johnston could not depend on large-scale military support from the southwest. However, the exploration of the unknown country was but a part of the impulse to unlock scientific knowledge. Not only did the MaComb expedition discover the whole drainage pattern of the San Juan and establish its relationship to the Colorado, it also proved that the Grand and the Green joined to form the Colorado. The fastidious Newberry mapped the numerous stratigraphic layers of the plateau, linked his findings with that of the Ives Expedition, and added a new dimension to western geology that "opened up a new and unknown country to the civilized world."[24]

But even while the MaComb expedition was edging its way along the Colorado Plateau, a second reconnaissance party had been sent from the Pacific Northwest to blaze a shorter wagon road from The Dalles of the Columbia River to Salt Lake City. The War Department's stepped-up activities in the arid wastes of Oregon had two interdependent strategic objectives—first, to provide a safe alternative to the old Oregon Trail and, second, to develop an all-weather supply line linking the Departments of Oregon and Utah.

In the planning stages of the expedition, General William S. Harney, commander of the Department of Oregon, faced multiplying problems. Dissension riddled his command when Captain Thorn, the ranking topographical officer in the Northwest, excused himself from the mission and selected Captain Henry D. Wallen to head the reconnaissance. Seeking an experienced engineer, Harney chose a young and very green lieutenant, Joseph Dixon of Tennessee, freshly graduated from West Point. The only man who could claim familiarity with the unsurveyed country was Lewis Scholl, a mountaineer, designated to lead the expedition through the dangerous and unknown territory. Indulging his passion for exploration, Harney assigned nine officers and slightly fewer than 200 men to the Wallen expedition. To maintain the column in the field, 38 horses, 344 mules, 121 oxen, 30 wagons, and an ambulance were drawn from the quartermaster's department.[25] This remarkable outfit was by far "the largest and best equipped of any engaged in wagon-road survey and construction for the United States Army in the American West."[26]

Leaving Fort Dalles in the morning of June 4, 1859, Captain Wallen directed his force south, past the silent sentinel of Mount Hood, along the west bank of the Des Chutes River, without noteworthy incident. The caravan continued along the waterway for sixty miles before crossing to the east bank, and reached the spur of the Blue Mountains, covered with a scattered forest of gnarled pine trees. After discovering the Crooked River, the party moved along its meandering banks until it emerged onto a stretch of level country hemmed in on the east by a wall of granite mountains.

Facing the contorted barrier, Wallen decided to cut himself free of his supply train. When the last of the supply vehicles reached the base camp, Captain Wallen ordered Lieutenant John C. Bonnycastle to return to Fort Dalles with the heavy wagons and all surplus equipment that would be of no further use to the expedition. The homeward-bound detachment of fifteen dragoons returned by way of the Blue Mountains, along the John Day River, in search of a wagon road through the mountains; but no passage was discovered.[27]

Looking southeastward from the flat plain, Wallen marched his men sixty or seventy miles through sloping country. He skirted Watumpa Lake and brought his men into camp along Lake Harney, named in honor of his departmental commander. Up to this point the physical hazards of the trail were never very great. The wilderness had no severe shortage of water, and grass for livestock was adequate. Although the trail was at times steep, especially through the spur of the Blue Mountains, there were no serious barriers to the development of an all-weather wagon road. But even while he made these observations, Wallen encountered a series of unexpected problems.

Following a course that ran northeast, the far-ranging expedition crossed over the crest of the Blue Mountains to the Malheur River and labored along its banks to discover its source. Forced against perpendicular mountain sides, Wallen concluded that it would be impossible for wagons to travel through the dangerous, narrow gorge. Leaving the river, the survey team veered north on a circuitous path through the narrow gateway leading to Fort Boise, the abandoned trading post of the Hudson Bay Company. From the safety of the virtually uninhabited region of the Owyhee River, Wallen dispatched Lewis Scholl, escorted by dragoons, to explore the country between the river and the Goose Creek Mountains for an undiscovered trail into Utah.[28]

Meanwhile, Wallen conducted the remaining troops south along the Oregon Trail. The captain found the trek across the waterless emigrant road depressing, sentiments that were echoed by his engineer, Lieutenant Dixon. The road was nothing more than a forest of sagebrush and other desert plants scattered rather thickly on both sides of the trail, giving an unnatural lushness to the otherwise dry and waterless country. Reaching the Raft River, Wallen rendezvoused with Lewis Scholl and his squad of explorers. Owing to the nature of the Snake River and the terrain east of the Raft Mountains, Scholl reported that only 100 miles could be saved by a newly discovered cut-off. Wallen's luck had not changed. After the Blue Mountain–Snake River surveys, he divided his command into three detachments—the first was sent northeast to reconnoiter the region between the Snake River and Fort Hall; the second was ordered to camp at Raft River, a tributary of the Snake; while the last element, reduced to twenty mounted soldiers, crossed the river and marched south to Camp Floyd, by way of the Steptoe road.

Nearly two months after leaving Fort Dalles, Captain Wallen entered Salt Lake City, much to the delight of the editor of the *Deseret News*, who prematurely claimed the mission a boon to the territory. "It is ascertained that emigrants going to Oregon will shorten the distance at least one hundred miles, between Salt Lake and Fort Dalles, by leaving the California road at Raft Creek Valley and following Raft Creek down to the second crossing, instead of passing up the Fort Hall road to its intersection with Colonel Lander's road from Fort Laramie."[29] Such praise did not lift Wallen's spirits, for during his stay at Camp Floyd he confessed to General Johnston that despite his efforts no practicable wagon road had been located that was an improvement over the old emigrant trail. The Oregon Trail was still mistress of the overland.

The dual failures of the Wallen and MaComb expeditions only stiffened Johnston's determination to join his department with surrounding military districts, and he refocused his energies on an east-west wagon road between Fort Bridger and California. The first link to be forged in this long chain was the development of an alternative wagon road through the Wasatch Mountains by way of Timpanogos Canyon. Fortunately, the road was in the first stage of development by the Mormons when they received news of the Utah Expedition. With the punitive force of federal troops successfully parried, the Saints accelerated their efforts to cut a road through Timpanogos Canyon to open the valleys east of the mountains as a refuge from the army. Twenty thousand dollars had been expended by the Timpanogos River Turnpike Company, a subsidiary of the Mormon Church, to build the first twelve miles of canyon trail.[30]

While General Johnston and his staff contemplated problems associated with the Mormons, Captain James Hervey Simpson assembled a surveying party at Camp Floyd to take the first step in one of the largest and most costly expeditions in the territory's history. A trained surveyor in the Topographical Corps, Simpson understood the special problems associated with soldiering in the arid West, having gained well-deserved recognition for his part in the military reconnaissance from Santa Fe to the Navajo country in 1849. Enjoying a series of rapid promotions, the wagon road engineer was recognized as one of the most promising men in the topographic service, although his career in the Minnesota territory was marred by political difficulties that spawned a wave of mounting pressure for his removal.[31] Angry opponents, protesting Simpson's location of important wagon roads and charging the army with misapplication of government funds, had forced his transfer to Fort Leavenworth where he was attached to the Utah Expedition. The change was a welcome relief for the restless captain, who, like many of his contemporaries, carried his taste for adventure into the western wilderness.

Striking out from Camp Floyd on August 25, 1858, escorted by twenty dragoons under Lieutenant Samuel F. Ferguson, Captain Simpson led his column north to the Jordan River, threading the northern shore of Utah Lake to the mouth of Timpanogos Canyon where he rendezvoused with his supply train that had moved out the day before. When dawn broke the following morning, the entire survey party marched over a sixty-foot toll bridge built earlier by the Saints. Here the captain noted the heavy construction cost of the span was defrayed by varying duties: wood wagons paid a toll charge of one dollar a cord; fifty cents was levied for a horse and carriage; one horse or mule and rider was charged ten cents; while five cents per head was charged for horses, cattle, and mules. Sheep and pigs were taxed at three cents a head.[32]

Turning upstream, the survey party paralleled the meandering Timpanogos River for twelve miles over an improved grade, crossed over the mountain into Round Valley, and bivouacked near the present site of Heber City. At times it was impossible to walk beyond the shadow of the campfires because of the rattlesnakes that infested the valley, making sleep almost impossible. The exhausted expedition resumed its eastern march the following morning, laboring along a narrow Indian trail to Silver Creek, a brawling tributary of the Weber River. Progress was slow but steady. After a hasty reconnaissance, Simpson took a small advance party and pushed on to the upper reaches of the Weber River to White Clay Creek, carefully taking into account the availability of timber and stone that could be used for future road construction. With great effort the survey team followed the sweep of White Clay Creek for thirty miles before crossing the divide to Bear River. Turning their backs on the mountains, the expedition members followed an unmarked trail to the northeast that terminated at Fort Bridger. The hardened soldiers had reconnoitered 155 miles of trail in nine days, traversing an immense and naked wilderness, and had driven another wedge through the Wasatch Mountains.[33]

Not content with these laurels, Simpson made preparations to turn a line on a topographical map into a practical wagon road. Attacking the problem on two fronts, Simpson directed Lieutenant Alfred T. A. Torbert to begin construction of the undeveloped western section of the road, while Lieutenant E. C. Jones was simultaneously dispatched from Fort Bridger with a work crew to widen the trace's upper stretches. Laboring against an early winter, ninety men worked simultaneously toward White Clay Creek. As September ebbed into

October, Simpson watched the construction of the road brought to a successful completion and detailed its progress to General Johnston in a series of handwritten dispatches carried by mounted dragoons.

While the last days of construction were under way Major Prince, traveling east to pay the troops at Fort Bridger, handed Simpson a message requesting the engineer to return to Camp Floyd. The captain left the project immediately and worked his way down the winding trail to Cedar Valley. Back at his home base Simpson reported that the new trail south of Echo was a marked improvement over the older trace. Not only was more grass and water available, but also the new road could be used for a longer season by pack animals and cattle. Anticipating the importance of the Simpson improvements, Russell, Majors & Waddell ordered its freighters to utilize the route immediately and found that the time saved more than compensated for the poor condition of the half-graded trail. Having summarily disposed of a new trail through the Wasatch Mountains, General Johnston turned his attention to the task of exploring the desert west of Camp Floyd.[34]

Like other military men who preceded him to Utah, the general's burning interest in wagon roads paralleled military, economic, and political considerations. The search for new grazing lands was never-ending, forcing the army to look west for additional winter range in the arid valleys bordering the military reserve. Also, 800 dangerous miles separated Camp Floyd from Carson City by way of the snaking detour north of the Great Salt Lake. To avoid this long journey, a central route was needed to cut the great interior desert in half, shortening by weeks the travel time to the western edge of the Great Basin. Moreover, Johnston considered building a military post near the sink of the Humboldt to control the renegades who operated along the overland trails, at the same time extending federal authority to the Sierra Nevada.[35] As his plans developed, the general found nothing in his orders that prevented him from making the distant territory more accessible to Gentiles, a cardinal benefit Johnston hoped would weaken Mormon control of the interior Basin.

Exuberantly, the high-spirited Simpson plunged into his new assignment. The advance into the western wilderness began during the middle of October when the expedition gathered on the parade ground of Camp Floyd. The field strength of the expedition included a Mormon guide, George Washington Bean, geologist Henry Engelmann, a score of laborers, and Lieutenant Gurden Chapin, who commanded a military escort of thirty-five soldiers, including ten dragoons. Behind the advance party five wagons carried foot soldiers, equipment and supplies, and in addition there was an ambulance loaded with astronomical instruments.

Working slowly westward through Camp Floyd Pass, separating Cedar and Rush Valleys, the expedition caught its first glimpse of the Johnston settlement, a small village of fifteen squalid buildings near the base of the Stansbury Range.[36] The Mormon hamlet, guarded by a handful of men, had been troubled from its beginning; Simpson observed that although the land around the settlement was rich in meadows, wild hay remained standing in the fields. Most of the original pioneers were gone, driven out by Indian raids the previous year. A dozen burned-out log cabins were left to the desert birds that flew in and out of the ruins without breaking flight. Moments later the topographical engineer showed considerable interest in a war party of Goshute Indians who arrived at the settlement when the expedition trooped in.

The situation was worse than Simpson had imagined and he was moved by the arrogance of the Indians who roamed freely through the village collecting tribute:

> The warriors were each well clad and armed with a rifle. Their manners appeared impudent and presuming towards the Mormons with whom they were conversing, and with hands full of bread, which, doubtless, they had levied upon some frightened citizen. They acted and talked as if they were entitled to anything they might ask for. The carriage of the Mormons towards them, I thought submissive and provocative of the very thing they would most depreciate, an attack upon them.[37]

Leaving the Mormons to settle their differences with the Indians, the half-mile-long column crossed the foothills of Rush Valley to the west, then labored up the steep ascent of Reynold's Pass that separated the Onagui and Stansbury Ranges.[38] Entering Skull Valley, Simpson led his men southward, noting the numerous isolated mountains and parallel ranges that divided the basin. The valley was a treeless plain that supported a heavy growth of greasewood and sagebrush, but vegetation suitable for livestock became more and more stunted. Two days later the expedition camped at Pleasant Springs, a small watering hole which Simpson renamed in his own honor, and there the captain plotted directions for a new trail to California. But a new crisis followed the soldiers into the wilderness.

No sooner had the reconnaissance reached Simpson Springs than a bitter quarrel broke out between the soldiers and their guide, rekindling old animosities.[39] Details of the episode are shrouded by time and conflicting evidence, but the outline is clear. The soldiers openly mocked with much heat and bitterness the whole spectrum of Mormon doctrine, belittling both Brigham Young and the entire population of Latter-day Saints. Predictably, the temper of the Mormon guide reached the boiling point. Damning the soldiers for their irreverence, the trail guide warned that he would leave the party if Simpson did not apologize for his men's remarks. Torn by dissension and racked by partisan feelings, the expedition was threatened with an untimely end. Somewhat offsetting his soldiers' militant approach to Mormonism, the commander excused the meddlings of his men and his own harsh treatment of Bean and his religion which he believed would in the long run bring more harm than good to the expedition. The scout accepted the left-handed apology and continued to function as guide.

In the continued search for a road through the Basin, Simpson broke a trail southwestward for twenty miles to the Thomas Mountains where he discovered a narrow slot that led to the valley beyond. After christening the gap Short Cut Pass, the train continued to the southwest across level land and encamped near the windswept House Range. The desperate thirst from which the party suffered forced Simpson to dispatch a squad of men to scout the trail ahead. After traveling thirty-five miles across White Valley the column returned, only to report no sign of water. Feeling the bite of winter in the breezes coming from the north, Simpson ordered his expedition to return to Camp Floyd.[40]

Choosing a different route from the original point of entrance into Rush Valley, the soldier-explorer made his way through the mountains south of Reynolds Pass, naming the narrow slit in honor of General Johnston. Merging with the outward trace, the column passed over Cedar Valley to the security of Camp Floyd.[41] Back at his home base, Simpson reported to General Johnston that the wilderness to the west was a series of parallel mountain ranges that split the territory into separate miniature basins, making entry from the east extremely difficult. On the other hand, the valleys were sometimes level and sometimes gently rolling, suitable for rapid overland travel. Eager to insure the progress of a wagon road survey through the Basin, Simpson reiterated his belief that a path south of the Humboldt River was highly feasible for military and civilian travel to California.

The significance of the Simpson survey was increased by the activities of George Chorpenning, who had contracted to carry the weekly mail between Salt Lake City and Placerville. To investigate the possibility of avoiding the dangerous ox-bow route around Goose Creek, the mail contractor sent his own investigating team, headed by an employee, Seth Taft, westward along the Simpson trace to Short Cut Pass. With a rough map of the route in his possession, Taft worked his way slowly to the House Mountains, noting possible sites for mail stations, then hastily returned to Camp Floyd to report his findings. Though the valleys were hardly the shimmering prairie that Chorpenning had been led to believe, the route avoided the blistering salt flats to the north and had sufficient water and grass for many hundreds of horses and mules.

With this account still fresh in his mind, Chorpenning, gathering horses, mules and whatever stores could be rapidly moved, transferred his operations from the Goose Creek route to the central trail.[42] The newly developed route assumed new importance when Howard Egan, later to be the most famous Mormon pony express rider of them all, developed an extension of Simpson's route between Short Cut Pass and the strategic Hasting's Road. From this point the route to the Humboldt was open.[43] In the words of Dale Morgan: "Although pack trains had to carry the mail by Hastings' old route between Ruby Valley and the Humboldt, it was plain that Chorpenning would soon have mail coaches running all the way to the desert river."[44]

With the work and experiences of the special task force to guide him, Simpson spent the remainder of the winter cloistered in Camp Floyd charting a new road from Short Cut Pass to Carson City. As the capstone of his military career, he presented his dual-purpose military and emigrant road proposal to the Secretary of War:

> It is believed that a direct route from this post to Carson Valley can be obtained which would avoid the detour by the Humboldt to the right and that by the Las Vegas to Los Angelas Route to the left and that it could be obtained so as to make the distance to San Francisco . . . 260 miles shorter than the Humboldt River route and 390 miles shorter than the Los Angelas route.[45]

Essentially two land expeditions were contemplated—one to explore a central route to the Pacific across the heart of the Great Basin, and a second to chart a trail connecting Utah to the headwaters of the Arkansas River where Lieutenant F. T. Bryan had laid out a road in 1855.

Significant to the success of the mission were the assorted talents and skills that Simpson drew into his command. Included in the expedition were two junior officers, Lieutenants J. L. Kirby Smith and Haldiman L. Putnam, both recent graduates from West Point who compensated for their lack of experience with unremitting energy and dedication. Also included in the party was Henry Englemann, a trained geologist and brother of George Englemann, the famous botanist who was associated with Lieutenant Bryan's trek across the front ranges of the Rockies. Representing the Smithsonian Institution was taxidermist Charles S. McCarty, a recent Irish immigrant. To record the forms of the desert and mountains on film, C. C. Mills arrived from Washington as the expedition photographer; however, since Simpson had little confidence in the "infant and unproven tool," H. V. A. Von Beck also was recruited to give his pencil and watercolor impressions of the trail.[46] The principal task of guide fell to John Reese, a pioneer pathfinder of the Basin who had established Mormon Station in Carson Valley four years after the Saints entered the territory. Ute Pete, formerly the Indian interpreter of Dr.

Garland Hurt, was taken along as interpreter, while the brother of Chief Arrowpeen (Arapeen) was hired as hunter.[47]

Added to the expedition to carry out purely military duties was Lieutenant Alexander Murry of the Tenth Infantry, commanding an escort of twenty men, divided equally between dragoons and infantrymen. As the expedition grew, twelve six-mule quartermaster wagons and two spring wagons were placed in the charge of fourteen teamsters. With so unwieldy a caravan, four Mexican herders tended the caravan's cattle while a wheelwright and a lone blacksmith were hired to keep the wagons and equipment in working order. Wagonmaster Henry Sailing was placed in command of the wagon train's auxiliary personnel. The youngest member of the party was seventeen-year-old William Lee, who had been farmed-out to the expedition by his wealthy and influential family to take part in the adventure.[48]

In the few days remaining before his departure, Simpson inspected the equipment, wagons, and provisions that would be vitally necessary to penetrate the hitherto forbidden Indian frontier to the west. Clearly it was a tremendous undertaking, and the army under General Johnston made an exceptional effort to assure the expedition's success.

After several months' delay occasioned by the sheer size of the expedition, Simpson led his men out of Camp Floyd in a southwesterly course toward Short Cut Pass during the early morning hours of May 3, 1859. At the Chorpenning Mail Station they observed the great herds of cattle owned by Russell, Majors & Waddell stretched across Rush Valley. Looking westward from Skull Valley, the explorer dispatched John Reese to make his way south to find a feeder road through or around the Sevier Desert. To the captain's disappointment the weary Mormon guide rejoined Simpson near the Thomas Range where he reported that the lack of pasturage made the southern crossing of the mountains unsuitable for wagon travel. Much of the country below Short Cut Pass, he reported, was a super-heated desert wilderness, torn by a labyrinth of valleys, occasional box canyons, and far-reaching isolated mountain ranges that blocked the western passage to California.[49]

From the Thomas Mountains, the mile-long procession plodded westward along the Chorpenning mail route, passing through a long series of mountain chains where Simpson described the Goshute Indians, commonly referred to as Diggers, as he found them in 1859:

They are the most wretched-looking creatures I have ever seen, and I have seen great numbers in various portion of our country. Both men and women wear a cape made of strips of rabbit-skins, twisted and dried, and then tied together with strings, and drawn around the neck by a cord. This cape extends to just below the hip, and is but a scant protection to the body. They seldom wear leggings or moccasins, and the women appear not to be conscious of any impropriety in exposing their persons down to the waist. Children at the best are perfectly naked, and this at a time when overcoats were required by us. The men wear their hair cut square in front, just above the eyes, and it is allowed to extend in streamers at the temples. The women let their hair grow at random. They live on rats, lizards, snakes, insects, grasses, and roots, and their largest game is the rabbit, it being seldom that they kill an antelope.[50]

By day the Goshutes dogged the army's herd and attempted without success to steal stray or weakened livestock. By night they gathered the entrails of slaughtered animals, feasting within the shadows of military campfires. As scavengers of the desert, they had no equal, wrote Captain Simpson in his journal. "Two rats make a meal. Like rabbits better than rats, and antelope better than either, but cannot get latter."[51] The sleeping habits of the nomadic Indians appeared as strange to the soldiers as did their eating rituals. "The way in which these fellows sleep," observed William Lee, "is singular, they had no lodges but lay entirely naked in a circle round a fire [each] with his head resting on the other—sometimes when it is very cold they lie in heaps one on top of the other spoon fashion."[52]

After a ceremonial exchange of gifts, Simpson set his course north by west to Ruby Valley where he encountered Howard Egan and Ball Robert, both of whom had established mail stations along the route. The station keepers told the engineer that they had tried twice without success to break a new trail south of the old emigrant road to Genoa. The rest of the one-sided conversation was more grim than the first. Egan warned that the land between Ruby Valley and the Humboldt sink was uncertain and hazardous, particularly the salt plains to the west, and hastened to add that the two men had passed the winter living on mule and coyote carcasses. Beyond the Ruby Valley death ruled the wilderness.[53]

The warnings of potential disaster were sobering but not intimidating. In clear weather the resolute captain passed through the spur of the Humboldt Mountains, veering south along the thirty-ninth parallel, determined to strike a new road to Genoa. The next leg of the epic journey took the expedition around and through a series of mountain ranges, streams, and valleys, memorialized with the names of members of the expedition, Simpson's close friends, and admired military supporters. In stifling heat the isolated caravan entered Reese Valley, two-thirds of the distance to Carson City.

Realizing that the safety of the new land route depended on the friendliness of the Diggers, Simpson did everything possible to maintain cordial relations with the Indians, though one incident threatened momentarily to destroy the peaceful coexistence. Shortly after Simpson arrived in the valley, the camp's mess cook was troubled by dust-coated Goshutes hov-

ering over his cook fires with their "unkept and lively hair." When one of
the warriors reached for an unattended piece of meat, the cook drew his
pistol and jokingly pointed it at the desert nomad. With the first click of
the weapon the Indians scattered into the brush, fleeing for their lives. In a
belated effort to take a grip on the matter, Simpson rushed across the
campground and cautioned his men to control their tempers in dealing
with the Indians, lest a fatal error in judgment bring the expedition to an
untimely end.[54]

Soon after this incident the entire party again moved westward. From
Reese Valley Simpson pushed through the Shoshone Mountains into
Woodruff Valley and camped at Smith Creek to await the return of their
guide. When John Reese failed to appear, Simpson sent a relief party of
four men headed by Ute Pete north to locate the missing scout. The
rescue team worked its way along Smith Creek, slowly advancing down a
newly discovered trail leading through the mountains, but failed to find
any trace of the missing guide. A second effort was ordered the following
day but returned with equally disappointing results.[55] To Simpson the
situation appeared bleak.

In the continuing silence of the third day, a half-hidden figure was
spied working his way through the sagebrush toward the expedition's
draft animals. From a distance he was mistaken for a marauding Indian,
and a squad of dragoons was ordered out to intercept him. Within minutes the soldiers surrounded the intruder; however, the dragoons, hardly
able to believe their eyes, found him to be their guide—a ragged corpse of
a man supporting his badly blackened body on two wooden sticks. Soon
after being taken back to camp, Reese lost no time recounting the terrible
calamities that had befallen him. On his return from the western slope of
the Lookout Mountains, a savage and desolate range seventeen miles and
two days from the main party, his scant provisions were about exhausted
when his mules gave out, forcing him to walk through a harsh belt of
mesquite desert. Without matches to kindle a fire, he endured the torment
of dropping temperatures until the next morning. Summoning up every
ounce of energy, he wandered on an unchartered course before he
encountered a friendly party of Digger Indians who reset his course
toward Smith Creek. Suffering from gnawing hunger, fatigue, and cold,
Reese was offered three fat rats by the Indians but could not bring himself
to eat them.[56] Summing up his experiences, he reported that the country
through which he had passed was an astonishing region that sweltered
under a burning sun that scorched everything in sight.

After much reconnoitering and searching along Smith Creek, the
expedition moved ponderously over the flats near Lookout Mountain and
rested at Middle Gate Creek. The character of the land from this point to
Carson Lake turned into a dry alkali sea, a lunar land of bald rock and
hard-baked white sand that extracted an incredible degree of suffering

from the men of the expedition. Because they were forced to watch the horizon until their eyes burned, Simpson devised special equipment to protect his men and animals from the blinding glare of the encrusted salt flats. All this scarcely deterred the commander, who believed the hard surface flats ideally suited for heavy overland traffic.[57] Still moving west, the expedition found almost no vegetation, and with the surrounding earth shimmering with furious heat, Simpson pressed forward toward the northern shore of Carson Lake. Reaching this position, the soldiers found a ribbon of lush, green marsh grass holding the desert at bay, but two large tributaries prevented the troops from circling around the large inland lake.

Moving as quickly as the weather would permit, Simpson retraced his steps south to the Walker River and proceeded northwestward to the bend of the Carson River. The south bank of the stream was followed for twenty miles to a point across the river from the Pleasant Grove mail station. Simpson found the normally lethargic stream a raging torrent—a boiling avalanche of water that prevented mules from standing against its current.

Across the river, the agent for the California Mail Company pulled down an abandoned building and constructed a cottonwood raft to ferry Simpson's men and equipment over the raging floodwaters. To reach the opposite shore tow ropes were taken across and lashed securely to prevent the wagons from drifting downstream. But despite this precaution the first vehicle capsized, throwing the cook and several teamsters into the icy river. Fortunately, the men managed to reach the opposite bank safely, after being carried a short distance downstream. The day dragged on. After seven hours the party succeeded in ferrying all of its wagons across the turbulent current to Pleasant Grove where the expedition regrouped before continuing its march.

From this point it was only a short distance to the mining camp of Chinatown, a cluster of squalid-looking buildings at the mouth of Gold Canyon, inhabited by fifty hardworking Asians. Here the engineer was intrigued by the sight of a foreign culture in the midst of the wilderness and could not resist wandering off into the sweet-smelling opium dens.

They were reclining, facing each other on a kind of platform the head supported by a stool or bench. Between them a lamp was burning. They had a pipe of about two feet long, the bowl of its being two-thirds of the distance from the mouth end. One or the other keeps the bowl, charged with opium, constantly applied to the lamp, and drawing hard, passes the smoke through the nose and mouth.[58]

Eight dollars worth of opium lasted two persons six months. "It stupefies," Simpson remembered in his journal, "rather than enlivens, and when endulged in excessively, perfectly paralyzes the energies."[59]

The lights of the rooms glowed faintly as the captain witnessed a unique form of Chinese gambling: "They have a large number of pieces, like dominos, and counters, and take a great deal of interest in the game; run through it with the greatest dexterity and rapidity." Concluding his remarks, he added, "They are represented as being very fond of gambling when they have nothing else to do, and not unfrequently lose all their earnings in this way."[60]

After a three-hour rest, the expedition left the mining camp and traced its way to the next settlement. Traveling through open country for twelve miles, the party reached Carson City, a mixed collection of twelve frame houses and two trading posts located at the base of the Sierra Nevada. The discovery of gold in the nearby canyons that would transform the poverty-plagued settlement into one of the most prosperous communities of the territory had not yet occurred. Halfway through the hamlet they were greeted by Major M. Ormsby, an important political figure of Eagle Valley. After an overnight stop the column swept on. When the exploring party took to the road again, they followed the well-traveled emigrant road and trudged into Genoa on the morning of June 13, shortly after dawn.

Amid a carnival whirl, Simpson led his men triumphantly through the heart of the town where their exploits were publicly acknowledged. The American flag fluttered, the local militia gave them a thirteen-gun salute, and the cheering people crowded around the exhausted marchers.[61] Later that day the captain was able to report to the enthusiastic audience that he had shortened the emigrant trail between Salt Lake and the Sierra Nevada by several hundred miles. After basking in the glow of well-deserved honors, the army moved through the crowds and camped a short distance from the southern edge of the town in the giant pine forests at the foot of the Sierra Nevada.

Here Simpson left his party for a "flying visit" to San Francisco, traveling in the company of Major Fredrick Dodge, Indian Agent for western Utah. The journey across the eastern slope of the Sierra Nevada to Placerville was a grueling eighty-mile-long mule ride over Dagget's Trail, south of Lake Tahoe. To their surprise, the pair encountered telegraph wires strung through the pine forest in an erratic line stretching across the green wilderness in the direction of the Great Basin. Crossing over to the western slope of the mountains with some relief and improved spirits, Simpson noted the incredible pine forests that guarded the trail like inanimate sentinels.

Presto, as soon as you place your foot on the Sierra Nevada a new order of nature appears. The eternal sagebrush, (artemisa) of which you have not for a day been out of sight since you left the Rocky Mountains, and the scrub cedar, which is the principle tree, disappear entirely, and in their stead lofty pines and firs become the characteristics. These attain an enormous size, the former being frequently seen as much as eight feet in diameter. The streams are more numerous, and appear as pure gushing rapids or cataracts, leaping over precipices, or beautiful lakes.[62]

A cool, pine-scented evening welcomed the two men to Placerville.

While in Placerville, Simpson visited Colonel Fred A. Bee, president of the Placerville and St. Joseph Telegraph Company, who had already taken positive steps to extend his lines into the Great Basin. For nearly an hour Simpson outlined his outward trace, attempting to enlist support for his new road, and he later received Bee's assurance that his firm would consider stringing its lines across the freshly blazed overland trail. But the engineer requested a delay in construction until variations of the route could be explored during Simpson's return trip to Camp Floyd.

Abandoning the saddle-worn mules, Simpson and Dodge traveled the next twenty-seven miles by stage to Folsom where they continued their journey by rail to Sacramento. The exuberant visitors noted that the river port had assumed new importance because of its proximity to the mines, but they tarried only long enough to board the shallow-draft river steamboat *Eclipse* bound for San Francisco. The captain filled his passing hours viewing the serenity of the surroundings which he attempted to describe to his brother in a letter later published in the *Valley Tan*. "California, I can only say, is, as I believe destined to be a great, if not the greatest, State in the Union. Her towns and cities vie with any east of the Rocky Mountains, and her population, like her soil, teems with a vigor which can only be comprehended by those who have been in her midst."[63] He continued:

> The people of the East can have no concept of the progress this young sister of the Confederacy has made in all the elements which go to make up a happy, powerful, and efficient State. The secret is in her climate, her soil, her productions, vegetation, cereal, mineral, her splendid rivers, her lovely scenery, her magnificent harbor of San Francisco, her relatedness to the commerce of the Indies and China, and the so-called Eastern World generally; all these have made her what she is, and as she grows in age so will all these advantages continue to cause her to grow in wealth and power.[64]

Landmarks of prosperity were everywhere apparent in San Francisco. Austerity had lost all meaning. Larger and more refined than Sacramento, the port city seemed to overflow with the rich products of the land— grain, wine, cheese, and ordinary staples were found in great abundance. The city was a hive of commerce and industry; international and urban with pretentions of culture, it was the metropolis of much of the Pacific Coast.

Walking along the streets as a common tourist, Simpson met several New Jersey acquaintances, and later he was interviewed by the owners of the *Alta California*. During his brief visit, the proprietors of the newspaper requested Simpson to allow one of their commercial correspondents in Sacramento, Walter Lowery, to return with the expedition to Camp Floyd. The unfortunate employee, struck with a fatal pulmonary disease, wished to return to his friends and relatives in Philadelphia before his expected death. The captain initially refused. With complete candor he pointed out that the return journey through unmapped country, with all of its unpredictable delays and dangers, promised to be as difficult as the original passage west. However, it was hard for Simpson to refuse, despite Lowery's physical condition and age; consequently, the correspondent was allowed to accompany the expedition as far as his health would permit. The hurried pace of San Francisco came to an end for the captain after two days. On his return trip to Genoa, he stopped in Sacramento where Colonel Bee introduced him to Lowery, who refused to be dissuaded from making the journey across the Basin.[65]

Before a week had run its course both men were subjected to night rides across the craggy mountains, having placed their lives in the hands of a drunken stagecoach driver with a warped sense of humor. Traveling the route safely, the pathfinder and his guest rejoined the expedition at Genoa. The harrowing experience infuriated Simpson, who later recommended to the War Department that Congress appropriate at least $30,000 to improve the Genoa–Folsom trace.

In the meantime, Carson City was preparing for Simpson's return with a formal ball in his honor. However, only two outfits of clothing were found suitable for the occasion among the explorers. When the celebration took place on the evening of June 23, the greater part of the expedition's members spent the night in their wall tents or around two barrels of whiskey that were set out for them in the streets by the town's merchants.[66]

The expedition was provided with extra rations by the citizens of Genoa, and the following morning it started the march eastward, taking advantage of the unheated mountain air. When the trail reached the Carson River, where they crossed without difficulty, Simpson dispatched John Reese to mark a trail around the southern shore of Carson Lake. However, after the expedition reached Pleasant Grove the guide reported the new trace offered one of the most formidable barriers of the entire route. By slow stages the expedition advanced eastward for eight days, detouring at unscheduled intervals to explore alternatives to their original trail. Resuming their march southeastward around the Lookout Mountains, the party was struck by violent columns of dust that whirled up into the air, driven by howling winds that stung the gloomy column with restless fury. Without a moment's rest, the slow, painful advance continued, snaking through a wild sea of moving desert.

From the Antelope Mountains, Simpson ordered John Reese, Ute Pete, and four dragoons, equipped with ten days' provisions, to examine the unexplored country south of Hasting's Pass seeking to discover a southern corridor to Camp Floyd. The advance scouting guides made their way through the desert with great difficulty before sending back word that a new route, well off the main trail, had been located. "The pass had been found by Ute Pete," Simpson penned in his journal, "who though he had been four days and nights without food, except roots, yet had been instrumental of finding us a pass, and thus enabling us to keep on our course."[67]

Threading through the last tortuous passage that cut the desert to the south, Simpson found cliff-rimmed canyons so deep that they hid strayed livestock, summer wind squalls that blew up without a moment's notice, and a short supply of water and grass. Twice the party retraced its steps to save the few remaining cattle from dying. "On one occasion the animals were without water for sixty hours," the engineer wrote, "and when they did drink could not be generally satisfied with less than eight buckets full."[68]

After what seemed an eternity of ploughing through the treacherous country parallel to the outgoing trace some fifty miles away, the tired soldiers passed through the Mon-tim Range by way of Horse Canyon and entered Steptoe Valley near its southern extreme. Working painfully eastward, traveling across the route developed by William Wall in 1857, Simpson noted that the region south of the House Range was a mountain of contorted rock, void of both water and grass, thinly covered with inedible desert foliage. The difficult return march through burning heat, dust storms, and unyielding terrain was faced with resolution and courage. In the midst of growing difficulties, the column's remaining foot-weary mounts stampeded, crazed by heat and thirst. Floundering, hopelessly lost in a raging thunderstorm, the expedition stumbled on unexpected good fortune—an Indian. The man on whom the fate of the expedition now depended was a middle-aged Indian, a quiet man with a distant look in his eyes. Though badly crippled and paralyzed, the former warrior "suffered himself to be taken up bodily and put on a mule and rode as a guide to the water twelve miles. . . ." Back on the trail again, the reconnaissance party camped at Good Indian Springs, named in honor of the good Samaritan, and took a well-earned rest. Some hours later, Simpson ordered his men to collect the milling herd in a narrow gorge, surrounded by dunes of coarse gravel.[69]

His mission concluded, the Indian volunteered the services of his son, apparently his only visible means of support, to guide the party through the mountains to Skull Valley. The grateful soldiers fastened together a pair of crutches, but soon realized that both the old Indian's legs were paralyzed from the waist down. Saddened by the sight, Simpson offered the Indian a bottle of "Schidedom Schnapps," but to the engineer's surprise, the warrior insisted that the liquor be massaged into his lifeless limbs. To ease his suffering, the crippled Indian was transferred to a spring wagon and driven east of the Thomas Mountains, where he and his son found shelter in a small valley.[70]

With the most dangerous section of the trail now behind him, the engineer divided his command and proceeded ahead to Camp Floyd with a small escort of dragoons. It was still light on the evening of August 4 when Simpson rode into the military reservation. Shortly after his arrival, he conferred with General Johnston and trumpeted his new highway to the Pacific as the western terminus of a new transcontinental wagon road.

The general was as good as his word. In less than twenty-four hours he dispatched Lieutenant J. L. Kirby Smith with a small construction crew to widen and straighten the last hundred miles of the southern road, to identify the overland with stakes and guide posts, and to build water tanks wherever possible. John Reese agreed to guide the expedition and interpret the rough map of the trail furnished by Captain Simpson. In that same week a half dozen California-bound emigrant trains were already following the trace, having been supplied with an itinerary at Camp Floyd. The road party of soldiers had scarcely left when Russell, Majors & Waddell laid plans to drive a thousand head of cattle over the route to California. Unfortunately, the firm delayed moving the livestock out of Rush Valley. Already weakened by the lack of good grazing land, 3,500 oxen were later caught in a severe blizzard that caused the death of two-thirds of the herd.[71]

Seven days after his triumphant emergence from the western desert, Simpson was on the trail again. Operating under modified orders largely due to the lateness of the season, the topographical engineer was instructed by General Johnston to explore a new road from Round Valley to Fort Bridger by way of the Uinta Mountains.[72] In the pre-dawn hours of August 9, Simpson and a vanguard of fifty-four men hurried up the road to Round Valley, trailing a caravan of eight quartermaster wagons, a spring wagon, one light ambulance, and ninety-eight animals. After an overnight stay at Heber City, a newly planted Mormon colony named after a member of the First Presidency, the expedition followed a tributary of the Timpanogos River to the foothills of the Uinta Mountains trying to find a suitable road across the base of the high range. Moving through a broken passage in the mountains to the headwaters of Potts Fork, the pathfinders followed the Duchesne River southward across a great interior plateau to the junction of the Uinta River. The long trek through the unpredictable country proved more difficult and dangerous than any

Simpson had surveyed to that point. The flurry of exploring activity through the broken foothills, exhausting men and animals, caused him great concern over the safety of the expedition. Facing the task of marking a passage over the Uintas, the engineer found a trail of long sloping grades that proved to be impracticable for wagon travel or pack trains without considerable investment of time and money.[73]

Retracing his steps to Round Valley, Simpson penciled a note to Johnston recommending a new reconnaissance north of the Uinta and Green Rivers, then eastward to the newly discovered gold fields of Colorado. Nearly a year later, in 1860, Captain Henry R. Seldon was authorized to make the military survey suggested by the engineer.[74] The rendezvous over, the engineer ordered a portion of his command under Lieutenant Alexander Murry to march directly to Fort Bridger across the route of 1858, while he and six men explored two shorter trails across the mountains. Neither survey proved important.

Seventeen days after leaving Camp Floyd, on August 29, 1859, the remaining elements of the expedition rode into Fort Bridger. Before a week had run its course, the column was on the trail to Fort Leavenworth; however, before Simpson reached Fort Laramie, he learned that his entire survey was under question.

No sooner had emigration crowded the trail, attracted by its shorter distance of 300 miles, than very disturbing reports reached Camp Floyd that the trace was far more troublesome than advertised.[75] Travelers found the desert east of the Lookout Mountains too difficult for ordinary wagon travel, which caused significant delays in the overland passage to California. Beyond Rush Valley the trail was generally drier than reported by Simpson, resulting in heavy losses of cattle and draft animals. Moreover, the heavy volume of traffic denuded the surrounding countryside of its natural pasturage, forcing the wayfarers to feed their livestock precious reserves of grain. General Johnston ordered Captain Henry F. Clarke to head a full-strength squad of dragoons to investigate these and other allegations.[76]

Several weeks later, Captain Clarke, having covered an estimated distance of 140 miles, reported that the emigrants' complaints had not been exaggerated and recommended no further use of the road for the remainder of the season. From Camp Floyd, the general sent a hurried dispatch to Captain Simpson at Fort Leavenworth directing him to halt immediately all attempts to turn the tide of migration from the Humboldt Trail until further study of the road could be made.[77] Nevertheless, Johnston was still optimistic about the newly forged link with California. Though the sweep of the trail proved inadequate for large-scale migration, the land route was of "real value for military and mail purposes, especially in the summer and late in the fall."[78]

In the final analysis, Simpson's brilliant wagon road survey did not provide the ultimate answer to western emigration to California—no single trail would. However, the Simpson road left its mark in the Great Basin. By charting every stream, waterhole, and mountain pass through central Utah, Simpson cleared the way for the Pony Express and helped further the western extension of the first transcontinental telegraph line. Furthermore, the central overland stage found the snaking trail to be the most practical route across the Great Basin to the Pacific before it closed its operation nearly a decade later. In the confusion that blocked the army's penetration of the Colorado Plateau, it was Simpson who stimulated future surveys that ultimately led to the beginning of a regular freighting service between Utah and Colorado. Collateral gains in the realm of pure science added to the storehouse of knowledge of the botanical, zoological, and meteorological data of the Great Basin. Writing during the centennial year of Simpson's survey, historian William H. Goetzman claimed that "by combining his discoveries on the Bryan expedition . . . he was able to get a cross section of the entire Mississippi West."[79] For generations professional scientists would focus their energies on unlocking the secrets hidden deep in Utah's canyon and plateau country.

The Simpson expedition exploded the myth that the intermountain Great Basin was suitable only as a wild haunt for the American Indian, and it laid the future foundation for Nevada's early cattle and sheep industry. As Simpson recorded in his final report:

> I will remark however that the idea that seems to have been generally prevalent that the country intervening the Great Salt Lake valley and Carson valley is a great desert, is a mistake; and that, so far from the portion we went over being so, it is on the contrary made up of mountain ranges, quite well supplied with water and valleys, along with run fertilising streams. . . . In addition to this, the mountains are covered with cedar, pine, fir, pinion . . . and mountain mahogany.[80]

Though his expedition brought Simpson no enduring personal fame, it was the high-water mark of his career and aided materially in pushing the American frontier to the Pacific.

Brigham Young. Photograph
taken about 1850.

General Albert Sidney
Johnston. Photo from
National Archives.

Government Train en route to Utah, 1857-58

Artist's rendering of Johnston's Army en route to Utah.

Daniel H. Wells

General Thomas L. Kane

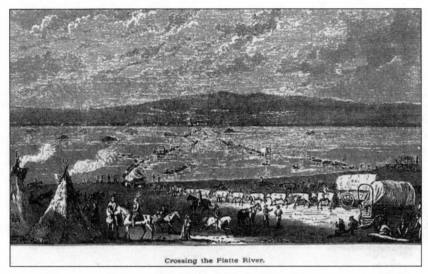

Crossing the Platte River.

Artist's rendering of Johnston's Army crossing the Platte River en route to Utah. Taken from *The Life of Gen. Albert Sidney Johnston* by William Preston Johnston (New York, 1878).

Artist's rendering of Johnston's Army en route to Utah caught in a snow storm.

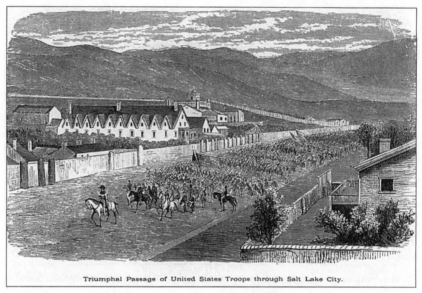

Triumphal Passage of United States Troops through Salt Lake City.

Artist's rendering of the entrance of Johnston's Army into Salt Lake City. Taken from *The Life of Gen. Albert Sidney Johnston* by William Preston Johnston (New York, 1878).

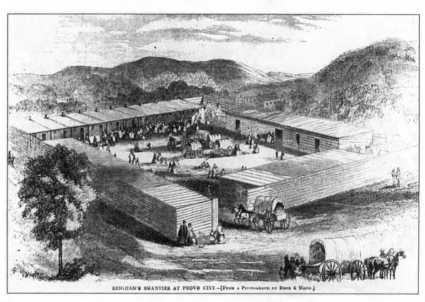

BRIGHAM'S SHANTIES AT PROVO CITY.—[FROM A PHOTOGRAPH BY BURR & MODO.]

Artist's rendering of the temporary shelters used by the families of Brigham Young when they left their homes in Salt Lake City and moved south at the coming of the Federal troops in 1858. From *Harper's Weekly*, October 9, 1858.

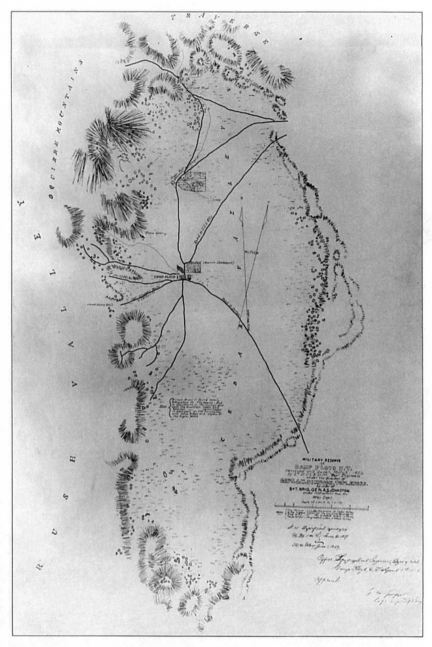

Map showing general location of Camp Floyd.

Camp Floyd. View of street between commissary buildings and regimental guardhouses, looking east. Photo taken by photographer of J.H. Simpson Expedition, January, 1859. National Archives.

Camp Floyd. View of Headquarters and ordinance quarters from the northeast. Photo taken by photographer of the J.H. Simpson Expedition, January, 1859. National Archives.

Drawing of Camp Floyd by Captain Albert Tracy from his journal.

Camp Floyd. View of street between the quartermaster's building and the commissary building from Headquarters, looking east. Photo taken by photographer of the J.H. Simpson Expedition, January, 1859. National Archives.

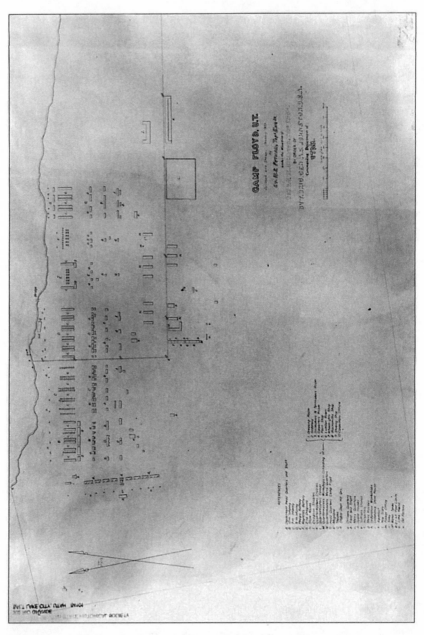

Map showing layout of buildings at Camp Floyd.

Camp Floyd. View of north end of Camp Floyd, looking northeast. This is the left-hand part of a three picture panorama. Photo taken by photographer of the J.H. Simpson Expedition, January, 1859. National Archives.

Camp Floyd. View of middle portion of panorama, looking northeast. Photo taken by photographer of the J.H. Simpson Expedition, January, 1859. National Archives.

View of the south end of Camp Floyd looking east. This is the right-hand view of the panorama. Photograph taken by photographer of the J.H. Simpson Expedition, January, 1859. National Archives.

Brigade Drill in Camp on Shore Utah Lake.

Brigade drill of Camp Floyd troops in camp at Utah Lake. Photo donated by Ruth Murdock.

Philip St. George Cooke.

Lieutenant Colonel Charles F. Smith, second commander at Camp Floyd.

The Bugle Corps of Johnston's Army at Camp Floyd. Photo donated by Nicholas G. Morgan.

Camp Floyd. View of regimental parade ground looking from middle point toward Headquarters. Photo taken by photographer of J.H. Simpson Expedition, January, 1859. National Archives.

Camp Floyd. View of regimental parade ground, looking east. Photo taken by photographer of J.H. Simpson Expedition, January, 1859. National Archives.

William (Bill) Hickman.
Photograph by C.W. Carter.

John D. Lee.

Mountain Meadows Massacre site seen from the top of the hill to the north and east of the camp. Includes a rock behind which Mormons hid while shooting into the emigrant camp which was just beyond the car in the distance.

Judge John H. Cradlebaugh.

Alfred Cumming, second Governor of Utah Territory (1858–1861).

THE SCENE OF THE MOUNTAIN MEADOWS MASSACRE, UTAH TERRITORY.—[FROM A RECENT SKETCH.]

Artist's rendering of aftermath of Mountain Meadows Massacre. Printed in *Harper's Weekly*, August 13, 1859.

Painting by C.B. Hancock showing the escape from the Mormons of Dr. Garland Hurt, Indian Agent for Utah Indians, in 1858.

Chief Walker (Wakara), painting by Solomon Carvalho.

Chief Kanosh of the Ute Tribe. Painting by Solomon Carvalho.

A group of Ute Indians including Arrowpeen (Arapene), head chief of the tribe. Photo taken on the outskirts of Camp Floyd looking northwest towards the Oquirrh Mountains. National Archives.

Camp Floyd site. Photo taken in March, 1931, by Everett L. Cooley.

Building believed to have been the commissary. Now restored as part of Camp Floyd State Park.

CHAPTER NINE

THE SEARCH FOR AN INDIAN POLICY

The present course pursued with the Indians of Utah is neither humane nor honorable. It is the curse to the white settlers and tends to the extermination of the Indian.

—Deseret News, *1858*[1]

As THE FEDERAL GOVERNMENT tightened its grip on the territory, another drama played itself out on the Mormon frontier—the disposition of the Indians of the Great Basin. Although controversy over land ownership helped precipitate the Utah War, the presence of Indians in the territory was not a formidable obstacle to white settlement and development. The basic Indian policy of the Mormons was formulated during the first decade of settlement and developed from the experiences of the frontier, relying on force rather than a fellow feeling between the Indians and the settlers. Although the Saints' beliefs, policies, and actions towards the Indians were unchallenged, many of their undertakings turned out badly.

In dealing with their nomadic neighbors in the Great Basin, the Mormons were no more responsive than the federal bureaucracy that governed both peoples. The national government had little understanding or sympathy for native rights. Consequently, in the decade before the military occupation of Utah, the Saints were given the widest latitude in dealing with the Indians. "The remoteness of Utah from Washington," wrote the Commissioner of Indian Affairs to Brigham Young, "and the little that is known of the Indians in that territory render it necessary that the management of our Indians Affairs in that quarter be left almost entirely to your discretion and judgement."[2] With this *carte blanche* as superintendent of Indian Affairs for Utah, Young was expected to develop and enforce rational policies for Indians who spoke a dozen or more languages and whose cultural diversity was overwhelming.

The Book of Mormon taught that the western tribes were "descendants from Joseph who was sold into Egypt, and that the land of America is a promised land unto them,"[3] which complicated the Mormons' feelings for them. Brigham Young expounded on his benevolent attitude toward the Indians in a statement to Isaac Haight during the troubled fall of 1858: "It is not to make their situation more intolerable that we pick up and sustain the poor, weak, and downtrodden race, but rather to strengthen, and so far as lies within our power, to redeem them from their low and degraded condition."[4] In the light of his conviction, the Mormon leader struggled to maintain a humane and just policy of peaceful coexistence based on the oversimplified philosophy "that it was better not to fight them but feed them well, treat them kindly and they will kill far less of our people."[5]

Well-meaning as the prophet's words were, the Mormons generally subscribed to the traditional feelings of frontiersmen toward the Indians. When the Mormons pushed into the desert and occupied vast stretches of land along the Spanish Trail, the Indians were unprepared to deal with them.

The origin of the Utah Indians is shrouded in mystery, and none of the Basin tribes approached the Plains or Atlantic Indian nations in group sophistication. Scattered over a wide geographic territory, neither understanding nor appreciating the concept of a powerful centralized government, they retained a traditional mode of life that was not always satisfactory to their white neighbors. They did not unite against a common foe, and thus fell victim to change on their own ground. Faced with the question of feeding and caring for the Indians, Young adopted various schemes to put public lands into the hands of white settlers at terms that Indians could not afford.[6]

The irresistible force the Indians felt was from a tide of missionary-settlers, armies of God who carried their weapons in one hand and the Book of Mormon in the other. They tried to assimilate the Indians into the mainstream of Mormon society, converting them to Christianity rather than killing them, but the Indians did not cooperate. The Saints took Indian land in exchange for products valued by the Indians—but the tribesmen continued to live in their traditional ways, and in hard times often on the edge of starvation. The territorial Indians ignored political and economic changes, continued to claim autonomy on their lands, and grew increasingly fearful that they were doomed to expulsion.

Meanwhile, no uniform pattern developed to deal with the Indians—the Mormons related to them as they thought conditions required. The Saints managed to gain control over the Indians by waging a series of brush-fire wars, scrimmaging with one tribe after another between 1850 and 1857. The Indians reverted to their old fighting ways to survive—raiding ranches, farms, settlements, and the overland trails. These acts brought punitive expeditions by the Nauvoo Legion, and in those campaigns Indian casualty rates were high.[7]

In the years without war, the Saints resorted to peace councils with their neighbors, making and remaking their Indian policy; but although Young had a deep and honest concern for the welfare of the Indians, his first duty was always to his followers. In the period before the Utah War, he negotiated with his charges as governor, Indian superintendent, and, more importantly, as Mormon spiritual leader. The contest was unequal. The widely dispersed, loosely organized bands of Indians lived in the past and did not always fully comprehend the meaning of agreements that ceded their hunting and fishing grounds near white settlements.

Those natives who chose not to retreat signed away their land in return for Mormon protection, and more often than not they existed by begging or by bartering. Whenever Indians stood in the way of land-hungry settlers, they faced a holy war. The Mormons were committed to the belief that Utah had been set apart as the Kingdom of God for the gathering of His children. Understandably, then, the pioneers closed ranks in dealing with the tribes and lived in constant fear of hostilities.

Periodically the Indians fought to keep their homes, but without success. Although the Saints generally tried to avoid conflicts and attempted to improve the lot of their aboriginal countrymen, the Indians caused the Mormons many problems. A twentieth-century Mormon historian wrote that "the more distant tribesmen proved either completely immune or only slightly affected by exposure to the superior culture, excepting to avail themselves of its weapons and vices."[8]

The territorial Indians reacted to Mormon policies in various ways, but the strongest and most warlike tribes in the north presented a serious challenge to pioneer settlement. Until the Saints extended their colonies to Brigham City, the Bannocks and Shoshone were relatively peaceful, but the Mormons' entrance into Indian hunting grounds brought swift retribution. Because of this bloodshed, the Brigham City settlers moved into two log stockades during the years 1853–1855.[9] The Shoshones, mounted on horses and well-armed, were at the peak of their power, and stubbornly resisted Mormon penetration of their frontier. War parties menaced travelers, sometimes stealing their livestock or taking their lives. The militancy of the Bannocks and Shoshones may have turned Brigham Young's thoughts to the more friendly bands in the Santa Clara country near the Colorado River.

No goal commanded more of his attention than the elimination of slavery among the southern tribes, a profitable practice that originated with Spanish traders from New Mexico. Powerful raiding parties from central Utah overran the Santa Clara villages, carrying off women and children and bartering them to the Spanish for horses, guns, and ammunition.[10] Mormon efforts to eliminate slave traffic between the territories were successful. Whatever the misgivings of the southern tribes toward Mormon infiltration of their land, open resistance to the Saints was scarce. The condition of the southern tribes improved slowly before the Civil War, although emancipation did not bring equality to Native Americans. Granting token protection to the southern Indians was profitable for the Mormons. Not only were they able to secure the right of passage through the Santa Clara country, but also they were permitted unrestricted settlement on land not occupied by the Indians.

Young proposed that Congress extinguish all Indian titles to the land, substituting a system of reservations throughout the settled parts of the territory.[11] Despite Washington's suspicions of the proposal, Brigham ordered three "Indian farms" to be laid out to grow food for the Indians. These farms were financed by private charity and Church funds. Indian affairs in Iron, San Pete, and Millard counties were managed by John A. S. Smith, James Case, and Anson Call, Mormon agents who provided crop and subsidy incentives for the Indians. In these early adventures the Saints were following their own best interests, wrote Gentile agents who publicized the weaknesses of Mormon policies:

> The Mormons . . . are making settlements, throughout the territory, on all the most valuable lands—extending these settlements for three hundred miles south, from this city Salt Lake City, and North to Mary's River, and Carson Valley. . . . The Mormons at first conciliated the Indians by kind treatment but when they once got foothold, they began to force their way—the consequence was a war with the Indians. This, they fear will again be the result, wherever the Mormons may make a settlement. The Indians having been driven from their lands and their hunting grounds destroyed without any compensation therefore, they are in many instances reduced to a state bordering on starvation.[12]

When Young sought to stifle criticism of his superintendency, federal officers blackened his name with accusations that he had plundered the agency's treasury, saddled the Indians with onerous treaties, and spawned dissension between his wards and the federal government.[13] They also claimed that he was responsible for Indian reprisals on the overland trails leading to the Pacific. Leaving these accusations to die a slow death in dusty departmental files in Washington, the Mormon superintendent voiced his own objections to bureaucratic bungling. Heading the list of his complaints were lagging federal appropriations, incompetent Indian agents, and the contradictory policy of encouraging the Mormons both to assimilate and segregate the Indians. The federal policies left Indian territorial affairs in a political limbo.

During this war of words, the federal government dispatched Doctor Garland Hurt to Utah in 1855 to help oversee the administration of Indian Affairs and to establish three reservations within the Great Basin. A supporter of cultural separatism and a strong advocate of Indian rights to their land, the young agent focused on the bitter struggle that engulfed the native tribesmen and their religious neighbors. His reaction to Mormon Indian policy was remarkably relaxed. In many respects Hurt carried out the program of Brigham Young, establishing a self-sufficient Indian farm economy adjusted to the white society's aims and institutions. The agent learned that agricultural accommodation was a slow process, with built-in shortcomings. Despite an empire of virgin soils, most Indians remained nomadic, reluctant to surrender their traditional ways for subsistence agriculture which they neither understood nor desired. Niggardly federal funds were a lean cushion against crop failures, so the reservation Indians were easily discouraged and became more dependent on government annuities. More seriously, perhaps, quarrels within the Utah agency hampered the conduct of Indian affairs, for Young was reluctant to yield any power to Gentile officials.

A new battle line was drawn when Hurt objected to Mormon missionary activity among the Indians. He accused the Mormons of creating dissension among tribal leaders and encouraging disloyalty toward the federal government. In a supplemental quarterly report that went over the head of Brigham Young, Hurt stated his fears. The missionaries "either accidentally or purposely created a distinction in the minds of the Indian Tribes of this territory, between Mormons and the people of the United States, that cannot act otherwise than prejudiced to the interest of the latter."[14] Countering this claim, Young answered that conditions on the overland during the California gold rush were responsible for the Indians' peculiar definition of settlers and overlanders:

> As regards Mormons and Americans the Indians themselves made the distinction when the California emigrants first made their appearance in this territory in 1849 and 50. They generally wearing so much more hair on their faces was one distinguishing which they soon learned but which was not of quite so much importance to the poor Indians as the following: they being in the habit of being shot by emigrants, and others traveling to California wher-

ever met by them, finding that the Mormons fed them and clothed them instead of killing them soon learned to enquire of every party they met whether they were Mormons or Americans, a distinction which they have and probably always will make.[15]

Hurt recommended to the Secretary of the Interior that Young be forbidden to regulate trade and intercourse with the Indians or carry out any activity that would extend Mormon influence on the reservations.[16] The message helped deepen the rift between Young and Hurt, each of whom was trying to maintain his own prestige and authority at the expense of the other.

Hurt began an investigation of Young's disbursal of agency funds. He warned that federal monies were being spent to further the interest of the Mormon Church and that a large part of the departmental budget was used to carry out religious missionary activity among the Native Americans.

There was also a flood of mail to Washington from embittered apostates and dissident Mormons requesting the removal of Brigham Young from territorial office. These complaints no doubt "influenced the government's decision to impose military occupation upon Utah."[17] Judged by its consequences, Hurt was largely responsible for the shelving of three Mormon proposals to Congress: Utah's admission to statehood, the removal of all Indians from white settlements, and the establishment of a land office to grant the Saints legal title to all settlements they occupied.[18] Predictably, Brigham reacted with a protest, voicing fresh objections to Hurt's activities in the territory. But Washington refused to reconsider. Hurt could not stand alone against the Mormon prophet, so he formed an alliance with David H. Burr, the territorial Surveyor General who had his own difficulties with the Saints.

The clash between Burr and Young raised in a new and spectacular form the question of Mormon claims to lands in the public domain without benefit of treaty, purchase, or congressional action. Almost from the day the Saints arrived in the Basin wilderness, Mormon editors had reminded Congress that primal and continued occupation of public lands entitled the people of the territory to the privilege of preemption.

> We have earned it faithfully and patriotically. We have earned it by our services against the nation from whose hands the land was wrested. We have earned it by the abandonment of happy homes in other lands. We have earned it by the blood of our brothers and sires and sons in its defense against the aboriginal savage. The extent and advancement of settlements and improvements testify whether we have not earned it by our industry. The graves of our kindred that form sorrowful guide boards on the path which led us here, testify whether we have not earned it by exposure and fatigue.

Besides there is no just reason why the preemption privilege should be withheld from Utah. Her citizens are a portion of the Commonwealth. Among them are a liberal number whose shares in the national danger extend back to the first wars subsequent to the revolution, and who inherit in a direct line a good share of the glory in the great struggle itself. Why should they now be refused a fair share in the national benefits and patronage?[19]

The fight for preemption was tied to Mormon expansion and added to Mormon discontent with the federal government and its agents in Utah. With the exception of a few thousand acres of land secured by land warrants by veterans of the Mexican War, the Mormons were squatters on the federal domain, although they monopolized the sale and disposition of territorial holdings by legislative fiat. Understandably, Burr's presence in the territory propelled him immediately into the limelight. Suspicious of the secrecy that surrounded his survey of central Utah, the Saints feared that he was only preparing for Gentile settlement of the territory. The Saints made his life singularly uncomfortable and "sought to impede the surveyor general's labor in every way possible, using intimidations, violence and their influence over the Indians."[20] Yet he continued to believe that in a test of strength he would prevail over the Mormons. It proved to be a nearly fatal error.

A traumatic event affecting Hurt and Burr occurred during the autumn of 1856, when the duties of their offices brought them both to the territorial capital at Fillmore. The two men and their aides rode down the Mormon corridor to inspect the Indian farm at Corn Creek. After visiting several sparsely settled and outlying Mormon villages, including Fillmore, they reached the reservation. Here they were informed by a reservation Indian that a Saint had warned the leading tribesmen that Burr planned to deprive them of their lands and, for good measure, would arrest a dozen warriors for the murder of Captain Gunnison the previous year. Not surprisingly, the surveyor denied the report, promising the Indians that he would use his influence to protect them against Mormon encroachment upon their reservation.[21]

The small party returned to the territorial capital, where they found every hotel and public inn closed. But before they reached the outskirts of town they were hailed by Peter Robinson, an old friend of Hurt's, who invited the weary travelers to spend the night at his home. They accepted the offer and followed Robinson to his home, which lay a short distance from the uncompleted capitol building. The host and his guests were not under shelter long before the arrival of another visitor, Edwin Pugh, an unprepossessing man who radiated the quiet strength of a mountaineer. The six men rehashed the Corn Creek Indian gossip about Burr. Finally, Pugh invited Burr's aides, R. W. Jarvis and James White, to spend the remainder of the night at his quarters. The offer was accepted and the three men walked the tree-lined streets to a small cottage where, behind shuttered windows, they resumed their conversation. Suddenly a volley of rocks came flying through the windows, striking a lighted coal-oil lamp and causing it to explode into a roaring fireball. The startled men rushed to extinguish the blaze before the fire could spread beyond the sitting room.

In the confusion that followed, a deep voice was heard in the night's blackness calling out Pugh's name and warning that, unless he appeared outside, the house would be burned to the ground. After a short period of time, Pugh stepped cautiously out of the small frame house and, peering out into the shadowed street, spied a half-dozen men standing around the front of the cottage.

"What are you doing with those damned Americans!" yelled one of the assailants.

"They are not Americans, but Mormons," replied Pugh in a quaking voice that left little doubt that he was a poor liar. The ringleader of the band stepped forward, and, pointing his finger in the direction of the house, warned that he had followed the Gentiles and had posted a guard to follow the their movements. A second man claimed that he had passed Hurt and Burr after the federal agents had departed from Corn Creek. A third man shouted that he had warned the Indians that the government had come to arrest them for the Gunnison Massacre. Again Pugh said nothing, and shortly afterwards the armed intruders called an end to the whole affair and disappeared into the night.[22] Reports of Mormon obstructionism soon found their way to Washington and relations between the two forces were rapidly reaching a breaking point.

Several months after this incident, unusually heavy emigration and massive crop failures severely tested the Mormon axiom that it was easier to "shoot Indians with tobacco and bread biscuits than powder and lead. . . ."[23] During the late winter of 1856–1857, a series of military skirmishes brought Indian-Mormon relations to a breaking point. The Saints answered the looting and intimidation by arming every able-bodied male and by imposing the Nauvoo Legion between the Indians and the settlers. Troubled by a series of Indian raids against his range cattle, one resident recalled that his rifle never left his side and was "always within arms length of his work bench in the day and near his bed at night."[24]

The pending invasion of Johnston's Army produced an immediate reversal of Brigham Young's attitude, aimed now not at warfare but at an alliance with the Indians against the approaching federal forces. Young's choice for negotiator with the Indians was Dimick Baker Huntington, a forty-nine-year-old frontiersman who had mastered a dozen Indian dialects and was a recognized authority on the habits of the western tribesmen.

Writing in his journal, Huntington complained that the Indians expressed a greater fear of the federal army than of the Mormon militia, and that they were determined to flee to the mountains and wait out the war. Huntington warned Chief Antero and eight warriors that if they did not fight the army alongside the Saints, they would have to face the troops alone if the Saints were defeated on the battlefield. But Antero answered that his tribe would not intervene.[25] Similar results grew out of conferences at Ogden, Tooele, Springville, Brigham City, and Salt Lake City. "I told him Arrowpeen [Arapeen] he might go as far as he could get but the Lord would fetch him out and he must do the work that God and the prophets has said they must do. Joseph's blood had got to [be] avenged and they had got to help to do it."[26] Arrowpeen refused to fight.

Next to Young, the man most concerned with Huntington's success or failure was Garland Hurt, one of the last Gentile officeholders in the territory. In his headquarters building at the Spanish Fork Reservation, the Indian agent viewed the Mormon activities with uneasiness. However, it was the news of the Mountain Meadows Massacre that brought Hurt to the decision to leave the territory. Unfortunately, the Mormons had their own plans for him.

The one sentiment shared by almost all Mormons was contempt for the unreconstructed Gentile official. In quieter times Hurt might have been overlooked as an innocent eccentric, but his extraordinary influence over his charges and his strong bid for leadership of the Gentile community made him an easy target for Mormon leaders who feared domestic intrigue. Furthermore, he refused to be run out of the territory like other officials, and remained a dangerous link between Washington and Utah. Obviously referring to Garland Hurt, Bishop Aaron Johnson of Spanish Fork complained: "It's raised the query in my mind if an influence for evil has not been used by some *one* in that quarter." Johnson also accused the agent of raising an army of Indians to be used against the Saints, and of trying to advance the Gentile cause in Utah.[27]

When word reached the Spanish Fork Reservation that Young had placed the territory under martial law, Hurt at last prepared to leave. Young's proclamation exaggerated with each retelling, and "put the Gentiles in the sweat," wrote John Lowe Butler, a high-ranking officer of the Nauvoo Legion.[28] Hurt cleared his desk of government business, inventoried the Indian property, and prepared to rendezvous with the Utah Expedition. But the Nauvoo Legion reacted swiftly against its adversary.

Early on the morning of September 15, 1857, a courier pulled up in front of the home of John Butler with the news "that Old Doc Hurt was going to skip his quarters and take up his abode in the mountains with the soldiers."[29] Describing subsequent events in his diary, Butler opened the story in more detail: "I went out and I called all the men in Spanish Fork together and told Colonel John S. Fulmer to take command of them, and go and take the Doctor. I knew it would take all the men we could raise for there was about two hundred Indians with him."[30] Mixed in with Colonel Fulmer's force were 250 men from the Springville and Payson militia. All of these troops gathered early the following morning at Spanish Fork and began the short march to the reservation. While the Nauvoo Legion moved along the road, an Indian runner was sent ahead with a message for the government agent. The note, suggesting that Hurt not leave the territory without a written pass from Young, warned that the Nauvoo Legion would "enforce the law at all hazards."[31]

Hurt was still not aware of the gravity of his situation and was in the process of thanking the messenger with a great show of kindness when another reservation Indian burst into the room yelling, "Friend, friend, the Mormons will kill you!" Aroused by this second alarm, Hurt left his desk, peered out the window, and experienced his worst single moment in the territory. "I saw from 70 to 100 armed dragoons stationed in the road about a mile from the house," he recalled, "and as I did not manifest quite so much concern as the Indians thought justified, they caught hold of me and gave me an understanding that they would not let me stay any longer."[32]

Hurt started to pack his official papers into two flour sacks, and was again interrupted, this time with a warning that the Mormons had blockaded Spanish Fork Canyon to prevent his escape. A third and then a fourth Indian entered the farm house with sharp messages that Springville and Payson militia were nearing Hurt's headquarters. From a second-story window the agent saw a force of grey-coated militiamen coming down the road, heading straight for the reservation.

Hurt saddled his horse and assembled a handful of trusted friends— Joseph P. Waters, Ute Pete, Sam, and Shower-Socket—and rode west toward Utah Lake while several hundred reservation Indians swarmed from hiding and charged the Nauvoo Legion. The militia fell back before them, offering no resistance. In the meantime, Hurt, Waters, and an escort of twelve Indian horsemen made their break for Spanish Fork Canyon and freedom.

Retracing their march to the mouth of the canyon, the military posse found themselves 400 yards behind the fleeing Gentiles. At last, after many hours in the saddle, Hurt ascended the mountain road and tried to cross the Spanish Fork River; but the stream was wider than he remembered. "I urged my horse," he reported later to his superior, "and he attempted to clear it at a single bound, but failing to reach the opposite bank with his hind feet, he fell back into the water and mud over the top of his hips. I alighted upon the bank over his head, and by pulling at the reins assisted him in extricating himself. . . ."[33] As soon as they got across the stream, Hurt and Waters stayed doggedly on the old trail through the mountains, followed closely behind by a rearguard of twelve warriors. In the gathering darkness, the horsemen rested for several hours, while Hurt remapped his strategy.

Unknown to the escaping Gentiles, the Mormons made little effort to continue their pursuit. "I knew it was no use to fight them for that would not bring the Doctor back," wrote John Butler, "so we held a council about what we should do. Some wanted to follow him and fight their way through, but the Doctor was on a horse as good a one as was in the Territory, and then he was well armed and had an escort of twelve Indians, the best warriors there was in the whole tribe."[34] Unfortunately, Hurt could not read the minds of the discouraged Mormon horsemen. Sometime before midnight he revised his plans and, although he was within a few miles of safety, he decided to return to the Indian farm where he hoped to restart his escape the following day.

Before the first light of morning, Hurt once more left the reservation and entered Spanish Fork Canyon, again escorted by 300 Indians who followed him through the Uinta Mountains, beyond the reach of his enemies.[35] When the party reached high country, an early winter storm took its toll in suffering. In deep ice and snow, they froze and starved for a month, and finally crawled miserably into Fort Bridger on October 23, 1857.

Having in a measure recovered from his ordeal, Hurt reported to Governor Cumming and General Johnston. Venting his personal quarrels with the Saints and his disgruntlement with Mormon Indian policy, Hurt painted a sordid picture of life in Utah under Brigham Young. Critics of the prophet were rare, he warned, which allowed federal laws and policies to be deliberately flouted. The army openly applauded Hurt's complaints. His strongly worded document warned that the Mountain Meadows Massacre was proof enough that a full-scale invasion of Utah was not only justified but necessary, if democratic institutions were to survive in the territory.[36]

While momentous decisions were in the making in Washington and at Camp Scott, Brigham Young increased his overtures to the Indians of the territory. The Indians, disgruntled by Mormon policies of the past, were unwilling to form new relationships with the Saints. Besides, they were convinced that the army would sweep the settlers from the territory and restore Indian control over the land.[37] Scattered bands of warriors, each bearing the bitterness of a decade, attacked isolated settlements and unprotected herds of livestock. Recounting his meetings with the Indians around campfires before this warfare, Dimick Huntington wrote:

> Pintuts sayed his Father had gone out to the soldiers and acted bad gut drunk and throwed him and the Mormons a way and said he had found out the American was good and the Mormons no

good Indians stole mutch of our stock in March, April, and May it was the Cumymbars and Gosha Uts the principle actors was Tabby-wepup, Ibim-muzup, Pooah-nan-kubbah Gosha Uts and Lego-ets Nara-coots and others of the Cunumbars May last or June 1 about 300 of the Uts came in to Utah Co down Provo canion from Camp Scot the principal men ware white Eye Tshappan-no-quint Tabby Anterro Tintick and commenced their stealing horses and killing cattle, Brother Brigham told me to give them some flour for they all came in to his office one by one and shook hands with him and the first Presidency they gave them nothing to eat and all they did was to use their squaws and had made them all sore when they had done talking I gave them 1200 lbs of flour and they mooved on to Springville whare Brigham gave them 6 beevs in a few days they mooved on to Spanish Fork and all the while they ware verry saucy and ugly Wah-toe-bict shot at Brother PH. L. Perry at Springville and shot at the Breathren at Spanish Fork and Pond Town stole the Breathrens horses cattle and sheep all the time. . . .[38]

Angry settlers suspected that the army was partially responsible for the sporadic violence marshaled against them, but Brigham was unsure of General Johnston's influence with the Indians. Young ordered his commanders to surrender all the livestock necessary to assure the neutrality of the Ute and Shoshone Indians. "We would prefer for you to say to the Indian," he wrote to Colonel Andrew Cunningham of the Nauvoo Legion, "if they have not enough of the Mormon cattle to come and get some more, but we would rather give them our cattle than to have them steal them."[39] As Indian resistance stiffened, Young emphasized the necessity of preventing further hostilities lest some unconsidered action drive the warriors into an alliance with the army. Continued fighting would paralyze the countryside. "Talk with the Indians," the prophet instructed his subordinates, "and exchange with them your wheat for cattle or things, make satisfactory arrangements with them. I have no objection but do insist that they shall be conciliated and not molested in consequence of this late affair by pursuing this course it will certainly have its influence after awhile and they will learn who are their friends."[40]

Such was the tone set by Brigham Young to all the military leaders under his command, including Church leaders throughout the Mormon frontier. "If any Indians in your neighborhood feel to carry out flour . . . you will furnish it from the tithing wheat in your possession and keep account thereof, and send word to Peteentneet, and all others who wish to come into our settlements and get something to eat."[41] Ultimately, the plan did not make the Indians into Mormon allies, or even keep them neutral.

The Indians seemed determined to play one side off against the other, unwilling to become pawns of either the Mormons or the army. The powerful northern Shoshone chieftain Washakie offered the services of his warriors to the army to drive the Mormons from the territory. Desperate to regain control of his homeland, he accused the Mormons of humiliating the Shoshone by driving them from their ancestral hunting grounds near Green River and robbing his intimate friend, Jim Bridger, of his trading post. He argued insistently that Brigham Young had attempted to alienate the Indians against the federal government, adding that the Shoshone were innocent of any wrongdoing against whites. Although the chief handed the army a powerful weapon, General Johnston gave Washakie's proposal a chilly reception, which reflected his own distrust of all Indians.

Listening half-heartedly to the warrior's complaints against the Saints, and giving some hope that the Indians could reclaim a part of their land, Johnston took the initiative to neutralize effectively the Indians. With studied tact and diplomacy, the general instructed the chief to stay clear of the Mormon pioneer settlements and not to obstruct the free passage of emigrants over the Oregon Trail. "Take your people to the buffalo country," Johnston advised the Shoshone chief, "do not connect yourself and people with the difficulties that exist between the Government and the Mormons."[42] Similar warnings were given to Ben Simons, a Delaware, and Little Soldier, a Shoshone sub-chief who controlled a small band of warriors around the present city of Morgan, Utah. In a council held by the army at Camp Scott, Johnston told the warriors: "Have nothing to do with existing difficulties; that the Great White Fathers did not wish them to connect themselves in any way with the Mormon trouble. . . ."[43]

Undaunted by this unsuccessful effort, the Indians pursued their own independent course against the Mormons, although rumors of an alliance persisted throughout the winter and lasted into spring. While the abrupt Shoshone exit from Fort Supply removed the immediate threat of an Indian-army alliance, reports circulated throughout Salt Lake City that Superintendent Jacob Forney had armed war parties near the Uinta Mountains with weapons superior to those carried by the Saints, preparatory to an attack against undefended Mormon settlements.[44] The fearful spectre of an alliance between the Indians and the army was reported by a Gosiute warrior, Dick Mooney. In part the tribesman claimed: "A big man named Forney in the Soldiers' camp . . . told the Weber Utes, that the soldiers were coming in with their big guns to kill all Mormons, all through the mountains; that Brigham had put a charm on Naracut's children, that made them die. . . ." No story was better arranged; however, the federal agent was ill-served by the remarkable statement that "Forney told them he could make medicine for Brigham and would kill him; that a long time ago he, Forney, had killed Joseph Smith very easy and he was a great deal bigger than Brigham, and that he could kill Brigham much easier. Naracuts said that Forney gave him a heap of powder for a buck-skin, and also gave them guns, and hats, and clothing."[45]

Brigham Young was hit hard by the worst attacks ever inflicted by the Indians on the Mormons and found it difficult to doubt the complicity of the army in these hostilities:

> When men are killed and scalped, and their horses, mules, and cattle are taken to the enemy's camp, and the Indians with their new blankets on their shoulders, guns and ammunition in their hands boast of having received these and other presents from the army, and themselves acting as their friends and our enemies, it proves, the charge of the President unfounded, as regards me and the people of this Territory, but saddles the foul slander most con-clusively upon the *immaculate soldiery* who have been sent to "cor-rect the morals" and teach a higher mode of warfare than practiced or known by the so-called "deluded fanatics and ignorant Mor-mons."[46]

Continuing to press his point, he catalogued Indian attacks on the western settlements in Tooele and Rush Valleys, as well as those in the north, where three Saints were killed, five wounded, and a considerable number of stock stolen. While these strikes were in progress, settlers in the region of south-central Utah braced themselves against imminent attack from the Uinta Utes, led by Garland Hurt.[47] Mormon morale plummeted, but the Indian sortie never materialized.

Although the army and the Mormons wasted a great number of words in counter-accusations, it soon became obvious to both parties that the Indians' strategy was to prolong hostilities in a desperate hope to regain control over the territory. Possessing neither the manpower nor the weapons to fight a modern war, the Indians verbalized their resent-ment of both the army and the Mormons as the situation demanded. More than one report substantiated this claim. While traveling the high-road between Fort Bridger and Salt Lake City, the federal peace commis-sioners reported numerous personal encounters with the Indians. At some point along the road near Green River, the caravan passed a band of Indians who asked Commissioner Powell if he was a Mormon. Powell replied he was not.

"Mormons no good!" the Indian answered in a forceful tone.

Moving down the trail a few miles, the party met still another group of warriors who asked the same question, but this time Powell answered he was a Mormon.

"Mormons, very good!" came the answer.

The story ended with Powell observing: "There was no confidence to be put in them."[48]

Immediately following the establishment of Camp Floyd, Johnston believed that nothing short of complete subjugation of all Indians was necessary before the final chapter of the frontier could be written. Viewing the long road of history, neither the Mormons nor the army believed that a permanent Indian homeland was to be found within the rim of the Great Basin.

CHAPTER TEN

A DEEPENING
INDIAN CRISIS

What the immediate future of the red men in this country will be is a question not so very easy of solution. Most of them persistently cling to their former habits and customs, and it requires a vast amount of patience to get along with them peaceably, and in all probability it will be a long time, especially under existing federal arrangements, before any material change in their condition will be effected.
—Deseret News, 1860[1]

THE EVENTS OF 1858 presented in microcosm all the difficulties that were to haunt the Mormons and the army in their handling of Indian relations during the next three years. But while the federal army moved to tighten its control over the territory, word of a different kind of Indian trouble reached General Johnston at Fort Bridger that spring. Rumors, followed by an unconfirmed report, claimed that Lieutenant Colonel Edward J. Steptoe, along with 156 officers and men, had been ambushed and killed by a large force of Indians near the mining town of Colville, Oregon Territory.[2] A Jesuit missionary, Father Adrian Hoecken, was the first outsider to give details of the disaster. Believing the uprising to be the entering wedge of a full-scale Indian war in the Far West, Johnston forwarded the document to Washington, adding pessimistically, "I do not doubt that the whole force has been destroyed."[3] News of the catastrophe prompted the Secretary of War to order the Sixth Infantry from Fort Bridger to Fort Walla Walla to reinforce the army along the Pacific. Under the command of Colonel George Andrews, the Sixth marched from the frontier post on August 21, 1858, on its long journey to Oregon.

A little less than a week later, the column reached a point eighty miles north of the Great Salt Lake, where it met local Mormon farmers hauling loads of food to sell to the army. The prices were outrageously high, wrote Private Eugene Bandel, a recent German immigrant. "It was the first time in four years that I saw fresh vegetables during the summer season. But we had to pay dear for them: 25 cents (about 10 silver groschen) for a pound of potatoes, 75 cents (somewhat over a thaler) for a dozen onions, $1.25 for a dozen eggs, $1.25 for a pound of butter, etc."[4]

The regiment advanced through the City of Rocks, a collection of stone monoliths set like huge chessmen, and reached the headwater of the Humboldt River by way of a well-defined road across Thousand Springs Valley. The expedition had hardly reached the desert waterway when it made its first contact with the Indians. Twice attacking forces slipped between the main column and straggling patrols. "In one instance a solitary soldier retreated before a band of Indians to a hill," wrote Private Bandel, "where he held off the savages with his gun all night. He was wounded in leg and arm by arrows. But the Indians were afraid of his gun and would not attack him. This fact saved him. Before the Indians could starve him out, as was apparently their intention, he was rescued by a party sent out to look for him."[5] Colonel Andrews avoided more trouble by distributing food and clothing to the natives. Fortunately, most of the river Indians proved to be more curious than dangerous.

The men moved across the desert to the Humboldt Sink and headed for the security of Carson City. After a brief rest in that small village, the long column of foot soldiers entered the Sierra Nevada, moving across low foothills for seven days, much of the time in driving rain. At higher elevations, rain gave way to snow, three feet deep. The supply wagons vanished in a turbulent storm, leaving the troops without tents, blankets, or food; but the men survived their ordeal by burrowing into the snow. After battling blizzards and near-starvation for several days, the Sixth Regiment crossed over the mountains, following the heavily traveled trail to Placerville, where the troops rested.

The regiment reached Benicia less than a week later, and got ready to join the battle, only to learn that peace had been restored in Oregon. Nevertheless, the Sixth Regiment had completed one of the longest continuous marches in frontier history, equaled only by General Kearny's trek across the Southwest during the Mexican War. Private Bandel wrote his own impressions of the march:

> If you should tell a journeyman in Europe to march two thousand miles (not ride) and not over a made road but over mountains and valleys, through sand and mud, over rocks and high grass, frequently through deep rivers and swollen streams after four days

without a drop of water, exposed to dry and wet weather, now the extreme heat and again to blizzards—in short, to march steadily along through all possible difficulties and hardships—I wonder what he would say.[6]

Meanwhile, from the eastern edge of the California Trail, reports filtered into Camp Floyd that bands of hostile Shoshone, Bannock, and Digger Indians had launched a series of raids against the Chorpenning mail stations. Dragoons were rushed to the headwaters of the Humboldt to quell the marauders, while undermanned companies of infantrymen pinned them down in the valleys between the fort and the open desert to the west. But the Indians tightened their grip on the overland trail, and the army was unable to send in enough troops to subdue them along the Humboldt River. Conceding Indian control of overland travel as well as river passage, General Johnston advised Chorpenning to close his operations for the season, and promised a strengthened escort for the mail service the following spring. Chorpenning stubbornly ignored the general's counsel, and managed to maintain a broken schedule between Placerville and Salt Lake City despite increasingly heavy pressure by the Indians; but potential tragedy was always in the air.

While the federal troops were establishing their sanctuary at Camp Floyd, John Mayfield drove the eastbound stage out of Placerville, carrying two passengers, Daniel W. Thomas and Washington Perkins. When the stage arrived in Carson City, incoming travelers told Mayfield that Indians had stopped all traffic between the headwaters of the Humboldt and Goose Creek. Outside the city, Mayfield met a wagon train of emigrants who had been robbed by Shoshone Indians near Thousand Springs Valley. Nevertheless, Mayfield elected to continue to Salt Lake City.[7]

The mail stage struck the California Trail, and the first 300 miles of the journey along the Humboldt River were uneventful. Deeper into Indian country, the driver discovered the decomposed bodies of several white emigrants who had been killed and mutilated by renegades.[8] At the mail station in Thousand Springs Valley, Mayfield received his second intimation of danger. Wandering through the station and yard, the driver found the outpost deserted. He decided to remain overnight anyway, and unhitched and corralled his horses. He and his passengers made themselves comfortable in the adobe station and plotted their remaining route to Salt Lake City. All at once, Mayfield spotted a large Indian war party making off with the company animals. He shouted at the Indians to stop, and attempted to pursue the warriors; but the war party drove him back into the station.

Mayfield decided to try to escape on foot before dawn, so the three men gathered the mail and a few personal effects and quietly slipped out of the earthen fort. They made it through the Indian lines in the lower fringes of the mountains, and headed in the direction of the Goose Creek Station, 100 miles to the east. Angered by the disappearance of their hostages, the Indians quickly took up the chase.[9]

Mayfield ordered his companions to drop all loose effects along the trail, including the federal mail. While the Indians argued among themselves over the disposal of the plunder, the mail party made good their escape from Thousand Springs Valley. It took almost a full week of difficult travel before the men reached the safety of the Goose Creek Station. Their fellowship in misfortune ended on August 28 when they arrived on foot in Salt Lake City.[10]

While hard-pressed to complete Camp Floyd before the first snows of winter, General Johnston responded to the Indian raid by ordering 150 mounted infantrymen to the first crossing of the Humboldt.[11] He instructed Captain James W. Hawes to establish temporary camp at Thousand Springs Valley, and patrol the California Trail eastward through the Goose Creek Mountains. The patrol scouted the mountains and deserts in search of hostiles, but the Indians had wisely withdrawn. Once in a while the army would see emigrants and escort them across the most dangerous places, but as autumn came on the flood of wagon traffic dwindled to a trickle.

After several weeks in the field and no contact with the enemy, the army intercepted Superintendent Jacob Forney and his sub-agent for the western district, Frederick Dodge, who were also investigating the Indian uprising along the California Trail.[12] Forney had traveled over a thousand miles to negotiate with the leading chieftains of the territory. Already he had clashed with both the army and the Mormons over the investigation of the Mountain Meadows Massacre. It was not as a visionary but rather as a government bureaucrat that earlier he had entered Farmington, a small village located north of Salt Lake City.

When the superintendent rode into the settlement he found the Indians friendly, especially Little Soldier, a subchief who operated throughout the northern half of the territory; but Farmington was infected by suspicions of fresh troubles with the Indians.[13] Little Soldier told Forney that the Indians of the Northwest had tried to enlist his support, as well as that of other Shoshone bands, to drive the Mormons and the federal army from the territory. The chief freely admitted that his tribe refused because the army had sufficient strength to overwhelm all the tribes south of the California Trail.

At Raft River, Forney was intercepted by two Indian riders who handed him a tattered slip of paper signed by Colonel Frederick Lander, the superintendent of the Honey Lake–Humboldt road. Lander urged Forney to meet with Chief Pocatello, also known as White Plume, at the warrior's encampment, one day's ride to the east. When Forney arrived at the Indian rendezvous, Pocatello had around him 150 armed braves. The Indians surrounded the superintendent and Pocatello demanded food, blankets, guns, and ammunition to carry his tribe through the winter; in exchange the Shoshone leader promised not to molest white settlements and not to interfere with overland emigration to the north.[14]

Forney told Pocatello that the Indian annuities had been left behind at Raft River, and they would be distributed to the tribesmen there. The statement was dangerously thin. Warriors tightened the circle to block the superintendent's possible escape, and Forney reacted sharply to the rude handling. He threatened the chief with military force if he interfered with emigrant passage through Shoshone country. The chief lapsed into silence, then motioned Forney to leave.

Forney and Dodge passed several days pleasantly at Raft River, distributing several hundred rations to the scattered bands of Shoshone Indians who visited their camp. The superintendent was shocked at the poor condition of his charges. "With the exception of the Chief and a few of the young men who are well provided with blankets," Forney wrote to his superior in Washington, "all are very destitute, many entirely naked."[15] The federal agents passed west through the high barrier overlooking Thousand Springs Valley and overtook a squad of dragoons returning to Captain Hawes's encampment.

They remained in the army bivouac for several more days, and then resumed their journey down the Humboldt River to Stony Point, escorted by twenty dragoons. The party spent the rest of the season parleying with roving river bands of Indians, sweetening speechmaking with a distribution of supplies. Forney observed that the Indians showed neither fear nor hostility toward the government. The superintendent missed no opportunity to impress upon the Indians their obligations to Washington; but he also believed that peace was frequently broken on the overland by the ill-tempered actions of white emigrants. "The Indians have been shot down for trivial causes. They have been robbed and have received other ill treatment from the whites," he wrote his superior in Washington, echoing similar charges voiced by Brigham Young when he filled the same office.[16]

Near Stony Point, 500 miles west of Salt Lake City, Frederick Dodge turned aside for Carson City. After dispatching food, clothing, and medicine to the surrounding tribes, Forney rejoined the main elements of Hawes's command; together they arrived at Camp Floyd during the closing days of October.[17]

While the expedition accomplished limited objectives, it accentuated the fundamental rift between the Indian service and the army. General Johnston retaliated against marauding war parties by creating an Indian no-man's-land on both sides of the Oregon and California Trails. Nonwhites found on the passages were considered hostile and treated accordingly. Jacob Forney considered Johnston's policies too warlike. He worked for enforceable Indian treaties, because he knew that without them permanent peace was impossible given the advance of the white frontier. Forney disapproved of both Mormon and military policies as possessing neither compassion nor justice. Opposing both the Church and the army diminished Forney's influence in the territory. He had scarcely affected public opinion when he learned that the army was gearing for an all-out Indian war, precipitated by the rape of a mother and daughter near Spanish Fork. The details of the crime brought a swift reaction from infuriated citizens who were prepared to believe the worst of all Indians.

The assault received widespread attention in the territorial newspapers, with no detail of the crime overlooked. Anna Maria Markham and her nine-year-old daughter were caught in an open field by two young braves who approached them. When Mrs. Markham turned to face the warriors to ward off the attack, they sprang from their horses and threw her to the ground, holding her hands and spreading her feet.

The horror she experienced was later recounted to the Indian Superintendent: "They took off my clothes and two took hold of my legs and tried to tear me open, they struck me several times, turned me over and over again and left me and went after my daughter."[18] Maddened by liquor, they fell upon the terrified girl and cruelly lacerated her womb with the cutting edge of an arrow before sexually assaulting her. Not until very late in the evening was she found moaning and screaming in the dark, hemorrhaging profusely before she lapsed into a coma.

The immediate result of this attack was increased aggressiveness against the Indians, expressed in demands that the governor arrest the criminals. Governor Cumming ordered Garland Hurt to Spanish Fork to apprehend the two suspects, identified as Moses (Pangunts) and Looking Glass (Namowah).[19] The peace officers arrived at the Indian farm early on the morning of September 14, but found the suspects had gone to Camp Floyd.[20]

The first notice of the rape came to General Johnston's desk in a dispatch from the governor, which requested the army to furnish troops to arrest the suspects. Further details of the crime reached Camp Floyd that afternoon when Hurt repeated the whole story as he had heard it from Mrs. Markham. For Johnston the worst feature of the incident was its poor timing. After several months of hard bargaining, he had assembled three of the most powerful chiefs of central Utah, Peteetneet, Sanpitch, and Tintic, in the first of a series of negotiations to end the Indian harassment of Mormon settlements. But the peace conference came to an abrupt end when Hurt presented the tribal leaders with the arrest order. The Indians rejected the warrant, replying that "they did not understand trying"; they would rather see "their warriors shot than submit to imprisonment."[21] Peteetneet turned to Johnston for assurance that the whole affair was a mistake, but the general advised the Indian leaders to comply with Hurt's demand. The chiefs finally consented to turn over the prisoners to the civilian posse at the Spanish Fork reservation.

The general, immensely pleased, allowed the Indians to leave Camp Floyd unmolested. First to arrive at the reservation the next morning was Peteetneet, who came riding in to the farm surrounded by a dozen armed warriors. Smarting over the treatment he had received at Camp Floyd, the chief refused to surrender the suspects, arguing that since the girl had not died, no crime was committed.[22] Completely bewildered, the agent listened patiently but could not bring himself to believe that the chief meant what he said. Outwardly Hurt was conciliatory, cool, and self-possessed as he repeated his request. Peteetneet's face remained wooden, and he refused to turn over the two warriors. The agent withdrew to his headquarters where he composed a letter to General Johnston requesting the immediate aid of a military posse.[23]

At dawn on October 2, 1858, the Indians at Spanish Fork found a force of 160 dragoons and infantrymen bivouacked around the farm, headed by Major Gabriel R. Paul. The commander's plan was to enclose all the reservation Indians into a contracting circle of soldiers until the suspects were identified and arrested. However, before the trap was closed, Tintic and Pintuts, the son of Arrowpeen, rode toward the eastern border of the reservation and charged through the line of soldiers. At first the troopers held their fire, but when the first Indian tore through the ranks, a dozen rifle shots sent Pintuts to the ground, mortally wounded in the head and chest. Tintic pulled up his horse and surrendered himself to Major Paul. Later, he agreed to exchange Moses and Looking Glass for his own freedom.[24] The two suspects were loaded into an army wagon and escorted to Camp Floyd to stand trial. The Indians had no particular friends in the federal court at Provo, but Judge Cradlebaugh eventually freed Pangunts and Namowah in a reaction against Mormon refusals to indict Mormon suspects of other crimes.

For the moment, the death of Pintuts overshadowed all other events in the territory. Not only did he urge reconciliation with the white settlers, he was also a friend of the Mormons. A warrior of great physical and mental strength, Pintuts was credited with saving the survivors of Gunnison's party from certain death in 1855.[25] A year later, he saved the lives of Garland Hurt and Surveyor General David Burr near the Sevier River. Angry over the death of his son, Arrowpeen (or Arapeen) stepped up his raids against army livestock in central Utah. His vendetta attracted an impressive number of subchiefs from central and southern Utah, including Tintic, Peteetneet, Sanpitch, and Kanosh. Couriers returning from California reported that Tintic was openly recruiting among the tribes on the western edge of the corridor to the Pacific.[26] There were other rumors that Arrowpeen had left for New Mexico to inflame the Navajos against the army.

The expected uprising began during the middle of October when Tintic and his warriors moved off the Spanish Fork reservation after an inglorious attempt to destroy the agency buildings by fire. Sanpitch and Peteetneet drove off the bureau's horses and cattle. Once safely out of striking distance of Camp Floyd, the Indians scattered southward to evade army patrols, then followed backcountry trails to Arrowpeen's camp near San Pete.

General Johnston notified his subordinates throughout the territory to prepare for a general Indian uprising. At Fort Bridger, Colonel E. R. S. Canby was ordered to be ready to reinforce Camp Floyd.[27] Major Paul was to remain in Spanish Fork, while two hundred reinforcements were divided equally between Springville and Pondtown.[28] While the army waited for the next attack of the Indians, the three chieftains led a large war party into the San Pete reservation to meet with Arrowpeen, who was still in Navajo country. The warriors streamed through the agency warehouse, carrying off food, blankets, and clothing. They fired the farm in a dozen places, and stampeded the farm's cattle and horses. Then they scattered to look for Arrowpeen.[29]

Even while the raiding parties stalked the countryside, many Mormon ranchers continued to live in a routine manner, relying on past good relations with Arrowpeen. Josiah Call and Samuel Brown tried to drive a herd of cattle from Juab Valley to Fillmore but were stopped by a band of warriors led by Tomac. Without warning, Tomac fired on the two Mormons, killing Brown instantly. Call got off a shot that mortally wounded Tomac and fled into a ravine, but his fate was never in doubt. Four days later an army search party found his and Brown's bodies, stripped and marked with a white flag tied to a spear. The *Deseret News* described the corpses:

> Mr. Brown was shot through the head, scalped and his throat cut. The birds had eaten the flesh from Mr. Call's bones with the exception of his leg below the knee and his left arm; but it was evident he had been shot three times; once through the right breast, the ball lodging in the back bone; once through the left ankle and once through the head, the ball entering the back part of the skull near the seam and coming out the left side of the nose.[30]

"It is supposed the throat was also cut," continued the report, "as the blood had run from where his neck lay and his right arm was entirely gone and was not found. They were both stripped of all their clothing except their underclothes, shoes and stocking."[31] Arrowpeen told

Brigham Young later that the Tomac war party believed they had killed two teamsters from Camp Floyd until they discovered the victims' religious undergarments, so they marked the site to insure recovery of the murdered Mormons.[32]

As the Indian war heated up, the army constructed four stone outposts west of Camp Floyd: Camp Tyler in Rush Valley, Camp Porter in San Pete, Camp Crosman in Tintic Valley, and Camp Eastman at Chicken Creek.[33] But the full-scale Indian uprising for which they prepared never materialized.

In November, Arrowpeen moved down off the mountains into the warmer valleys of central Utah. The army learned that he had asked Jacob Forney to help end hostilities. Forney agreed to meet him that week at San Pete, a safe distance from Camp Floyd.[34]

When Forney reached San Pete, he found the smoldering reservation still deserted, with Arrowpeen nowhere to be found. Bewildered, Forney turned his troops around and started back to Camp Floyd. They were overtaken by a lone Indian rider who waved the superintendent to a halt. In broken English, aided by sign language, the brave indicated that he had been sent by Kanosh, chief of the Pahvants, to tell Forney that Arrowpeen waited to receive him at his campsite near the Corn Creek reservation. The wary Forney sent word to the renegade chief that he must appear at San Pete immediately and without his warriors.[35]

Arrowpeen arrived at San Pete, surrounded by armed braves. The sight of military pickets patrolling the farm's perimeter angered the chief, and he demanded that the troops be pulled back. The superintendent refused. Forney justified the dragoons as his personal guard, denying that they were sent to arrest Arrowpeen. The superintendent brought up the Navajo alliance, warning Arrowpeen that his warmongering was a dangerous course; it would not only endanger Mormon colonization but would cause privation for the tribesmen. The American government ordered the Indians to lay down their arms and return to their reservations, Forney said. The terms were unconditional.[36]

Arrowpeen denied responsibility for the death of the two Mormon herdsmen; instead, he blamed Kanosh and the Pahvant. The warrior-chieftain promised to return to the San Pete reservation with his entire band during the last week of November. That was all that he had hoped for, so Forney promised to deliver enough food, blankets and clothing to carry the tribe through the winter, providing Arrowpeen kept his word.

Forney also questioned Kanosh about complicity in the recent uprisings and of the murders of Brown and Call. Kanosh blamed the murders on Arrowpeen. He offered to return the horse and saddle of one of the victims, claiming that they had been left behind by the Utes. Speaking through the government interpreter, Peter Royce, Kanosh told Forney that

Arrowpeen is greatly enraged and is determined to kill and plunder all travelers who pass this way to California, he says he will have revenge for the Indian that was killed at Spanish Fork by the soldiers. He says there is only two ways to settle the difficulty and that is for Colonel Johnston to give up the man that shot the Indian at Spanish Fork, or to send a committee and pay him. . . .[37]

The Pahvant chief also reported that "Arrowpeen has got at his command the Utahs, Piutes, and Piedes and Snakes, and most of his band which he could not control because 'they are so mad.' "[38]

Forney and his aides returned to San Pete to reconvene their counsel with Arrowpeen. When the caravan finally reached the reservation, Arrowpeen arrived without Tintic, Peteetneet, or Sanpitch, who had decided to wait out the conference in the mountains near Fish Lake.[39]

Forney accused the chief of betraying his trust. Disregarding Arrowpeen's protests that he had little control over his subchiefs, he demanded that they return immediately to the reservation or they would all face the consequences. Angry and frightened, Arrowpeen complained that the army had weakened his control over his tribe and brought hunger and disease to his wandering people. Forney said that the Indians had brought the trouble on themselves and warned Arrowpeen that if his tribe did not return to their reservation and lay down their weapons the army would destroy them all. Arrowpeen guaranteed nothing, but agreed to try to coax his people back onto the reservation.

The superintendent gladly relinquished the responsibility of the Indians to the army until the following spring. A month later, Forney penned his feelings concerning the Indians to his superior in Washington. The tribesmen were "entirely devoid of any principle of thanks but are full of treachery, murder, thieving and ingratitude to the very hands that fed them." His sense of outrage grew as he wrote: "by their acts . . . one might be led to believe they had not one redeeming quality."[40] This judgment, however, proved premature.

Scarcely had he recorded these impressions when the reservation Indians began drifting leaderless into their farming grounds in small groups of twos and threes. Tintic, Peteetneet and Sanpitch followed their people into San Pete.

Half-frozen elements of the Tenth and Seventh Regiments of Infantry spent the winter of 1858–1859 near the austere reservations, imprisoning the Indians on three farms. By consent of both the army and the Indian department, no tribesman was permitted to leave the agency without written permission from the superintendent. The truce held. Food shortages, common to reservation life, disappeared when the army opened up its warehouses to its new charges. Neither Forney nor Cumming objected to the army's new role in curtailing the "dangerous nuisance."

Knowing that surveillance and the dole could not be maintained indefinitely, General Johnston tried his hand at Indian diplomacy. One of his first moves was to convene a council at Camp Floyd, summoning chiefs of all tribes within fifty miles of the fort.

The chiefs and warriors presented themselves at the general's head-quarters in early January, flanked by interpreters and government agents. The army promised to safeguard deeded reservations and Indian hunting grounds not already occupied by settlers. In exchange for this guarantee, the Indians promised to stay clear of Mormon villages and all territorial roads that passed through their lands. Later, Johnston personally escorted the Indian dignitaries throughout the camp, pointing out the artillery pieces in a long line near the north end of the fort. The usually immobile face of Arrowpeen showed fear. Awestruck, he confessed "that his little band of Utes couldn't whip the soldiers."[41] That evening the Indians were invited to the command dining hall where they were served a lavish dinner with visiting dignitaries and the ranking officers of the fort. The tribal leaders were also honored guests at the regimental theater where they witnessed a sham battle staged by the soldiers' circus.

The military holiday continued into the following day. Again the Indians were witnesses to the army's opulence when the quartermaster's storehouse was thrown open to the warriors and they were allowed to take away all that they could carry.[42] Little more is known of this council apart from the fact that the tribal leaders returned peacefully to their reservations; but the warriors had scarcely recovered from the banquet wine when the army's policy drew fire.

The main source of opposition came from territorial Indian agents, who feared that all Indians might view Johnston's dole as a reward for their insurrection. Garland Hurt urged Forney to continue the Indian farm experiment, arguing that annuity payments were unproductive and subject to graft. In Forney, Hurt found a convert willing to reestablish the prestige of the farming-reservation system.

Believing that the tribes could not exist as islands in a sea of white settlement, Forney suggested that the Indians be trained in agricultural and mechanical arts. With advanced technology, the nomadic tribes could become a progressive part of territorial society.[43] Forney set aside as much unoccupied agricultural land as he could, first laying out the Gosiute farm at Deep Creek near the present Utah-Nevada line. A second Indian settlement followed in Ruby Valley, 250 miles west of Salt Lake City. The farm system of his predecessors had depended heavily on white farmers, but Forney's new system came to rely exclusively on tribal labor.[44]

It was difficult, however, to interest the Indians in the plow and mule. Farming was of little importance to the territorial Indians before the Mormons came, and these Indians believed that "it was the man's business to hunt and the business of the women to do what little farming was done.

To take up the hoe or the plow was considered degrading, and a man who would do such a thing was thought to be effeminate."[45]

Though he worked hard to achieve nominal independence for the Indians in their own land, Forney experienced a continuing string of failures that eventually forced his resignation. A major weakness in the new program was the tendency of non-farming tribesmen to regard the harvest of the five farming reservations as the property of all Indians, regardless of tribal affiliation. Equally distressing was the practice of the farming Indians of trading their food to settlers for whiskey.[46] The tribes relied more and more on federal subsidies or begged from Mormon settlers.

Forney's resignation was an aftermath of the struggle between the army and the federal judges on one hand and the Mormons and the governor on the other. Governor Cumming advocated the extension of Mormon settlements, thus assuring support for his political ambitions in the territory. He had become a friend of the Saints and believed that development of the farm-reservation system would weaken Mormon claims to their painfully conquered holdings. Of the two claimants to the same land, Cumming supported the Mormons against compensation to the Indians for tribal grounds.

High commodity prices, burdensome transportation costs, and an antiquated federal banking system combined to cripple the territorial Indian bureaucracy. Forney lost his temper over alleged manipulation of agricultural prices, wrote a resident of San Pete:

> Bro Jermiah Hatch, Indian farmer from San Pete, called upon Dr. Forney. Forney told him he wanted to settle his accounts with him, and that he would allow them; and told the clerk to make out the bills, upon which he left the room. When he returned he took the bills and tore them, saying the "Mormons" in San Pete were a set of damned robbers, to charge such prices. Hatch told him, they had sold to him cheaper than to the army.[47]

Brigham Young had a free hand in colonizing the remaining unsettled valleys of northeastern Utah because in any confrontation between the Indians and the white settlers the army protected the interests of white homesteaders. As a result, the Great Colonizer established fifty-one settlements during the three-year operation of Camp Floyd, as compared with only ninety-eight in the whole decade before military occupation.[48] Ironically, Johnston had strengthened the hand of his enemy, and Young enjoyed his moment and made the most of it.

CHAPTER ELEVEN

TROUBLES ON THE OVERLAND

On the northern California and Oregon road, Indian depredations might be punished; but such as those committed . . . this year can scarcely ever be prevented, notwithstanding the strenuous efforts and watchfulness of the army however strong. With white men (painted when in action) to aid them, and to indicate the position of troops, and to mislead that latter a small body of Indians can slip in between any two detachments and take advantage of the careless and straggling emigrant.

From the South Pass to the Sink of the Humboldt, some eight hundred miles, many places favor an ambuscade so many that an enormous army would be required to guard them and patrol the country.

—Deseret News, 1859[1]

I N THE AFTERMATH of the Move South, Mormon settlers began to spread cautiously northward, planting fields across the flat expanse of land in the lower Bear River country of what is now Box Elder County. Looking to establish cattle ranching operations in Cache Valley, the Church organized its first communities there as well as exploratory settlements in the Malad Valley. These sorties into the northern frontier of the Great Basin would later involve the Saints in the most active Indian difficulties America would face in the years just before the Civil War. The Shoshones found themselves pressed from all sides and determined to play a dangerous game of harassing overland travel while dealing inscrutably with both dogged Mormons and often frustrated federal authorities. As a result, the military establishment at Camp Floyd, supposedly in Utah to control the Mormons, found itself increasingly burdened with Indian problems.

For the Mormons, Indian depredations along the overland to the north of them served as a continual reminder that they were building God's kingdom in the midst of a perilous frontier. The northern villages along the Wasatch Mountains found themselves in 1859 still in fear of violence from warrior bands along the overland trail. The people of Brigham City never forgot these tragedies, vividly brought home to their doors by survivors or by the Indians themselves.[2]

The drama began to unfold during the summer of 1859 when Indian trading parties arrived at the Mormon village with goods and livestock stolen or bartered from passing travelers. A score of men watched a small party of Shoshone Indians descend a mountain road and enter the town trailing a small herd of livestock—twenty head of oxen, mules, and horses. In a trading session, the Shoshone produced a dozen Colt revolvers, a few watches, jewelry, gold coins, and a daguerreotype family portrait in a small baroque brass frame. A Mormon merchant identified the photograph as one belonging to an emigrant party that had passed through the city a few days before.[3]

The Saints asked the Indians how they came into possession of the goods. Through a translator, a Shoshone warrior volunteered the story that "six sleeps ago, at or near the Goose Creek Mountains, four lodges of the Flat Head Indians were camped near the California road; that two of their number went to a small emigrant train to swap some buckskins. . . ." Instead of trading, the translator continued, "the emigrants fired upon and killed them both; the others of their party, learning this statement, applied to the Shoshones for help, and a company of Flat Heads and Shoshones, in the number of twenty, attacked the train and killed five men and two women, only two men and one woman making their escape." The combined war party plundered the wagons, stealing the grazing animals and baggage of the train.[4]

After telling the story, the Indians left the hamlet and rode north. The Mormons' sense of outrage grew, and a small posse tracked them northwest to the Goose Creek Mountains; but the Indians eluded pursuit. In the heat of the afternoon of the following day, the posse overtook the Shepard party—the train that had been attacked. They escorted the wagon train until the evening camp, and the surviving emigrants told their version of the incident.[5]

The Shepard train had made its way across the plains with little difficulty, encountering only friendly Indians. Quitting the northern branch of the Oregon Trail, the long column curved westward along the Sublette Cutoff to Cold Springs, where they left the main road to rest and fill their water kegs.

At twilight, a war party of Bannocks crowded into the bivouac, demanding food and clothing in exchange for safe passage through their country. Perceiving danger, the wagon master ordered the warriors fed. "Having obtained some bread," one victim later reported to the Commissioner of Indian Affairs, "they started to a hill where cattle were herded by two men. After saluting the cattle guards, then passing them, one of the Indians suddenly turned his pony, lowering his rifle, shot one of the men Mr. Hall, through the heart, killing him instantly; the other man fled to the camp. The Indians were in the mountains running off nine head of cattle and two horses."[6] The Bannocks ran off at the arrival of the second and third sections of the train.

At dawn, the combined train proceeded to Goose Creek Canyon, a dangerously narrow passage of the California Trail. Following the banks of the river that gives the canyon its name, the trail snaked through a series of sage-walled gorges, squeezing traffic into vulnerable single columns. The train passed into the canyon during the closing days of July. Suddenly, Indians poured out from both sides of the road, sounding battle cries. The Bannocks fired a deadly rain of arrows and bullets into the slow-moving columns, instantly killing three outriders: Bill Driggs, Clayborn F. Rains, and William Shepard.[7] Caught in a deadly ambush and heavily outnumbered, the terrified survivors fell back in a wild retreat towards Cold Springs.

Several women and three children hid beneath wagons, too weak to run with their men down the trail. One survivor, Mrs. Wright, watched the raiders tear the train apart, taking $1,800 in gold and other spoils, including horses, mules, and dairy cattle. Minutes later she was dragged from hiding, holding her infant daughter tightly against her breast. Fearing she would be murdered or "worse," the panic-stricken woman fell to her knees and begged for mercy, but the sight only whipped the Bannocks into a frenzy. Without warning, a warrior pulled the baby from the mother's arms, tomahawked the child and threw the mutilated body against the canyon wall. With what little strength remained, the bereaved woman made a feeble attempt to save herself. Once again she was caught, dragged to the ground, stripped of her clothing, and repeatedly raped. The Indians fired a quiver of arrows into her body and left her for dead. Although horrified by the sight of this atrocity, a second child managed to crawl out from under the wagon and escape.[8]

After seizing a great quantity of goods and burning what stores could not be carried, the war party rode east along the California Trail to attack the second train, still camped at Cold Springs. From where they halted on a bluff overlooking the encampment, they were spotted by a lone picket who sounded the alarm—three loud explosions of rifle fire that brought the pioneers to their feet. Having lost the advantage of surprise, the Indians swarmed out of hiding and launched a frontal assault against the emigrants in their entrenchments. All along the emigrant firing-line rifles went off, killing six warriors. The Bannocks, thinking that the emigrant force was smaller than theirs, regrouped and sent a second charge against the wagons, but lost four warriors to expert marksmanship. Unnerved by their unexpected losses, the Bannocks broke off the engagement and disappeared from the battlefield.[9]

For some reason, the third train failed to reach Cold Springs until dark, although it was within earshot of the battle. After a night filled with terror, the caravan of 54 wagons and 200 men, women, and children followed the Goose Creek road along the moving water until the smell of death revealed the massacre site. They found four dead bodies bloated by the heat into grotesque forms. Smoldering wood and canvas, human hair, and clothing dangling from the sagebrush were inanimate witnesses to the horror that spread across the overland.

A hurried search for survivors uncovered an eight-month-old infant boy, hidden in a small swale by his mother, Mrs. Shepard, who was too weak from loss of blood to carry the child to Cold Springs. A further search turned up the remaining members of the Wright family, hidden under a partially burned wagon. In a remarkable display of endurance, the woman had managed to drag her mangled body to where her dying child lay and had carried the battered infant to the nearest wagon for shelter. Equally heroic was the Wrights' five-year-old son who, unlike the emigrant guards who had abandoned the survivors, returned to the massacre scene to keep his parents alive by nursing them with water.[10] As evening came, the party placed the victims' corpses in wagons and carried them eighteen miles across the bleak trail to be buried in a common grave. Ten days later, James Wright died and was buried near Thousand Springs Valley. Farther west along the river road of the Humboldt they met the eastbound stagecoach and made their first report of the disaster.

In the dining room of the California House in Salt Lake City, Jacob Forney heard the Mormon and stage drivers' versions of the Shepard massacre.[11] He left the hotel for the Staines mansion where he reported it to Governor Cumming. Cumming sent an urgent dispatch to General Johnston requesting a punitive expedition against the Bannocks and northern Shoshone. The following day a courier brought Cumming's message to Camp Floyd.

Military response to the attack on the Shepard train was delayed while political scores were settled. The War Department's criticism of the Cradlebaugh-Provo incident still rankled, and Johnston bluntly reminded the governor that he had no authority to call for troops. He added that, since he judged that there were good military reasons for dispatching troops to the northern frontier, the army would do all in its power to prevent further massacres.[12] Two companies of dragoons commanded by Lieutenant Ebenezer Gay were earmarked for the campaign against the Indians.[13]

Quitting Camp Floyd on the morning of August 7, 1859, the special force worked its way north to Brigham City, patrolling the countryside for hostiles; but none were found. A messenger reported a large concentration of Shoshone in Cache Valley. A second dispatch convinced the lieutenant that this was the band responsible for the Goose Creek Massacre.

Gay elected to attack the war party before dawn. Leaving his heavy supply wagons and surplus animals heavily guarded, Gay turned his forty-two dragoons east into the mountains toward Cache Valley. Guided by Sheriff Sheldon B. Cutler, one of the first settlers of the village, the detachment hoped to destroy the Indians while they slept.[14] After four hours in the saddle the army stumbled right into the Indian camp, which was pitched in the middle of the road. By the time the dragoons had recovered from their surprise, the hundred Indians had retreated up the mountain.

Taking command of the high ground, the Shoshone launched a fierce counterattack and prevented the dragoons from following them up the mountain. Gay ordered his men to the south side of the road where they fought from deep dugouts.

The skirmish raged until dawn. Finally, the Indians ceased firing and ran away. In a hurried search of the heavy undergrowth six casualties were found, and Sheriff Cutler was missing and presumed dead. Twenty Shoshone warriors were killed or wounded and twenty horses captured, including one that was later identified as belonging to the ill-fated Shepard party.[15]

The army retraced its steps towards Brigham City, and by sunup the troops were out of the heavy dust of the high trace. Along the way, a noncommissioned officer noticed Abraham Hunsaker standing near his ranch talking to the missing sheriff. Gay rode to where the two men stood, and ordered Cutler to explain his defection from the battle. The sheriff met the officer's accusations with protestations of innocence. According to Cutler, he had been swept away by the confusion of battle, but he had not left the battle site until the Indians had retreated. The lieutenant rejected Cutler's explanation, lashed out at him for his cowardliness before the enemy, and accused him of leading the troops into a trap.[16]

Just then a dragoon passed through Hunsaker's pasture nearby, where an Indian named Lemuel sat astride a chestnut mare branded with federal initials. Lemuel was Hunsaker's devoted Indian herdsman, and had been with him for years. Before Hunsaker could explain that the horse had been borrowed from the sheriff, the trooper reined up alongside the Indian and ordered Lemuel to surrender it. The

Indian dismounted and nudged the mount against the dragoon's horse, audibly commenting, "Take your god damned horse." When the infuriated soldier reached for his pistol, Lemuel flipped himself into the saddle and rode in the direction of the canyon.

The dragoon pursued him down the road. Lieutenant Gay saw the trooper close the distance to twenty-five yards, and the Indian lean forward over the horse's neck to avoid the soldier's fire. Suddenly the sound of gunfire exploded across the valley. The suspected horse thief bounced backward in the saddle, swayed to one side, and crumpled to the ground with a mortal wound in his back. Lemuel's death generated a wave of protest throughout the Mormon community, but the outrage was only temporary.[17]

Gay turned his soldiers north to rendezvous with the command of Major Lynde, who was camped near the first crossing of the Bear River. Pitching camp at Hampton's Crossing, a short distance from Brigham City, the patrol learned that a large war party was planning an attack against Lynde's forces. The information came from a mountaineer who claimed that a concentration of two hundred Bannock and Shoshone Indians had gathered in Cache Valley for the assault. The account alarmed Gay, and he sent a call to Camp Floyd for reinforcements.[18]

The lieutenant learned that a war party had followed the patrol through Malad Valley. A dozen yards from the Bear River, a scout discovered a warrior hiding in a thick patch of rushes. When the prisoner was brought into camp he was identified as Chief Pocatello. Gay questioned Pocatello about his activities along the California Trail and his relationship with the warring bands then gathered in Cache Valley. The chief appeared confused and bewildered by the questions, but he probably realized that Gay would send the Indian version of the story to Camp Floyd for evaluation. Pocatello denied having interfered with overland emigration or knowing about the Shoshone and Bannock activity in Cache Valley. Gay was convinced that Pocatello was lying. He ordered the chief placed under protective custody.[19]

Satisfied that large bands of Pocatello's tribe were in the region, Gay sent a squad of nine men to reconnoiter the northern half of Malad Valley. If trouble was coming, he would meet it head-on. The scouts searched through rough country for several days, but failed to find the Indians. Later, on a stretch of the river road, the reconnaissance party met two Indian traders riding out of the high country. The traders claimed that there was a camp of fifty Indian lodges on a small stream flowing into the Malad River. The war party was waiting for the return of their chief, Pocatello, "the worst Indian in this country. . . ." When this report reached Lieutenant Gay, Pocatello was arrested, shackled with leg irons, and placed in a supply wagon under heavy guard.[20]

The commander ordered his men to attack the Indian encampment; but when the army arrived at the site the warriors retreated into a wooded canyon and the women and children drove the horses and cattle into a narrow gorge. The Shoshone sent twenty-five mounted warriors to protect the noncombatants and the supplies and ammunition in their pack train. Realizing that if the warriors regained the rocky ledges it would be difficult to dislodge them, Gay tried to decoy the Indians. The dragoons broke ranks and retreated to a small ravine where a line of troopers had been barricaded to await the warriors. But the Indians refused to be drawn.

The lieutenant, following the action with field glasses, ordered the army's mules unpacked and left in the open ground that separated the two forces, hoping to entice an attack. Again his strategy failed. Pulling his men into one fighting unit, Gay led his troopers in a headlong charge across the open battleground and drove the warriors back into the hills. However, in the opening moments of the battle, the Shoshone women and children slipped through the canyon beyond the reach of the army. The Indian strategy had been magnificent, and the American soldiers had learned a valuable lesson in Indian fighting.

Breaking camp the following dawn, the detachment moved north, reaching the first ford of the Bear River on August 17, 1859. For two days the forces under Gay remained near the crossing, waiting the return of Major Isaac Lynde's command and Lieutenant G. A. Gordon's reinforcements from Camp Floyd. Once the three commands had safely rendezvoused, Major Lynde reported on his two-month patrol of the overland.

The campaign had started at Camp Floyd on the morning of June 12, 1859.[21] Moving his two companies of soldiers to Salt Lake City, Lynde escorted several families of emigrants for four hundred miles. After a rest of two days at Gravelly Ford, Lynde detached fifty-five men to follow the north bank of the Humboldt River for ninety-six miles to search out and destroy hostile Indian bands. The river trail itself seemed hostile, the major observed: "The greater part of this distance the valley, which does not average more than three-fourths of a mile in width, was covered with water, and deep sloughs running parallel to the river render it dangerous for the animals to drink it, and the mosquitos and flies worse than I ever saw them before."[22]

The idea of a head-on assault against the Indians soon evaporated, for none were found. The reunited command retraced its steps along the river road to the headwaters of the Humboldt—the western gateway to the Goose Creek Mountains. Here Lynde observed the poverty of the regional tribes and absolved them of much of the blame for their predations. "The Indians," he observed in his report to General Johnston, "in this part of the country are miserably poor, nearly naked, and subsisting on squirrels and nuts that they dig from the ground, they beg from the emigrants the cattle that die from disease, and eat them."[23] The Digger Indians had many faults as well as virtues, but were generally friendly to passing emigrants and the Mormons, he wrote to his superior.

The high point of his adventure occurred on August 4 when the army discovered the Shepard train encamped near Thousand Springs Valley. Recounting their ordeal, the emigrants claimed that they had recognized at least three white men costumed as Indians in the attacking party, one of whom appeared to be leading the Bannocks. The presence of "white Indians" in the country complicated the army's problem. "During the season of emigration many persons located themselves along the different roads with a few goods for the avowed purpose of trading with the emigrants," warned Major Lynde, "but in fact, I believe, for the purpose of inciting the Indians to plunder the trains, and assisting them in these outrages. They are then enabled to purchase for a trifle the Indians share of the spoil. This practice, I think, must stop."[24]

Tales of "white Indians" had followed the path of emigration across the California Trail. For a decade travelers along the Humboldt had suffered violence at the hands of these renegades who, in alliance with true Indian confederates, worked their evil along the river highway. Writing in 1852, Major Jacob H. Holeman, an Indian agent, warned that the white brigands were the more dangerous: "The renegades, deserters, and thieves, who have had to fly from justice to California, have taken refuge in the mountains, and have associated with the Indians are more savage than the Indians themselves. By their cruelty to the whites, they have stimulated the Indians to acts of barbarity, which they never know to be guilty before. . . ."[25] The army soon added new evidence to these charges.

Lynde reorganized his command into the Bear River Expedition. Dropping his planned offensive against the Indians, he divided his 400-man force into three defensive fighting units. Captain L. McLane was responsible for the safety of emigrant traffic over the Fort Hall road; Captain T. H. Neil had patrol duty north of Cache Valley; Lieutenant Gay controlled the trail between the first crossing of the Bear and Gravelly Ford. Lynde turned his attention to Chief Pocatello.

The commander feared that Pocatello's continued imprisonment would bring the "Snake nation, if not others, upon us."[26] In Gay's report the commander found little evidence to sustain a charge against the chief, except that he was haughty and verged on insolence. Lynde released the chief after receiving his promise that the Shoshone would stay clear of the overland trails and not interfere with westward migration. The chief warned that his young men were angry; they would not be restrained by wise counsel and had joined renegade bands of Bannocks operating south of the Snake River.[27]

The Wallen Expedition felt that anger near the Raft River, when a combined force of Bannock and Shoshone warriors almost succeeded in overrunning them. The survey party managed to turn back the attack but lost most of its livestock.[28]

News also reached Camp Floyd of the appearance in the south of a mysterious prophet called Warahikah.[29] Little Soldier identified him as War-I-Gika, a Bannock witch doctor who claimed to be guided by underworld spirits in a holy crusade to drive the whites from the northern rim of the Great Basin. F. W. Lander assumed the warrior-priest to be Pash-e-co, a leader of the Snakes who espoused the cause of Indian unity and was a pillar of strength against the white tide of settlers.[30]

Like the Ghost Dancers of a later decade, Warahikah's followers were inspired by a fanaticism that grew stronger as the Indian way of life grew weaker.

> The story runs that his mother scarcely had time to encase him upon her back, before his limbs had grown so large that they snapped the buckskin thongs and he stood before his astounded mother full grown. He was described as being very large and perfectly developed, but did not resemble the people of his tribe. He claimed the power to heal the sick, by blowing his breath upon them, while every variety of wild animal were under his control as well as the elements of fire and water. He made powder and bullets out of dirt, and he was impervious to the arrows of his enemies. Upon one occasion, when in battle he fell and after it was over his comrades sought for his supposed dead body, but in vain. After returning to the village they found him in his wigwam quietly smoking his pipe. Waragikah kept himself secluded, thus adding prestige and more mysterious curiosity to his supposed miraculous powers. . . .[31]

This was the glittering reputation of the Indian leader that struck panic along the Mormon frontier, but he proved to be a false prophet. The Indians south of the Snake River continued their war in small bands of ten to fifty hostiles who roamed over the overland routes killing every white man they could. Relying on the element of surprise and their superb knowledge of the geography, the Bannocks and Shoshone were lords and masters of the California Trail, Major Lynde complained: "The country was so rough that the redskins could manage to escape when the soldiers were within twenty-five miles of them."[32] As autumn dragged to an end, other tragedies were in the making on the overland.

On the twentieth of August, an Iowa emigrant train, later identified as the Beal party, paused near the Porter trading station on Marsh Creek where they reprovisioned with fresh supplies and equipment. Returning to the sluggish stream, the train formed a stockade of wagons on a grassy meadow and waited out the night.

Soon after sunrise Porter saw a contingent of Shoshone warriors trailing a pack train heavily loaded down with buckskins and other hides. The band of young warriors appeared eager for a fight and well-armed, and demanded rifles and ammunition in exchange for their goods. Porter told the Indians that he had sold the last of his gunpowder to the emigrants, now slowly making their way west. Following the pointing finger of Porter's outstretched hand, the braves watched the diminutive caravan laboring along the trail. Leveling his rifle at the white trader, the Shoshone chief ordered Porter to leave the country within three days. Then the war party remounted and disappeared into the foothills.[33]

Porter worked through the day preparing to abandon his profitable wilderness outpost. That night he was interrupted by the sight of the battered survivors of the Beal party staggering into the station. Disaster had come unexpectedly in the bleak hills near a bend in the river, where hostile Indians fired without warning at the white-topped wagon train. The emigrants held their ground for ten minutes, then retreated along the brushy riverbank. The Indians fired into the bullrushes and willows, wounding four men. Several hours later, they crawled out of hiding and scrambled back to the trading post.

In the darkness Porter loaded the wounded into his wagon. The remaining emigrants made a fort of the cheerless station, armed with rifles, shotguns, and provisions for three days. The frightened trader left his outpost with his supply wagons and the four wounded men and worked his way northwestward along the main-traveled road. Less than forty-eight hours later he met the Bear River Expedition. While the military surgeon, Dr. Covey, worked to mend the wounds of the overlanders, a handful of dragoons rode out to the Porter Station. They found that the emigrants had managed to hold their position and were unharmed. Because his men and animals were exhausted from the forced march over the parched trail, Lynde decided against pursuing the war party into the mountains. The Beal party returned to Salt Lake City with the expedition before continuing to California.[34]

Indian summer was the most dangerous time on the road. Major decisions faced travelers: either collect at the Bear River Crossing and be escorted by the army to Gravelly Ford, sacrificing time for safety, or go on alone, trusting to chance that they would escape the snows of the Sierras and the cruelty of the Indians. One train that chose the dangerous second alternative was the Harrington-Miltmore caravan.

Reaching the Hudspeth Cutoff during the closing days of August

1859, the Harrington company stopped its westward march near the Portneuf Bridge, a short distance from the Snake River. Several miles downtrail, the Miltmore party toiled ponderously to overtake the lead section of the train before nightfall. Shortly before twilight the Harrington company heard distant firing, and saw an Indian war party on a ridge. A small boy stumbled toward their wagon corral, holding his mangled arm against his stomach. While shots were exchanged, a rescue party sprinted across the open ground and managed to drag the child into the enclosure without casualties.

The Miltmore wagons had become too far separated from the Harrington train. Strung out on the cutoff, they pushed forward as fast as their tired animals would allow, unaware of three Indians working their way forward through the unguarded livestock at the rear of the column. When the Indians came near the wagons, the cattle stampeded into the foothills, exposing the intruders. Edward Miltmore sounded the alarm, but instead of retreating, the hostiles approached the captain. In this silent and empty land, all men were considered dangerous, and the three strangers looked more deadly than most to the emigrants. The captain observed that the strangers' hair was chestnut colored, streaked by the sun, and cropped to the skull. Although they were dressed as Indians, the men appeared taller than Indians, with light eyes and long, ill-kept beards. They also spoke perfect English.

"Where are you going?" asked their leader.

"To California," Miltmore answered.

The intruder grinned menacingly and said, "No you are not!"

After pronouncing this death sentence, the three men walked straight ahead and disappeared from sight. The emigrants resumed their journey with new urgency and got within a thousand yards of the main party before disaster struck. At a point where the trace narrowed to a dozen feet, they found their way blocked by renegades. Without warning, Indians swarmed from a shallow draw, killing or wounding five settlers before the emigrants could fire a shot.

Unable to find cover in that narrow place, a handful of men threw down their weapons and ran for the river, abandoning their women and children. However, before the Indians could close the trap, the rest formed a moving firing line and fought their way to better positions on the embankment south of the trail. Tiring of the battle, the renegades pulled away and returned to the wagons, allowing the emigrants to escape.

The survivors followed the river for three days, past the Portneuf Bridge, where they met the advance guard of Lieutenant Henry B. Livingston's detachment, escorting the Wallen Expedition. Elements of the Third Artillery under Captain John Reynold and an emigrant party destined for Walla Walla were also included in the column. Lieutenant

Livingston sent nine dragoons to the scene of the massacre to search for survivors.[35]

The rescue column found the plundered wagons, and, near the road, the bodies of four men feathered with arrows, their heads scalped and mutilated beyond recognition. Stunned and horrified, a dragoon paused over the mutilated corpse of a five-year-old child. The attackers, apparently taking delight in torturing the child in the presence of her mother, had cut off her legs, gouged out her eyes, severed her ears from her head, and tomahawked her. From all appearances she had been forced to walk, despite her amputation, "for the sole purpose of gratifying the hellish propensity of savage barbarity."[36] Three of the victims, Mrs. Miltmore and her two children, were never found, and were presumed to have been carried into captivity by the Shoshone.

The Harrington-Miltmore massacre provoked protest from frightened white settlers, and pressure mounted for a military campaign against the northern Shoshone and Bannocks. But additional testimony gathered by General Johnston clearly showed that the Indians were not entirely to blame for the tragedies. The problem of "white Indians" again complicated the army's task. The rumors were given new life by Lorenzo Suberr who ran into the "white Indians" head-on.

Working his way west to California, Suberr caught up with the Harrington-Miltmore train near Fort Laramie and traveled with the caravan to the Sweetwater Mail Station. At a saloon in Green River, a dozen rough-looking strangers joined him and displayed interest in the Harrington-Miltmore train. That night Suberr was kept busy answering questions about everything associated with his journey from the Missouri River. One of the strangers told him that the Harrington-Miltmore party would never reach California alive. Untroubled, he watched the twelve strangers saddle their horses and return to the trail, riding in the direction of the Miltmore party. Despite that hint of disaster, Suberr continued to Utah without a pang for his former traveling companions.

In Salt Lake City Suberr enjoyed the saloons, gambling halls, and brothels. During one of his pleasure excursions he was cornered by one of the toughs he had met at Green River—a swarthy, unshaven man, marked by a deep scar below his left eye. The man initiated a conversation on the subject of white Indians, but Suberr grew increasingly uncomfortable over his confession of murder, violence, and theft on the overland. The bandit invited Suberr to join his band of 125 white men and 350 Indians at their camp in Goose Creek Valley. He promised Suberr he "would make a pile."[37]

Suberr kept discreetly silent on the outlaws' activity in the territory until the Harrington-Miltmore massacre, when he reported what he knew to the army. General Johnston did not act on it at once. His Indian patrol was still out, and he waited for their report so long that the last of the season's transcontinental migration had cleared the trail. He then ordered the Bear River Expedition back to Camp Floyd, and the northern frontier was left to the Indians.

That winter General Johnston reviewed the sorry failure of the federal government's Indian policy in Utah and the bitter struggle that had erupted in Washington over it. The War Department had trimmed Camp Floyd's complement of troops to fewer than 1,000 men because President Buchanan wanted to avoid Republican criticism of his budget. Besides, he never bestirred himself over territorial emergencies.

The first casualty of the budget cut was the overland patrol, reduced to three companies of dragoons to control the dangerous trace from the first crossing of the Bear River to Gravelly Ford. Johnston deplored the War Department's economizing. He feared it would facilitate Indian raids against the overland and place the uncontrolled tribes beyond federal justice. "From the facilities afforded in an open mountainous country of watching the movement of the troops," he wrote, "frequent opportunities are afforded the Indians for making attacks without risking an encounter with any portion of the troops, and, after having perpetrated a robbery, by scattering in retreat, successfully elude both search and pursuit."[38]

Johnston recommended to General Lorenzo Thomas that the War Department abandon the easily avoided punitive patrols. Instead, he recommended temporary cantonments in key sections of the northern trails, garrisoned during the height of the overland emigration season by a well-equipped force of front-line effectives. The first control point should be at the first crossing of the Bear River, where new arrivals of emigrants would collect before continuing their journey west, he argued. This post would not only control the eastern entrances into the territory but, situated as it would be in the heart of the Shoshone country, it would help pacify them. To the west he envisioned a post near Soda Springs, and he planned a third at the mouth of Goose Creek Canyon, from which the army would operate a shuttle service to the Sinks of the Humboldt River. He recommended that the Oregon Trail by way of Fort Hall be permanently abandoned and that emigrant trains be required to travel with a complement of at least fifty mounted riflemen, civilian or military.[39]

This last proposal came about because of the claim of Major Isaac Lynde that every wagon train attacked by the warring tribes had failed to take adequate protective measures. "The Indians watch the trains from the hills," he complained to his superior, "and if they see a train well armed and watchful, they do not molest them. I have seen many trains on the road during the summer who had plenty of arms, but they carried them on their wagons; and, in many cases without being loaded. They would laugh at me when I told them of the necessity of always having their arms ready for instant use."[40]

Reorganization of the western military districts also occupied the general. There had been continued Indian depredations near the Snake River, so he recommended that the jurisdiction of the Department of Utah be extended over the Oregon Territory below the forty-fourth parallel. Soldiers stationed at Camp Floyd were to be responsible for the California Trail between Fort Bridger and the junction for the southern routes to the Pacific. To forestall raids north of this line, the commander urged General Harney to reopen Fort Boise or establish a series of summer garrisons from the Snake River to Solomon Falls.[41]

Johnston suggested that the Department of the Interior establish a separate Indian agency to shepherd the Bannocks and northern Shoshone along the Snake River. Johnston believed that these federal Indian agents should live with their respective tribes and watch over them. Equally important, the agents were to relocate all northern bands away from the overland trail since it was difficult to discriminate between friendly and unfriendly Indians. Then, any Indian found near the California Trail would be intercepted and destroyed. This policy, Johnston maintained, "was absolutely necessary to avoid involving the Government in a general war with the mountain tribes."[42]

As for the problem of white Indians, the commander acknowledged the wrongs inflicted on the northern tribes by white brigands. He recommended that all commercial activity with the Indians emanate from fixed stations or else that all trading posts be subject to federal licensure. "Many of these men," the general observed, "were supposed to be instigators if not participants in the robberies perpetrated on the route. . . ."[43]

However, nothing came of Johnston's proposals. Instead, Washington further reduced the strength of Camp Floyd. The influence of the army waned, and the long-smoldering troubles between the Paiutes and whites leaped into flame. In the minds of the policy makers in Washington, Camp Floyd existed as a result of the Utah War, which had to do with Mormons and not Indians. The white intrusion into the ancestral homeland of Native Americans would have to follow its natural and inevitably dangerous course.

CHAPTER TWELVE

PAIUTE AND SHOSHONE UPRISINGS

In the very heart of our settlements, the war-club and tomahawk are swung in wild defiance; the quiver of the red-man is replenished full with the sharpened arrows of destruction; powder-horn and bullet-pouch are supplied afresh with the preparations of death; and all forebode a time of attack and war, and blood and slaughter.
—The Mountaineer, *1860*[1]

INCREASINGLY FRUSTRATED by the continuing loss of their best lands and confused over inconsistent white policies toward them, Native American groups within the Utah Department's territory picked up the pace of their resistance. Mormons and other whites in the area usually exacerbated the problem with shortsighted and self-centered reactions. Caught in the middle, the garrison at Camp Floyd had little chance of doing much to pacify the region. Any hopes that the army may have had of containing Indian uprisings within the northern portion of the territorial frontier were dashed by further troop reductions at Camp Floyd during the winter of 1859–1860. Not comprehending that he was surrendering Utah's unprotected borders piecemeal to the Indians, the Secretary of State informed Governor Cumming that "it is deemed very desirable to reduce the large numbers of United States troops now in Utah, if it can be done consistently with the tranquility and general interests of the territory. . . ."[2] The message dismayed the governor no less than it pleased the Saints.

The governor pointed out the territory's chronic troubles with the Shoshone and Bannock along its northern border, saying that the "Indians of this Territory are numerous, well armed, and somewhat

218

warlike." He warned that "the withdrawal of the entire army from this territory seems to me injudicious and unjust, both to the resident population, as well as to the emigration through the country." Trying to prolong the life of Camp Floyd, Cumming requested that "five hundred soldiers should be retained here, and be established at such points as are deemed desirable by the officer in command."[3]

The War Department denied Cumming's proposal in General Order Number 10, which reduced the garrison at Camp Floyd to a handful of untried frontier regulars and relieved General Johnston of his command there. Colonel Charles F. Smith succeeded him.[4] The Buchanan administration conducted its Utah Indian policies as obstinately as it handled the Mormons in 1857. There was little effort to protect territorial citizens or emigrants. Few leaders in the nation's capital foresaw the human costs of this decision.

The change in command proceeded rapidly during the spring of 1860. While General Johnston's train was still en route to California, Smith tried to neutralize the Indians on the northern border with the undermanned department he had inherited. The War Department's penny pinching hampered everything, and a series of Indian raids swept the territory.

The Interior Department responded no better to the territorial challenge and failed to come forward with any remedies for Indian problems under their jurisdiction. Like Colonel Smith, Indian Superintendent Jacob Forney was ignored and underfinanced.

Most of Forney's troubles were caused by the growing strength of the anti-Mormon faction in Washington and a corresponding loss of prestige of Cumming's faction in Salt Lake City. Forney's budget came under fire, and everyone found out about it when Surveyor General S. C. Stambaugh appeared in Salt Lake City on official business during the spring of 1859. The superintendent must have realized that he was being forced out of office. His fears were not dispelled when Colonel Stambaugh opened public hearings on May 6, 1860, at the Farnham House. Although Judge Cradlebaugh had indicted Forney for returning false vouchers, Cradlebaugh did not attend the inquiry before Stambaugh, nor was his evidence made available to the defendant.[5] Nevertheless, Cradlebaugh's influence was unmistakable in the way the case proceeded, and a presumption of Forney's guilt clouded the investigation from its beginning. Stambaugh audited the agency's internal accounts with more political ingenuity than accuracy, and claimed to find evidence of fraud and corruption. Forney denied the allegations and painstakingly buttressed his claims of innocence with documents and agency records submitted to Stambaugh by his Mormon attorney, Hosea Stout.[6] Forney pressed Stambaugh for a full list of charges, only to be told that the final document would be forwarded to Washington without private or public disclosure. Forney was powerless.[7]

Time ran out for him on June 14, 1860, when he was suspended from office. One week later, he boarded the stage for Washington to present his case before the Secretary of the Interior.[8] Although he would return briefly that summer, he had no more effect on Indian problems in the territory.

Governor Cumming was appointed acting superintendent to repair the damage sustained by the Indian department. Painfully aware that he could not escape either declining governmental expenditures or the political morass through which defenders of Indian rights had been dragged, Cumming counseled the complete abandonment of the Indian farm system. Viewing his new responsibilities with the same one-sided economic commitment that characterized his tenure as governor, Cumming plainly intended to remove farming Indians from white villages. "The whole system of farming for Indians," he wrote, "whether for encouraging their inclinations for industrial pursuits, or any economical arrangement, is unreasonable and utterly at variance with the experience of the past." Never really reconciled to Indians and Saints living together harmoniously, he charged that the farm system was unreliable and only advanced the interests of the non-Indian bureaucracy. Predictably, he believed that male Indians "cannot be induced to labor, under any circumstances."[9]

Complicating the issue further was the question of land ownership. The governor and the Mormons believed that whites should move freely into unsettled land. Further, Cumming believed that ancestral Indian claims had been invalidated by the joint resolution that annexed Texas as well as by the Treaty of Guadalupe Hidalgo that added the Mexican Cession to the American empire. As a result, the governor proposed a drastic limitation on the size of native land claims. In an effort to enforce this policy, he suggested "that treaties be held with the various tribes occupying or roving over the Territory, for the purpose of defining their boundaries, making suitable compensation for concessions, and holding the tribes respectively responsible for any outrages committed by them."[10]

Yet, despite the fact that such ideas could only benefit the Saints, the *Deseret News* speculated whether the Indian Department of Utah existed in name and salaries only. "The superintendent Forney has undoubtedly traveled and talked much; perchance has taken many sketches of Indian life and customs; but a very important portion of his career lately has been devoted to squabbles about his balance-sheet at Washington."[11] Debauched and swindled by unscrupulous agents, the article continued, the Indian presented "himself at our door in his aboriginal breech-cloth, and with the rags of blanket, the gift of ten years ago, asks for bread. The hungry savage cannot be turned over to the dogs; but, may we ask, has not the Great Father, the Government paid for his eatables and new shirts and blankets?"[12]

The normally friendly and hospitable Indians of San Pete abandoned their reservation because of lagging appropriations, making a bad situation worse. Comparable conditions at the Spanish Fork and Corn Creek reservations produced dissension and partisan feuding. The governor nevertheless continued to refuse food and supplies to hungry Indians.

As spring approached, starved and alienated Indians began moving off the desert reservations of Ruby Valley and Deep Creek. Shortly after the exodus started, an unidentified traveler described conditions among the desert tribes for readers of the *Deseret News.* "Indians in that vicinity were assuming a threatening and hostile attitude towards the few settlers, in consequence of the singular conduct of someone connected with the Indian department here." Dismayed by the inroads of fear, disease, and famine, the account painted a dreary picture of tribal life. "I was informed, however, the Indians were starving," the article continued, and "had killed one of Mr. Severe's oxen . . . and that they were exasperated at the non-distribution of the few goods which had been sent out there for them, and had expressed their intention of taking them by force." Agent Harrison Severe, discouraged because neither the national government, the army, nor the Mormons would feed the Indians, abandoned his post and took his family to Camp Floyd.[13]

Near the foothills of the Sierra Nevada, along Pyramid Lake and the Walker River, Agent Frederick Dodge warned that the Paiutes had learned from long and bitter experience to be suspicious in dealing with the white man. "The Indians of my Agency linger about the graves of their ancestors," wrote Dodge to the Commissioner of Indian Affairs in Washington,

> but the game is gone, and now, the steady tread of the white man is upon them, the green valleys too, once spotted with game are not theirs now, necessity makes them barter the virtue of their companions as a commodity of the market, and the bitter contemplation burn[s] in their bosoms the stern reality of their fate. Driven by destitution they seek refuge in crime, and show themselves unsparing because they have been unspared.[14]

However, the figures of "white Indians" were never absent from the resultant carnage, he cautioned. "I sincerely hope that those asylums will be made for them [the Indians] where they can be free from the influence of the *White Brigands* who loiter about our great overland mail and Emigrant routes,—using them as their instruments to rob and murder our citizens."[15]

Pondering over these and other points, the western agent urgently requested changes in budgetary appropriations for his district, complaining that the 6,000 Indians under his charge had received only a fractional share of federal monies appropriated for the territory. "Nearly *three hundred thousand dollars* has been appropriated for the Territory of Utah since 1853. And yet almost the entire amount has been squandered or exhausted in the vicinity of Salt Lake City—without . . . securing any aims or objects of the same. And while this is the case, two-thirds of the Indian population reside west of Salt Lake."[16]

But even while Major Dodge penned these words, the Paiute War echoed back across the Basin into the very heart of Mormon country. Bewildered by the rapid changes brought to their land by prospectors, the western Paiutes found themselves engaged in an Indian war forced upon them. In 1859, several bands of Paiutes encircled a force of more than a hundred whites, ambushing and killing seventy of the gold hunters. At the eastern end of the trail the Gosiutes raided the newly opened mail stations on the Simpson road traversing their country. From the standpoint of the Indians, the cause of the Paiute War on the central overland was purely economic.

The Gosiutes suffered at the hands of an army of Mormon settlers who appropriated the best agricultural and grazing lands near the mail stations, and produced a conflict between native traditions and white desires.[17] This friction led to furious Indian assaults against travelers and Pony Express relay stations along the central route. Emboldened by each new success, according to one writer, "howling like wolves, a band of a hundred or more would swoop down on a lonely post, killing keeper, hostler, and guards; pillaging, burning buildings and haystacks, and driving away relay horses."[18]

Station masters and settlers yielded ground, demanding that Camp Floyd secure the Simpson route from Indian attack. Colonel Smith responded by establishing a military depot at the northern end of Ruby Valley where the terrain offered protection for the overland mail and emigrant traffic. He ordered into the field a mounted company of soldiers drawn from the Fourth Artillery and led by Lieutenant Delavan Duane Perkins, a fledging graduate from West Point unaccustomed to Indian fighting or the Utah terrain.

Smith had no desire to embark on a ruinous Indian war. He cautioned Perkins to conciliate the Gosiutes, even to the extent of authorizing any concessions necessary to assure the safety of the Simpson road and the new Mormon settlements in Tooele Valley. He dispatched a second patrol of dragoons toward Ruby Valley under the leadership of Lieutenant Stephen H. Weed. Before the patrol got under way it was joined by

Howard Egan, a veteran mail carrier, who offered his services as guide and interpreter.[19]

The company marched westward, but less than a day later a friendly Indian hailed Lieutenant Weed to report that a Paiute war party had burned the Deep Creek mail station—wounding several keepers and driving off a score of horses and mules from the valley pastures. The main body of warriors retreated north to the Humboldt River. The soldiers gathered at the abandoned Deep Creek station and settled into bivouac.[20]

At daybreak, sentinels discovered a lone Indian watching the soldiers' movements. The warrior was quickly captured and escorted into camp for questioning. The brave refused to reveal the location of his band, and even attempted an escape, although surrounded by troops. As later reported in the *Deseret News*:

> There were two sentinals guarding him. He requested one fetch him a drink of water; while he was gone, the Indian gathered a handful of ashes and threw it in the eyes of the other sentinal, and then thrusted to his heels. The bullet brought him down; about thirty yards from the camp. The ball passed through his thigh after which he received three through the head, yet strange to say, he is in a fair way to recover! When first shot, he pretended to be dead, or would doubtless have been put out of his misery.[21]

The warrior either died from his wounds or was executed, for no prisoner was reported taken back to Camp Floyd.

Peter Niece, station keeper of the Schell Valley relay post, came to Ruby Valley on the stagecoach. Having survived one Indian attack himself, he reported that most of the relay posts along the overland were abandoned, bringing mail service to a standstill. The story of his escape from the tightening ring of warriors varied only in detail from tales of other tragedies heard by the soldiers of the overland. Late in the afternoon of June 8, Niece and a dozen men were busy repacking several thousand pounds of provisions for distribution along the mail road when thirty warriors surrounded the station. The war party demanded the supplies and immediate evacuation of the post. Niece refused to consider the request, turned his back to the tribal leader, and walked toward the building.

The chieftain signaled to his band to open fire, but Niece managed to reach the stockade safely. The Indians attempted to fire the building and lost several braves before withdrawing. Niece decided to trade the provisions for safe passage out of the country. The warriors scrambled through the outpost stealing provisions as well as horses, sheep, and cattle before burning the station.[22]

The survivors painfully made their way west through the open country, eventually hailing the California-bound stage driven by John Smith and Nathan Slater. After sending the remainder of his party on to Ruby Valley, Niece continued west by stage to Deep Creek. When the coach arrived at the station, Niece found the bodies of three Paiute warriors on the road near the ransacked and burned-out building. No trace of the post's personnel or livestock was found, although the immediate country was scouted. After burying the dead Indians in a common grave, the three men turned the stage around and returned to Ruby Valley, where Slater reported the Paiute uprising.

No sooner had Perkins established control of Ruby Valley than a courier arrived from Camp Floyd with orders for his column to return to Deep Creek, where a train of 250 emigrants had collected before crossing the desert to Carson City.[23] The column halted briefly at Schell Creek where fourteen soldiers were detached to protect civilians who were rebuilding the destroyed depot. Several times on their way they left men behind to protect civilians. Greatly reduced in strength, the small detachment continued its journey to Deep Creek, where the young lieutenant met the emigrant train and escorted it west to Carson City. Caked with dust and bone-tired from their long ride across the desert, Perkins and his charges arrived safely and he bade the emigrants farewell. After a brief rest, his depleted forces left their camp at the base of the Sierra Nevada and retraced their steps across the overland toward Ruby Valley. For the next six weeks the patrol provided escort service to passing emigrants whenever it was not required elsewhere.

Locked away in Cedar Valley, isolated from the events to the west, Colonel Smith chafed under the military restrictions imposed on his command by the War Department. With several hundred of his troops protecting the central overland, and half that number ranging along the California Trail, the commander was obliged to protect the government's multimillion dollar investment in Camp Floyd with fewer than fifty soldiers. Moreover, he was showing remarkable skill in controlling the entire intermountain Basin with fewer than 400 men, but he fell victim to squabbles in Washington over the effectiveness of his command. The Secretary of War sent a blistering communique charging that the Utah Department had done little to insure the safety of emigrants passing through the territory. Backlash from the Paiute War spread from California to Washington, and from Washington the federal government voiced demands for action by the Utah Department to improve its western Indian policies.[24]

An ardent apostle of the army's point of view, Colonel Smith rejected the flood of bureaucratic criticism, which he felt placed a straitjacket on his command. While the situation in Utah went from bad to worse, he reminded eastern congressmen that it was impossible for his undermanned army to control 2,000 square miles of primitive terrain.[25] Furthermore, the Indian warriors could not be crushed, for their mobility and knowledge of the desert and mountains made action by a small force useless. He angrily withdrew all patrols from the eastern section of the territory and stationed his troops along the overland at Ruby Valley, Willow Springs, Egan Canyon, Dry Creek, and Smith's Creek. Protection of the California road west of Smith's Creek was left to the Carson Valley volunteers. Soon after redistributing his command, Lieutenant Perkins became gravely ill and turned over his responsibilities to Lieutenant Weed for the remainder of the fall campaign.[26]

The Paiute War reached its peak during the sweltering summer of 1860, when Indians raided an army supply train near Antelope Springs. Teamsters in the train broke the Indian attack, wounding a dozen braves without suffering casualties. Lieutenant Weed was ordered east to Willow Springs, where a small force of Indians had been reported. But his march was interrupted by a Pony Express rider who reported that 200 warriors had surrounded the Egan Canyon station and had demanded powder and lead. The letter carrier warned that the Paiutes were heavily armed with modern weapons and had taken strategic positions on the crest of a ridge overlooking the road approaching the scattered buildings.

Weed ordered his men to work their way down the road, timing their march to surprise the Indians. But an Indian sentinal posted on the high ground opened fire before the troopers reached the crest of the ridge. Weed ordered an immediate charge across the foothills, forcing the Indians back. Then, however, the troopers panicked and fled for cover, leaving several soldiers wounded on the field. The skirmish continued until evening, when the Paiutes moved out. The valley was quiet again.[27]

Weed reported one soldier killed and two wounded in that encounter. No Indian body count was listed. In many respects the engagement demonstrated the Paiutes' fighting ability and endurance. So Weed withdrew his troops to Egan Canyon, where his patrol could provide escort service for express riders traveling west to Willow Creek. But the determination of the Paiutes would not be quelled; the Indians struck the Spring Valley Station farther to the east.

After one of his fights with the Paiutes, Sergeant Bishop reported to his superior that on the night of August 11, 1860, his patrol was awakened by gunfire. "I immediately but very quickly, awoke the men; divided them four with the horses; two skirted one side of the hill, Mr. Rogers (Indian Agent) and myself on the other; the moon just arose; we startled one Indian; he turned and fired a rifle; Mr. Rogers and I fired, and just struck him, but he was too near the hills to follow him."[28] Swift to follow up any small success, the troopers traced the wounded warrior from Spring Valley to Deep Creek. There the sergeant learned that the Indians had demanded the outpost's supply of food, clothing, and weapons and had threatened the station master's life when he refused the request. Unknown to the Indians, the soldiers corralled their horses and spent an uneasy night sleeping in hay wagons, half listening to a thousand small sounds that might hint of the warriors' return. The sun was scarcely over the desert horizon when the sergeant spied several dozen Paiutes coming out of the brush in a dead run for the relay post. Before the warriors reached the station, Bishop yelled at his men to commence firing. A single volley killed four attackers before they could discharge their weapons. The dumbfounded Indians broke and fled, abandoning their dead and wounded.[29]

The smoke of that battle had scarcely cleared when a raiding party of Paiutes again attacked the Schell Creek Station during the dawn hours of August 12. The mail carriers rallied and made a successful retreat into the station without suffering casualties. The Indians then divided into two parties. The first encircled the station and crawled as near as possible to attack the inner defenses. While they fired into the building, the second wave of attackers drove the outpost's livestock into the surrounding hills. One hour into the battle, Lieutenant Weed and his men, patrolling near Schell Creek, heard the firing and came racing down the road to investigate the shooting. The young officer coolly ordered his mounted artillerymen to form a battle line and open fire on the Paiutes. When the dust and smoke of the fight cleared, seventeen Indians lay dead on the battlefield, and there were as many wounded. The mauled Paiutes retreated to remake their strategy, having gained a healthy respect for the federal dragoons.[30]

Undaunted by heavy losses in the field, or by the persistent pressure of the overland patrol, the Paiutes ambushed the biweekly stage traveling from Camp Floyd to Salt Lake City. The raiding party emerged from a wall of undergrowth that screened the road four miles west of Lehi and, in a daring flank attack, shot the lead horses of the heavy Concord stage. The remaining animals, their legs bruised and bleeding from the doubletree they kicked to pieces, brought the coach to a halt. Aware that the Indians were about to close the trap, the driver yelled at the lone passenger to open fire, but he refused to join the fight. Later, a rescue party found the mutilated bodies of the two men. Apparently "the renegades shot both the driver and the passenger and took both their scalps which they mounted on the ends of two long sticks and rode off on the west side of Utah Lake toward Goshen."[31]

During the remainder of the year and continuing into 1861, numerous small skirmishes occurred. Nearly half of the twenty mail stations within the Great Basin were destroyed, and only a few protected miles of the overland trail were free from sporadic Indian raids. Nevertheless, in this brief and desperate struggle, the army's deep probes stunned the insurgent Paiutes, and fostered the development of the Pony Express. Yet the Indians faced their enemies courageously.

Emigrants began to fear that the Mojave Indians would ally themselves with the Paiutes. The Mojave showed little disposition to attack travelers or to extend the Indian troubles into California, but panic-stricken emigrants spread exaggerated stories of Indian uprisings. This fear intensified after the death of Thomas S. Williams, murdered by southern tribesmen. On March 18, 1860, Williams and Parmeno Jackson led a caravan of a dozen wagons along the Mormon Corridor to Bitter Springs, 135 miles east of San Bernardino. They met a band of unpainted Mojaves who agreed to take them to a small watered valley four miles beyond the springs in exchange for a small amount of trading goods. The traders followed the natives into a box canyon where they were ambushed by a waiting war party, each receiving two or three serious wounds in the assault. Holding stubbornly to his saddle, Williams was carried by his horse to Bitter Springs, too weak from loss of blood to tell what had happened. Jackson was shot from his horse. A rescue party, alerted to his plight by Williams's appearance, rode forward and discovered him stretched out on the ground, alive but seriously wounded. Later that night Thomas Williams died and was buried at Bitter Springs.[32] The Mojave and Paiute Indians never did join forces, although isolated violence made travel over the southern road to California extremely hazardous.

Such outbursts of violence clearly underscored the mounting Indian troubles throughout the territory, especially in smaller Mormon settlements along the Wasatch Mountains. Taking advantage of the army's preoccupation in the western desert, the Indians methodically demoralized poorly protected villages with lightning guerrilla strikes. In one such assault, a war party of Shoshone raided the farm of Ezra and Lachoneus Barnard near Farmington on the eleventh of April, seriously injuring both men before driving off a small herd of cattle.[33] This was followed by an attack on the farm of Edwin Pugh, where raiders mauled a herder who attempted to prevent the theft of a horse and some harnessing equipment. Shortly after the attack, Pugh's son followed the renegades to the Weber River, but instead of recovering the stolen property, the boy narrowly escaped with his life.

As conflicts with the Indians multiplied, the outraged editor of the *Deseret News* demanded an investigation into the attacks.

> Many of the Indians in this territory complain that the promises made to them by the Superintendent and Agents have not been fulfilled. That is a matter between the "red skins" and the government agents, and may be true or not, but it has been thoroughly demonstrated that if agreements made with or promises made to any of the American race are not carried out by the party dealing with them, a spirit of revenge is at once enkindled which cannot be satisfied till they commit some depredation and often not without the shedding of blood.[34]

Still the raids continued. A band of Shoshone warriors raided several farms near Kingston's Fort, a short distance from Ogden. Among the victims of the tragedy was Thomas Miles, who on the afternoon of April 13, 1860, was confronted by three Indians armed with bows and iron-spiked war-axes. Anticipating the worst, the settler tried to escape into the farmhouse but was felled by eight arrows in his back. Calling forth every ounce of energy his body could command, the wounded farmer grabbed one of the war clubs and managed to drive off his attackers. Miles dragged himself to the nearest settlement, where his wounds were treated by the local physician, Dr. Higgins. Miles recovered, and later recalled the weapons used by the Indians. The bow was "about four feet long, and one and one-half inches thick, painted with blood, and in one end is fixed a piece of buckskin with a lock of human hair attached to it. There are also thirty-six notches cut in the club which, it is said, denote the number of persons they have killed, the number of scalps they have taken."[35]

To stem the flood of violence in the northern settlements, the commander of the Weber County Militia, General Chauncy West, concentrated his forces along the Weber River. The home guard failed to find any sign of a war party, or any trace of the large number of animals reported stolen. Nevertheless, a steady flow of intelligence indicated that one of the guilty warriors had returned to his tribe, now camped a short distance from Brigham City. Responding to the reports, General West dispatched Colonel James W. Cummings and Captain Alvin Nichols from Ogden to arrest the fugitives and to recover any stolen property in their possession. Captain Nichols led a company of militiamen into the Shoshone camp and arrested the suspected warrior. Despite protests from the band's leader, the renegade was placed in irons and escorted back to Brigham City, where his actions were described to the local probate judge, who jailed the Indian in a storage room attached to the rear of his house. Several hours later, a squad of Shoshone braves entered Judge Smith's office, threatened the life of the magistrate, and forced their comrade's release. The town swarmed with Indian horsemen. The Mormons, once considered by the Indians to be militarily invincible, were put on the defensive and challenged to come out of their homes and fight. The Saints refused, and the Shoshones galloped home to their wickiups near the edge of the village.[36]

The following dawn, in a last endeavor to intimidate the settlers, a small war party laid siege to the house of Sheriff Cutler, firing into the dwelling to draw him from the building. Fortunately, the sheriff had already left. Moving north, the Shoshones raided Willow Creek, where they again attempted to draw the Mormons into battle. Parading through the streets, the Indians yelled out insults to the hidden settlers. Again the Saints refused to take up the challenge.[37]

Although the actual damage inflicted by the Indians was not great, the attacks had a tonic effect on the northern warrior bands, which now fell upon defenseless ranches and farms. Meanwhile, the freshly triumphant Indians roved northward unhurriedly, appropriating herds of Mormon and emigrant cattle as they made their way to the Shoshone homeland between the Snake River and the California Trail.³⁸

Other raids plunged Cache Valley into mourning. Indian reaction to the Saints' attempt to resettle the rich farmland in 1859 was instantaneous, violent, and more widespread than in previous years.³⁹ The settlement of the valley had been a long, torturous experience for the Saints. Starting in 1856 with the establishment of the village of Wellsville by Peter Maughan, the northward probe of Mormon colonization was beset by troubles. The first settlement ended the following year with the call to return south amid the Saints' growing concern over Johnston's Army.

Despite severe political problems and the increased presence of Indians, the Mormons reoccupied Cache Valley in 1859, attracting a heavy migration of poor, inexperienced, and uneducated English converts from Liverpool.⁴⁰ The Saints could foresee problems associated with the resettlement, yet they stepped into the task with characteristic confidence. Past experience with the Indians did not prepare the hardworking settlers for the drama and tragedy that followed. Trying to hold territory they could not hope to control, the Mormons suffered heavy losses from Indian attacks. Still more alarming was the colony's weak military posture that left the settlers without the protection of either the federal army or the territorial militia.

Disturbed by the resurgence of Indian strength, Superintendent Forney signed a peace treaty with the valley warriors during the spring of 1860. But even while the Saints were breathing a sigh of relief over the tenuous agreement, new dangers loomed on the horizon. The chief source of the Indians' unhappiness lay in their resentment over the planting of new colonies. Indians laid siege to Smithfield when one of their warriors was arrested for horse stealing. The one-eyed prisoner was detained in the schoolhouse, guarded by several men.

As the Saints started their summer harvest, a small band of northern Shoshone rode into the village and attempted to negotiate the release of the Indian. But when the Saints flatly refused to turn over the prisoner, the band's leader shouted at the prisoner to leave the building, assuring him that the Mormons would not interfere with his escape. Inside the jail the captain of the guard warned the Indian not to move, and he instructed the armed sentinel to kill the prisoner if he left the building. The threat only inflamed the prisoner, who, during a momentary lapse of vigilance, made a wild scramble for freedom. A single shot from the guard's musket brought the Indian to the ground, mortally wounded in the back. Crazed by the sight of their fallen comrade, the rescue party returned fire without hitting anyone, then retreated to reload their weapons. Three settlers near the edge of town were surrounded by a second band of Shoshone. Before the Mormons could draw their weapons, the Indians opened fire, killing John Reed and severely wounding Samuel Cozens. The Saints of Smithfield rallied and forced the Indians to withdraw to the mountains, where they met Ira Merrill and his brother coming down the canyon. The Indians killed Ira Merrill and seriously wounded his brother. Their wagon was looted and burned before the Mormon posse arrived.

Taking to the trail again, the posse located the Indians several hundred yards away, snaking their way down a steep incline. Moving closer to their targets, the Mormons fired a volley of shots in the direction of the warriors, knocking one Indian from his horse. Frightened by the soldiers' marksmanship, the Indians hurried east to join other Shoshone.[41]

As the struggle for control of Cache Valley became more intense, Brigham Young warned the Saints in the north to use a full measure of caution in dealing with the Shoshone. Agonizing over the Smithfield incident that darkened the fall of 1860, he wrote Peter Maughan not to dabble in strategy that endangered the lives of settlers.

> I was pleased to learn, that the brethren proved so prompt and well prepared as they did but with that same one, aware of the beginning of the affray, could have had forethought enough to have timely warned those in the canyon, or sent assistance to them. But the lives of the killed cannot be recalled, and it only remains that their deaths profit the living, by prompting to increase an unrelaxing vigilance and wariness on the part of all in your valley and its neighborhood.
>
> I hope that the brethren will learn that a horse or two is not so much value as the life of a person.[42]

Meanwhile, trouble continued to plague the army's meager forces stationed near the Portneuf Bridge, charged with the responsibility of maintaining the safety of the California Trail. Commanding three reduced companies of dragoons, Colonel Marshall Saxe Howe continued to provide escort service for emigrants and to patrol the dangerous battle zone from the crossing of the Portneuf River to Thousand Springs Valley.[43] The little force succeeded in conveying the great bulk of traffic safely through the northern passage with minimal losses of life or property. Yet, as the Civil War started, the great question of who would control the overland was still not answered.

CHAPTER THIRTEEN

UNSAINTLY CITY

There is silence in Zion; no warning voice in the streets, nor in the Tabernacle of the Lord; everyone is left to go his own way, and many are running away from the Lord; and in this hour of temptation and darkness, it is our duty to live our religion. . . .
—Journal History, *1858*[1]

THE END OF THE FIFTIES was not a saintly time in the city of the Saints. Domestic unrest engulfed the Mormon kingdom. The city was divided, Mormon against Gentile, each suspicious of the other, and both factions often in revolt against law and order. The center of this brawling Basin crossroads was the Gentile-dominated business district, a post-frontier collection of shops, warehouses, gambling halls, brothels, and saloons, populated by a colorful collection of carpetbaggers who referred to the red-light zone as Whiskey Street.

It was a critical time in the history of the Saints—their control of the territory and their existence as a separate people were at stake. The army's presence and the Gentiles' intractability undermined Brigham Young's control of the territory. Living in the Lion House, protected by armed guards around the clock, the Mormon prophet said nothing publicly about the growing menace. With the evils of the army's occupation in mind, he warned his people "to keep clear of Whiskey Street," and let "civilization take its course."[2] Yet the events of the summer of 1858 realized many of the worst fears of the Saints. The city was torn apart by an unprecedented wave of drunkenness, gambling, and shooting, according to Luke Gallup, who lamented that the saintly and blessed were rare: "If there are any devils in this world they are there in Salt Lake City. They are all strangers here and not wanted, we are down on them in our feeling and some may be glad to leave next spring, as we can spare them comfortably."[3] Mormon feeling against the army and Gentile hatred of local police ran so high that

231

men in uniform were afraid to be seen in the streets. Anarchy threatened.

The problem of crime and violence reached into every household of the city. A generation of young ruffians left their wild experiences blazoned in the editorial columns of the territorial newspapers or in descriptive passages in books by world travelers. "A few youths of rather a rowdyish appearance were mounted in all the tawdriness of western trappings," wrote the famous explorer-journalist, Sir Richard Burton,

> —Rocky Mountain hats, tall and broad, or steeple-crowned felts, covering their scalp-locks, embroidered buckskin garments, huge leggings, with caterpillar or millepede fringes, red or rainbow-coloured flannel shirts, gigantic spurs, bright-hilted pistols and queer-sheathed knives stuck in red sashes with gracefully depending ends."[4]

Ruffians raced through the streets unchallenged, the editor of the *Deseret News* wrote:

> If some of those who are in the habit of yelling and whooping like savages, as they pass through the streets on their nocturnal excursions in sleighs, on horseback, or gratify their pedestrian propensities, were made to answer therefor, they might learn a lesson that would be beneficial to them in afterlife, even if it did not have a tendency to cure them at once of brawling in the streets when riding or on promenade.[5]

Riding horseback down Main Street in a kind of witch's sabbath, young renegades at times made the avenue impassable. Breaking the night's silence by firing weapons, they roamed the shuttered streets, breaking into shops or robbing nocturnal travelers. "The Headquarters of rowdyism is on East Temple St.," wrote George A. Smith to a friend. "There have been two murders within the last week, and several men badly wounded; a good many have been badly bruised who chose to use other weapons than revolvers."[6] Still later, he described a night in Salt Lake City in a letter to T. B. H. Stenhouse. "Last night some gamblers galloped through the town, firing pistols, shouting like Indians, issuing military orders, as though commanding soldiery, and uttering blasphemies, which gave evidence of their Christian origin."[7]

Brigham Young, searching for ways to stop the sudden revolt against law and order, requested the municipal government of Salt Lake City to increase its police force from 40 to 200 peace officers. The city council passed the desired action without a single dissenting vote.[8] The following evening, September 16, 1858, the new recruits were assembled near the livery stable of the Beehive House and inducted into their new offices. The Church leader spent the greater part of the meeting speaking apologetically of the lawlessness of many young Saints who were now cast adrift to suffer the same penalties as erring Gentiles.[9] The news of the enlarged police force rumbled through Whiskey Street. "After dark no Gentile walks the streets alone. Everyone, night and day, is armed to the teeth. Daily we expect to hear of a row," wrote Captain Jesse Gove.[10]

It was a bad year in every way for the city jailer, William Cooke. He was a favorite target of ambush gunfire, frequently finding himself surrounded by drunken mobs attempting to storm the prison to release friends or fellow travelers. He came unscathed through the summer of 1858, but one autumn night a gunman named McDonald, alias Cunningham, and two companions, identified later as Foster and Ingram, knocked on the door of the jail and asked permission to visit two of the inmates. Cooke failed to disarm the desperadoes before he allowed them to enter the inmates' cell. The young roughnecks watched the officer leave the room and walk to the front of the jail to wait out the visit. Cunningham pulled from his pocket a key to the prison's front door, but to his surprise the convicts refused it.

Cunningham drew his pistol on one of the reluctant inmates, warning him to come out of the jail or be killed on the spot. The convict complied. Cooke met the gunman near the entrance of the building and went for his gun. The crack of a revolver rang through the jail, and Cooke collapsed, shot twice in the chest. While the jailer bled to death, Cunningham and his gunmen started for Fort Bridger, where they hoped to spend the winter disguised as teamsters from Camp Floyd.

News of the murder reached the army outpost in a matter of days, with the eastbound mail carrier, Edwin P. Jones, known affectionately as "Scottie." Though Jones had brought along a description of the killer, he had shared a meal and several drinks with the outlaws without connecting them with the penned impressions. Scottie realized his mistake on the road to Green River, exchanged routes with a westbound stage driver, and headed back.

He found Cunningham gambling with a handful of mountaineers, apparently deserted by his partners. As Jones approached him, Cunningham turned abruptly in his chair and drew his gun. Both men fired. The fugitive dropped to the floor mortally wounded, bleeding profusely from a gaping neck wound. Even though he had a wound in his left arm, Scottie took out his bowie knife and scalped Cunningham's lifeless body. Grinning, he held the scalp aloft for all to see.[11]

Throughout 1858, nervous Salt Lake City peace officers at times contributed to the civic lawlessness. T. B. H. Stenhouse, then a confidant of Brigham Young but later a vocal enemy of the Church, claimed that "Resistance to an officer, of the slightest attempt to escape from custody,

was early seized, when wanted, as the justification of closing a disreput-
able career, and in more than one case of this legal shooting, there is much
doubt if even the trial excuse was waited for."[12]

The writer charged that the "Salt Lake police then earned the reputation of affording every desperate prisoner the opportunity of escape, and,
if embraced, to a 'halt,' and saved the country the expense of a trial and his
subsequent boarding in the penitentiary. A coroner's inquiry and cemetery expenses were comparatively light."[13] Although Stenhouse's accusations were colored by the bitterness that often accompanies apostasy,
newspaper accounts of the period seem to substantiate his claims.

Many of the desperadoes shot while trying to escape were thieves, like
A. B. Baker, a notorious rustler who operated between Salt Lake City and
Fort Bridger. On June 30, 1860, Baker stole a pony from an emigrant
near Ham's Fork and escaped westward on the road to Salt Lake City. A
posse followed him into Echo Canyon, where he was overtaken the next
day and wounded after a prolonged shooting match. The *Deseret News*
handling of the story was not unbiased.

> When too late, he pled for life, and said if they would not kill him,
> he would tell them where there was a band of a thousand stolen
> horses. He was buried by those who thus meted out to him sum-
> mary justice, not exactly according to law, but upon a more
> speedy, economical and salutary principle, and a stake placed at the
> head of his grave, on which was inscribed—"*A.B. Baker, shot for
> horse stealing, July 1st, 1860.*"[14]

Trouble loomed as large for Davis Skeen of Lehi, a young man
arrested in Logan on June 29, 1860, for stealing a horse that belonged to a
neighboring farmer. In the absence of a jail he was confined in the local
schoolhouse under guard to prevent his escape. Three days later the jailer
heard a loud rapping outside the building and, aroused by curiosity,
looked out into the street and saw three men with blackened faces peering
into the building. Believing the strangers were attempting a release of the
prisoner, the jailer rushed from the building and attempted to arrest them,
but they managed to escape. "In the tumult of the moment, Skeen made
an attempt to get away, but met with a detainer in the form of nine rifle
balls, rendering any further proceedings in his case, especially under the
habeas corpus act, entirely unnecessary."[15]

Although a reign of lawlessness seemed to engulf Utah, official penitentiary records reveal that only thirty-six territorial criminals were committed to confinement between 1858 and 1861, and of those, ten were
pardoned, twelve were released on writs of *habeas corpus*, while three were
left to serve out their sentences.[16]

Local police often took justice into their own hands, and even the
staunchest Church supporters feared that some individuals were assassi-

nated to satisfy personal vengeance or to answer for earlier violations of the law for which they could not be held legally accountable.[17] The tragic case of Andrew Bernard cast a dense fog of distrust over the Salt Lake police force.

Born deaf and dumb, Bernard was frequently the source of public amusement, relentlessly hounded by every Salt Lake City street urchin. Long before the army arrived in the territory, Bernard was considered a public nuisance, tolerated by the local police, though it was a matter of common knowledge that he was a petty thief.[18] In Salt Lake's booming prosperity, Bernard had graduated to practicing grand larceny. During the autumn of 1858 a teamster named Henry C. Smith charged him with stealing fifty-five dollars in gold, but before the order could be executed, Smith departed for California.[19]

N. L. Christiansen, a sober Dane newly deputized assistant marshal, jailed the deaf-mute and bound him over for trial under the old warrant, but a sympathetic court remanded the prisoner to the custody of his mother. At first, Bernard admitted stealing eleven dollars to buy winter clothing but denied any knowledge of the teamster's gold. He later spoiled his credibility by agreeing to return the unspent loot, but when he escorted a police officer to his mountain cache he had only seven dollars hidden there.

Bernard never returned to Salt Lake City. His mother searched the byways of the city, but nobody knew her son's whereabouts. After a week of worry, the woman recognized Marshal Christiansen walking in the shadows of Whiskey Street, apparently attempting to avoid her. She demanded to know what had happened to her son. Christiansen said that her boy was unharmed, adding that he intended to return him to the city the following morning. Unconvinced, the mother said she had heard that her son was dead, killed by Christiansen. The lawman then admitted that he had killed her son, but claimed he did it in self-defense.

The story was publicized in a series of unsigned letters in the *Valley Tan*, raising the ugly suspicion that the boy had fallen victim to "blood atonement," a philosophy of payment for sins by the voluntary death of the sinner, once thought to be a Mormon practice. A second letter printed alongside the first, apparently written by a Saint, contradicted the blood atonement theory and stated "that Dummy had been killed up the canyon near Eph Hank's cabin by a policeman from the city." The writer added, "he himself did not believe, as some of the brethren do, that it necessary to kill a person to save his soul."[20]

The murder inflamed partisan feelings. Newspapers kept the rumors circulating. Finally a full-scale investigation was opened in Salt Lake City, directed by Judge Sinclair. Brigham Young, believing that the investigation was an effort to drag him through the courts, viewed the soft-spoken judge's actions darkly. "The malicious and vindictive spirit of Judge Sinclair," he wrote to a close companion, "is an insult to the whole of the civil officers of this city and an outrage on the community."[21] The angry prophet said that Sinclair was trying to worsen the relationship between the territory's hostile factions so that the federal army could be brought into play against the Saints.[22]

The morning of December 16, 1858, Assistant Marshal Christiansen gave his version of the Bernard killing to the grand jury. He countered almost every bit of testimony that would link him with the murder. The way he told the story of Bernard's death, the two men had arrived at the unoccupied mountain cabin of Ephraim Hanks late on the evening of December 8. The next day they climbed a steep canyon to reclaim the money Bernard had hidden. At a bend in the trail, Bernard attacked Christiansen with a knife, striking him in the side just above the hip. The heavy-bladed knife glanced off Christiansen's belt buckle, he testified, which probably saved his life. The marshal drew his pistol and fired four times. Shot in the breast, arm, and hand, the boy ran down the mountain to Hanks's cabin, pursued by the Mormon deputy. At the cabin, Christiansen testified, Bernard attacked him with a cast-iron wheel hub on a rope and chased him into the cabin, where he hid until he was rescued by C. Bacon, who was camping nearby.

Christiansen testified that he and his recaptured prisoner were headed down Emigration Canyon when they met Ephraim Hanks, who convinced Christiansen to go back and search for the missing money. Christiansen left Hanks in the freight wagon and escorted the prisoner out of sight. He claimed that this time, when they rounded a small bend in the pathway, Bernard picked up a large rock and hurled it at him, barely missing him, so enraging him that he drew his knife and put an end to the man's life. Christiansen said he and Hanks buried the body in a small ravine and returned to the city, where they reported the killing to Peter Clinton, justice of the peace, and Andrew Cunningham, captain of the municipal police. Clinton, Hanks, Christiansen, and the county coroner loaded a wooden coffin into Hanks's wagon and reclaimed Bernard's body. They performed a candlelight inquest at the burial site, and then the corpse was wrapped in a white shroud and transported to Salt Lake City for interment.

The police tried to hide the incident, but by the end of the month the *Valley Tan* had chronicled the dark and senseless killing. "You will see by the 'Valley Tan' what they are striving for," wrote Brigham Young to George Q. Cannon, "—the Danites with the complicity of the Mormon authorities have done it. They have not yet decided what for. You will notice two letters purporting to have been written by Mormons endorsing that filthy sheet and answering the enquiry after Dummy & co." The Church president described the letters, written under the pen names of "Utahns," as the work of Judge Sinclair, Marshal Dotson, and Indian

Agent Craig, all of whom he accused of crusading to implicate the Mormon community in Christiansen's actions. The Gentile community forced Judge Sinclair to set the issue before the grand jury.[23]

In the end, however, Christiansen's restrained and carefully reasoned arguments won his acquittal, a verdict of justifiable homicide.[24] When the twelve-to-six decision of the grand jury was announced, Seth M. Blair had to eject several Gentiles who attacked the Mormon defense attorney. The acquittal sharply divided public opinion, and several dozen army officers met at the Globe Inn to re-try Christiansen for murder. They were stopped short by Governor Cumming, who had feared that bedlam would follow the grand jury's verdict. He visited the officers and other Gentiles associated with the incident and managed to prevent them from taking the law into their own hands.[25] Gloom settled over those Gentiles who believed that the brutal murder of Bernard was the work of the Danites, or "Brigham Young's Destroying Angels." The editor of the *Valley Tan* wrote: "The Destroying angels or rather the avenging devils that are peculiar to the hierarchy and theocracy that has so long prevailed in this Territory should bear in mind that Heaven is not only retributive, but that temporal laws can and will be enforced." The interest of the territory and the political relationship of Utah with the federal government were at stake, he added, demanding "that no concealment should be made but that crime no matter from what source it comes should be exposed and punished. . . ."[26]

Though this initial protest against Brigham Young failed to gain much public support, reports of a secret society of assassins made people uneasy. The Danite organization began in Missouri when a Mormon guerrilla band attempted to rescue some Saints from a frontier mob. One of the most famous exiles from Mormonism, William A. Hickman, popularized the Danites in his brief autobiography published in 1872, nearly ten years after his excommunication.[27] He wrote with unrestrained irony and scorn, generally giving little evidence to support his accusations. Hickman related incidents of death or exile at the hands of this phantom army. Passing the edge of truth, he charged that few enemies of Brigham Young were not in terror of midnight visitations.[28]

Reflective men saw the Danites as a creation of commercial journalism. Writing a decade after the abandonment of Camp Floyd, T. B. H. Stenhouse claimed that daylight street killings received only passing attention, while unexplained midnight assassinations attracted the willing pens of hostile Gentile reporters who "created a sensation of terror in the minds of all who were inimical to the priesthood."[29] But Brigham Young's own words added to the myth of the "Destroying Angels": "If men come here and do not behave themselves, they will not only find Danites of whom they talk so much about, biting the horses heels, but the scoundrels will find something biting their heels. In my plain remarks, I merely call things by their right names."[30] Such outbursts fed Gentile fears, and even gave their author second thoughts after the death of Frank McNeil.

McNeil arrived in Salt Lake City during the summer of 1857, as war clouds hovered over the territory. His close association with the few remaining Gentiles in Salt Lake City and his aggressive behavior toward the Saints drew the attention of the Mormon militia, and he was arrested and charged with spying for the army, as were his companions, Charles Miles, W. H. Fabens, and a Mr. Brown. In the presidential pardon and general amnesty of 1858, they were released; but the incident was not forgotten. McNeil sued Brigham Young and others for damages amounting to $25,000. The bill of indictment alleged that Brigham Young had illegally detained him in irons and had denied his constitutional right to a writ of *habeas corpus*, as well as to a jury trial. The case moved sluggishly through the court, and the public divided itself into McNeil supporters and opponents. But time ran out for McNeil. The night before the civil suit was to be heard, he was fatally shot from ambush while he walked along Main Street, the busiest thoroughfare of the city.[31]

When word of the murder went out, Brigham Young became the prime suspect, although it soon turned out that McNeil was simply the victim of an outlaw quarrel. Well before the troubled spring of 1859, McNeil had joined a gang of cattle rustlers who specialized in stealing government cattle. Leaders of the band were Joe Rhodes, a prominent Gentile outlaw from California, and "Billy" Hickman, who had also left behind a trail of homicides and other crimes. It is doubtful whether McNeil ever played more than a minor role in the outlaw band, but Hickman and Rhodes accused him of holding money out on them. He wounded several members of the gang sent to retrieve the money, and went into hiding. After a few weeks, the marked man tired of his self-imposed confinement and headed for a Whiskey Street saloon. No sooner had he entered the unlighted avenue than Joe Rhodes came out of the shadows and demanded the return of the stolen money. McNeil tried to run and Rhodes shot him. When McNeil fell, Rhodes leaped on him and struck him in the chest and head with his pistol, inflicting a dozen serious wounds. Spectators rescued him and he survived temporarily.[32]

Years later Hickman, a co-conspirator in the plot, wrote another version of the tragedy. "I came to town one afternoon, and heard he McNeil was upstairs at Sterritt's Tavern drunk. Darkness came on and we got the chamber-pot taken out of his room, so that he would in all probability come down when he awoke with whisky dead in him." Urged by nature, McNeil left his room, followed by three or four members of the gang. "Rhodes followed him around the house and shot him in the alley," Hickman wrote. "McNeil lived until the next day, and died, not knowing who shot him; neither did any other person, except those who sat by the side of the tavern."³³

Hickman was mistaken. Before McNeil died, he informed the Territorial Attorney, General Alexander Wilson, that Rhodes had shot him from ambush, although he was reluctant to sign an affidavit to that effect. The controversy faded from public attention when the coroner's inquest found no evidence linking Rhodes with the murder, and he was released. The court's indecision left Gentiles free to blame Brigham Young.

That winter assassination took a heavy toll of Utah's outlaws. Joe Rhodes fell out with Hickman and joined a rival band led by the colorful Joaquin Johnston. It proved to be the most costly mistake of Rhodes's short criminal career, but for the moment Hickman's attention was focused on other problems. In the decade following the Utah War, reports of Hickman's crimes and scandals dominated the territorial newspapers.

Born in 1815, the grandson of a veteran of the Revolutionary War, the self-confessed Danite matured in the quiet back country of Franklin, Missouri.³⁴ Destined to become one of the legendary villains of Utah, Hickman was below average height and thin, yet he was an impressive physical figure. His hair was coal black and brushed to the side, his face was drawn and swarthy, and his eyes were deeply recessed under a prominent forehead. His double set of incisor teeth helped give him a demonic appearance, adding to his reputation as one of the most dangerous men on the frontier.

All attempts to pigeonhole William A. Hickman have failed, mainly because it is difficult to isolate his lawlessness from the violence of the Mormon frontier. In quieter times Hickman might have lived out his life in relative obscurity, but his fortunes took an abrupt turn when he joined the Mormon Church and moved to Nauvoo, where he won his way into the heart of Joseph Smith. He escaped anti-Mormon vigilantes in Illinois, killing his first man while escaping from prison. He followed the Mormon migration west to Utah, traveling over the California Trail to the gold fields four years later.³⁵

One of the wiliest and most ruthless Indian fighters in the entire Mormon frontier, he rid the Green River Crossing of mountain men and their native allies, thus clearing the way for the successful Mormon occupation of that emigrant crossroad in 1853. This bloody job left the outlaw permanently scarred both in mind and body. Not only was his anger razor sharp, but he used it ruthlessly, collecting enemies like so many bad debts. A contemporary who penned his name "Justitia" remarked that "Bill Hickman and his increasing band are a terror to the people. No man's life is safe with him, and he is gathering around him others that believe he is authorized in all his acts."³⁶ Hickman blamed Church authorities for the violence in order to clear his own name.

Through spies, informers, and sympathizers, Hickman kept abreast of outlaw activities within the territory, securing information about missing stock, which he would recover for a fee. He worked with the leaders of outlaws, passing on the cost of their information to grateful merchants. One such finder's fee was received by Joe Rhodes for information about Joaquin Johnston. Suffering extraordinary losses in cattle and horses during the summer of 1859, the firm of Gilbert and Gerrish hired Hickman to recover a sizable herd of livestock hidden several miles south of Salt Lake City. But Hickman failed to locate the stolen property, so he offered Joe Rhodes fifty dollars for information leading to its recovery. Rhodes told Hickman that the stolen cattle could be found fifteen miles up the Jordan River, hidden in a small canyon.

Hickman dispatched his men southward along the river, headed by his son-in-law Jason Luce, one of his trusted lieutenants. They found the unguarded cattle and drove the herd back to the city, where they collected a sizable reward from Gilbert and Gerrish. Then Rhodes, uneasy over his own safety, confessed to Joaquin Johnston that he had told Hickman about the stolen herd. He told Johnston that he had relinquished the information only because he believed that Hickman never interfered with the stealing of Gentile cattle. Nothing was mentioned of the bribe.[37]

The resulting gang war, the most dramatic event of the holiday season, reached a peak when Hickman returned to Salt Lake to celebrate Christmas with friends and relatives. He was dining at his daughter's house when he saw a tall man with a gun entering the yard. Hickman answered the door to Lot Huntington, a member of the Johnston gang. The slender fighter was outwardly calm, except for a slight awkwardness in explaining his visit, which lasted only a few minutes. Hickman suspected that the Christmas call had graver motives. Huntington reappeared at the doorstep a dozen hours later. Hickman cocked his gun and opened the door. But, to his relief, Huntington only explained that he had been sent by Joaquin Johnston to iron out the division of stolen property. Hickman agreed to meet his rival at a later date.

A few days later, Hickman went to call on John Wakeley. To Hickman's disappointment, Mrs. Wakeley said that her husband was out, but she insisted that Bill should stay for breakfast. They were joined by a second guest, Bill Woodland. Moments later, ten grim-faced men led by Lot Huntington and Cub Johnson knocked at the Wakeley door and demanded to see Hickman. Hidden behind the door, Hickman heard Huntington tell Mrs. Wakeley angrily that Hickman was responsible for sending Porter Rockwell and a Mormon posse south to recapture Joaquin Johnston's stolen cattle. Mrs. Wakeley convinced the mob that Hickman had left with her husband, and Huntington continued his search for Hickman elsewhere.

Hickman collected a cadre of men and prepared to leave the city for safety. In front of a dry goods building they ran head-on into Lot Huntington and a half-dozen minions of Joaquin Johnston. The two gangs backed apart, allowing their leaders room. Conscious of his superiority in men and firepower, Huntington rehearsed a catalogue of charges against Hickman and added that Hickman was a liar and scoundrel, punctuating his words with a loud demand for the return of his stolen property.

Hickman drew his bowie knife and lunged at Huntington; Huntington drew his pistol and fired. The bullet struck Hickman's watch, splintering it into shrapnel that pierced his leg, and the shock sent him to the ground. The gunfire brought Hickman's men pouring into Main Street, yelling and firing as they came, driving Johnston's gang into the nearby buildings. After exchanging shots, Huntington's desperadoes fled, leaving their leader to escape as best he could. Huntington limped down the street, pursued by Hickman's gunmen. He emptied his pistols at them and then took refuge in the house of George D. Grant.[38]

While bullets were still flying, the fallen Hickman was carried to the home of his son-in-law, a Mr. Butcher, where he was treated by two Mormon physicians whose unpolished medical skills almost cost him his life. "They split the flesh on the inside and outside of my thigh to the bone hunting the ball," Hickman later wrote, "and finally concluded they could not find it, then went away and reported I would die sure."[39]

After three weeks the wound swelled from the effects of gangrene, but Hickman again cheated death. Hickman's wife brought her cousin, Dr. Hobbs, an army surgeon, along with a number of physicians from Camp Floyd, to Salt Lake City to inspect the inflamed wound. The military surgeons found a cotton compress sewed into the patient's body, which was badly infected. His condition improved under the watchful eye of Dr. Hobbs, but the specter of death was never far away.

By the new year, 1860, when it was apparent that he would survive, Joe Rhodes appeared at the Butcher doorstep and attempted to force his way into Hickman's room. Hickman raised himself from his bed and yelled at his bodyguard Ormus Bates to "get Rhodes away." The other guard, Jason Luce, sprang at Rhodes and drove his bowie knife into his heart. Bates seized Rhodes's pistols and struck several blows to his head. The two bodyguards carried Rhodes's body to City Hall, where Luce surrendered himself to the municipal police. The following day he was tried before Judge Clinton, but was acquitted on grounds of justifiable homicide.[40]

The body of the California outlaw remained in the municipal building for public viewing for several days. Before it was interred in a pauper's grave, a reporter for *The Mountaineer* described its macabre condition: "It was a horrible sight. Four fearful looking cuts, within a circle of six inches right over the breast, four others on the right side very close together under the ribs, two cuts on the left side and one on the left shoulder."[41]

Brigham Young watched the public resentment rapidly spread; he ordered Seth Blair to investigate the affair. Two days later Blair reported that both parties had agreed to a truce. Still, Brigham Young was troubled by Hickman's claims of outraged innocence. Absorbed though he was in more pressing problems, the Mormon leader moderated several turbulent meetings between the two factions, and, although no written account of these sessions is available, it is apparent that Brigham Young brought the full weight of his office to bear on the enemies.

No one was louder in his dissatisfaction with Hickman's conduct than Mayor A. O. Smoot, who urged Brigham Young to sever his personal ties with the outlaw. In a conversation with the president, he explained that visits to the Church offices by the wayward Mormon cast doubts on the integrity of Young's leadership and exposed him to criticism of the most dangerous kind. "Dogs were necessary to take care of the flock but if the Shepherd's dogs hurt sheep it would be time to remove them," he warned. Brigham Young sidestepped a direct reply, answering: "Whether he was wounded or whether he recovered or whether he died these events were in the hands of the Lord."[42] Giving second thoughts to Smoot's warning, Brigham relayed his disapproval to Hickman in a message delivered verbally by the outlaw's brother. A glimpse of that message was revealed by Hickman's response, penned from his sickbed: "When my brother told me what you said it made the cold sweat run off me and I almost sank under it. . . ."[43]

The Hickman affair faded from the public mind, but the winds of violence continued to buffet Salt Lake. Revulsion, fear, and disgust followed in the wake of the murder of two spiritualists, Charles M. Drown and Josiah Arnold. Assuming that the spiritualists were victims of sectarian partisans, the *Valley Tan* filled its pages with anti–Mormon accusations that appealed to the Gentile reader.

The territory saw a minor outbreak of spiritualism in 1859, a period when differing religious and political ideas enjoyed a renaissance. In its purest form, spiritualism held that the dead communicated with the living and that living communicants could send messages to their loved ones or receive instruction from beyond the grave. Heading the fledgling Utah spiritualist organization was Ivy Eddy, a self-styled prophet who lectured on spiritualism until he left the territory in 1859. The prophet's style attracted a handful of early converts, including Josiah Arnold, author of a book on spiritualism that was selling well in Salt Lake City.[44]

The book offended the town's religious community because Arnold claimed he wrote it under the divine authority of Jesus Christ, who transmitted His thought to the author. Spiritualism was an irritant to the Saints, and they treated it with the same caution as they did the other religions in their community, although there were rumors of heretical conspiracies in Salt Lake City.[45] Young dismissed the spiritualist movement as just another minor annoyance, but its influence nevertheless reached into the Beehive House.

Charles Drown, Josiah Arnold, and their wives met at the home of Ivy Eddy on the evening of August 27, 1859, to conduct spiritualist services. The meeting was warm and cheerful, and at the close of the séance the couples retired to separate bedrooms for the evening. Eddy was awakened by a loud knocking on the front door. He answered it and found a young man standing in the darkness asking for hot coals to start a fire. Eddy politely refused. The sleepy prophet was awakened a second time by the same caller, this time surrounded by armed men demanding to see Drown. Eddy slammed the door and placed his shoulder against it. Awakened by the confusion, Drown added his weight against the door, but the top hinges split from the door casing and then the door burst violently open. Drown fell to the floor with a fatal stomach wound. Eddy managed to crawl to safety, unaccountably escaping the murderous cross fire from the door and side window.

The first shots brought Arnold running out of the stables where he had gone after the first visit, apparently believing the night callers were horse thieves. He drew his pistol and screamed, "Murder." After firing three or four wild shots, he raced toward the street in a desperate run for his life, but he was stopped by a single rifle shot. Minutes later a crowd of people poured out of nearby houses to investigate the noise and found Arnold leaning against a building, bleeding from a wound in the leg. The following day Arnold was carried from Eddy's home and driven home by carriage. As he drew closer to his destination he slipped into a deep coma. A Mormon physician, Dr. French, examined him and warned Brigham Young that the wound would prove fatal. Less than a week later, on September 2, 1859, the patient entered the spirit world quietly in his sleep.

Arnold's death sent shock waves throughout the city. One rumor had it that Arnold had been poisoned by order of Brigham Young. A post-mortem examination conducted in the presence of Territorial Attorney General Alexander Wilson and a Mormon attorney, Hosea Stout, found that the victim had died of complications related to his wounds.[46]

The dual assassination raised speculation about the identity of the men responsible for the killings. All through the difficult winter of 1859 three names were most frequently associated with the crime: Brigham Young, "Billy" Hickman, and Rodney D. Swazey. To further complicate matters, Hickman himself was Brigham Young's prime accuser and, to camouflage his own involvement, carried out a long campaign of character assassination against the Church leader, charging that the killings were religious executions.[47] "It is a singular fact," the outlaw would write after his excommunication, "that there is no other form of apostasy the Mormon Priesthood so fear, hate, and curse, and no kind of mysticism to which apostate Mormons are so prone, as 'spiritualism.'"[48] The facts appeared simple to the outlaw and to J. H. Beale, an anti-Mormon lawyer who helped Hickman write his autobiography. Yet their judgment was not sustained by later findings. To the contrary, when Drown and Arnold were excommunicated for spiritualism by their stake council in July 1858, they appealed the decision to Young, who promptly reversed the findings of the lower ecclesiastic court. At the time of their deaths both men had been reinstated to full membership, and there is no proof that their status within the Church had changed at the time of their murders.[49]

On the other hand, however, there were aspects of Drown's life in Utah that gave Young grave concern. Shortly after his arrival in Salt Lake City in 1855, he was disfellowshiped for involvement with a gang of horse thieves.[50] After an unaccountable absence from the historical records, Drown returned to the territory with the arrival of the army in 1858. Fragmentary evidence suggests that Drown assumed the leadership of a gang of young outlaws largely recruited from the Mormon community, among whom were Rodney Swazey, James Warthers, and Ike Hatch.[51] With Drown dead, Swazey was able to assume control of the brigands, a benefit which placed him high on the list of suspects with a motive. Swazey was arrested for Drown's murder but was later released although there was a considerable amount of circumstantial evidence against him.[52]

Hickman had the best financial reason for wanting Drown dead. Just before he was killed, Drown had obtained a judgment against Hickman for five hundred dollars. Hickman denied any implication in the crime, claiming he was attending a party in honor of the editor of *The Mountaineer* at the time, although he admitted being close enough to the murder scene to hear the shooting.[53] The only surviving witness, Ivy Eddy, contradicted Hickman's alibi in a letter to Wilford Woodruff about the murder night. "'Billy' Hickman and his gang broke into my cottage in Salt Lake City, fired off their pistols that were aimed at me, but as I made a step aside the bullet entered the body of Drown who fell dead at my side. My wife-Sister Ruby, jerked me behind the big chimney and saved my life. . . ." In the same letter, however, he remembered, "Bill Hickman was so sorry at his orders that he, at Camp Floyd offered to save my life when I started for California."[54] Thus the strange affair came to an end with Hickman escorting to safety the very spiritualist he claimed that Brigham Young had ordered him to destroy.

The last link of this chain was forged by Jason Luce, shortly before he was executed for another murder, the bowie knife killing of Samuel Benton. In a packed jail cell, filled with friends and peace officers, Luce swore to Wilford Woodruff that Hickman and two unidentified conspirators were responsible for the deaths of Arnold and Drown.

Bill Hickman's career as a criminal had repeatedly made a fool of justice, and a more illogical candidate for the bar could not be imagined; yet, shortly after the army entered the territory, Hickman joined a young attorney, Thomas S. Williams, in establishing a law office in Salt Lake City. He attracted few paying clients in his career within the law, and one of the few men to trust him to handle his legal affairs became the first man to be legally executed in the territory, Thomas Ferguson.

A small shop on Temple Street was robbed of $600, setting the scene for Hickman's career as a defense attorney. The theft was still under investigation on the evening of September 16, when several men drifted into the stage office of P. Jackman. The callers included Alexander Carpentar, the owner of the plundered store, and Thomas Ferguson, the prime suspect for the robbery. After a period of heavy drinking, Carpentar accused Ferguson of being one of the robbers, and, while Jackman and others watched, Ferguson drew his pistol and fired point blank, killing Carpentar instantly. The coroner found that the bullet had gone through the victim's breast and lodged in the wall.[55]

After the killing, Ferguson moved quickly through the office into the street, but a crowd of armed spectators cornered him and took him to the Salt Lake jail, where he was chained to the wall. Charles L. Walker penned in his diary his impressions of the murderer. "He looked pale and thin and a wild look about the eyes. . . . He would smile and sometimes laugh but his smile was ghastly and his laugh was hollow, quick, and short as though a fiend had power over him."[56] Bound over for trial and defended by Hickman and Williams, Ferguson was found guilty of first-degree murder by a mixed jury of Mormons and Gentiles and was sentenced to be hanged. By a curious oversight, Judge Sinclair set the day of the execution for Sunday, September 4, 1859, a date that drew the scorn of the Mormon community, forcing a postponement until October 28. Public excitement did not die down in the meantime.

On the appointed day, Marshal Peter Dotson, heading a detail of 100 members of the Nauvoo Legion commanded by Lot Smith, loaded the twenty-seven-year-old prisoner and his coffin into an unmarked wagon. The small army marched through lesser-used streets to the north bench overlooking the city, a short distance from the public cemetery. From every house the caravan passed, from every small shop and store, people poured out to look at the prisoner, for they could not resist seeing territorial history in the making.

At the gallows the prisoner's handcuffs were removed, and Ferguson was allowed to unscrew his own leg irons. Standing on the scaffold and facing the hooded executioner, Ferguson raised his voice in anger for the first time. The prisoner made no attempt to plead his innocence to the close-packed circle of listeners; instead, he "censured Judge Sinclair for not allowing him an impartial trial and accused the Judge of being drunk when he passed the sentence."[57]

His most bitter remarks were reserved for his defense attorneys, whom he charged with mishandling his defense and failing to obtain a stay of execution from the governor. Ferguson reviewed his short, tragic stay in Utah, the unfairness of his trial, and Sinclair's violation of the territorial statute that gave a prisoner the privilege of being hanged, beheaded, or shot. The prisoner said he would have preferred to die before a firing squad.

Then the condemned man requested a prayer. After some delay, Henry Jacobs, a Mormon elder, climbed the platform and knelt with Ferguson, carrying out the last request. With his eyes gentled by the experience, the prisoner looked at the crowd, smiled, and said, "Gentlemen I bid you all farewell."[58] The crowd hushed, mesmerized by the sight of the gallows cap being drawn over the doomed man's head. Lot Smith sprang the trap door and Hickman's client plummeted to his death.

Hickman's full role in the Ferguson-Carpentar case was never discovered. According to Wilford Woodruff's *Journal*, Jason Luce claimed that Hickman robbed the Carpentar store, delivered the stolen property to accomplices for safe keeping, and eventually sold the merchandise from his ranch near Camp Floyd. Hickman, claimed Luce, "then told Ferguson if he would kill Carpenter [*sic*] he would clear him that he should not lie in jail one day. Furguson [*sic*] killed Carpenter [*sic*] and was hung for it and Hickman made him believe that he would be liberated up to the last minute." Telling all he knew about Hickman's activities in Utah, Luce added that he "was at the head of a band of thieves that have stolen as high as one hundred head of cattle at a time from Camp Floyd and gone out onto the prairie and divided them and taken them to different parts of the Territory." Describing events with the authority that only a member of the same gang could command, he continued: "Hickman had many men around him that had to be fed and the men under him would go onto the range, drive up a beef and kill, eat it, and sell the hides or make them into Larretts or throw them away as the case might be without any regard to whom might be the owners." Years later, in the last minute before his own hanging, Luce remarked that "Hickman had been his ruin and the ruin of others."[59]

Certainly the wild career of William Hickman testified to the sorry state of law and order in Salt Lake City by the end of the 1850s. The Mormon dream of building a separatist utopia in the Great Basin had disappeared under the weight of frontier events. Johnston's Army had conquered Utah without firing a shot.

CHAPTER FOURTEEN

DISQUIET IN ZION

*I believe that if all who have been unfortunate in crossing the
River Styx, and, if hell itself had been raked, and more mean
miserable low degraded set of miscreants, rascals and sneaks could not
have been found.*

—Journal History, *1859*[1]

PLEASURE IN UTAH could often be had for a price: the bodies, the spirits, and the games of chance in Salt Lake City were a perpetual temptation to men seeking forgetfulness or excitement. The army, however, faced a chronic shortage of hard specie, caused by an inadequate federal banking system, and paid its public indebtedness by issuing drafts drawn against governmental subtreasuries in St. Louis and New York. These drafts were accepted by local merchants, but at a discounted rate. This system had conspicuous shortcomings. The "paper" was not safe from the oldest confidence game in the world—counterfeiting. Camp Floyd's drafts offered opportunities in plenty for counterfeiters.

In the winter of 1858, while the army was still engaged in building its fort, rumors of a plot to forge quartermaster drafts began to circulate through the territory. The story implicated members of the Mormon Church. The army operated on the assumption of Mormon complicity, and General Johnston and his quartermaster, Colonel George Hampton Crosman, launched an investigation. Over the next few months a more clear picture emerged, but the army made no effort to suppress the plot, so the counterfeiting scheme continued unchecked. Eventually the army determined that three men were involved—John M. Wallace, Myron Brewer, and David McKenzie.[2]

The most active conspirator was Wallace, a California gambler in the habit of wearing black, a preference he hoped would create the impression that he was a gentleman of good breeding and intelligence. Before arriving in the territory in 1858, Wallace had pressed energeti-

247

cally for an invasion of Utah from California and a war of attrition against the Saints. He believed that the Mormons were guilty of the Mountain Meadows Massacre, and had convened several mass meetings in Los Angeles to discuss avenging the deaths of the emigrants.[3]

Following the army into the Basin, he served as a juror in Judge Sinclair's court and ran successful saloons in Salt Lake City and Fairfield. A witness to his activities at Fairfield described him as possessing "all the stoicism, sangfroid, and deep cunning shrewdness . . . necessary to success in the profession." Wallace met the challenge of the gambling table in intrepid fashion, the writer continued: "He can sit and lose thousands without evincing the slightest perturbation, feeling upon the subject and can pocket the last dollar, which make[s] the 'gold fascinated dupe,' a beggar, with equal sanssouci."[4]

It was toward the latter part of the monotonous and unsatisfying winter of 1859 that the gambler found his fortune taking a dramatic turn for the worse. "Business became dull, money scarce, and the gambling operations unfortunate so that in a few months [he] became worth nothing."[5] Wallace then concocted the scheme to defraud the federal government, taking in an accomplice, Myron Brewer, an attractive and able Mormon convert.

The boyish-looking Brewer was born near the newly settled edge of the frontier, a short distance from the Missouri River, and suffered the disadvantages of being in a society with an underdeveloped economy. He met with Wallace when the latter boarded at his parents' home. Brewer enlisted as a private in the artillery at Fort Monroe, Virginia, and deserted the army during the Mexican War, making his way back to Iowa just in time to participate in the Mormon trek across the plains.[6] Converting to the new religion, he solicited Brigham Young for financial assistance to establish a "Gymnastic Performance, and Minstrel Club," but was refused.[7] He later volunteered his services to the Nauvoo Legion but was assigned instead the inglorious position of musician in the territorial militia. During the height of the Utah War he made elaborate proposals to form a company of archers to stop the advance of Johnston's Army, but when the conflict collapsed he returned to obscurity.[8] Brooding over imagined wrongs at the hands of his own people, Brewer reestablished his friendship with Wallace. The promptness with which the gambler gained the loyalty of Brewer revealed a basic weakness in the young Mormon's character. To those who knew him well, he was a youth of "confiding nature, relying upon the apparent honesty and good faith of others, and consequently often becomes the victim of misplaced confidence."[9] Brewer often proved a greater enemy to himself than to anybody else. The daring of Wallace's counterfeiting plan appealed to Brewer, and the two men refined their scheme to defraud the government.

They invited into their conspiracy a gifted twenty-five-year-old engraver of the Deseret Currency Association, David McKenzie, who was a respected member of the Mormon community. McKenzie had engraved plates for William B. Martin, an enterprising Gentile merchant-speculator who proposed the issuance of an independent currency to manipulate the territorial economy. Martin proposed to raise capital by issuing private mercantile scrip in exchange for staples, especially cattle. By monopolizing the commodity market, he hoped to create an artificial food shortage. As prices rose, he reasoned, the value of the scrip would decline because of over-circulation. Then his paper money could be redeemed at the new low level while real money could be made by the sale of agricultural products at inflated prices.

Local sentiment against Martin's trade was slow to develop. Nevertheless, the dishonesty in the plan was soon apparent to Brigham Young, who watched Martin's moneychanging with disapproval and warned his followers not to accept the Martin scrip. This pronouncement by the Lion of the Lord brought the scheme to a quick end.[10]

Although he labored hard at being an engraver and a clerk as well as a practical craftsman, McKenzie never seemed to make enough money to answer his growing needs. As poverty sharpened its claws on his career, he developed a friendship with the visionary Myron Brewer, who tested his future partner very carefully. He appealed to the engraver's vanity, praising the craftsmanship of the notes he made for Martin. Pride and greed quickly fused the two men into one spirit. Eventually McKenzie sprang his own trap, after Brewer threw out the bait in the form of a question about the workmanship of the Martin notes. "This I consider a very indifferent piece of work," McKenzie mused, "and yet considering the purpose for which it is made, may perhaps compare somewhat fairly, with others of much greater importance. Take for instance the U. S. Treasury Draft, which I look upon as a very trifling affair, taking into the results that would attend a successful effort to counterfeit it."

Brewer asked, "And do you apprehend that such a thing could be so easily accomplished?"

"Yes," replied McKenzie, "and that too without the cost of much serious effort."[11]

As McKenzie talked, Brewer was obviously pleased; abandoning all subtlety, he asked McKenzie to forge the government drafts, and McKenzie agreed to engrave the plates and print the counterfeit bills on the press of the Deseret Currency Association. Brewer was to pass the forged drafts to merchants in Salt Lake City and Fairfield, and Wallace was to channel the bogus paper into the hands of gamblers and other itinerants leaving the territory.[12] However, in the space of several weeks the plot turned into a nightmare.

Toward the latter part of April 1859, Colonel Crosman rode across Cedar Creek to the gambling saloon of John Wallace, then walked directly to the owner and told him that the army was on to him. Crosman admitted that the army's investigation lacked hard evidence against its main target, Brigham Young. He said that if Wallace would cooperate with the government all charges against him would be dropped. Wallace agreed to the colonel's terms.[13]

Several weeks later, on May 18, 1859, a document was drawn at Camp Floyd that summarized the conspiracy. It was signed by two sutlers, Henry D. Sherwood of the firm of Miller, Russell & Co., and C.A. Perry of Gilbert and Gerrish. In part it read:

> This certifies that Mr. John M. Wallace has this day informed me [Colonel Crosman] that he has been solicited to join a party, now being organized in this Territory for the purpose of defrauding the United States Treasury of large sums of money by the process of counterfeiting the drafts made by the Deputy Quarter Master Gen. on the Asst. Treasuries at New York and Saint Louis and he has further informed me that he has consented to act with that party, for the sole purpose, however, of learning the names of those engaged in the nefarious transaction, and obtaining specimens of their work, together with any other evidence of guilt; it is his wish and intention to lay the whole matter before the proper authorities and aid and assist in bringing the guilty to justice.[14]

In keeping with his pledge to the gambler, Crosman inserted a short paragraph clearing Wallace of future prosecution. "Mr. Wallace informs me that I am the only person to whom he has communicated these facts, and has asked this certificate from me, that he may use it as evidence, of the purity of his motive for taking part in the above mentioned transaction, should that motive be called into question." Attesting to the gambler's character, the officer testified: "I am well acquainted with Mr. Wallace, and have every confidence in the honesty of his intentions in this matter; and judging from the character of the man, feel satisfied that if he receives proper encouragement from the United States Authorities of this Territory, will expose a most villainous scheme to defraud the Government and bring offenders to justice."[15]

The ease with which Wallace changed alliances was shown by his willingness to keep the army abreast of the progressing fraud. On June 17, he wrote the general that the plates were half-finished and in his judgment the engravings were "a dangerous counterfeit."[16] Three weeks later he reported that the drafts had been printed and that, for reasons unknown, Brewer had decided to circulate the paper in California.[17]

Two days later, July 11, 1859, Brewer walked into Wallace's saloon, ignoring a small group of soldiers milling near the bar, and stopped in front of his two-faced partner, who appeared absorbed in playing cards with three other men. Wallace drew back from the table, inconspicuously signalling the infantrymen, and put out his hand to Brewer for the counterfeit drafts. Brewer pulled the bogus bills from his jacket and placed the small bundle in the cardsharp's outstretched hand. Before a word had passed between the two men, Brewer was arrested by one of the officers who had watched the transaction from the bar.

Brewer was allowed to escape prosecution, provided he turn state's evidence against McKenzie and Brigham Young. The young Mormon's testimony made no difference to the final outcome of the trial; nevertheless, it did add to the confusion over Young's role in the conspiracy. The army ordered Pete Dotson to arrest David McKenzie, who was transported in irons to the Camp Floyd stockade.[18] But the army was still not satisfied; the evidence uncovered against Young was not really damaging. When McKenzie appeared before Judge Eckles at Camp Floyd, he was polite, repentant, and communicative, confessing his part in the conspiracy. Much to the chagrin of the army, he failed to implicate the Mormon leader and refused to be tempted to do so by a promise of freedom.

McKenzie's trial received full treatment from the press. Convicted on one count of fraud, he was sentenced to two years in the territorial penitentiary.[19] Even his most bitter critics were dissatisfied with the outcome of the case and petitioned Governor Cumming for his release. The governor refused to pardon the luckless engraver, allowing him to serve out the full term of his sentence.

The aftermath of the trial proved as bizarre as all of the previous events combined. While the government's case was being developed against Brigham Young, Marshal Dotson raided the office of the Deseret Currency Association, carrying out bank notes, currency bills of various denominations, records, and engraved plates. When he realized that none of it was related to the forged McKenzie drafts, he attempted to return it; but Young refused to receive the confiscated property, and sued the marshal for damages, claiming the engravings had been damaged beyond use.[20]

When the civil case finally came to trial, Dotson was found guilty of willfully destroying private property and directed to pay Young $2,300.[21] The court ordered Dotson's private residence sold at public auction to pay the judgment, a judgment that was harsh, vindictive, and an outright miscarriage of justice. Dotson sent a scathing letter of resignation to President Buchanan, and a whole concatenation of charges relating to his trial reached the desk of the president weeks later. But the marshal's words were not widely read in the official circles of Washington, because Buchanan chose to suppress the whole issue rather than stir the smoldering embers of territorial politics.

The Saints celebrated Dotson's departure, but the political infighting continued, and violence remained a part of everyday life in Salt Lake City.

Wanton murder occurred during the summer of 1859 with the cold-blooded killing of Sergeant Ralph Pike, a tragedy that grew out of a dispute over control of grazing lands in central Utah. In its struggle to reassert federal sovereignty over the Great Basin, Washington converted the Mormon rangelands of Skull, Rush, Tintic, Cedar, and Goshen Valleys into a military reservation. The Saints then reasserted their claim to this heartland, creating a dispute with grave economic ramifications. With the seizure of these enormous tracts of land, the army forced the Mormons to reduce the size of their herds at a time when the demand for cattle was increasing. The Saints also faced the loss of these valleys' grazing revenue from Russell, Majors & Waddell and other commercial freighters.

Relations between the army and the settlers remained stable, in the main because General Johnston had allowed a handful of ranchers to share pasture lands reserved for military livestock. In the late winter of 1858, one of the Mormon ranchers, Bishop Daniel Spencer, filed a series of complaints against the army at Camp Floyd. Delivering his charges personally before General Johnston, he claimed that several head of his cattle had been butchered by soldiers guarding the government range, and several of his outbuildings had been torn down for firewood to warm patrols in the northern end of Rush Valley.

Johnston was cool toward the rancher's petition and countered with some army complaints against the bishop. First, Spencer had erected permanent structures on the Rush Valley Reserve contrary to his agreement with the army; secondly, he was herding livestock of non-Mormon freighters on land reserved for domestic use; and, third, he willingly allowed the vending of whiskey by turning his log cabin "into a tavern and a place of resort for a band of horse thieves."[22] Their confrontation was followed by a series of letters from the pro-Mormon Governor Cumming, after which Spencer was notified that his grazing privileges had been revoked. The bishop denied the army's allegations and asked for a stay of his eviction, pending a second appeal to the governor.

Letter after letter passed between Salt Lake and Camp Floyd; in the meantime the ranch foreman, George Reeder, attempted to drive Spencer's cattle from Rush Valley, a task made difficult by a severe storm that raged through the third week of March. Before the roundup was completed, Reeder received a message from Daniel Spencer that under no condition was he to comply with the military orders. The army responded to the challenge on March 22, when it ordered Lieutenant Louis Henry Marshall and a company of Tenth Infantrymen to clear the valley of all nonmilitary livestock. The lieutenant drew up his troops within sight of the ranch house and handed Reeder General Johnston's edict.[23] Lieutenant Marshall, however, stayed the order until all the livestock had been safely corralled.

The lieutenant and bishop retired to a comfortable Sibley tent where they were later joined by Lieutenant Alexander Murry and Sergeant Ralph Pike. Each man professed his expertise on a wide spectrum of topics, including the many problems that had reduced the territory to a battleground. Their enchantment with their own eloquence was interrupted by the arrival of Howard Spencer, the nephew of the owner of the controversial herds. The cordial atmosphere soon changed dramatically. Lieutenant Murry stared hard at Spencer, then asked when he planned to move his uncle's cattle from the government reservation. Spencer read aloud the territorial code under which his uncle claimed part of Rush Valley and declared that the army had no authority to remove civilian cattle from public ranges. Angered by the Mormon's defiance, the peppery lieutenant demanded that the cattle be removed from the reserve before the next dawn, threatening that the army would confiscate the herd if his orders were not met. Spencer returned to his uncle's headquarters and reported that he had been talked down.

The following day began badly. An hour after sunup Murry, Pike, and a small escort of infantrymen arrived at the Spencer ranch. The lieutenant reprimanded Spencer for making no effort to comply with General Johnston's orders, and he requested an explanation of the nephew's actions. Unexpectedly, the younger Spencer called a troop of armed men out of hiding, refused to give up the land his uncle had worked seven years to improve, and declared that the time had arrived for the Mormons to stand up and fight for their rights. Murry, believing Spencer had suddenly gone mad, returned to his military headquarters and reported the incident to his superior, Lieutenant Marshall, who immediately led a forced march to the Spencer ranch.

The soldiers found the ranch swarming with men who quickly surrounded them while the two leaders exchanged insults. At this stage in the story there is a complete lack of agreement as to what happened. According to the Mormon version of the affair given by Reeder, Spencer had paused "from his work and chatted with the Lieutenant, after which he agreed to leave the premises the following morning." Writing several weeks after the event, he informed probate judge Jeter Clinton that Marshall "asked those present if they wanted to resist their authority on the Government reserve." In response Howard Spencer answered, "No we do not." Independent of this action, Pike arrived at the spot, raised his musket, and knocked Howard Spencer to the ground with a crushing blow to the skull.[24]

The army's account was at considerable variance with the Mormon account, and no doubt each side exaggerated at the expense of the other. Lieutenant Marshall's report to General Johnston said: "I sent Lieutenant Murry to tell the party that the house was no longer a tavern, and that at eight o'clock in the morning they must leave it. Lt. Murry was treated by

Mr. Spencer with so much insolence, that he says had he been armed he would have saved Sergeant Pike the trouble of breaking his head." He added, "Spencer's whole line of conduct, both before and since . . . has been that of a perfect bully."[25] Marshall reported that he had ordered his men to drive the sheep and cattle from their corrals to the open range when, to the army's surprise, Howard Spencer pushed his way through the troops and blocked the gate of the livestock enclosure. The commander moved immediately, ordering Pike to arrest him and to deliver him to the regimental stockade at Camp Floyd. The indefatigable Spencer picked up a pitchfork, straightened up, and gave a hoarse shout, "No two men can take me to the guard tent."[26] Young Spencer sprang clear of the soldiers and attempted to strike the arresting sergeant. Reacting to the danger, Marshall said, Pike lunged at Howard Spencer, knocking him to the ground with a single blow of the butt end of his musket.

Within minutes soldiers carried the critically injured victim into the ranch house, where they attempted to stop the flow of blood by stuffing the wound with pieces of their uniforms and window curtains. Meanwhile, the company commander dispatched a rider to Camp Floyd for a military physician. Sometime during the night, Dr. Charles Brewer entered the wounded man's room. The young Spencer's pulse had slowed alarmingly, accompanied by body spasms and deep and slow breathing, all of which were diagnosed as threatening paralysis. After administering an opiate, the surgeon cleaned the wound of foreign material that had been crushed against the brain, which brought an immediate improvement in the patient's pulse rate. With the physician's work completed, the unconscious man was allowed to fall into a deep sleep. Eight hours later Spencer was out of danger and continued to improve, much to the relief of the army.[27]

Regaining consciousness the following morning, Spencer dragged himself out of the cabin and reopened the raw wound before he was caught and returned to his bed. Brewer was summoned to dress the fracture once again, but the patient refused further treatment. Pride prevented Spencer from consenting to be taken to Camp Floyd for more intensive care, although Bishop Johnson and several companions urged it. Reluctantly, the surgeon watched the patient loaded into a carriage for the long passage to Salt Lake City, expecting never to see Spencer alive again. News of the incident traveled quickly through the Mormon community.

Spencer's injury took on more prominence in August, when a grand jury ordered Sergeant Pike to stand trial in Salt Lake City for the attempted murder of Howard Spencer. The barracks received the news with incredulity. Colonel Smith, convinced of Pike's innocence, permitted the summons to be served. General Johnston did not argue the point. Though his patience with the legal system governing the relationship between the army and the Mormons was running out, he ordered Acting

Adjutant General Major Fitz John Porter to supervise every detail of the sergeant's defense. Having prepared his case, Porter led an entourage to Salt Lake City, accompanied by John Bigler, a Mormon deputy marshal. On the morning of August 11, Sergeant Pike appeared before Judge Sinclair and entered a plea of not guilty.[28] At midday the court recessed, barely allowing the prosecution to open its case; meanwhile Major Porter, the defendant, and four soldiers walked down Main Street to a nearby boarding house where they ate a light meal.

It was nearly one o'clock when the party rose from their table and left the building to return to the courtroom. As the soldiers passed the familiar site of Reese's Bakery, Pike heard his name called out. The sergeant raised his eyebrows and moved in the direction of the voice. "I turned to see who was speaking," Pike later recalled. "I saw a man advancing towards me from the street; in his approach I did not at first recognize him: as he came near he said: 'Are you the man who struck me in Rush Valley?' Then I knew him: I knew him by his features; I recognized him as Howard Spencer." The rancher stopped contemptuously in front of Pike and drew his revolver. "My pistol holster," the soldier added, "was buttoned, and I knew he could fire on me first; I retreated behind a post in order to have a chance for self-defence; just as I turned around I heard the report of the pistol, and felt the shock in my side: I then ran to the entrance of the stables; I felt faint, and, feeling myself about to fall, I retired to the sidewalk of the street and asked, 'Will some one help me to my room?' "[29] The soldiers spied Spencer running down the street, howling like a madman. When one trooper leveled his pistol at him, an unidentified peace officer nudged the weapon, sending the shot wide of its mark. While a crowd gathered around the stricken man, Spencer scaled a fence into a nearby lumber yard "where a horse stood ready saddled, and mounting this, he put spurs, and fled up the valley."[30] Lorenzo Brown marveled in his journal, "although· seen by hundreds no one knew him [Spencer] and no two gave the same description of him."[31]

The stricken soldier was carried to the Salt Lake House where he gave his dying statement to Judge Sinclair before lapsing into a coma from which he never awoke. Outside the room, Major Porter ordered his soldiers into the streets to search for the killer. With uncontrolled passion the major instructed his men: "If any man *looked* at them, to draw their pistols, and ask the person what he was looking at, and if he did not turn round and walk off, to shoot him down. . . ."[32]

Pike's murder shocked and outraged the Gentiles of the territory. Two hours before sundown an express rider reached Camp Floyd carrying the news of the shooting, then a second rumor reported the death of four soldiers at the hands of Mormon assailants. Major Porter wrote General Johnston that a riot was expected momentarily, for "no one who has offended this people regards himself free from assassination."[33] The rumor, however, was just a rumor. After the first burst of anger subsided, Johnston refused to move against the Mormons, and when a clearer picture of the situation drifted south to Camp Floyd, he sealed off Cedar Valley from the outside world. Writing from his quarters, he ordered all leaves canceled and all soldiers confined to the fort, reducing the provocation to civil war. The atmosphere of crisis took a long time to dissipate, however.

Additional sentinels were posted around Camp Floyd to prevent soldiers from venting their frustrations on nearby settlements. Nevertheless, guerrilla activity against isolated army detachments threatened to reopen the tragedy's festering wounds. Basil Norris, an army surgeon sent to treat Sergeant Pike, was turned back to Camp Floyd by a band of armed horsemen, and forced to restart his trip under the escort of a company of dragoons.[34] The delayed physician failed to save the young sergeant, who died three days after he was shot.

Pike's body was wrapped in a white shroud and returned to Camp Floyd where it was received with the posting of General Order No. 63:

> It is with much regret the commanding officer announces to the regiment the death of that excellent soldier, First Sergeant Ralph Pike, of company I, late last night, the victom of Mormon assassination, through revenge for the proper discharge of his duty.[35]

Soldiers by the hundreds attended an outdoor mass celebrated by Father Bonaventure Keller. The flag-draped coffin was placed on a caisson and driven slowly down the dust-covered road to a small plot of land designated as the military cemetery, escorted by an honor guard of the Tenth Infantrymen.

Having buried their comrade, the troops of the Tenth Infantry looked to avenge him. Unfortunately their target was the small farming community of Cedar Fort, five miles north of Camp Floyd, where the name Howard Spencer was relatively unknown. A score of infantrymen slipped past the fort's pickets in twos and threes that moonless night and waded across Cedar Creek to rendezvous near the outskirts of Fairfield. The combined force marched north and quickly encircled Cedar Fort. They fired two stacks of hay and several wooden outbuildings before the smoke roused the Saints from their sleep, and in minutes the village swarmed with riflemen. For the next fifteen minutes both sides exchanged a fusillade of gunfire, but neither side inflicted casualties on the other. Then all was silent.[36]

The fleeing figures picked up their old trail through the darkness, and in less time than they took for their outward journey, the soldiers crossed Cedar Creek to safety. There they found General Johnston, Colonel C. F. Smith, and Colonel Crosman awake and waiting their return. The three officers signaled the infantrymen to return to their barracks.[37]

The soldiers had scarcely left the sentry post when a Mormon posse of three men rode into the light of the sentry's torch and requested permission to talk with the duty officer. The general motioned the Saints into the camp. The men introduced themselves as settlers of Cedar Fort and reviewed the raid on their settlement. Their words fell on unsympathetic ears. Staring contemptuously at the visitors, Colonel Smith ridiculed the idea of his men's involvement, declared that the outrage was the work of gamblers, and later reported the incident as such to the War Department. Taking his cue from his superior officer, Crosman agreed, adding that the gamblers of Fairfield were known to possess military uniforms and had reason to dislike the Saints. Johnston said: "I cannot guarantee safety to you nor to any one in Fort Cedar. There are so many outrages committed by this community that we cannot control the soldiers, when such outrages are committed!" The general said that Mormon property would be respected and promised that a squad of dragoons would be dispatched to the settlement to maintain order. After a last stern look, General Johnston returned to his quarters. The episode was officially closed.[38]

Rumors of preposterous proportions reached the Lion House. Brigham Young was told that soldiers at Camp Floyd were relieved of their duties in order to destroy various properties of Mormon merchants, including the Beehive House. For want of additional excitement they were said to have hanged William H. Kimball, the son of a member of the First Presidency. Young remarked, "But as W. H. Kimball was seen walking down the streets of Salt Lake City on the day of the supposed hanging it was presumed the story a 'Hoax.' "[39] Nevertheless, ugly and confusing tales circulated through Salt Lake City.

To the army and the Gentiles, Salt Lake City remained enemy country, a fact demonstrated by the clashes between the municipal police and non-Mormons. The shooting of two army officers excited general attention and indicated how darkly the shadows of passions lay across the city. The issue precipitating the event was an unrequited love affair between a Mormon woman and an army surgeon, Dr. Edward Covey, who had his own special grievance with the Saints. According to Mormon accounts of the incident, the physician was annoyed by local bishops who spoiled several of his amorous adventures into various Church wards. Dr. Covey "threatened to maul Bishop Sheets within an inch of his life for daring to caution the girls against his arts."[40]

Dr. Covey and Captain P. T. Turnley dined at the Globe, where they engaged the Mormon innkeeper David Candland in an injudicious conversation on polygamy and the related question of statehood. Making no secret of his feelings toward the Saints, Turnley poured out a spate of words with all the hatred he could command, wrote Candland. He "threatened if we dared any of us to crook our finger he and the army would deal with us in the most summary manner and he would be God damned but blood ought to shed in those streets and old Buchanan would find the Army was not such fools to pardon a damned set of polygamists for we were a stink in the nose and he hoped yet to see old Brigham hung." Dr. Covey swore he would resign his commission, forswear his country, and do all he could to break up the federal government if the Mormons were admitted into the Union. The gates of hell were open, he remarked, "and he was glad of it and he did not care if blood was shed and it was his business to shed blood and he did not care how God damn quick it was done either."[41]

Growing tired of the argument, the surgeon walked through the somber streets to the store of Livingston and Bell, where he was joined by Charles A. Kindead and a number of army officers and camp followers. A few minutes later, their evening of pleasure ended with the sound of shouting from the street. The front door was thrown open, and the Gentiles recognized Marshal John Sharp and several deputies, including William Hennefer, outside. Sharp and Kindead argued loudly. Their quarrel turned into a brawl when Sharp attempted to arrest the Gentiles for disturbing the peace. The peace officers in the streets opened fire, wounding the surgeon and another officer, Lieutenant Saunders. Although both officers recovered, the incident echoed unpleasantly in Camp Floyd.

For the next seventeen months few people outside the army saw or heard very much of Dr. Covey until May 1860, when he was transferred to New Mexico along with various companies of dragoons and infantrymen. The detachment's outward line of march from the territory followed the narrow passageway along Yellow Creek Canyon, where the soldiers were divided into two separate columns, the first led by Colonel Morrison, the second commanded by Major Isaac Lynde. At the same time, William Hennefer and a small party of Mormons, including William I. Appleby, departed for Fort Bridger to establish a blacksmith shop to service the overland emigration. Hennefer followed the same trail selected by the army.[42]

In one of the narrowest parts of Echo Canyon, the Mormon train caught up with the rear guard of the second army column as it was ferrying an ox train across the river. When Morrison's troopers crossed to the east bank of Yellow Creek, Lynde ordered his men into camp on the opposite shore, splitting the expedition's livestock into small herds to assure adequate grazing on both sides of the river. The Mormons followed the army's lead column and forded the stream, after receiving Colonel Morrison's permission to camp alongside his command.

It was still daylight when Lieutenant Gay left the bivouac of the advance column and rode across Yellow Creek to tell Covey that the policeman who had wounded him back in Salt Lake City was now within a few hundred yards of him.[43] What occurred next was retold by an eyewitness, William I. Appleby, to the editor of *The Mountaineer*: "Just at twilight, while we were preparing to tie up our cattle, and while W. M. Hennefer was sitting in the front of his wagon, James Hennefer examining one of the oxen's hoofs (which was sore), Wm. Ward sitting under the waggon, and I standing at the end of the waggon-tongue, Dr. Covey, Lieut. Gay, and an attache of the army, rode up to the waggon." The physician dismounted and, tying his horse to a wheel, went to the rear of the conveyance where he met James Hennefer, the brother of the intended victim, who directed Covey to W. M. Hennefer at the front of the wagon. Covey ordered the ex-police officer down from the wagon. Hennefer refused. While the infantrymen stood watching, the physician drew his revolver from under his uniform coat and aimed it at Hennefer with the words: "Get out of that waggon, you G-d d—d son of a bitch, or I'll blow your G-d d—d brains out; I'm in earnest."[44] William Hennefer jumped from the wagon box, unarmed and fearing for his life.

The rancher was offered a pistol to defend himself, which he refused. Almost at the same moment, the Mormon was stripped half-naked by three soldiers and was tied, spread-eagled, to the wagon wheel. The excitement drew the attention of many soldiers who collected around the encampment to witness what would occur next. "Covey then stepped up to Hennefer, and with a leather riding-whip (a stock about eighteen inches long, and the lash of about the same length, formed by braiding four lashes together, and knotting them as they are braided), gave Hennefer seventy lashes, before he swooned and fell, his breast striking the hob of the wheel."[45] When his brother attempted to stop the beating, the soldiers "pounced on to him like a pack of hounds knocked him down; and as he got up, they kicked him down again."[46] He escaped to the express station in Echo Canyon as did most of the other Mormons, but Appleby remained behind to plead for Hennefer's life.

The whipping went on, irrespective of Appleby's protests, until Covey grew tired and stopped. "There, G-d d—m you, go into town and show the stripes to Brigham Young, and tell him that I did it; and if he was here I would serve him the same," the officer yelled.[47]

As a final act of defiance, everything in the Mormon wagons was either thrown into the creek or destroyed, including over a thousand dollars' worth of blacksmith's tools, clothing, blankets, and provisions belonging to the two brothers. The Mormons were understandably incensed over the incident, but their protests fell on deaf ears.

The Hennefer incident illustrated the extent to which the brief presence of the army had changed forever the Mormon dream of sovereignty over the Great Basin. When the army left the territory, the treasure hunters descended, and the Mormons were left to assess with bewilderment the effects of the outsiders on their kingdom in the mountains.

CHAPTER FIFTEEN

THE ECONOMIC IMPACT OF THE UTAH WAR: AN ANALYSIS

Cattle cheap and money plentyful. The bullets the troops brought to shoot at us turned out to be gold Eagles and landed in our pockets.
—William Laud[1]

WITH TERRITORIAL VIOLENCE came economic advantages that initiated a new era of prosperity for the Saints. The Utah War and the establishment of Camp Floyd opened the door, partially at least, for Utah to come to economic accommodation with the world beyond its borders.

Not since the California gold rush had there been so much to threaten Mormon economic independence. "The entrance of Johnston's army," a Mormon critic observed, "with the government contracts thereby rendered necessary, and the more complete establishment of the Overland Stage, mark a point of departure, so to speak, between the old and the new, separating ancient and modern history."[2] Military expenditures gave the territory unprecedented economic growth, but it was the Gentile merchants who did the most to mold a new financial outlook for the Saints.

The effect of their influence was staggering, bringing complaints that Gentiles were benefiting more from the new opportunities than were the original settlers of the territory themselves. Throughout the early period of Utah's history, the mercantile economy fell by default to non-Mormon businessmen, mainly because Brigham Young failed to encourage this type of activity among his own people. The Saints

260

believed that agricultural production and home industries would provide work for every honest and upright citizen, and lead to Mormon self-sufficiency. As a result, Utah's economy rose and fell erratically for ten years, influenced by weather, politics, and a shortage of hard currency.

The windfall brought on by Camp Floyd came none too soon for the Saints, already reduced to proud poverty by a decade of agricultural and commercial disasters. The economic problems of the Saints were many. The high cost of mastering the wilderness, chronic shortages of working capital, inadequate production capacity, decreasing capacity to pay secular taxes and Church tithes, a shortage of skilled labor, and heavy immigration outlays strained the Mormon economy. The dollar drain caused by the mass movement of converts to Utah was highly deflationary and slowed the rate of economic growth within the territory. Since the majority of converts were too impoverished to pay their own way, money was advanced by the Church through the Perpetual Emigration Fund, established in 1849 to aid immigration to the Great Basin. This involvement influenced the rapid population growth of the territory, but financing it imposed an increasingly heavy economic burden on the treasury of the Saints. In other words, immigration drained private and Church revenues alike, accelerating the outward flow of hard currency Utah so desperately needed to develop its local economy. Brigham Young failed to create stimulative financial policies to overcome these setbacks and check gold outflow from the territory.

Likewise, supplying the local militia to fight the Indians took money, which caused more poverty and economic depression in the Mormon kingdom. Militia expenses probably absorbed one-fourth of the liquid capital of the Saints, and, in addition, thousands of dollars were spent for the upkeep of the Nauvoo Legion. Neglected agricultural and domestic industries did not prosper the Saints as they had hoped. With few direct secular taxes to meet ballooning expenditures, and with a reluctance on the part of the federal government to meet the needs of territorial defense before 1858, the Saints dug deeper into their financial reserves to defend themselves.

The patient, industrious, and disciplined Saints turned to the tithe to fund their indebtedness. The tithe, like other religious levies, was not a sophisticated fiscal instrument, inasmuch as it did not produce residual income or monetary expansion. Consequently, it did not generate new industrial or economic activity that would have enabled the Saints to compete successfully with the products imported from the outside world. Over the years the economic aspirations of individual Saints were shunted aside to accommodate the broader struggle of establishing a secure foundation for Zion, which imposed a heavy restraint on overall economic development for the territory. Brigham Young further sapped the strength of the fledgling economy when he failed to ask for advice in fashioning new fiscal policies.

The leaders of the Mormon community appeared not to desire any close check on Gentile trade, so the territory's economy was kept on the verge of bankruptcy. Ben Holladay parlayed an investment of less than $70,000 into a small fortune in Utah, which eventually allowed him to establish a stagecoach empire across western America. High profits also attracted traders Livingston and Kinkead, who in 1849 took in several thousand dollars a day in gold until their supply of goods was exhausted.[3] While the exact profits of this firm are not known, they were sufficient to impress Brigham Young. "I saw several brass kettles under it [the counter], full of gold pieces—sovereigns, eagles, half-eagles, etc. One of the men shouted, 'Bring another brass Kettle!' They did so and set it down, and the gold was thrown into it, clink, clink, clink, until in a short time, it was filled."[4]

The firm's booming prosperity continued until the Utah War, when, in dread of an austere wartime economy, the mercantile house closed its accounts. But less than a year later Livingston and Kinkead were once again doing business in Salt Lake City, this time in a store leased from Young for $2,500 a year.[5] Although he accepted their rent, the Church leader criticized the firm for its inflated prices, its close cooperation with Gentiles, its uncontrolled speculation that affected the well-being of the Saints, and its indifference to Young's efforts to curtail the lawlessness that swept the city. Livingston had, up to this time, lived a charmed life among the Mormons, but Brigham accused him of trading the blood of the Saints for gold and silver. The Church leader sermonized that although Livingston had resided "in the midst of this community, and [was] sustained by their custom and enriched by their traffic, [you] are never heard in the public papers of our country contradicting the lies and misrepresentation perpetrated upon this people, nor even publishing one line in our behalf."[6] Young's statement triggered a personal confrontation with Livingston that aborted their long-standing friendship and drove Livingston into the enemy camp.

The territory's economic prospects increased rapidly in 1858 as the volume of military and civilian freight flooded Salt Lake and Camp Floyd. The spectacular development of Gentile merchandising interrupted Mormon ideas of self-sufficiency. Partners Livingston and Kinkead freighted slightly less than 300 tons of freight to Utah in 1858, estimated at an aggregate value of $300,000. An equal quantity of merchandise was delivered to the Salt Lake warehouse of Miller, Russell and Company, while G. A. Perry, Radford and Cabot, Kit

Brannon, and J. M. Hockaday shared smaller profits from the domestic trade.[7] The firm of Gilbert and Gerrish collected huge financial rewards for five succeeding years, "their sales on one particular day amounting to $17,000 in gold."[8]

Salt Lake City prospered as the economic center of the territory. This became evident to the young Mormon missionary John Orton, who arrived in the territory shortly after the army established Camp Floyd, and found that the Saints had shed their austere way of life.

> Goods rolled in plentifully by ox and mule teams—wagons, new, stood here and there, for sale cheap. Oxen, poor from unmerciful usage of unskilled drivers $25.00 per yoke as winter approached. Passing along busy Main St. almost any time, proprietors of shoe shops sought to engage me "Cash down." Destitute as I was I was enabled to save up more by Christmas, about five and one half months, than in eighteen months in New York City.[9]

Hundreds of settlers rushed to Camp Floyd offering to supply the army with building materials, wheat, and animal forage. The army molded its marketing policy to discriminate in favor of poorer citizens and small bidders, a practice condemned by Brigham Young, who charged that General Johnston was bringing dissension among the Saints by a "judicious distribution of federal gold."[10]

Though Church discipline grew weaker during this period, Young was not reluctant to make major economic commitments to maintain high prices for domestic foodstuffs. He instructed his bishops to establish a minimum price for all commodities marketed at Camp Floyd. He brought heavy pressure on members of the Mormon community to sell their products at prices prescribed by the Church First Presidency. To insure compliance, "all wards and settlements were advised to trade through officially recognized associations, committees, and agents."[11] Simultaneously, the *Deseret News* published a price schedule advising the Saints not to sell grain below three dollars a bushel or flour below ten dollars a hundred pounds.[12]

The Saints often attempted to pool their bids, distributing profits in proportion to investments. The vast timber holdings of Brigham Young and a dozen other leaders brought them a fortune when they supplied lumber to the army for the construction of Camp Floyd.[13]

Young's effort to maintain high agricultural price levels was complicated by the extraordinarily large wheat harvests of 1858 and 1859; but, fortunately for the Saints, the surplus was absorbed by the steadily increasing Gentile population, estimated between eight and fifteen thousand people. Also, 150,000 bushels of wheat were sold at Camp Floyd and more still was purchased by Russell, Majors and Waddell for their military contracts with the War Department.[14]

The Saints, however, often failed to exercise caution in disposing of their stores of food. The flaws in their marketing system became evident to Erastus Snow, who cautioned:

> I will tell you what you will see in Provo. You will see men and women and children in the streets begging for bread within twelve months, and when they can't get it they will go to the Gentiles and sell themselves, their wives and children for bread and then think that was a good loop hole to creep out of Mormonism. This is a time that many are starving for want of word of life, and men are selling the last bus. of grain they have, they will perish for bread.[15]

The demand for labor created by the federal government combined with an inflated commodity market brought acute suffering to citizens who could not keep up with the high prices. As the cost of wheat, barley, oats, beef, and timber reached record levels and threatened to go higher, shortages developed. Ninety percent of the people of Salt Lake City were without enough wood for heating and cooking during the winter of 1859, while "cows kept in the city [were] like walking skeletons, having little or nothing to eat."[16]

Church leaders understandably were alarmed by what they thought were dangerous excesses in the wage structure of the economy. Working as casual day-laborers, or as skilled craftsmen, members of the Mormon work force saw their monthly wages escalate from fifteen to fifty dollars, payable in gold rather than in Church scrip or produce. While Brigham Young preached self-sufficiency, crops remained in the field because farmers deserted their farms for the big money to be made at Camp Floyd.[17] None of the Church's arguments could counterbalance this lure, or prevent the emergence of public sentiment that favored the free market system. This independence often showed up in quarrels within Mormon towns and villages. Fort Ephraim was torn apart when Benjamin L. Clapp and a handful of Saints allowed the army to rent their corrals and stables, after contracting to furnish hay at fifteen dollars a ton and wheat at slightly more than a dollar. After conferring with Brigham Young, the stake president called the local Saints together and warned that "they were selling their hay and grain too cheap, they ought to have 25 or 30 dollars a ton for hay and the higher price for their wheat, and that the army would just as soon give $3 as 1.30 for wheat, but it was not right to feed wheat to mules when their brethren would be short of bread." Clapp objected, "claiming $1.30 was enough for wheat and $15 was a great price for hay, and the brethren might as well have money for their wheat as to keep it to feed other settlements with, and left the council in a rage and went to the Soldiers and asked the officers for protection."[18]

Reduction in the rural labor force produced secondary problems, remembered Church Historian George A. Smith:

I put into the hands of a man four and a half bushels of flax seed, gave him a piece of land, and told him there was a chance for him to raise a fine crop of flax. The first thing I knew about it was that the flax was gathered, but the man told me he had no time to attend it; he had been to Camp Floyd trading a little, he had let it all rot, not nobody would swinger, break or work it out, because it was so much easier and cheaper to do some kind of trading and get a little something out of the store.[19]

Brigham Young was informed by Edmund Ellsworth that Gentile laborers were being employed at a salary of thirty dollars a month to finish various Church projects in City Creek Canyon. The Mormon foreman "had tried to hire 'Mormon boys,' but they told him they could get $50 a month at the soldiers camp, and they would rather work for ten dollars less in the camp than in the canyon."[20]

Increased demand for labor permitted urban Saints to profit from the rapid expansion of Gentile merchants, the new territorial government, and the nonmilitary needs of Camp Floyd. With the economic boost the Church encouraged immigration and advertised the territory's new prosperity throughout the mission fields of Europe. "There are so many who need female help that the demand far exceeds the supply," wrote George A. Smith, "a hint to the sisters in foreign lands that here there is no fear of want of labor, good pay therefore, and comfortable situations." These expectations had a profound effect on the structure and operation of the mission program, especially in the depressed industrial countries of Europe.

The brethren who arrive and desire employment are at once engaged at fair prices and find good homes in our peaceful gathering retreats. This is doubtless a wide and favorable contrast to the situation of many of our brethren and sisters in foreign lands, and we trust that all consistent effort will be at home and abroad, by all parties concerned especially by those who wish to come, to further the transportation of the Saints from foreign shores to our own. . . .[21]

High wages concentrated non-agricultural employment at Salt Lake City and Camp Floyd and its economic satellite, Fairfield. An important result was the steady deterioration of home industries, which increased Utah's commercial dependence on the outside world.

Wherever people gathered, a new order of things was abundantly evident. Discomfort had been taken as a matter of course, wrote William Jennings, noting that as "clothing became exhausted, women were so scantly dressed as scarcely to cover their nakedness, barefooted and bleeding too, with no means for supplying their needs. They dressed sometimes in sacking or with remnants of rag carpets thrown round them."[22]

Accounts of the changing economy found their way into Mormon journals, and few pioneers were dismayed to report: "The settlers replaced
their sewing equipment of horse hair and thorns with real thread and
needles. They picked up shoes discarded by the soldiers which were much
better than their own. Some even were barefoot. Their dried squash and
bread diet was varied with more palatable foods."[23] In the newly found
prosperity, Saints were no longer satisfied with heavy homespun clothing
but demanded high quality machine-woven wool, linen, and calico, or an
occasional dress trimmed with lace. Factory shoes marked a degree of
indulgence that the Saints had not known since Nauvoo.

The Saints' deep sense of frugality gave way to an orgy of spending
during the last months of 1858. Although the Church attempted to place
some restrictions on domestic consumption of nonessential imports, one
writer claimed, "a fresh opening of a season's stock of State's goods by
our merchants, for instance, was quite sufficient to kill a whole year's
preaching on home manufactures."[24] Such moments were all too frequent,
remarked the editor of the *Valley Tan*: "The shelves of the merchants
present a lagging account of emptiness, all having sold out . . . and the
several Gentile firms, rather than wait for supplies from the Missouri
were ordering their goods directly from California."[25] The Pacific trade
had two major advantages over freighting from the east: it was closer by
several hundred miles and the southern route through the territory was
open to year-round traffic.

Trade goods came over the two coastal traces relatively slowly because
of the mountain barriers in the north, the waterless deserts in the south,
and the Indian menace along both the California and Spanish trails. The
central overland was the mainstream of Mormon emigration and an
important source for imported goods into the territory. The remarkable
growth in overland freighting between the Mississippi Valley and Utah
was noted by A. B. Miller, who told Young that "there were 1100 merchant wagons besides the Suttler's [sic] trains on the road to this place, and
more than half of them were 3 ton wagons 2 million dollars worth of
goods at cost & carriage are on the way to Utah."[26]

The overland Utah trade declined sharply in the summer of 1859,
partly because the territorial market had been saturated, and partly
because of the increased number of merchants competing for the Salt
Lake trade. Economic activity during the first half of 1859 was also
slowed by substantial investments in goods from California, which eventually depressed the price of merchandise freighted from the Missouri
River. This slight dimming of the economic picture was a cause for concern, but retail prices leveled off and a more disciplined pattern of consumption took hold among the Saints.

By midsummer of 1859, merchants were closely following the fluctu-
ations in the economy and working with a narrow profit margin, pain-

fully aware of increased costs of transportation, high interest rates from eastern banks, and an oversupplied market. In marked contrast with the preceding year, the price of manufactured goods steadily declined after October. The *Deseret News* took particular pleasure in announcing:

> Peradventure some have had other inducements also for visiting the city; to behold with their own eyes and hear with their own ears the evidences that *we*, that is the citizens of Great Salt Lake City, are basking in the sunshine of Christendom and rally luxuriating in the blessings of Christian civilization; to participate with us in the opportunities of purchasing *cheap goods* at cost and 15 cents freight, i.e., to buy sugar at 40 cents per pound; coffee at 45 cents; tea at $1.50 to $2.50; sheeting at 20 to 25 cents per yrd; calicos at 20 and 30 cents; stoves at $175 and $150. . . .[27]

Some of these changes in the territorial price structure were accelerated by the August sale of surplus commodities from the quartermaster's warehouses at Camp Floyd, forcing the majority of merchants to sell their goods at cost.[28] "Many useful implements and clothing are obtained cheap," wrote R. L. Campbell to George A. Smith. Campbell reported that when a newcomer "commenced selling in Jordan street, at the west end of the city, his prices were moderate; shortly a messenger came along and priced his sugar and on being told informed the emigrant he would take what he had to spare at that price."[29]

Feeling the pinch of declining business, many restaurants, taverns, stores, and trading establishments closed their doors for want of paying customers, who began their exodus from the territory during the winter of 1859–1860. Among the most prominent restaurants to close its doors was the "Globe," a Mormon enterprise owned by David Candland and a handful of Church leaders. Predictably, the Saints took pleasure in the outward movement of the carpetbag residents.

> With few exceptions, the hotels and other kindred establishments in this Territory and more particularly in this city, have hitherto received most of their patronage from the transient and mobile class of people, who come and go, like birds of passage, arriving in the spring or summer and departing in the fall or before it is too cold to continue their journey, or retrace the way by which they came in safety.[30]

Paralleling the long-predicted movement was the belief that federal power over the purse was tantamount to sovereignty over the territory. "If another enormous amount of money could be appropriated and expended to gratify those who are constantly howling about the crimes and abominations committed and practiced by the people of Utah," wrote the *Deseret News*, "for the sole purpose of inducing the Government to make further appropriations for the benefit of speculators and gamblers, some of those who have migrated lately would unquestionably return in order to secure a share in the spoils, a greater one, if possible, than they obtained before." Reflecting the consensus of its reading audience, the paper added, "but there will surely be no sorrowing if their faces are seen no more in the valley of the Great Salt Lake."[31]

As trade waned and commercial activity became somewhat spartan, a handful of Mormon capitalists were attracted into the market, purchasing the entire stock of unsold Gentile stores.[32] Following the example of the Walker Brothers, who had grown wealthy through their retail outlets at Camp Floyd and Fairfield, Charles Woodmansee, William Staines, J. C. Kimball, W. S. Godbe, J. C. Little, and others saw opportunities to extend Mormon influence over the commercial sector of the territory. Exchanging imported manufactured goods for frontier produce and domestic livestock that were eventually consumed locally or sold to the army at Camp Floyd, these local merchants emerged as examples of prosperity to future Mormon entrepreneurs. But they were aware that they could not escape the consequences of their unfamiliarity with trade requirements, an inadequate banking system, and a lack of liquid capital.

However, the need for new markets was partially met in 1860 by the Colorado and Nevada gold strikes. Although Utah lacked the capacity to increase its exports dramatically, full employment and high incomes were generated by fortune hunters moving in and out of the new gold fields. Momentarily at least, Salt Lake City became the major trading center between St. Louis and San Francisco, a marketplace that attracted a fair share of domestic and foreign merchants. The importance of its geographic position, approximately the same distance from Denver as was the Missouri Valley, gave the city an early edge as an important supplier of staples to the eastern Rockies. Commented *The Rocky Mountain News*:

> There arrived yesterday a vast quantity of fresh eggs, butter, a large quantity of onions, barley, oats, etc., only fifteen days from the city of the Saints. . . . We hear also of twelve thousand sacks of Utah flour now on the road; five thousand bushels of corn, a large quantity of barley, onions, etc., now enroute for this city in the trains of Miller, Russell and Company. This is a new unexpected branch of trade. Nobody here dreamed of any supply of provisions coming from the west.[33]

The newspaper criticized the War Department for not promoting the Utah market, or maintaining an economic atmosphere in which commerce would flourish.

> The fact that the army supplies for Camp Floyd are still transported from the Missouri River, even the corn and oats that is fed to stock, being hauled from western Missouri and Iowa, makes it seem strange that Utah is now able to ship thousands of sacks of

flour eastward to this country. The Mormons must be prospering, and Uncle Sam must be very shortsighted, or some of his agents are great rascals.[34]

The combination of regional marketing problems sent Denver prices soaring. During the last weeks of September, forty-five heavily loaded wagons from Utah rolled through the busy streets of the mining capital, adding to the total tonnage of trade arriving at the mile-high city from the Mississippi. "Utah is becoming quite important as a supply point for the gold regions, and we are pleased to see the above firm Miller and Russell taking the initial steps for opening a trade," commented the editor of *The Rocky Mountain News*.[35] Unfortunately, the remarkable success of these early trains from Utah did not last. By late fall, freighters experienced a rapid decline in agricultural prices. Wheat dropped in value by forty percent—to a price scarcely enough to cover the cost of freight from Salt Lake City. In 1861, commodity exports from the Missouri Valley flooded the gold fields, further depressing the market.

While markets in Colorado diminished in importance, Utah trade with the Mississippi Valley remained attractive, mainly because it continued to be a source of missionary and immigration traffic. William H. Hooper, territorial delegate to Congress, attempted to establish a joint-stock company to carry freight from the Missouri to Utah, combining private interest with Mormon necessity. Under his proposal, the company would sell shares at one hundred dollars each, redeemable in three years, drawing an annual interest rate to ten percent, and payable in hard currency. To encourage Mormon investment capital, business was to be conducted "on a wholesale principle, and open a ledger account with each article, showing profit and loss to each member of the association his share of the profit, pro ratio of goods and cash."[36] To Hooper's words, E. D. Woolley added:

> It was time something was done to stop the bleeding of the people in regard to means . . . there was a prejudice existing against any "Mormon" who will embark in the business of merchandising, but there was no prejudice against any persons who did not belong to us, no matter how much they [non-Mormons] imposed upon the peoples, and when trouble came upon us, would pack up their goods and the immense fortunes they had made, and leave us to ourselves to bear the burden.[37]

But a movement of another sort was already established that would fix the Mormon pattern of freighting until the advent of the railroad in 1869. Lacking money to expand either immigration or freighting, Brigham Young conceived a plan to increase the volume of goods brought into the territory by the Saints, while at the same time saving thousands of dollars by transporting converts to Utah. In an entrepreneurial vision, the Church president considered shipping the freight trains by water to the headwaters of the Missouri, where a Mormon settlement would be established. "The annual expense of our freight and immigration across the plains is so great that I again call your attention to the subject of the highest point of navigation on the Missouri or Yellow Stone," he wrote to W. H. Hooper in Washington, "and I wish you to try to hunt up Richard R. Hopkins (who is running on the Missouri) or some one who will engage in the upper trade and attend to our freighting." Continuing, he added: "They will perhaps require boats that can run where the ground is a little damp so as soon as we learn the practicability of that route, we intend to make a settlement at the head of navigation and save the enormous cash expenditures to which we have so long been subjected."[38] The water route, however, was dropped as being too costly and impractical.

Young then proposed that, instead of purchasing wagons and supplies at the Missouri Valley, Mormon trains be sent east from Salt Lake City with provisions and other exports, mainly livestock and surplus wagons. Round trip freighting proved successful for a variety of reasons. First, the cost of wagons and livestock which could be collected in the territory was only a fraction of the price that the same items were in Missouri. The Saints could purchase hundreds of wagons from Russell, Majors and Waddell for ten dollars each, about one-seventeenth of the cost of their manufactured price. Also, the deactivation of Camp Floyd reduced retail prices of ox-teams by fifty percent, half the cost demanded at the eastern end of the Oregon Trail.

The plan also relied on voluntary labor of "missionaries," who "were credited on the tithing books with the value of the service rendered."[39] The plan was only a limited success, however, for it could hardly meet the demands of the rapidly increasing population, or succeed in matching the commercial efforts of Gentile and private Mormon merchants. Nevertheless, the first missionary freighting teams of thirty wagons and fifty men left Salt Lake City on April 27, 1860, and arrived at the Missouri the first day of July. After a delay of twenty-three days caused by the late arrival of freight, the train started its return journey to Utah, arriving in the territory on the third of October.[40]

Having established the feasibility of his plan, Young weighed its strengths and weaknesses. The draft animals were in "far better shape than teams that crossed the plains once. However many of the missionaries did not know what was expected of them," complained the Church president. "They had an idea they would be allowed on tithing for their trip and have the privilege of loading up goods at the Missouri and get their pay for freighting to this place too." To correct this misunderstanding, Brother Brigham suggested that local merchants send extra wagons for local communities, so they would not sacrifice the Church program of missionary freighting.[41]

The direct effect on the Utah economy of the sale of Camp Floyd and the surplus goods of Fort Bridger is not clear. Although $4 million worth of stores and livestock was sold for less than $100,000, the profits from the public auction fell into the hands of a small group of speculators and had a limited effect on the pace and character of the territorial economy. The month-long sale, commencing on July 16, 1861, generated price levels that were remarkably low: flour was sold at less than six cents a pound, sugar at twice that, nails at six cents a pound, horse and mule shoes at less than a cent, while mule collars were disposed of at forty-one cents each. Comparable bargains were found on all perishable and durable goods.[42] To give the Saints optimal advantage from the government sales, Brigham Young appealed to them not to bid against each other and thus force the price up. "I would like a few tools, a mowing machine, etc., as we spoke of before you left, but not enough to bid against the brethren and run articles up, for I had rather have you return without having made single bid, than to bid against the brethren; I trust the wisdom of this counsel will at once be seen and practiced upon by all the brethren who may be there. . . ."[43] The sale was limited because consumer desires exceeded their meager incomes, so there were only limited opportunities for small investors to participate in the one-time bonanza.

As the dazzling economic prosperity came to an end, Brigham Young's problems remained. His obsession with economic self-sufficiency kept him in its grip throughout most of the 1860s, weakening an already overburdened credit structure and allowing only a small improvement in domestic merchandising. George A. Smith voiced his thoughts on the effect of Camp Floyd on Utah's economy:

> How did it made us rich? You got their old iron, and that put a stop to the manufacture of iron here; you got the rags they brought here to sell, and that put a stop to our home manufactures; hence I do not think that, financially, our condition was much improved. The Government is said to have expended forty millions in bringing that army to Utah and in establishing Camp Floyd, yet most of it went into the hands of speculators, and very little into the hands of the actual settlers of this country.
>
> I do believe, however, that if the little means then accumulated by the people had been used with wisdom it would have resulted in permanent benefit to the community, but as it turned out it educated us into the idea that we must buy what we needed from abroad.[44]

The Mormon dream of developing a unique regional economy was already dimming as Congress debated the construction of a transcontinental railroad. Again, the brief tenure of the army in Utah had changed forever the course and nature of the Mormon experience.

CHAPTER SIXTEEN

EPILOGUE

On arriving at the rim of Cedar Valley I turned to look at the small region of the globe where an entire year and more of my life had been spent like a blank, and which I hoped I might never see again.
—William Phelps[1]

THE HISTORY OF CAMP FLOYD drew to a close in an atmosphere of prosperity and violence. During the first months of 1860, President Buchanan concentrated on problems in the territories that hampered any reconciliation between the federal government and the people in Utah and Kansas. He considered bringing the Mormons under martial law as his federal judges had requested, and he also considered completely deactivating the military department of Utah and letting history run its course. The seriousness of his dilemma was underscored in Congress by the Covode Committee, an immensely powerful collection of anti-administration congressmen who deeply troubled the president by their investigation into the Kansas question and its implications in the Utah War. There was division within the president's own cabinet on the course to be pursued in the western territories and the way to bridge the dangerous chasm of sectionalism. Grievances against the Saints were voiced by the fire-breathing Secretary of War, John B. Floyd, who viewed the Mormon question as an irresolvable difference between conflicting cultures. This view drew support from the Commissioner of Indian Affairs, A. B. Greenwood, who denounced the Saints for their part in the Mountain Meadows Massacre. Counteracting these powerful pressures and expressing qualified support of the Saints, Secretary of State Lewis Cass cited the benign influence of Brigham Young in developing the Great Basin. More than any other member of the cabinet, Cass urged the president to stabilize the territories, and Buchanan chose to try this in Utah.

Buchanan announced that he would hand Utah back to the Mormons by reducing the troop strength of the Department of Utah from

272

thirty-four companies, composed of slightly more than two thousand men, to eight companies, totaling less than three hundred soldiers.[2] What persuaded Buchanan to reverse his position toward the Saints is not entirely clear, but, abandoned by his own party and suffering criticism from abolitionists and Republicans, Buchanan renounced his policy of forceful military intervention in the territories. Kansas and Utah had forced him to face the complexities of territorial politics. In the next twelve months, the lame-duck president would refuse to disturb the delicate balance between war and peace, thus ending his interventionist politics and, ironically, leaving himself helpless to save the Union he had so desperately tried to preserve.

General Johnston was the first soldier to leave Utah under the withdrawal orders.[3] The duties of military life in the territory had severely restricted his private life, had drenched his career with homesickness, and had disheartened his thoughts with bitterness and disappointment. Having requested a leave of absence shortly after arriving in the territory, the general had grown tired of the monotony of camp duty and the frustration of his efforts to bring Utah under tight federal control. "I have no news for you from this far away region," he wrote to his daughter. "I believe I told you in my last letter how time is disposed of in camp life and so far there has been not an incident to vary the routine—the history of a day is the history of the year, we have our duties and our amusements, all of which I have mentioned— but our life, has great contrasts, liable to shift suddenly from dull routine to one of toil and activity, for this change we hope and without it I think we despair."[4]

For seven weeks Johnston put his military and personal affairs in order, carefully grooming his replacement, Colonel C. F. Smith, on the operation of the department. When preparations were finished, he announced that he would depart for California on the morning of March 1, 1860, a date that saw 2,000 troops turn out on their snow-covered parade ground to pay their last respects to their departing commander. Amid the clash of artillery, the general rode from his headquarters to review his troops for the last time. In an emotionally charged atmosphere, the general addressed his troops from the saddle. He thanked his men warmly for their service in the Utah Expedition and for their loyalty during his difficult command. Turning to face Colonel Smith, he relinquished command and joined his escort. The regimental band played "Come Out of the Wilderness," and the combined force rode west through the desert, pulled uphill toward General Johnston's Pass, and disappeared over the cloud-fringed horizon. The general's career in Utah had come to its official end.[5]

As the flood of carriages, wagons, horses, and soldiers followed the Simpson trail to California, Johnston contemplated the events of his three-year tour of duty in the territory. "Like much of Johnston's previous career," a later historian would write, "his experience as commander of the Utah expedition was one of enthusiasm turned to frustration. He gave up the command feeling that his true mission in Utah was unfulfilled."[6] Yet, like a phoenix arisen from the desert floor, Johnston was actually approaching his zenith, and he was destined to be thrust into the political limelight as one of the country's most able generals. "It is generally remarked," wrote an unidentified correspondent, "that no other military commander of the American army ever left a military department carrying with him so universally the high regards and good wishes of those under his command, as well as their approval of his official conduct."[7]

Johnston was approached to run for the presidency of the United States. "My friends, some of them in the States say that a glittering prize is within my grasp. . . ," he wrote to his son William Preston Johnston. "If I had you to write my answer declining profered [sic] honor if any chance it should be offered, I could by displaying the folly of our people in selecting men for public office without any regard to their education & training for the particular duties they are called upon to perform more entitles myself to their good opinion than by accepting." He added, "My education, my taste & my ambition, if I have any, would find nothing congenial in the performance of the duties of a civil office. . . ."[8] But in 1860 his candidacy was again given careful attention by his friends. "Take care, old fellow," wrote James Love from Texas, "or you will be President after awhile, a station no honest man in these desperate days ought to hold."[9]

Meanwhile, the well-meaning and personable Colonel Smith supervised the rapid deactivation of Camp Floyd, reduced by the following summer to a field strength of slightly more than 300 soldiers. Transferred to New Mexico were elements of the Second Dragoons, the Seventh Infantry, the Tenth Infantry, and the Fifth Infantry. Company C of the Tenth Infantry was ordered to Fort Laramie, while B and G Companies were transferred to Fort Bridger.[10] The remaining elements were ordered to Fort Garland under the command of Lt. Colonel E. R. S. Canby.[11]

The military posture of the Department of Utah remained unchanged during the next sixteen months, although the departmental command was reassigned to Colonel Philip St. George Cooke when Colonel C. F. Smith was transferred to Washington. Operations at Camp Floyd were disturbed by news of Southern secession, which sharply divided the officer corps in Cedar Valley and produced heated confrontations in the barracks. Colonel Cooke approached the secession crisis with a distinctly Republican frame of reference, yet rumors claimed he would resign his commission when his native state of Virginia left the Union. The commander's efforts to reunite his officers ended in failure, partially because he believed he would not raise his sword against Missouri, his adopted state, if she joined the Confederacy. "Mere hatred of the South becomes now, especially in these noncombatants—a zealous patriotism," wrote Cooke to his superior officer in Washington, "which they exalt, as worthy of great applause."[12] When Cooke showed no sign of leaving federal service, his most personal, most intimate relationships came under close examination by the pro-Union officers serving under his command. Tired and harassed, he continued, "Instead of sympathizing with the unhappiness of my family division—one of the great miseries of the times— and the patriotic fidelity of many so sorely tried as to be impelled to battle against their own flesh and blood—a generosity with which I credit the unscheming mass of my fellow country men of the west and north—they travel and impute it as a crime!"[13]

Cooke experienced a wave of "defections" of former friends, who now openly questioned Cooke's relationship to his son, John R. Cooke, and his son-in-law, J. E. B. Stuart, both of whom had followed their native states into the Confederacy. "The department, I doubt not, knew better than they—" he wrote of the heartbreaking experience, "even than I do, of the acts of my far distant, long absent, unhappy son but gloating in my misfortune, they did not stop to observe the malice betrayed but I dismiss the subject with loathing."[14]

For southern officers the hardest blow came in December of 1860, when the War Department changed the fort's name to Fort Crittenden and demanded signed pledges of loyalty to the Union.[15] This directive had an adverse effect on the closing days of Camp Floyd. The majority of the remaining officers resigned their commissions and offered their swords to their native states of the South. Meanwhile, as General Scott had ordered, Cooke was preoccupied with disposing of military property to the best advantage of the federal government.

As the sale of the remaining surpluses quickened, Colonel Cooke received orders to evacuate Fort Crittenden whenever the public properties could be sold, but not later than August 1, 1861.[16] While Cooke reduced the fort's operations, soldiers destroyed the remaining unsold government property, including all ammunition and small arms, an obvious attempt to prevent military weapons from falling into the hands of the Mormons. "Minie rifles Yager revolvers all the ordinances stores & much other property, that it was thought would be of use to the citizens of the Territory if left in the country [were destroyed]," wrote Judge Elias Smith. "A more damnable act," he continued, "could not well be done but it was such a one as might be expected from the Government of the United States which has long sought the destruction of the Saints, and would of course do nothing that would enable them to defend themselves from the assault of the savages who surround them in these mountains nor from the lawless acts of bandits who might make depredations upon their unprotected settlements."[17]

One day past the third anniversary of the army's march through Salt Lake City, the last link in the ring of steel around the Saints dissolved. Abandoning Camp Floyd to the desert waste, Colonel Cooke marched his small detachment out of Cedar Valley for the last time on the morning of July 27, 1861. Two months earlier the last Gentile federal official, Governor Alfred Cumming, had departed for Georgia, and with his exodus the first carpetbag administration of Utah came to an end.

But the federal government was not to allow the Saints to pursue an independent life west of the Rockies, for the old problems of Indian affairs, poor political appointees, and jurisdictional conflicts were not yet resolved. However, these conflicts were "only symptomatic of the primary cause of dispute," wrote Norman Furniss, "the Mormons' angry insistence on the right to manage their own affairs, which to them included most of the temporal as well as religious business of the Territory, and their opponents' antithetical desire to reduce the Church's authority." The investigation of the Mountain Meadows Massacre remained, as did the criticism of polygamy, and "while the shifting currents of political tides of the nation might wash different men into the Territory's secular offices . . . the changes failed to bring a diminution of hostility."[18]

There was a final touch of irony in the history of Camp Floyd—a saga that was told in the careers of the officers and men who were to fight in the Civil War. No soldier would be untouched by the drama that unfolded across the bloody battlefields of that conflict. The soldiers of Camp Floyd marched together away from Utah to glory and death that would find them as they fought against each other.

Marching east towards the frontier, adding to his column several companies of infantrymen from Fort Bridger, Colonel Cooke learned that General Johnston had resigned his command of the Department of the Pacific and was hurrying across the Southwest to offer his services to the Confederacy. Before Cooke reached the Mississippi, Johnston had joined the Texas troops under General Baylor and had taken temporary command of the southern forces headquartered at Mesilla, New Mexico Territory.[19] After tarrying a week, Johnston left for San Antonio by stage and continued toward Houston, where he arrived during the middle of August. Learning that the Union naval blockade made a sea voyage impossible, Johnston traveled overland to New Orleans, then by rail to Richmond, where he conferred with the president of the Confederacy, Jefferson Davis.

Davis expressed concern over the vulnerability of the Confederacy west of the Appalachian Mountains, adding that a citizens' committee from Memphis had petitioned him to name Johnston commander of that department. Moreover, Lieutenant General Leonidas Polk, in command of the militia regiments along the northern border stretching from eastern Tennessee to Indian Territory, supported the request: "I know of no man who has the capacity to fill the position, who could be had, but General Johnston."[20] Johnston's appointment to command the Confederate Department Number 2, with a rank second only to that of dotty Adjutant General Samuel Cooper, ended the confusion that had beset the western command of the Confederacy. In Johnston the South found a general whose knowledge of military affairs was respected on both sides of the battle line. "His contemporaries at West Point," General Ulysses S. Grant would write in his memoirs, "and the officers generally who came to know him personally later and who remained on our side, expected him to prove the most forcible man to meet that the Confederacy would produce."[21]

Johnston became increasingly aware that the Confederacy could not defend a 300-mile border from the Cumberland Gap to Columbus, Kentucky. His worst fears were realized in February, when a coordinated Union land and water assault forced the surrender of Fort Henry and Fort Donelson, and secured for the North the entire length of the Tennessee and Cumberland Rivers. Falling back to a line that snaked from the Cumberland Mountains to Memphis, Johnston remapped his strategy to carry the war to the North. On April 2, he drew up plans to advance against the Union army at Pittsburg Landing, a short distance east of Shiloh Church.

The Confederate army took three days to cover a distance of twenty miles. "Almost everything that could go wrong went wrong. . . . The soldiers did not know how to make a cross-country hike and most of their officers did not know how to direct them."[22] Johnston's exasperation boiled over. But his forces had not been detected by Union pickets, and on the evening of April 5, he gave the order to attack the enemy's encampment the following morning.

The first streaks of dawn opened one of the most critical battles of the Civil War. At five o'clock the Confederate forces advanced on three fronts and found the Union army commanded by William T. Sherman scattered and unprepared for their assault. General Grant, recovering from injuries sustained in a painful fall from his horse, arrived at Pittsburg Landing three hours after the fighting began and saw near disaster. By the middle of the morning the Union's right and center lines had given ground, but from positions along a wooden wagon road General Benjamin Prentiss was able to put up a good defense and drive back repeated Confederate charges.

Throughout the first hours of battle, Johnston was confident of victory. Riding from one end of the skirmish line to the other, reconnoitering enemy positions and conferring with his corps, division, and brigade commanders, the indefatigable general ordered his troops to press the attack. The enemy line still held, despite two direct assaults against its front and flanks; however, Johnston was determined to hurl the enemy from its positions. Moving to the center of the Confederate line on his horse, Fire-eater, he pointed to his soldiers' bayonets, dulled by the black smoke of battle, and yelled encouragement to his men: "These will do the work. . . . Men, they are stubborn; we must use the bayonet."[23]

Pointing to the Union column, he added, "I will lead you!" The Confederates pushed forward like lions, but were answered with bullets, one of which struck the charging general. Soldiers stationed to the rear again heard the sharp crackling of rifle fire; Johnston reeled in agony as a second wound was opened in his left leg, severing an artery below the knee.

Ignoring his injuries, Johnston remained in the battle and ordered Breckinridge's battery to silence a line of federal artillery in the woods to his left. Precious minutes slipped by. His leg streaming with blood, the commander slumped to one side of his saddle and was helped to the ground by his aide. Facing the downed, blood-soaked general, the man asked Johnston if he had suffered a vital wound. The commander answered, "Yes, and I fear seriously."[24] Minutes later he was dead, and with him went all hope of Confederate victory.

No battle was more decisive. The bruised and battered Southern army had failed "to turn the tables, to recoup what had been lost along the Tennessee-Kentucky line, to win a new chance to wage war west of the Appalachians on an equal footing. . . . After this, the Southern nation could do no more than fight an uphill fight to save part of the Mississippi Valley—the great valley of American empire without which the war could not be won."[25] A thousand miles from the adobe ruins of Camp Floyd, immortality finally came to Albert Sidney Johnston.

Fate also tracked the career of Colonel Charles F. Smith in the Union forces. Following his successful campaigns that led to the fall of Forts Henry and Donelson, his military reputation rose considerably. Temporarily superseding his former student at West Point, Ulysses S. Grant, Smith commanded the federal army's thrust down the Mississippi, but the former commandant was destined not to lead his forces against General Johnston. While the battle of Shiloh raged, Smith lay dying from an accident that had occurred near his headquarters in Savannah, Tennessee. Nineteen days after Johnston was killed, Smith followed his former commander into immortality, ending the thirty-five-year military career of the man General Lew Wallace called "by all odds the handsomest, stateliest, most commanding figure I had ever seen."[26]

Throughout the course of the Civil War the officers and men of Camp Floyd served in every major campaign on both sides of the battle line. In the borderlands of the Southwest, Edward R. S. Canby and his Confederate brother-in-law Henry Hopkins Sibley led opposing armies battling for control of the Rio Grande. The Confederate general would be one of the last men to surrender his command during the Civil War. Surviving the rebellion unscathed, E. R. S. Canby was murdered in 1873 by a band of Modoc Indians while engaged in peace negotiations with Keintpoos, better known among the white settlers as Captain Jack. The death of an army general at the hands of the Indians shocked the nation, and in subsequent heavy fighting the Modocs were overwhelmed and Captain Jack and a handful of his followers were hanged.

The former commander of the Department of New Mexico, Colonel William Wing Loring, joined the Confederacy and transferred valuable equipment and munitions to its cause. Tragedy struck Major Isaac Lynde, the veteran campaigner of the California Trail, and he ended the war in disgrace—a victim of poor judgment and hard luck. Forced to abandon Fort Fillmore in southern New Mexico to a superior force led by Colonel John Baylor, Lynde moved up the river to Fort Stanton, about one hundred miles northeast. Although ordered to destroy the fort's supply of liquor, his soldiers filled their canteens with whiskey and brandy, and when the Confederate forces overtook the Union column in the mountains, the "fainting, famishing soldiers threw down their arms . . . and begged for water."[27] Without Lynde's reinforcements, the Union forces had to abandon Fort Stanton.

Throughout those violent days, no battle was more costly to human lives than the one fought at Gettysburg, Pennsylvania, a small farming hamlet surrounded by rolling hills. Here two armies met by accident, dramatically altering the course of the Confederacy. The campaign got off to a slow start a little west of the town on the morning of July 1, 1863, when General Henry Heth's division of General A. P. Hill's corps met and engaged General John Buford's Union cavalry, along with advancing elements of infantry commanded by General John Reynolds. As young officers attached to the Utah Expedition, both Heth and Buford had suffered the hardships of wintering in Camp Scott in 1857–1858, as did General Reynolds. A skillful military leader and fearless in battle, Reynolds was offered command of the Army of the Potomac, but he refused. He was killed during the pitched fighting of Gettysburg's first day. Although

Buford was wounded for the second time during the fighting, he survived until December, when he died from exposure and exhaustion.[28] When the guns of Gettysburg were silenced, the federal army listed its losses at more than 3,000 killed and 20,000 wounded; the Confederates counted 3,900 killed and 24,000 wounded.

During the war, the former soldiers of Camp Floyd dearly bought their laurels. When casualties were counted, the regimental colors that once had flown over Utah were stained with the blood of its soldiers. Although many officers and men were detached from their original regiments or resigned to join the Confederacy, making it difficult to estimate the exact number of deaths among the soldiers who were at Camp Floyd, the figure ran into the hundreds.[29] Listed among the distinguished Union generals to fall in battle were Jesse L. Reno, after whom the Nevada town was named, William P. Sanders, Jesse A. Gove, and Stephen Weed. Counted in the ranks of Confederate losses were Generals George B. Anderson, Lewis A. Armistead, James Deshler, John Dunovant, and John Pegram. Also marked among the Confederate dead was President Buchanan's peace commissioner and Mexican War veteran Benjamin McCulloch.

Before Appomattox put an end to the campaigning, many young soldiers were thrust into national prominence, but none became more notorious than a former Camp Floyd mess cook, William Clarke Quantrill. Under the guise of serving the Southern cause, Quantrill operated independently in Kansas, but came under Confederate suspicion and was arrested. Outlawed by the Union as well because of his indiscriminate banditry, he escaped to Texas, where in 1865 he drew up a fantastic plan to assassinate Lincoln. Carving a path of bloody violence in attacks as far as Kentucky, Quantrill was eventually surprised and killed.

At the close of the Civil War, Camp Floyd lay in ruins. Ceiling beams were carried off to help build homes and farm buildings in the adjoining Mormon communities, allowing the winter snows and spring rains to wash away the adobe walls that gradually melted back into the earth. Vandals pillaged stone foundations and dismantled the arsenal, the regimental jails, and the remaining wooden structures spared by the weather. Camp Floyd breathed its last. The military reservation was turned over to the Interior Department, under whose jurisdiction it remained until 1892, when the land was thrown open for homesteading.[30]

The spirit of Camp Floyd was never absent from the land, however. The army retained ownership of the final resting place of its fallen dead, later converting it into a national historic site. Recently, because of the revival of interest in the fort among the inhabitants of

Utah, one monument has been restored to mark the presence of Johnston's Army—the commissary building in which the final auction sale was made. The army's long shadow, somewhat softened by time, still falls over Cedar Valley, a ghostly reminder of the furious controversy that once shook the Mormon kingdom.

NOTES

NOTES TO CHAPTER 1

1. Andrew J. Allen, "Diary," February 3, 1958 (typescript), University of Utah, p. 32.

2. Wallace Stegner, *The Gathering of Zion: The Story of the Mormon Trail* (New York: McGraw-Hill Book Company, 1964), p. 1.

3. Paul I. Wellman, *The House Divided: The Age of Jackson and Lincoln, from the War of 1812 to the Civil War* (Garden City, New York: Doubleday & Company, Inc., 1966), p. 215.

4. Brigham Young to Samuel Brannan, July 7, 1846, *Brigham Young Papers*, Manuscript Collection, Church of Jesus Christ of Latter-day Saints, Salt Lake City. Hereafter this archive is identified as C.H.O.

5. Ibid.

6. Ibid.

7. Henry W. Bigler, "Journal," January 24, 1848, Manuscript Section, C.H.O.

8. D.W. Meining, "The Mormon Culture Region: Strategies and Patterns in the Geography of the American West, 1847–1964," *Annals, Association of American Geographers*, LV (June, 1965), p. 198.

9. At least one historian claimed that to guarantee the perpetuation of the ideals of the political Kingdom of God, a "Council of Fifty," created by Joseph Smith as an advisory group in 1844, was given complete religious and political control of the State of Deseret: "The Council of Fifty, in creating the State of Deseret, paid lip service to the doctrine of sovereignty of the people and the democratic practices of a constitutional convention and free elections. Actually, the new government was formed through the highly centralized and autocratic control of its own organization." Klaus Hansen, *Quest for Empire: The Political Kingdom of God and the Council of Fifty in Mormon History* (Lansing, Michigan: Michigan State University Press, 1967), p. 127.

10. Meining, "The Mormon Culture Region," p. 198.

11. Howard Roberts Lamar, *The Far Southwest, 1846–1912: A Territorial History* (New Haven: Yale University Press, 1966), p. 328.

12. Arnie Podervaart, "Black-Robed Justice in New Mexico, 1846–1912," *New Mexico Historical Review*, XXII (April, 1947): p. 137.

13. Church of Jesus Christ of Latter-day Saints Journal History, manuscript history of day-by-day events, compiled by Andrew Jensen and others, Manuscript Section, C.H.O., September 7–20, 1851; henceforth labeled *Journal History*.

14. T. B. H. Stenhouse, *The Rocky Mountain Saints* (New York: D. Appleton and Company, 1873), p. 276. President Taylor rejected the petition of the State of Deseret for admission into the Union in 1847, possibly with the remark that Utah was the Sodom and Gomorrah of the West.

15. *Journal History*, September 7–10, 1851.

16. *New York Times*, May 18, 1857.

17. Jules Remy, *A Journey to Great Salt Lake City: Being a Sketch of the History, Religion and Customs of the Mormons* (2 vols., London: W. Jeffs, 1861), vol. 1, p. 469; Morris R. Werner, *Brigham Young* (New York: Harcourt, Brace, and Company, 1925), p. 381.

18. Mrs. C. V. Waite, *The Mormon Prophet and His Harem: An Authentic History of Brigham Young, His Numerous Wives and Children* (Chicago: J. S. Goodman and Company, 1867), p. 49; *Millennial Star* (Liverpool) XVIII (1856): 204–205.

19. *Journal History*, December 12, 1857; Brigham Young to G. A. Smith, January 3, 1857, *Brigham Young Papers*, Manuscript Section, C.H.O.

20. *House Executive Document*, No. 71, 35th Congress, 1st Session, Serial 956, X, pp. 212–214.

21. Although Drummond's letter was dated March 30, 1857, Buchanan had already received a dispatch from the judge on March 17, 1857. *Chicago Tribune*, April 23, 1858.

22. *New Orleans Courier*, April 3, 1857.

23. W. W. Drummond to D. J. Thompson, April 2, 1857, *Drummond Papers*, Manuscript Section, C.H.O.

24. *Chicago Tribune*, April 20, 1857.

25. Ray Allen Billington, *The Far Western Frontier* (New York: Harper and Row, 1956), p. 213.

26. Lawrence, *Herald of Freedom*, July 4, 1857.

27. Brigham Young to George Taylor and others, June 29, 1857, *Brigham Young Papers*, Manuscript Section, C.H.O.

28. Brigham Young to Thomas L. Kane, June 29, 1857, *Brigham Young Papers*, Manuscript Section, C.H.O.

29. *New York Times*, December 29, 1857.

30. Roy Franklin Nichols, *The Disruption of American Democracy* (New York: The Macmillan Company, 1948), p. 100.

31. John M. Bernhisel to Brigham Young, (no date), *Brigham Young Papers*, Manuscript Section, C.H.O.

32. Wellmen, *The House Divided*, p. 385.

33. Philip G. Auchampaugh, *Robert Tyler, Southern Rights Champion* (Duluth, Minnesota: Hinman Stein, 1934), pp. 180–181; David A. Williams, "President Buchanan Receives a Proposal for an Anti-Mormon Crusade, 1857," *Brigham Young University Studies*, XIV (Autumn, 1973): 103–105.

34. William I. Appleby to Brigham Young, April 13, 1857, *William I. Appleby Papers*, Manuscript Section, C.H.O.

35. George A. Smith to Brigham Young, April 15, 1857, *George A. Smith Papers*, Manuscript Section, C.H.O.

36. *New York Times*, July 6, 1856.

37. Thomas F. O'Dea, *The Mormons* (Chicago: University of Chicago Press, 1964), p. 79.

38. John Hyde, Jr., *Mormonism: Its Leaders and Designs* (New York: W. P. Fetridge and Company, 1857), p. 145.

39. A striking example was his loyalty to William A. Hickman, an accused killer, sought by federal authorities for shooting an Indian in Nebraska Territory, a loyalty Young abandoned in the 1860s.

40. Edward W. Tullidge, *Tullidge's Histories, Containing the History of All the Northern, Eastern, and Western Counties of Utah: Also the Counties Idaho with a Biographical Appendix of Representative Men of the Cities and Counties and a Commercial Supplement, Historical* (Salt Lake City: Juvenile Instructor, 1889), vol. 2, p. 28.

41. Stenhouse, *Rocky Mountain Saints*, p. 352.

42. Ibid.

43. *Journal of Discourses*, 26 vols. (London, 1854–86; reprint ed., Salt Lake City, 1967), 5:77–78 (hereafter JD); *Deseret News*, July 29, 1857.

44. Stenhouse, *Rocky Mountain Saints*, p. 352.

45. Lieutenant General Daniel H. Wells to district military commanding officers, Nauvoo Legion, August 1, 1857, Military Records Section, Utah State Archives; "Records of Orders, returns and court martials etc. of 2nd Brigade, 1st Division Nauvoo Legion: Headquarters, 14th Ward G.S.L. City," August 6, 1857 (typescript copy), Brigham Young University, pp. 2–3. The reorganization of the Mormon Militia into the Nauvoo Legion took place April 20, 1857, with a district muster, election of officers, and a parade. *Deseret News*, April 29, 1857.

46. An estimate based on the Legion archives in the Church Historian's Office places the strength of the Mormon army at five thousand men although only twelve hundred front-line effectives faced the federal forces during the winter and spring of 1857–1858.

47. *New York Times*, December 15, 1857; although a later *Times* article dated October 9, 1858, reported "a case of Colt's pistols and rifles, manufactured at the public works of the Church, in this city Salt Lake for the use of the Mormon Army none of these weapons have been discovered." Church sources also indicate "the manufacturing of weapons . . .commenced this week to make revolving pistols at the public works in the shop put up from portion of the Wheelwright shop—David Sabin and William Naylor employed with others." Brigham Young's *Office Journal*, August 8, 1858–January 31, 1862, Manuscript Section, C.H.O.

48. Brigham Young to George Q. Cannon, August 4, 1857, *Brigham Young Papers*, Manuscript Section, C.H.O.

49. Brigham Young to Silas Smith, F. D. Richards, Edward Partridge, August 4, 1857, *Brigham Young Papers*, Manuscript Section, C.H.O.

50. Brigham Young to Orson Pratt, September 12, 1857, *Brigham Young Papers*, Manuscript Section, C.H.O.

51. *Deseret News*, September 23, 1857.

52. General Harney to Brigham Young, July 28, 1857, *Letters Sent*, Department of Utah, Records of the War Department; House Executive Document, No. 71, 35th Congress, 1st Session, Serial No. 956, X, p. 25, henceforth identified as "Utah Expedition."

53. *Deseret News*, September 23, 1857.

54. Ibid.

NOTES TO CHAPTER 2

1. *New York Times*, April 20, 1858.

2. Jesse A. Gove, *The Utah Expedition, 1857–1858: Letters of Capt. Jesse A. Gove, 10th Inf., U.S.A. of Concord, N.H., to Mrs. Gove and Special Correspondence of the New York Herald*, edited by Otis G. Hammond (Concord: New Hampshire Historical Society, 1928), p. 66; "Utah Expedition," pp. 24–26.

3. Ibid. [*sic*], p. 66.

4. Gove, *Letters*, p. 64.

5. John I. Ginn, "Mormon and Indian Wars, the Mountain Meadow Massacre and Other Tragedies and Transactions Incident to the Mormon Rebellion of 1857, Together with the Person Recollections of Civilians Who Witnessed Many of the Thrilling Scenes Described" (typescript), Utah State Historical Society, pp. 9–10.

6. Brigham Young to Daniel H. Wells, John Taylor, George A. Smith, October 4, 1857, *Brigham Young Papers*, Manuscript Section, C.H.O.

7. John M. Bernhisel to Brigham Young, November 2, 1857, *John M. Bernhisel Papers*, Manuscript Section, C.H.O.

8. For a complete list of the stores burned by the Mormon cavalry see *Utah Expedition*, pp. 106–107.

9. Gove, *Letters*, pp. 75–92.

10. Brigham Young to D. H. Wells, October 23, 1857, *Brigham Young Papers*, Manuscript Section, C.H.O.

11. Gove, *Letters*, p. 81.

12. Ibid., pp. 84–89.

13. Ibid., p. 92.

14. Ibid.

15. Keene Abbot, "The Sound of Running Water," *Outlook*, IC (October, 1911): 486.

16. Ibid.

17. Albert G. Brackett, *History of the United States Cavalry, From Formation of the Federal Government to the 1st of June, 1863* (New York: Argonaut Press, 1965), p. 178.

18. Samuel W. Ferguson, "With Albert Sidney Johnston's Expedition to Utah, 1857," *Kansas Historical Collections*, XII (1911–1912): 10.

19. Brigham Young to D. H. Wells, C. C. Rich, G. D. Grant, November 8, 1857, *Brigham Young Papers*, Manuscript Section, C.H.O.

20. Brigham Young to William Cox, December 4, 1857, *Brigham Young Papers*, Manuscript Section, C.H.O.

21. John M. Bernhisel to Brigham Young, December 17, 1857 (typescript copy), *John M. Bernhisel Papers*, Manuscript Section, C.H.O.

22. Ibid.

23. J. M. Bernhisel's account of conversations with President James Buchanan was referred to in a letter dated January 18, 1858, addressed to Brigham Young, *John M. Bernhisel Papers*, Manuscript Section, C.H.O.

24. General Order No. 1, January 8, 1858; No. 4, January 16, 1858; *Order Book*, Department of Utah, Records of the War Department.

25. When the Utah War was brought to a successful and bloodless conclusion, Harney was placed in command of the Department of Oregon where he remained until 1860. With his transfer, General Johnston became commander of the Department of Utah.

26. Norman Furniss, *The Mormon Conflict, 1850–1859* (New Haven: Yale University Press, 1960), p. 172.

27. Ibid.; for a more detailed study of the role played by Russell, Majors and Waddell in the Utah War see Raymond W. and Mary Lund Settle, *War Drums and Wagon Wheels: The Story of Russell, Majors and Waddell* (Lincoln: University of Nebraska Press, 1966). A shorter discussion may be found in Henry Pickering Walker, *The Wagonmasters: High Plains Freighting from the Earliest Days of the Santa Fe Trail to 1880* (Norman: University of Oklahoma Press, 1966).

28. Brigham Young to J. M. Bernhisel, February 4, 1858, *Brigham Young Papers*, Manuscript Section, C.H.O.

29. Thomas Kane to Brigham Young, February 19, 1858, *Brigham Young Papers*, Manuscript Section, C.H.O.

30. L. A. Bertrand, *Memoires D'Un Mormon* (Paris: E. Dentu Libraire, 1862), p. 122.

31. Richard D. Young, "Major General Thomas L. Kane," *Millennial Star*, LXXII (February 24, 1910): 130.

32. Ibid.

33. J. K. Kane to Tom, January 4, 1858 (typescript only), *Thomas L. Kane Papers*, Manuscript Section, C.H.O.

34. This massacre will be treated in its entirety in Chapter Seven.

35. Ebenezer Hanks to Brigham Young, February 6, 1858, *Thomas L. Kane Papers*, Manuscript Section, C.H.O.

36. Amasa Lyman, "Journal," February 1–25, 1858, Manuscript Section, C.H.O.

37. Thomas L. Kane to Brigham Young, March 5, 1858, *Thomas L. Kane Papers*, Manuscript Section, C.H.O.

38. Amasa Lyman, "Journal," February 1–25, 1858, Manuscript Section, C.H.O.; the Mormons mistakenly believed the survey party under the direction of Captain W. P. Blake—commonly called the Ives Expedition—was the fore-runner of a larger army.

39. Ibid.

40. Wilford Woodruff, "Diary," February 25, 1858, Manuscript Section, C.H.O.

41. Brigham Young to Thomas L. Kane, February 25, 1858 (typescript), *Thomas L. Kane Papers*, Manuscript Section, C.H.O.

42. Stenhouse, *Rocky Mountain Saints*, pp. 382–383.

43. Unidentified letter, not dated, *Brigham Young Papers*, Manuscript Section, C.H.O.

44. Ray Benedict West, *Kingdom of the Saints: The Story of Brigham Young and the Mormons* (New York: Viking Press, 1957), pp. 263–264.

45. Fitz-John Porter, "Diary," March 13, 1858, Barret Collection, Tulane University. Captain John W. Phelps's account of the incident varies only slightly: "without looking right or left he moved straight forward to the commanding officer's tent and seemed as if he wished to ride into it instead of stopping outside, so near did he urge his horse to that opening. Someone—probably a servant— knocked and informed the Colonel that someone wished to see him. The Col. was engaged in conversation and did not come out immediately and this delay was compared with the man's forwardness seemed to look and be felt as a check. Presently the Col. came partly out; being stopped entirely by the man's horse whose head was nearly in the opening, and looking up in a crouched attitude, his own head being near the horses' head said 'Who are You?'" John W. Phelps, "Diary," March 13, 1858, Manuscript Section, New York Public Library.

46. F. J. Porter to Gen. A. Johnston, March 17, 1858, *Letters Sent*, Department of Utah, Records of the War Department; Johnston to Cumming, March 17, 1858, *Albert Sidney Johnston Papers*, Barret Collection, Tulane University.

47. Fitz-John Porter, "Diary," March 20, 1858.

48. A. Cumming to Col. Thomas L. Kane, March 22, 1858, *Alfred Cumming Papers*, Duke University.

49. *New York Times*, March 16, 1858.

50. *Millennial Star*, LXXII (March 3, 1910): 132.

51. Fitz-John Porter, "Diary," April 2, 1858.

52. Ibid.

53. Mrs. Cumming to Alfred Cumming, April 21, 1858, *Alfred Cumming Papers*, Duke University.

54. Cumming to Lewis Case, Secretary of State, May 2, 1858, U.S. State Department Territorial Papers, Utah Series, April 30, 1853, to December 24, 1859; Gove, *Letters*, p. 147.

55. Stenhouse, *Rocky Mountain Saints*, pp. 389–390; this incident is described by Ebenezer Couch, who witnessed the episode as a member of the Mormon militia: "In the meantime Col. Callister ordered a number of men to climb the mountains and to gather dry wood and pile it up in heaps and to be ready to fire the piles, when the first gun was fired. He also posted men at the bottom of the mountain, armed with U.S. muskets.

"About eleven o'clock at night they were to pass our camp. The company I belonged to was posted on each side of the creek. As the Governor and escort came abreast of the picket guard, the guard fired. This was the signal for the men on the mountain to put fire to those heaps of dry wood. Immediately at the firing of the pickets the mountains were to all appearances covered with men, and the light from the fire on the tops of the mountains reflected in the canyons, making it light as day.

"When the Governor arrived at the creek where I was stationed with the advanced guards, Capt. Scott challenged the company which stopped.

"Major Hagan gave the sign. Then they were allowed to pass. As they went through our lines, we presented arms." Ebenezer Couch, "Autobiography of Ebenezer Couch" (typescript), Brigham Young University, pp. 64–65.

56. One of the first notices of the move came in a letter from Brigham Young addressed to the officers north of Great Salt Lake City, Ecclesiastical, Civil, Military: "As you will perceive by pointed instructions herewith forwarded that we have concluded to vacate this city. We are intending to send families, grain, stock &c., forthwith to different locations South where we can sow grain, plant potatoes, sugar cane, corn, and other vegetables and recommend you do likewise. We intend to move a part of the way and return and bring another load and so on until all are removed. The young brethren will generally remain to water and take care of grain and property." March 24, 1858, *Brigham Young Papers*, Manuscript Section, C.H.O.

57. "History of Brigham Young," March 21, 1858, Manuscript Section, C.H.O., p. 268.

58. Orson F. Whitney, *History of Utah* (Salt Lake City, Utah: George Cannon and Sons Co., 1892), p. 677.

59. Andrew Love Neff, *History of Utah 1847–1869* (Salt Lake City: Deseret News Press, 1940), p. 498.

60. Cumming to Lewis Cass, May 2, 1858, U.S. State Department, Territorial Papers, Utah Series; *Journal History*, April 12, 1858.

61. Cumming to Johnston, May 21, 1858, *Alfred Cumming Papers*, Duke University.

NOTES TO CHAPTER 3

1. T. B. H. Stenhouse to George A. Smith, July 7, 1858, *T. B. H. Stenhouse Papers*, Manuscript Section, C.H.O.

2. *Journal History*, June 7, 1858.

3. Ibid., June 10, 1858.

4. Gove, *Letters*, p. 175.

5. "The Utah War: Journal of Albert Tracy, 1858–1860," edited by J. Cecil Alter, *Utah Historical Quarterly*, XII (1945): 17.

6. James M. Merril, *Spurs to Glory: The Story of the United States Cavalry* (New York: Rand McNally & Company, 1966), p. 100.

7. Tracy, "Journal," p. 18.

8. Ferguson, "With Albert Sidney Johnston," p. 311.

9. Ibid.

10. Nels Anderson, *Desert Saints: The Mormon Frontier in Utah* (Chicago: University of Chicago Press, 1942), p. 185.

11. Tracy, "Journal," pp. 27–28; most of the verses are unprintable.

12. Ibid.

13. *Journal History*, June 26, 1838.

14. John R. Young, *Memoirs of John R. Young: Utah Pioneer, 1847* (Salt Lake City: The Deseret News Press, 1920), p. 115.

15. Harold D. Langley, ed., *To Utah with the Dragoons and Glimpses of Life in Arizona and California* (Salt Lake City: University of Utah Press, 1974), p. 96.

16. Ibid., pp. 96–97.

17. Charles Roland, *Albert Sidney Johnston: Soldier of Three Republics* (Austin: University of Texas Press, 1964), p. 185.

18. Francis B. Heitman, *Historical Register and Dictionary of the United States* (Washington: U.S. Government Printing Office, 1903), 1, p. 324.

19. The Saints apparently purchased Fort Bridger from Louis Vasquez without Bridger's knowledge or consent. Although the Latter-day Saints had proof of purchase, the War Department maintained ownership of the property until it was sold to a third party long after the entrance of Johnston's Army.

20. Gene Caesar, *King of the Mountain, the Life of Jim Bridger* (New York: E. P. Dutton, 1961), p. 258.

21. Heitman, *Historical Register*, 1, p. 895.

22. The command was originally assigned to Colonel Pitcairn Morrison who was removed for reasons not entirely clear after several months in the territory.

23. Gove, *Letters*, p. 278.

24. Ibid.

25. George Hammond, ed., *Campaigns of the West: The Journal and Letters of Colonel John Van Deusen* (Tucson: Arizona Pioneer Historical Society, 1949), p. 69.

26. James Sweeney, "Narrative" (typescript), privately owned, p. 2.

27. Although the marching order of the regiments has frequently been described, each report seems to be in contradiction. The following narration is heavily dependent on contemporary accounts, yet this writer does not deny the possiblility of error in reconstructing the parade.

28. Keene Abbott, "The Sound of Running Water," *Outlook*, IC (October, 1911): 438.

29. Tracy, "Journal," pp. 26–27.

30. *Journal History*, June 26, 1858.

31. Gove, *Letters*, p. 371.

32. Elizabeth Cumming to Anne, July 9, 1858, *Alfred Cumming Papers* (typescript), Duke University.

33. *Journal History*, July 27, 1858.

34. Ibid.

35. Gove, *Letters*, p. 378.

36. David Candland, "Documents," August, 1856, November, 1856, March, 1858, May, 1858, February, 1859, June, 1860. The construction of the Globe commenced in August, 1858, and was financed by Brigham and Brigham H. Young. Opening three months later under the management of David Candland and William C. Staines, the saloon enjoyed a profitable business catering to the Gentile trade until March of 1858, when it closed its doors because of a depressed

money market. With the arrival of the army Candland reopened the Globe, but ten months later, in February, 1859, he again concluded to close the business. Although the saloon was reopened for a brief three months' interlude in 1860, unpaid bills and the withdrawal of the troops from the territory forced the Globe to close its doors forever.

37. W. Eugene Hollon, *Beyond the Cross Timbers: The Travels of Randolph B. Marcy, 1812–1887* (Norman: University of Oklahoma Press, 1955), pp. 230–231.

38. Ibid.

39. Elizabeth Cumming to Anne, July 9, 1858, *Alfred Cumming Papers*, Duke University.

40. Gove, *Letters*, p. 371; Tracy, "Journal," p. 28.

41. Norman Furniss, *The Mormon Conflict*, p. 202.

42. Although the site is somewhat difficult to pinpoint, the temporary cantonment was near the present village of Copperton, on Brigham Creek; John Bennion, "Journal," July 2, 1858, Manuscript Section, C.H.O.

43. Tracy, "Journal," July 1, 1858–July 7, 1858.

44. Ibid., July 4, 1858.

45. Ibid.

46. Brigham Young to James Ferguson, June 27, 1858, *Brigham Young Papers*, Manuscript Section, C.H.O.

47. Senate Executive Document, Number 1, Part 2, 35th Congress, 2nd Session, Serial No. 975, 131. Although the directive, General Orders Number 17, was dated July 29, 1858, Mormon missionaries had picked up the rumor ten days before the dispatch became official.

48. *Journal History*, June 30–July 3, 1858; Gove, *Letters*, p. 372.

49. Furniss, *Mormon Conflict*, p. 203.

50. Stenhouse, *Rocky Mountain Saints*, p. 399.

51. *New York Times*, August 13, 1858.

52. Henry S. Hamilton, *Reminiscences of a Veteran* (Concord, N.H.: Republic Press Association, 1897), p. 108.

53. *New York Times*, August 13, 1858.

54. Ibid.

55. Ibid.

56. *Journal History*, July 6, 1858.

57. Gove, *Letters*, p. 185.

58. Johnston to son, September 23, 1858, *Albert Sidney Johnston Papers*, Barret Collection, Tulane University.

59. George Laub, "Diary," August 11, 1858.

60. *Boston Semi-Weekly Advertiser*, November 13, 1858.

61. Glen F. Harding and Ruth Johnson, *Bernard White Family Book* (Provo: Brigham Young University Press, 1967), p. 216.

62. *Boston Semi-Weekly Advertiser*, November 13, 1858.

63. J. E. Farmer, *My Life with the Army in the West*, edited by Dale F. Giese (Santa Fe: Stagecoach Press, 1967), p. 23.

64. Tracy, "Journal," pp. 51–52.

65. Johnston to son, September 23, 1858, *Albert Sidney Johnston Papers*, Barret Collection, Tulane University.

66. Tracy, "Journal," p. 53.

NOTES TO CHAPTER 4

1. *Valley Tan*, February, 1860; "tiger" was a form of poker game.

2. Manuscript History of the Fairfield Branch of Lehi Stake: 1855–1989, Manuscript Section, C.H.O. Fairfield was named in honor of Amos Fielding who was entrusted with the location of the settlement. The first pioneers were William Berdshall, Amos Fielding, James Gally, John Clegg, James McFate, John Carson, William H. Carson, George Carson, David Carson, Washington Carson, Henry Morgan, Samuel Broadearth, Majes Barrow, John Barrow, Robert Barrow, Frank Hodge, Patterson Griffiths, and William Cunnington.

3. David H. Carson, *A Brief History of Fairfield* (Salt Lake City: no publisher listed, 1955), p. 4.

4. Ibid.

5. Ibid.

6. Ibid.

7. Ibid.

8. Ibid.

9. Johnston's personal animosity toward the Saints was expressed in a letter to his son: "The Mormon question is not freed from a single difficulty that existed twelve months ago. The only change is presence of an army a seeming acquiescence on the exercise of the duties of the civil corps, they are not opposed or disturbed that I know of in any way; but admitting this, what is gained? The theocracy exists, the obligations to which are in as full force now as before, the people are as much bound to go by Council now as before or in other words, which better express their relation to those in authority. 'To do as they are told'— Do you believe that the laws can be properly administered with such inside pressure. . . ." A. S. Johnston to William Preston Johnston, September 4, 1858, *Albert Sidney Johnston Papers*, Barret Collection Tulane University.

10. *Marlington* [West Virginia] *Journal*, September 15, 1860.

11. Charles Bailey, "Diary," p. 34, Manuscript Section, C.H.O.

12. Henry S. Hamilton, *Reminiscences*, p. 110.

13. Sir Richard Burton described Fairfield in 1860 as a bazaar cantonment "teeming with gamblers and blacklegs, groghouse-keepers and prostitutes: The revolver and the bowie-knife had nightly work to do there, and the moral Saints were fond of likening Frogtown to certain Cities of the Plains." Richard F. Burton, *The City of the Saints and Across the Rocky Mountains to California*, ed. Fawn M. Brodie (New York: Alfred A. Knopf, 1963), p. 373.

14. John Young Nelson, *Fifty Years on the Trail: A True Story of Western Life* (Norman: University of Oklahoma Press, 1963), pp. 131–32.

15. Ibid., p. 132.

16. Ibid.

17. Ibid.

18. Ibid.

19. Ibid.

20. Phelps, "Diary," November 5, 1858.

21. Robert West Howard, ed., *This Is the West* (New York: The New American Library, 1957), pp. 104–105.

22. The term is used loosely to denote the full range of personnel associated with wagon freighting.

23. Phelps, "Diary," October 9, 1859.

24. Richard Thomas Ackley, "Across the Plains in 1858," *Utah Historical Quarterly*, ed. J. Cecil Alter, IX (October, 1941): 213.

25. Ibid.

26. Ibid., p. 214.

27. Ibid., pp. 214–15.

28. Ibid., pp. 215–16.

29. Ibid., pp. 212–213.

30. Settle, *War Drums and Wagon Wheels*, pp. 55–56.

31. Ackley, "Across the Plains," pp. 218–219; *New York Times*, September 4, 1858. The *Times* correspondent reported the name of the victim as Peale, and listed the place of Rucker's birth as Tennessee; *New York Herald*, January 14, 1860.

32. Ibid. [*sic*]

33. Phelps, "Diary," October 28, 1858.

34. Cumming to Johnston, October 21, 1858, *Alfred Cumming Papers*, Department of Utah, Records of the War Department.

35. Johnston to Cumming, October 31, 1858, *Letters Sent*, Department of Utah, Records of the War Department.

36. F. J. Porter to C. F. Smith, January 17, 1859, *Letters Sent*, Department of Utah, Records of the War Department.

37. *Deseret News*, April 20, 1859.

38. Cumming to Johnston, May 9, 1859, *Alfred Cumming Papers*, Department of Utah, Records of the War Department.

39. *Valley Tan*, June 29, 1859.

40. *Valley Tan*, March 18, 1859.

41. *Journal History*, February 16, 1859.

42. *Journal History*, November 22, 1858.

43. *Journal History*, November 10, 1858.

44. *Valley Tan*, July 7, 1859; Phelps, "Diary," July 3, 1859; *Deseret News*, July 6, 1859.

45. *Valley Tan*, July 9, 1859.

46. Richard Wilds Jones, "Diary," July 3, 1859, microfilm copy, Utah State Historical Society.

47. Phelps, "Diary," June 17, 1859.

48. George Laub, "Diary," Manuscript Section, C.H.O., I, 35–36.

49. *Deseret News*, May 2, 1860.

50. D. R. Eckles to James Buchanan, August 17, 1859, "Appointment Files, Utah, 1857–1861," Department of Justice, R.G. 60, N.A.

51. Horace Greeley, *An Overland Journey from New York to San Francisco in the Summer of 1859* (New York: C. M. Saxon, Barker, & Co., 1860), p. 202.

52. Robert West Howard, ed., *This Is the West*, p. 102.

53. *Deseret News*, September 28, 1859.

54. Ebenezer Crouch, "Autobiography of Ebenezer Crouch" (typescript), Brigham Young University, p. 14.

55. Ibid., pp. 14–15.

56. Ibid., p. 15.

57. Ibid., p. 17.

58. General Order Number 37, October 15, 1858, *Order Book*, Department of Utah, Records of the War Department.

59. Brigham Young to Thomas L. Kane, September 10, 1858, *Brigham Young Papers*, Manuscript Section, C.H.O.

60. Bailey, "Diary," pp. 35–36.

61. Ibid.

62. Charles L. Walker, "Diary of Charles L. Walker, 1833–1904" (typescript), Brigham Young University, I, p. 8.

63. Kate B. Carter, *Military Forts of the West* (Salt Lake City: Daughters of the Utah Pioneers, 1941), III, p. 167.

64. Ibid.

65. Charles S. Peterson, "A Historical Analysis of Territorial Government in Utah Under Alfred Cumming, 1857–1861" (unpublished Master's thesis, Brigham Young University, Provo, Utah, 1958), p. 85.

66. James Rodeback, November 25, 1858, *Brigham Young Papers*, Manuscript Section, C.H.O.

67. Clarence E. Bennett to R. K. Johnston, May 19, 1859, *Letters Sent*, Department of Utah, Records of the War Department; *Journal History*, June 23, 1859.

68. "General Elections, 1859," *Territorial Executive Records*, Territorial Papers of the United States, Utah Series, 1848–1863, National Archives.

69. Gustive O. Larson, "The Mormon Reformation," *Utah Historical Quarterly*, XXVI (January, 1958): 44–63.

70. *Valley Tan*, August 3, 1859; *New York Times*, August 31, 1859. Token opposition had been offered by the Gentiles in 1858.

71. Ibid.

72. *New York Times*, August 31, 1859.

73. Peterson, "Alfred Cumming," p. 133.

74. Ibid.

75. *Deseret News*, August 2, 1859. Judge Eckles was the leading figure of Gentile opposition to Brigham Young, and his role in the aftermath of the Utah War will be detailed in a later chapter.

76. Peterson, "Alfred Cumming," p. 132; see abstract and letter of Zerubabbel Snow reporting the contested election, "General Elections, 1859," *Territorial Executive Records*.

77. Harold P. Fabian, *Camp Floyd at Fairfield*, address at the dedication of a monument to first Masonic Lodge, June 21, 1959 (Salt Lake City: privately printed, 1959), p. 2.

NOTES TO CHAPTER 5

1. Phelps, "Diary," August 20, 1859.

2. L. A. Bertrand, *Memoires*, p. 122.

3. Court Martial Return: Camp Floyd 1858–1861; Proceedings: Board of Survey, December 17, 1859, Department of Utah, Records of the War Department.

4. Registry of Trials by Garrison and Regimental Courts Martial, Adjutant General's Office, Department of Utah, Records of the War Department.

5. "John Lowe Butler Tells His Story," Vol. II of *Our Pioneer Heritage*, edited by Kate Carter, 17 vols. (Salt Lake City, Utah: Utah Printing Company, 1959), pp. 20–21.

6. Ibid.

7. *Valley Tan*, December 7, 1859.

8. J. E. Farmer, *My Life with the Army in the West*, p. 28.

9. *Valley Tan*, December 7, 1859.

10. Everett Dick, *Vanguards of the Frontier: A Social History of the Northern Plains and Rocky Mountains from the Fur Trades to the Sod Busters* (Lincoln: University of Nebraska Press, 1967), p. 81.

11. *Valley Tan*, May 17, 1859.

12. *Valley Tan*, March 17, 1859.

13. General Order No. 10, September 16, Headquarters Book, Department of Utah, Records of the War department.

14. *Valley Tan*, April 19, 1859.

15. *Deseret News*, June 8, 1859.

16. John W. Phelps's "Diary" provides an excellent example of the range of fantasy that was typical of the mind of the frontier soldier.

17. W. G. Binney to Johnston, November 4, 1858, *Albert Sidney Johnston Papers*, Barret Collection, Tulane University.

18. *Valley Tan*, February 1, 1859; Ackley, "Across the Plains," p. 225.

19. Hamilton, *Reminiscences*, p. 110.

20. Ibid.

21. Ibid., p. 111.

22. Ibid., pp. 111–112.

23. Phelps, "Diary," November 10, 1858, January 31, 1859, April 27, 1859; during the Civil War General Patrick Conner would rediscover these finds.

24. *Valley Tan*, November 12, 1858.

25. Ibid.

26. Personal interview with John Hutchings, May 31, 1967.

27. Ibid.

28. *Deseret News*, November 10, 1858; *Valley Tan*, November 12, 1858.

29. *Valley Tan*, November 9, 1859.

30. Ibid., October 5, 1859; however, at least one Shakespearean tragedy was performed. Details of these Utah tragedies will be discussed in subsequent chapters.

31. Ibid., September 14, 1859.

32. Ibid., September 7, 1859
33. Ibid.
34. John S. Lindsay, *The Mormons and the Theatre* (Salt Lake City: n.p., 1905), p. 16.
35. *Valley Tan*, January 25, 1859.
36. Ibid.
37. Lindsay, *The Mormons and the Theatre*, pp. 16–17.
38. *Valley Tan*, September 7, 1859.
39. Ibid.
40. Johnston to daughter, February 15, 1860, *Albert Sidney Johnston Papers*, Barret Collection, Tulane University.
41. *Valley Tan*, October 5, 1859.
42. Johnston to daughter, February 15, 1860, *Albert Sidney Johnston Papers*, Barret Collection, Tulane University.
43. Phelps, "Diary," March 15, 1859.
44. *Valley Tan*, September 28, 1859.
45. Ibid.
46. Ibid.
47. *Valley Tan*, October 12, 1859, November 23, 1859.
48. Ibid. [*sic*]
49. *Valley Tan*, May 24, 1859.
50. Phelps, "Diary," May 24, 1859.
51. Special Order No. 16, January 24, 1859, Headquarters Book, Department of Utah, Records of the War Department.
52. Jerome Stoffel, "The Hesitant Beginnings of the Catholic Church in Utah," *Utah Historical Quarterly* (Winter, 1968): 52.
53. Ibid.
54. Lieutenant W. A. Mehle to Captain Henry F. Clark, August 11, 1859, Post Letters, Department of Utah, Records of the War Department.
55. Thomas A. Bailey, *The American Pageant: A History of the Republic* (Lexington, Massachusetts: D. C. Heath and Company, 1971), p. 348.
56. Phelps, "Diary," June 6, 1859.
57. Ibid.
58. The Keller story is marked by a successful ending. "Returning to the East, he left his mark in Utica, New York, and Louisville, Kentucky, and in the first Provincial Chapter of his religious order in 1872 was elected to the office of Provincial and confirmed in that office by apostalic rescript, guided the destinies of his Province until his death April 5, 1877." Stoffel, "The Hesitant Beginnings," p. 55.
59. Historian's Office Journal: June 11, 1859–December 25, 1859, Manuscript Section, C.H.O., p. 45.
60. *Journal History*, June 18, 1859.
61. *Deseret News*, June 22, 1859.
62. Charles Walker, "Diary," p. 89.

63. Historian's Office Journal, June 11, 1859–December 25, 1859, Manuscript Section, C.H.O., p. 54.

64. Phelps: "Diary," June 26, 1859. Of course, Phelps believed all women were not ladies, especially the wives of enlisted men who served as laundresses. Many of the officers' wives arrived during July and August, 1859. Major Lynde was patrolling the northern California Trail at the time of his daughter's wedding.

65. Phelps, "Diary," July 30, 1859.

66. Special Order No. 140, Headquarters Book, Department of Utah, Records of the War Department.

67. Sam Henry Goodwin, *Freemasonry in Utah, Rocky Mountain Lodge Number 205* (Salt Lake City: Grand Lodge of Utah, 1934), p. 17.

68. Ackley, "Across the Plains," p. 224.

69. Farmer, *My Life with the Army*, p. 25.

70. Phelps, "Diary," April 27, 1859, May 2, 1859, June 1, 1859, July 3, 1859, July 30, 1859.

71. Tracy, "The Utah War," p. 36.

72. Unidentified newspaper clipping dated March 14, 1859, *Alfred Cumming Papers*, Duke University.

73. *Senate Executive Document*, Number 52, 36th Congress, 1st Session Serial No. 1035, pp. 317–325.

74. Tracy, "The Utah War," pp. 69–70.

75. Ibid.

76. Ibid.

77. Ibid.

78. Ibid.

79. Ibid.

80. Ibid., pp. 54–55.

81. Ibid., p. 55.

82. Ibid., p. 56.

83. "Soldiering on the Frontier," *Annals of Wyoming*, XXXV (April, 1963): 83–84.

84. Ibid.

85. Farmer, *My Life with the Army*, p. 38.

86. Langley, *To Utah with the Dragoons*, pp. 83–84.

87. Ibid., pp. 104–105.

88. Smith to the Adjutant General, May 7, 1859, *Letters Sent*, Department of Utah, Records of the War Department.

89. Farmer, *My Life with the Army*, p. 38; Langley, *To Utah with the Dragoons*, p. 25.

90. Phelps, "Diary," February 19, 1859.

91. Hamilton, *Reminiscences*, p. 44–45.

92. Ackley, "Across the Plains," p. 224.

93. Captain J. M. Hawes to Lt. C. E. Bennett, December 28, 1858, Post Letters, Department of Utah, Records of the War Department.

94. Ackley, "Across the Plains," p. 225.

95. Farmer, *My Life with the Army*, p. 38.

96. *Valley Tan*, February 11, 1859.
97. Ibid.
98. Roland, *Albert Sidney Johnston: Soldier of Three Republics*, p. 236.

NOTES TO CHAPTER 6

1. John C. Cradlebaugh, "Utah and the Mormons: Speech of Hon. John Cradlebaugh, of Nevada, on the Admission of Utah as a State, Delivered in the House of Representatives" (privately printed, 1863), p. 15.
2. R. N. Baskin, *Reminiscence of Early Utah* (Salt Lake City: privately printed, 1914), p. 59.
3. James B. Allen, "The Unusual Jurisdiction of County Probate Courts in the Territory of Utah," *Utah Historical Quarterly* XXXVI (Spring, 1968): 134.
4. Furniss, *The Mormon Conflict*, p. 166.
5. Ibid., p. 97.
6. *New York Times*, September 6, 1858; January 3, 1859.
7. Ibid., September 20, 1858.
8. *Journal History*, September 11, 1858.
9. *New York Times*, November 13–15, 1858.
10. Ibid., January 3, 1859.
11. Ibid.
12. Ibid.; Brigham Young's *Office Journal:* August 8, 1858–January 31, 1862, December 31, 1858, Manuscript Section, C.H.O.
13. Heber C. Kimball, Daniel H. Wells, Orson Pratt, George A. Smith, John Taylor, Wilford Woodruff, Willard Richards, *Journal History*, December 3, 1858; Ibid. Barely substantiating Herbert Bancroft's claim that the grand jury was composed of mainly Mormons, a newspaper account listed its composition as twelve Mormons and eleven Gentiles. *New York Times*, January 3, 1859.
14. *Journal History*, December 1, December 3, 1858.
15. *New York Times*, January 3, 1859.
16. Ibid.
17. *Deseret News*, January 12, 1859.
18. Cumming to Cass, Secretary of State, January 28, 1859, U.S. State Department, *Territorial Papers*, Utah Series, April 30, 1853, to December 24, 1859.
19. *Deseret News*, August 3, 1859.
20. *Journal History*, February 26, 1859.
21. Ibid., November 4, 1858.
22. Ibid.
23. George A. Smith to Brigham Young, March 10, 1858, *Brigham Young Papers*, Manuscript Section, C.H.O.
24. Furniss, *The Mormon Conflict*, p. 208.
25. Ibid.
26. Stenhouse, *Rocky Mountain Saints*, pp. 404–405.
27. Ibid.
28. Phelps, "Diary," January 8, 1859.

29. General Order No. 37, March 6, 1859, *Post Orders*, Department of Utah, Records of the War Department.

30. Furniss, *The Mormon Conflict*, p. 215.

31. Heth to Bennett, March 12, 1859, *Post Letters*, Department of Utah, Records of the War Department.

32. *Valley Tan*, March 15, 1859; *Journal History*, March 9, 1859.

33. *Journal History*, March 18, 1859.

34. Ibid.

35. *Deseret News*, March 30, 1859; there were three or four petitions during March, all of which were basically similar.

36. Johnston to Thomas, March 10, 1859, *Letters Sent*, Department of Utah, Records of the War Department.

37. Moses Franklin Farnsworth, "Diary," Huntington Library, p. 7.

38. Ibid.

39. *Journal History*, April 5, 1859.

40. Ibid., March 18, 1859.

41. Ibid., March 19, 1859.

42. Johnston to Paul, March 19, 1859, *Post Letters*, Department of Utah, Records of the War Department; Phelps, "Diary," March 19, 1859.

43. Tracy, "The Utah War," March 23, 1859, p. 61; F. J. Porter to Major Paul, March 22, 1859, *Post Letters*, Department of Utah, Records of the War Department.

44. Tracy, "The Utah War," p. 60.

45. Ibid., p. 61.

46. Ibid., p. 62.

47. Ibid., p. 64.

48. Ibid.

49. The *Journal History* entry of April 27, 1859, lists the number of men who fled to the "Mountains of Hepsedam" and "Colob." Hans Jensen Halls noted: "When the soldiers in Camp Floyd got out of hand and would jail some of the brethren we men would go from Sanpete into the western mountains. This lasted three weeks. . . ." Hans Jensen Halls, "Autobiography," March 10, 1859, Manuscript Section, C.H.O.; Henry Ballard, "Journal," April 26, 1859, records the same entry: "A company was called to march to the low mountains to watch army."

50. Reports of Orders, Return Etc. Nauvoo Legion, Brigham Young University.

51. James Garnmell to Charles E. Sinclair, March 29, 1859, *Albert Sidney Johnston Papers*, Barret Collection, Tulane University.

52. Brigham Young to Governor Cumming, April 23, 1859, *Brigham Young Papers*, Manuscript Section, C.H.O.

53. Johnston to Cumming, March 22, 1859, *Letters Sent*, Department of Utah, Records of the War Department.

54. U.S. State Department, *Territorial Papers*, Utah Series, April 30, 1853, to December 24, 1859.

55. *Journal History*, March 30, 1859.

56. *Deseret News*, March 30, 1859; *Valley Tan*, March 29, 1859.

57. Ibid. [*sic*]

58. *Valley Tan*, April 5, 1859; *Deseret News*, April 6, 1859.

59. *Millennial Star*, XXI, p. 481.

60. Tracy, "The Utah War," p. 65.

61. *Journal History*, April 8, 1859.

62. David A. Burr to C. E. Sinclair, May 5, 1859, *Albert Sidney Johnston Papers*, Barret Collection, Tulane University.

63. James Garnmell to Charles E. Sinclair, March 29, 1859, *Albert Sidney Johnston Papers*, Barret Collection, Tulane University.

64. Affidavit of Mr. Hickey and Tomlinson, July 10, 1859, *Albert Sidney Johnston Papers*, Barret Collection, Tulane University.

65. Ibid.

66. Hurt to Johnston, May 1, 1859, *Albert Sidney Johnston Papers*, Barret Collection, Tulane University.

67. John Kay to Cumming, May 16, 1859, U.S. State Department, *Territorial Papers*, Utah Series, April 30, 1852 to December 24, 1859.

68. David A. Burr to C. E. Sinclair, May 5, 1859, U.S. State Department, *Territorial Papers*, Utah Series, April 30, 1853 to December 24, 1859.

69. Ruggles to F. J. Porter, June 2, 1859, *Cole Collection*, Yale University.

70. *Journal History*, April 24, 1859.

71. Ibid.

72. Ibid.

73. Ibid.

74. Ibid.

75. Ibid.

76. Ibid.

77. Ibid.

78. *Journal History*, April 24, 1859.

79. Governor's Proclamation, May 9, 1859, U.S. State Department, *Territorial Papers*, Utah Series, April 30, 1853–December 24, 1859; *Deseret News*, May 18, 1859.

80. Furniss, *The Mormon Conflict*, p. 229.

81. Johnston to Thomas, March 31, 1859, *Letters Sent*, Department of Utah, Records of the War Department.

82. House Executive Document, 35th Congress, 21st Session, Volume X, p. 79; *Deseret News*, June 29, 1859; *Valley Tan*, June 29, 1859.

83. *Valley Tan*, June 29, 1859.

84. Ibid.

85. *Valley Tan*, May 24, 1859.

86. The Cavode Committee would issue its critical finding shortly before the beginning of the Civil War.

87. William Preston Johnston, *The Life of Albert Sidney Johnston* (New York: D. Appleton & Company, Inc., 1878), p. 240.

NOTES TO CHAPTER 7

1. John C. Chatterley to Andrew Jenson, September 18, 1919, *Mountain Meadow Massacre*, Manuscript Section, C.H.O.

2. Juanita Brooks, *The Mountain Meadows Massacre* (Palo Alto: Stanford University Press, 1950), p. 42.

3. Brigham Young to George Q. Cannon, October 4, 1856, *Brigham Young Papers*, Manuscript Section, C.H.O.

4. Ibid.

5. Ibid.

6. Ibid.

7. John Ward Christian, "Reminiscences," Bancroft Library, University of California.

8. Ibid.

9. John C. Chatterley to Andrew Jenson, September 18, 1919, *Mountain Meadow Massacre File*, Manuscript Section, C.H.O.; Gustive O. Larson, a Mormon historian, discounts the doctrine as a leading cause of the massacre in "The Mormon Reformation," *Utah Historical Quarterly*, XXVI (Spring 1958): 62; however, William C. Stewart, one of the participants in the massacre, believed that the Reformation was a contributing factor leading to the tragedy.

10. *Journal History*, June 23, 1857; Samuel Pitchforth: "Diary," June 25, 1857, Brigham Young University.

11. Hoffman Birney, *Zealots of Zion* (Philadelphia: The Penn Publishing Company, 1931), p. 141.

12. Andrew Love Ness, *History of Utah: 1847 to 1869* (Salt Lake City: Deseret News Press, 1940), p. 577.

13. Fanny Stenhouse, *Tell It All: The Story of a Life's Experience* (Hartford, Connecticut: A. D. Worthington & Co., 1874), p. 326.

14. Brigham Young to Lewis Robinson, August 4, 1857, *Brigham Young Papers*, Manuscript Section, C.H.O.

15. "Parowan Historical Record," August 7, 1857, Manuscript Section, C.H.O.

16. Jesse Lewis Russell, *Behind These Ozark Hills: History–Reminiscences–Traditions, Featuring the Author's Family* (New York: Hobson Bank Press, 1947), p. 98. The rendezvous site was also known as Beller's Stand and was located within a short distance of the present city of Harrison, Arkansas.

17. Ralph R. Rhea, *The Mountain Meadow Massacre and Its Completion as a Historic Episode* (Harrison, Arkansas: privately printed, ca. 1957), p. 3. Among the families that took part in the western migration that was to end in tragedy at Mountain Meadows were the Fancher, Baker, Michell, Beller, Deshago, Prewitt, Camerons, Dunlap, and Cecil famlies, all from Carroll County. From Marian County came another Dunlap family, the Woods, and the Wilsons; and from over the mountains emigrants from Johnson County—the Joneses, Tackets, Millers, and Huffs—joined the caravan. Later, while en route through the rolling countryside of western Arkansas, the Fancher train grew to include nearly a dozen more pioneer settlers.

18. Ibid.; Russell, *Behind These Ozark Hills*, p. 98; Brooks, *Mountain Meadows Massacre*, p. 203.

19. Brooks, *Mountain Meadows Massacre*, p. 203.

20. Rhea, *Mountain Meadow Massacre and Its Completion*, p. 5.

21. Ibid.

22. Baskin, *Reminiscence of Early Utah*, pp. 179–180.

23. T. B. H. Stenhouse, *Rocky Mountain Saints*, p. 427.

24. Ibid.

25. This is the precise wording as found in *Mountain Meadow Massacre File*. No other identification is offered, but A. J. Allen, a Mormon in Salt Lake City, wrote in his journal, "I ware in Salt Lake City, saw a train of emigrants going to California, men, women and children. Great stir in states." A. J. Allen, "Diary," August 5, 1857, University of Utah.

26. John A. Ray, a letter, apparently unpublished, to the editor of *The Mountaineer*, December 4, 1859, *Mountain Meadow Massacre File*, Manuscript Section, C.H.O.

27. Ibid.

28. A half-dozen Mormon journals and numerous affidavits, never intended for public view, confirm this report. A non-Mormon source, the *Alta California* of October 27, 1857, substantiates the poor behavior of the Fancher party or at least of the Missouri party: "They were free in speaking of the Mormons. Their conduct was said to be reckless and they would commit little acts of annoyance for the purpose of provoking the Saints." Mary L. Campbell to Andrew Jenson, January 24, 1892, *Mountain Meadow Massacre File*, Church Historian's Office. According to another writer: "An aged lady in Beaver, resident in Cedar City in 1857 [reported that] before the company arrived here [Cedar City] they heard that they had poisoned the springs and beefs in passing through Millard County and that they intended to take to the Meadows and fatten for the soldiers, hence the people expected what to expect."

29. Confidential affidavit, circa 1892, *Mountain Meadow Massacre File*, Manuscript Section, C.H.O.

30. Ibid.

31. Memo signed William Palmer, n.d., *Mountain Meadow Massacre File*, Manuscript Section, C.H.O.

32. S. B. Aden to Brigham Young, March 14, 1859, *Brigham Young Papers*, Manuscript Section, C.H.O.

33. Ibid.

34. Juanita Brooks, *John Doyle Lee: Zealot–Pioneer Builder–Scapegoat* (Glendale, California: The Arthur H. Clark Company, 1962), p. 206.

35. William R. Palmer to Dabney Otis Collins, February 26, 1959, *Mountain Meadow Massacre File*, Manuscript Section, C.H.O.

36. *San Francisco Daily Bulletin Supplement*, March 24, 1877.

37. Elias Morris to Andrew Jenson, February 2, 1892, *Mountain Meadow Massacre File*, Manuscript Section, C.H.O.

38. Ibid.; Mary H. White in an undated letter agreed in part with this statement: "White was a member of this High Council but opposed the killing of the

company, and he was not in the council meeting that decided to kill the company." *Mountain Meadow Massacre File*, Manuscript Section, C.H.O. There seems to be no doubt of Haslem's ride. One witness recorded, "an express went threw yesterday from Iron County to President Young bringing the information that the emigrants who went through a short time ago was acting very mean." Samuel Pitchforth: "Diary," September 9, 1857.

39. Ibid. [*sic*]

40. Elias Morris to Andrew Jenson, February 2, 1892, *Mountain Meadow Massacre File*, Manuscript Section, C.H.O.

41. Nephi Johnson to Anthon H. Lund, March 1900, *Mountain Meadow Massacre File*, Manuscript Section, C.H.O.

42. Ibid.

43. John C. Chatterley to Andrew Jenson, September 18, 1919, *Mountain Meadow Massacre File*, Manuscript Section, C.H.O.

44. Affidavit of Sam Knight, no date circa 1896, *Mountain Meadow Massacre File*, Manuscript Section, C.H.O.; Abraham H. Cannon: "Journal," June 15, 1895, University of Utah.

45. Mary Campbell to Andrew Jenson, January 24, 1892, *Mountain Meadow Massacre File*, Manuscript Section, C.H.O.

46. Mary White; ibid. [*sic*]

47. Ibid. [*sic*]

48. Ibid. [*sic*]

49. Francis Hayes to Andrew Jenson, October 27, 1935, *Mountain Meadow Massacre File*, Manuscript Section, C.H.O.

50. Unidentified note, *Mountain Meadow Massacre File*, Manuscript Section, C.H.O.

51. Ibid.

52. Ibid.

53. Elias Morris, op. cit.

54. Ibid.; William Barton, op. cit.

55. William Barton, op. cit.

56. *San Francisco Daily Bulletin Supplement*, March 24, 1877.

57. Brooks, *Lee*, p. 211.

58. Brigham Young acknowledged the death of William Aden in a letter dated July 12, 1859: "Since my reply, of April 27, to your letter of enquiry concerning your son William A., also advertising in the current number of the Deseret News to learn his whereabouts, from all I can hear I am induced to believe that he joined the emigrant company that was massacred at Mountain Meadows. In all the reports that I have heard, or seen published, agree in the statement that none of that company were saved, except some sixteen very young children, it becomes my painful duty to inform you that, in case your son was in that company, I know of no reliably stated fact or even report upon which to ground the least hope that he is now alive.

"With the kindest sympathies in your affliction and holding myself ready to furnish you any additional information concerning your son William A. that may come to my knowledge, I have the honor to remain, very respectfully." *Brigham Young Papers*, Manuscript Section, C.H.O.

59. Mary L. Campbell, op. cit.; John C. Chatterley to Andrew Jenson, September 18, 1919, op. cit.

60. San Francisco *Daily Bulletin Supplement*, March 24, 1877.

61. Ibid.

62. William R. Palmer to Dabney Otis Collins, February 26, 1959, *Mountain Meadow Massacre File*, Manuscript Section, C.H.O.

63. Albert R. Lyman, *Biography: Francis Marion Lyman 1840–1916: Apostle 1880–1916* (Delta: Printed and published by Melvin A. Lyman, 1958), p. 37.

64. Brigham Young to Isaac Haight, September 10, 1857, *Mountain Meadow Massacre File*, Manuscript Section, C.H.O.

65. Jacob Hamblin to Brigham Young, November 13, 1871, *Mountain Meadow Massacre File*, Manuscript Section, C.H.O.

66. Ibid.

67. Ibid.

68. Ibid.

69. Unidentified note dated 29th, *Mountain Meadow Massacre File*, Manuscript Section, C.H.O.

70. Brigham Young to Thomas L. Kane, December 15, 1859, *Brigham Young Papers*, Manuscript Section, C.H.O.

71. Ibid.

72. Garland Hurt to Jacob Forney, December 4, 1857, *Letters Received*, Office of Indian Affairs, Records of the Department of the Interior.

73. Ibid.

74. Ibid.

75. *New York Times*, November 30, 1857.

76. Ibid.

77. Ibid.

78. Ibid.

79. Ibid.

80. *San Francisco Daily Evening Bulletin*, October 12, 1857.

81. U. S. Senate Executive Document, No. 42, 36th Congress, 1st Session, pp. 42–43.

82. T. B. H. Stenhouse, *Rocky Mountain Saints*, p. 460.

83. Mary L. Campbell, op. cit.

84. "Historian's Office *Journal:* June 11, 1858–December 25, 1859," April 13, 1859, Manuscript Section, C.H.O.

85. Brooks, *Lee*, p. 225.

86. Ibid.; Historian's Office *Journal*, April 13, 1859.

87. *Valley Tan*, February 15, 1859.

88. Alexander Wilson to Jacob Thompson, March 28, 1859, Department of Justice, RG 60, N.A.; Juanita Brooks, *Mountain Meadows Massacre*, p. 174.

89. Ibid. [*sic*]

90. Forney to James Buchanan, May 12, 1859, Department of Justice, RG 60, N.A.

91. *Deseret News*, May 11, 1859.

92. Ibid.; the exact number of victims probably will not be known with any degree of accuracy, but it would seem that the figure was close to a hundred.

93. Ibid.; J. Forney to J. Hamblin, August 4, 1858, *Letters Received*, Office of Indian Affairs, Records of the Department of the Interior.

94. Ibid.

95. Brooks, *Lee*, p. 246.

96. J. Forney to Col. A. S. Johnston, June 15, 1859; F. J. Porter to Col. G. H. Crosman, June 20, 1859, *Letters Sent*, Department of Utah, Records of the War Department; U. S. Senate Executive Documents, No. 42, 36th Congress, Session 1, p. 49; *Valley Tan*, May 17, 1859.

97. Phelps, "Diary," June 26, 1859; *Deseret News*, June 29, 1859; *Journal History*, June 28, 1859.

98. J. Forney to A. B. Greenwood, October 6, 1859, *Letters Received*, Department of Indian Affairs, Records of the Interior Department.

99. Abraham H. Cannon, "Journal," May 2, 1895, University of Utah. Cannon's journal states: "We gave some consideration to the correspondence of G. C. Williams of the Mexican Mission, who feels that he has been badly treated by some of his brethren, and also feels to condemn the Church for allowing Isaac Haight who is said to be one of the leaders in the Mountain Meadows Massacre to remain in the Church after his participation in that terrible crime. In that massacre, Williams is said to have lost fourteen relatives. He is himself considered a very good man, but because of the matters mentioned above he desires to be dropped from the Church."

100. Brooks, *Mountain Meadows Massacre*, fifth printing, pp. xv-xvi.

101. John L. Herrick to J. G. Tolman, April 13, 1910, *Mountain Meadow Massacre File*, Manuscript Section, C.H.O.; Louise Linton gave only her married name.

102. *Deseret News*, May 11, 1859.

103. U. S. Senate Executive Document, No. 42, 36th Congress, 1st Session, p. 32.

104. Black was later a strong defender of the Mormons during the anti-polygamy crusades of the 1870s. Black (now a private citizen in Pennsylvania) fervently defended the Saints' right to practice their religion without governmental interference.

105. *Deseret News*, June 29, 1859.

106. Ibid.

107. Ibid.

108. Ibid.

109. The exact amount was $128,000, a far cry from the anticipated payroll of $650,000; *Journal History*, May 4, 1859.

110. Major J. H. Carleton, "Mountain Meadows Massacre," 57th Congress, 1st Session, House Document Number 605, p. 1.

111. A. S. Johnston to L. Thomas, April 27, 1859, *Letters Sent*, Department of Utah, Records of the War Department.

112. Ibid.

113. *Journal History*, John Jacques to Brigham Young, April 22, 1859.

114. *Valley Tan*, February 29, 1860.
115. Ibid.
116. A. F. Cardon, "Mountain Meadow Massacre Burial Detachment, 1859: Tommy Gordon's Diary," *Utah Historical Quarterly*, XXXV (Spring, 1967): 143–146.
117. Nelson, *Fifty Years on the Trail*, p. 129.
118. R. P. Campbell to F. J. Porter, July 6, 1859, *Letters Sent*, Department of Utah, Records of the War Department.
119. Ibid.; Cradlebaugh, *Utah and the Mormons*, p. 32.
120. Cradlebaugh, *Utah and the Mormons*, p. 17.
121. Carleton, "Mountain Meadows Massacre," p. 14.
122. A. F. Cardon, "Mountain Meadow Burial Detail," p. 146; Major Prince reached Camp Floyd on June 1, 1859.
123. Carleton, "Mountain Meadows Massacre," p. 15.
124. Brooks, *Lee*, p. 248.
125. Nelson, "Fifty Years on the Trail," p. 130; Isaac Haight wrote that he had been warned of Cradlebaugh's approach. "May 1 a messenger came to us and said Judge Cradlebaugh with 200 U. S. troops were at Beaver coming south with the intentions of taking me and some of the brethren and hanging us without trial for supposed crime. . . ." Isaac Haight, "Diary," (typescript) Utah State University; Cedar City was occupied by twenty or thirty families, the majority of which were in the process of moving to Salt Lake City, "Historian's Office Journal, June 11, 1859–December 25, 1859," April 13, 1859, Manuscript Section, C.H.O.
126. Cradlebaugh, *Utah and the Mormons*, p. 43.
127. Nelson, "Fifty Years on the Trail," p. 130.
128. Ibid.
129. Elijah Everett, "Diary," Utah State University, p. 20.
130. Cradlebaugh, *Utah and the Mormons*, p. 20.
131. Isaac Haight, "Diary," Utah State Historical Society, September 29, 1859.
132. Phelps, "Diary," June 4, 1859.
133. *Deseret News*, June 8, 1859.

NOTES TO CHAPTER 8

1. Hodding Carter, *Doomed Road to Empire: The Spanish Trail of Conquest* (New York: McGraw-Hill Book Company, Inc., 1963), p. 5.
2. W. Eugene Hollon, *Beyond the Cross Timbers*, p. 216.
3. James Sweeney, "Narrative," p. 2.
4. Ibid.
5. Ibid.
6. Ibid.
7. Ibid., p. 4.
8. Randolph Barnes Marcy, *Thirty Years of Army Life on the Border* (New York: Harper Brothers, 1866), p. 243.

9. The exact figure is somewhat unclear. One officer reported 1,100 mules, 200 horses, and 100 oxen. Gove, *The Utah Expedition*, p. 315.

10. Gove, *The Utah Expedition*, p. 315.

11. Ibid., p. 316.

12. Ibid.

13. Ibid.

14. Sweeney, "Narrative," p. 4.

15. Gove, *The Utah Expedition*, p. 316.

16. William H. Goetzmann, *Army Exploration of the American West, 1803–1863* (New Haven: Yale University Press, 1959), p. 377.

17. The route somewhat south of the old Oregon Trail but north of Hedspeth's Cutoff was later completed by Frederick W. Lander from South Pass to City of Rocks.

18. Gove, *The Utah Expedition*, p. 239.

19. B. F. Ficklin to Major F. J. Porter, April 21, 1858, *Albert Sidney Johnston Papers*, Barret Collection, Tulane University.

20. Phelps, "Diary," April 10, 1858, typescript, Utah Historical Society.

21. John N. MaComb, *Report of the Exploring Expedition from Santa Fe, New Mexico, to the Junction of the Grand and Green Rivers of the Great Colorado of the West in 1859* (Washington: U. S. Engineer Department, 1876), Part II, p. 53. Newberry penned the geological portions of the MaComb *Report*.

22. Ibid., p. 96.

23. Ibid., p. 97.

24. Goetzman, *Army Exploration*, p. 397.

25. Senate Executive Document 34, 36th Congress, 1st Session (1859–1860), pp. 4–5.

26. W. Turrentine Jackson, *Wagon Roads West: A Study of Federal Road Surveys and Construction in the Trans-Mississippi West, 1846–1869* (New Haven: Yale University Press, 1965), p. 85.

27. Ibid., pp. 18–22.

28. Ibid.

29. *Deseret News*, August 17, 1859.

30. William H. Hooper to J. H. Simpson, December 9, 1859, *William H. Hooper Papers*, Manuscript Section, C.H.O.

31. Jackson, *Wagon Roads West*, pp. 48–70.

32. James Hervey Simpson, *Report of the Secretary of War Communicating, in Compliance with a Resolution of the Senate, Captain Simpson's Report and Map of Wagon Road Routes in Utah Territory* (hereafter cited as Simpson, *Wagon Roads*), Senate Executive Document No. 40 (1858–1859), 35th Congress, 2nd Session, pp. 4–5.

33. Ibid., pp. 8–13.

34. Ibid., pp. 23–24.

35. F. J. Porter to Captain James H. Simpson, April 26, 1859, *Letters Sent*, Department of Utah, Records of the War Department.

36. "The Fort was known as Johnston's Fort. The walls of the fort were about two feet thick, about twelve feet high and enclosed about one acre of land. In the northwest, and southwest corners, they built tall two story buildings called bas-

tions. The bastions had port holes where the men used to take their turns standing guard or as watchman to protect themselves and the families from hostile Indians. They built their homes on the inside of the fort, using the wall for the back of the house. The land in and around the fort was either meadow or swamp with very little that could be used as means of support of many families and as a result, the task of building the fort rested on a very few men, the main one being Laban Morrill, James and William Dalley. There was a well in the center of the fort where they all drew water for culinary purposes." Sarah Ann Dalley Hulet, "Biography of James Dalley," Biographies of Mormon Pioneers, Manuscript Section, C.H.O.; Simpson, *Wagon Roads*, p. 27.

37. Simpson, *Wagon Roads*, p. 27.

38. The pass was named in honor of Major John F. Reynolds, who had camped near the pass while with the Steptoe expedition in 1855. It was Reynolds, now stationed at Camp Floyd, who enlisted the services of the redoubtable desert guide, George Washington Bean; Bean, p. 135.

39. Ibid.

40. Ibid., pp. 24–25.

41. Ibid.

42. *Valley Tan*, November 19, 1858.

43. Howard Egan, *Pioneering the West 1846–1878: Major Howard Egan's Diary*, edited by Wm. M. Egan (Richmond, Utah: Howard R. Egan Estate, 1917), pp. 194–195; George Chorpenning to Forney, November 9, 1858, *Letters Sent*, Department of Utah, Records of the Office of Indian Affairs.

44. Dale L. Morgan, *The Humboldt: Highroad of the West* (New York: Farrar and Rinehart Incorporated, 1943), p. 271.

45. James H. Simpson, *Report of Explorations Across the Great Basin of the Territory of Utah for a Direct Wagon-Route from Camp Floyd to Genoa, in Carson Valley in 1859* (Washington, Government Printing Office, 1876), p. 41; hereafter cited as *Exploration of the Great Basin*.

46. Ibid., pp. 41–44.

47. Ibid.; J. Forney to Captain J. H. Simpson, February 22, 1859, *Letters Sent*, Department of Utah, Office of Indian Affairs; apparently Reese was permitted to bring his son along to join in the adventure, *Deseret News*, August 17, 1859.

48. Simpson, *Wagon Roads*, pp. 41–44.

49. Ibid., p. 47.

50. Ibid., pp. 52–53.

51. Ibid., p. 25.

52. William Lee, "Diary," May 10, 1859, *William Lee Papers*, Library of Congress.

53. Simpson, *Wagon Roads*, p. 61.

54. Ibid., pp. 67–68.

55. Ibid., pp. 80–81.

56. Ibid., pp. 80–84.

57. Ibid.

58. Ibid., p. 90.

59. Ibid.

60. Ibid., pp. 90–91.

61. Ibid., p. 93.

62. *Valley Tan*, November 16, 1859.

63. Ibid.

64. Ibid.

65. Walter Lowery died at Fort Laramie while endeavoring to return to his home.

66. William Lee, "Diary," June 24, 1859, *William Lee Papers*, National Archives.

67. Simpson, *Wagon Roads*, p. 113.

68. *Valley Tan*, November 16, 1859; Simpson, *Wagon Roads*, pp. 124–130.

69. Ibid. [*sic*]

70. Ibid. [*sic*]

71. Settle, *War Drums and Wagon Wheels*, p. 106.

72. F. J. Porter to Captain James H. Simpson, August 5, 1859, *Letters Sent*, Department of Utah, Records of the War Department.

73. Simpson, *Wagon Roads*, p. 141.

74. C. F. Smith to Assistant Adjutant General, July 9, 1860, *Letters Sent*, Department of Utah, Records of the War Department.

75. *Deseret News*, September 14, 1858.

76. F. J. Porter to Captain Henry F. Clarke, September 16, 1859, *Letters Sent*, Department of Utah, Records of the War Department.

77. Porter to Simpson, November 16, 1859, *Letters Sent*, Department of Utah, Records of the War Department.

78. Ibid.

79. Goetzman, *Army Explorations*, p. 404.

80. Simpson, *Wagon Roads*, p. 851.

NOTES TO CHAPTER 9

1. *Deseret News*, November 17, 1858.

2. Luke Lea to Brigham Young, February 20, 1852, *Letters Received*, Office of Indian Affairs, 1824–1881, "Utah Superintendency 1849–1880." Cited hereafter as *Letters Received*, O.I.A.

3. Joseph Fielding Smith, ed., *Teachings of the Prophet Joseph Smith* (Salt Lake City: Deseret Book Co., 1967), p. 17.

4. Brigham Young to Isaac Haight, October 8, 1858, *Brigham Young Papers*, Manuscript Section, C.H.O.

5. Wilford Woodruff, "Journal," November 2, 1858, Manuscript Section, C.H.O.

6. Joseph H. Holeman to Luke Lea, September 22, 1851; Ibid., March 24, 1852; S. B. Rose to Luke Lea, March 31, 1852, *Letters Received*, O.I.A.

7. Ibid. [*sic*]

8. Neff, *History of Utah*, p. 371.

9. Milton R. Hunter, *Brigham Young, The Colonizer* (Salt Lake City: The Deseret News Press, 1940), pp. 270–71.

10. *Deseret News*, March 6, 1852.

11. Brigham Young to Luke Lea, June 30, 1852, *Letters Received*, O.I.A.

12. Joseph H. Holeman to Luke Lea, March 24, 1852, *Letters Received*, O.I.A.

13. Jacob H. Holeman to Luke Lea, September 21, 1851, *Letters Received*, O.I.A.

14. Hurt to Mannypenny, May 2, 1855, *Letters Received*, O.I.A.

15. Brigham Young to J. M. Bernhisel, November 4, 1856, *Brigham Young Papers*, Manuscript Section, C.H.O.

16. Hurt to Mannypenny, May 2, 1855, *Letters Received*, O.I.A.

17. Furniss, *Mormon Conflict*, p. 47.

18. Neff, *History of Utah*, p. 384.

19. *Deseret News*, October 27, 1858.

20. Furniss, *Mormon Conflict*, p. 45.

21. Garland Hurt to Brigham Young, October 31, 1856, *Letters Received*, O.I.A.

22. Ibid.

23. Leland Creer, "The Activities of Jacob Hamblin in the Region of the Colorado," *University of Utah Anthropological Papers*, XXIII (May, 1958): 3. The emigration of that year was estimated to be slightly less than five thousand men, women, and children, *Millennial Star*, XVIII (June 14, 1856): 377.

24. Hyrum Derrick, "Diary," Utah State Historical Society, p. 3.

25. Dimick B. Huntington, "Journal: 1857–1859," August 16, 1857, Manuscript Section, C.H.O.

26. Ibid., September 20, 1857.

27. A. Johnson to D. H. Wells, August 18, 1857, *Daniel H. Wells Papers*, Manuscript Section, C.H.O.

28. John Lowe Butler, "Diary" (typescript), Manuscript Section, C.H.O.

29. Ibid., pp. 70–71.

30. Ibid.

31. Hurt to Johnston, October 24, 1857, *Letters Received*, O.I.A.; *New York Times*, November 27, 1857.

32. Ibid. [*sic*]

33. Ibid. [*sic*]

34. Butler, "Diary," p. 72.

35. Ibid.

36. Hurt to Johnston, October 24, 1857, *Letters Received*, O.I.A.

37. Dimick B. Huntington, "Journal: 1857–1859," May 3, 1858, Manuscript Section, C.H.O.

38. Ibid.

39. Brigham Young to Andrew Cunningham, March 10, 1858, *Brigham Young Papers*, Manuscript Section, C.H.O.

40. Ibid.

41. Brigham Young to Aaron Johnston, March 10, 1858, *Brigham Young Papers*, Manuscript Section, C.H.O.

42. Senate Executive Document No. 1, 35th Congress, 2nd Session, Serial 975, Vol. 1, Pt. 2, pp. 82–84; F. J. Porter, "Diary," April 28, 1858.

43. Ibid. [*sic*]; F. J. Porter to Dr. Forney, April 26, 1858, *Letters Sent*, Department of Utah, Records of the War Department. After enlisting Washakie's support to protect the ferries on the Green River and Ham's Fork, General Johnston warned Forney not to use the Indians for any other purpose.

44. Affidavit signed by Hosea K. Whitney and Elias Smith, March 24, 1858, *Brigham Young Papers*, Manuscript Section, C.H.O.

45. Ibid.

46. Brigham Young to Commissioner of Indian Affairs, April 5, 1858, *Letters Received*, O.I.A.

47. Ibid. One pioneer recalled: "Last night the indians stole 100 head of horses from Bro. Nails hird ground, the indians that were stealing at Samon River has come to Cash Valley and stolen 70 bushels of wheat. The people are leeving that give[s] the indians a chance to steel. We believe the U.S. officers at Bridger are putting them up to it." Andrew J. Allen, "Diary," April 13, 1858.

48. *Journal History*, June 16, 1858.

NOTES TO CHAPTER 10

1. *Deseret News*, February 22, 1860.

2. Robert Ignatius Burns, *The Jesuits and the Indian Wars of the Northwest* (New Haven: Yale University Press, 1966), p. 239; although Burns has revealed the complex causes for this unrest, a contemporary account by Major John Owens to Brigham Young attributed the Indian war to the influence of Johnston's Army and the Jesuits. Brigham Young: "Office Journal, August 8, 1858–January 31, 1862," October 8, 1858, Manuscript Section, C.H.O.

3. A. S. Johnston to East, July 29, 1858, *Letters Sent*, Department of Utah, Records of the War Department.

4. Eugene Bandel, *Frontier Life in the Army, 1854–1861*, ed. Ralph P. Bieber (Glendale, California: The Arthur H. Clark Company, 1932), p. 228.

5. Ibid., pp. 229–230.

6. Ibid., p. 229.

7. Unless otherwise noted, the following account is based on John I. Ginn, "Mormon and Indian Wars, the Mountain Meadows Massacre and other Tragedies Incident to the Mormon Rebellion of 1857, together with Personal Recollections of Civilians who witnessed many of the thrilling scenes described" (typescript), Utah Historical Society.

8. Brigham Young, "Office Journal, August 8, 1858–January 31, 1862," August 28, 1858, Manuscript Section, C.H.O.

9. Ginn, "Mormon and Indian Wars," p. 160.

10. *Journal History*, August 28, 1858; "Historian's Office Journal: August 8, 1859–January 31, 1862," August 28, 1858, Manuscript Section, C.H.O.

11. A. S. Johnston to A. Cumming, September 17, 1858, *Letters Sent*, Department of Utah, Records of the War Department; F. J. Porter to J. Forney, September 3, 1858, *Letters Sent*, Department of Utah, Records of the War Department; "Historian's Office Journal: August 8, 1859–January 31, 1862," August 28, 1858, Manuscript Section, C.H.O.

12. J. Forney to C. E. Mix, November 5, 1858, *Letters Received*, O.I.A.

13. Ibid.

14. J. Forney to C. E. Mix, September 22, 1858, *Letters Received*, O.I.A.

15. Ibid.

16. Ibid.; *Journal History*, October 30, 1858.

17. John W. Phelps, "Diary," October 25, 1858. The command reached Camp Floyd on Sunday, October 24, 1858.

18. J. Forney to A. Cumming, September 18, 1858, *Letters Received*, O.I.A.; David Dority to Garland Hurt, September 20, 1858, Indian Affairs Book, *Brigham Young Papers*, Manuscript Section, C.H.O.; *Valley Tan*, December 24, 1858.

19. A. Cumming to G. Hurt, September 24, 1858, *Letters Received*, O.I.A.

20. G. Hurt to A. Cumming, September 24, 1858, *Letters Received*, O.I.A.

21. Ibid.

22. Ibid.

23. F. J. Porter to P. Morrison, September 30, 1858, *Letters Sent*, Department of Utah, Records of the War Department; Special Order No. 37, *Order Book*, Department Of Utah, Records of the War Department.

24. G. Hurt to A. Cumming, October 3, 1858, *Letters Received*, O.I.A.

25. Brigham Young to George A. Smith, November 11, 1858, *Brigham Young Papers*, Manuscript Section, C.H.O.

26. John Lowery to Capt. A. F. Garrison, November 11, 1858, *Letters Sent*, Department of Utah, Records of the War Department.

27. F. J. Porter to Col. E. R. S. Canby, November 11, 1858, *Letters Sent*, Department of Utah, Records of the War Department.

28. A. S. Johnston to A. Cumming, October 5, 1858, *Letters Sent*, Department of Utah, Records of the War Department; F. J. Porter to P. Morrison, October 5, 1858, *Letters Sent*, Department of Utah, Records of the War Department.

29. J. Forney to C. E. Mix, December 3, 1858, *Letters Received*, O.I.A.

30. *Deseret News*, November 3, 1858.

31. Ibid.

32. "Historian's Office Journal: August 8, 1859–January 31, 1862," December 16, 1858, Manuscript Section, C.H.O.

33. The foundation and collapsed walls of one of these outposts was discovered by Dr. Everett Cooley of the University of Utah.

34. J. Forney to C. E. Mix, December 3, 1858; Jeremiah Hatch to J. Forney, November 12, 1858, *Letters Received*, O.I.A.

35. Ibid. [*sic*]

36. J. Forney to C. E. Mix, December 3, 1858, *Letters Received*, O.I.A.; *Valley Tan*, December 10, 1858.

37. Peter Royce speaking for Kanosh to Jacob Forney, November 15, 1858, *Brigham Young Papers*, Manuscript Section, C.H.O.

38. Ibid.

39. *Valley Tan*, December 10, 1858.

40. Ibid.

41. *Valley Tan*, January 25, 1859.

42. Ibid.
43. J. Forney to J. W. Denver, February 15, 1859, *Letters Received*, O.I.A.
44. J. Forney to J. W. Denver, March 9, 1859, *Letters Received*, O.I.A.
45. Everett Dick, *Vanguards of the Frontier*, p. 114; this statement has no application to the prehistoric Indians of southeastern Utah.
46. J. Forney to J. W. Denver, March 9, 1859, *Letters Received*, O.I.A.
47. *Journal History*, November 1, 1858.
48. Milton R. Hunter, *Brigham Young, The Colonizer* (Salt Lake City: The Deseret News Press, 1940), pp. 361–362.

NOTES TO CHAPTER 11

1. *Deseret News*, December 21, 1859.
2. In 1858, Brigham City was officially known as Box Elder City.
3. Samuel Smith to J. Forney, August 1, 1859, *Letters Received*, O.I.A.; J. Forney to A. Cumming, August 2, 1859, *Letters Received*, O.I.A.; *Deseret News*, August 3, 1859.
4. *Deseret News*, August 3, 1859.
5. Ibid.; Isaac Lynde to F. J. Porter, August 20, 1859, *Letters Sent*, Department of Utah, Records of the War Department.
6. *Deseret News*, August 3, 1859; Affidavit of Anton W. Tjader, James R. Shepard, Oscar T. D. Fairbanks, George Everst, September 2, 1859, *Letters Received*, O.I.A.
7. Major Isaac Lynde to F. J. Porter, August 20, 1859, *Letters Sent*, Department of Utah, Records of the War Department; *Deseret News*, August 3, 1859; *Valley Tan*, August 10, 1859.
8. *Valley Tan*, August 10, 1859.
9. *Deseret News*, August 3, 1859.
10. Ibid.
11. The incident was also reported to Forney by Alvin Nichols.
12. Johnston to Cumming, August 5, 1859, *Letters Sent*, Department of Utah, Records of the War Department.
13. F. J. Porter to Lieutenant E. Gay, August 6, 1859, *Letters Sent*, Department of Utah, Records of the War Department.
14. *Valley Tan*, August 17, 1859; *History of Box Elder County* (Box Elder County, Utah: n.p., ca. 1935), pp. 150–151; *Box Elder Lore of the Nineteenth Century* (Brigham City, Utah: Box Elder Chapter of the Sons of Utah Pioneers, 1951), pp. 63–64.
15. E. Gay to F. J. Porter, August 13, 1859, *Letters Sent*, Department of Utah, Records of the War Department; *Valley Tan*, August 17 and 24, 1859.
16. E. Gay to F. J. Porter, August 13, 1859, *Letters Sent*, Department of Utah, Records of the War Department; *Deseret News*, August 17, 24, and 31, 1859; *Valley Tan*, August 24, 1859; *History of Box Elder County*, pp. 150–151.
17. Ibid. [*sic*]; *Journal History*, August 19, 1859.
18. *Journal History*, August 19, 1859.

19. E. Gay to F. J. Porter, August 13, 1859, *Letters Sent*, Department of Utah, Records of the War Department.

20. Ibid.

21. F. J. Porter to Major Isaac Lynde, June 5, 1859, *Letters Sent*, Department of Utah, Records of the War Department; Special Order No. 142, May 30, 1859, *Order Book*, Department of Utah, Records of the War Department; *Valley Tan*, June 1, 1859.

22. U. S. Senate Executive Document No. 2, 36th Congress, 1st Session, Vol. 2, Pt. 2, p. 241.

23. Ibid., p. 242.

24. Ibid.

25. Jacob Holeman to Luke Lea, May 2, 1852, *Letters Received*, O.I.A.

26. Major Isaac Lynde to General A. S. Johnston, August 28, 1859, *Letters Sent*, Department of Utah, Records of the War Department.

27. Ibid.

28. *Valley Tan*, August 24, 1859.

29. Ibid., November 12, 1859.

30. Virginia Cole Trenholm and Maurice Carley, *The Shoshones, Sentinels of the Rockies* (Norman: University of Oklahoma Press, 1969), p. 184.

31. *Valley Tan*, November 12, 1859; two years earlier a somewhat related story was reported by Dimick Huntington: "Some Bannocks from Oregon City came in to see Brigham one Chief by the name of Piut & chief by the name of Koroko-kee they sayed that the Banak Prophet had sayed a great many things of late about Gods cutting off the Gentiles and that the tribes must be at peace with one another and that the lariat of time was to be broke that the sun was a going to fall and the Moon to be turned into blood that the Lord had cutt off all the Gentiles and throwed them all away. . . ." Dimick B. Huntington, "Journal: 1857–1859," September 16, 1857, Manuscript Section, C.H.O.

32. Ibid.

33. *Valley Tan*, September 7, 14, 1859; *Deseret News*, September 7, 1859.

34. Ibid. [*sic*]

35. D. R. Eckels to J. Thompson, September 23, 1859, *Letters Received*, O.I.A.; *Deseret News*, September 21, 1859.

36. *Deseret News*, September 21, 1859.

37. Unless otherwise stated, the following story is based on an affidavit signed by Lorenzo Suberr, September 20, 1859, *Letters Received*, O.I.A.

38. A. S. Johnston to Lorenzo Thomas, November 2, 1859, *Letters Sent*, Department of Utah, Records of the War Department.

39. Ibid.

40. Major Isaac Lynde to General A. S. Johnston, October 24, 1859, *Letters Sent*, Department of Utah, Records of the War Department.

41. A. S. Johnston to Lorenzo Thomas, November 2, 1859, *Letters Sent*, Department of Utah, Records of the War Department.

42. John B. Floyd to Jacob Thompson, January 23, 1860, *Letters Received*, O.I.A.

43. Ibid.

NOTES TO CHAPTER 12

1. *The Mountaineer*, April 21, 1860.

2. Cass to Cumming, December 2, 1859, *Cumming Papers*, Duke University; House Executive Document Number 78, 36th Congress, 1st Session, Serial No. 1056, p. 41.

3. Cumming to Cass, February 2, 1860, *Cumming Papers*, Duke University; *House Executive Document*, Number 78, 36th Congress, 1st Session, Serial No. 1056, p. 46.

4. Cooper to A. S. Johnston, January 1, 1860, *Letters Sent*, Adjutant General's Office, Records of the War Department; General Order Number 10, February 29, 1860, *Order Book*, Department of Utah, Records of the War Department.

5. *Journal History*, May 7, 1860; *Deseret News*, June 13, 1860.

6. Hosea Stout to Colonel S. C. Stambaugh, June 16, 1860; Colonel S. C. Stambaugh to Hosea Stout, June 16, 1860, *Letters Received*, O.I.A.

7. J. Forney to A. B. Greenwood, July 3, 1860, *Letters Received*, O.I.A.

8. *Deseret News*, June 27, 1860.

9. A. Cumming to J. Forney, February 15, 1860, *Letters Received*, O.I.A.

10. Ibid.

11. *Deseret News*, April 21, 1860.

12. Ibid.

13. *Deseret News*, March 5, 1860.

14. F. Dodge to A. B. Greenwood, November 25, 1859, *Letters Received*, O.I.A.

15. Ibid.

16. F. Dodge to A. B. Greenwood, March 6, 1860, *Letters Received*, O.I.A.

17. LeRoy Hafen and S. Lyman Tyler, "Lands of the Western Shoshoni and Gosiutes" (unpublished manuscript), Brigham Young University Library, Provo, Utah, p. 21.

18. Ralph Moody, *The Old Trails West* (New York: Crowell Co., 1963), p. 297.

19. C. F. Smith to S. Weed, May 25, 1860; C. F. Smith to A. Cumming, May 26, 1860; C. F. Smith to A. A. G., May 26, 1860; Senate Executive Document, Number 1, 36th Congress, 2nd Session, Serial No. 1079, pp. 77–78.

20. *Deseret News*, June 13, 1860.

21. Ibid.

22. Ibid.

23. C. F. Smith to Assistant Adjutant General, August 1, 1860, *Letters Sent*, Department of Utah, Records of the War Department. A Mormon train of 190 men, women, and children made up the bulk of the caravan.

24. Senate Executive Document, Number 1, 36th Congress, 2nd Session, Serial No. 1079, pp. 87–88.

25. C. F. Smith to Assistant Adjutant General, August 16, 1860, *Letters Sent*, Department of Utah, Records of the War Department.

26. *Deseret News*, August 15, 1860; *Senate Executive Document*, Number 1, 36th Congress, 2nd Session, Serial No. 1079, pp. 87–88.

27. Ibid.

28. *Deseret News*, August 15, 1860; Senate Executive Document, Number 1, 36th Congress, 2nd Session, Serial No. 1079, p. 99.

29. *Deseret News*, August 15, 1860.

30. Ibid.

31. Raymond Duane Steele, *Goshen Valley History* (privately printed 1960), p. 16.

32. *Sacramento Union*, April 2, 1860; *Los Angeles Star*, March 26, 1860; *Deseret News*, April 25, 1860; *Journal History*, April 18, 1860.

33. *Deseret News*, April 18, 1860.

34. Ibid.

35. Brigham Young to Horace Eldredge, April 19, 1860, *Brigham Young Papers*, Manuscript Section, C.H.O.; *Deseret News*, April 18, 25, 1860.

36. *Deseret News*, April 18, 25, 1860.

37. Ibid.

38. *Deseret News*, April 25, 1860.

39. Senate Executive Document, Number 1, 36th Congress, 2nd Session, Serial No. 1079, p. 71.

40. Hunter, *Brigham Young, The Colonizer*, p. 277.

41. Ibid., July 24, 1860; *Deseret News*, August 1, 15, 1860, September 1, 1860; "Brigham Young's Office Journal: August 8, 1858–January 31, 1862," July 26, 1860, Manuscript Section, C.H.O.

42. Brigham Young to Peter Maughan, July 26, 1860, *Brigham Young Papers*, Manuscript Section, C.H.O.

43. C. F. Smith to Acting Adjutant General, May 5, 1860; C. F. Smith to Colonel M. T. Howe, May 22, 1859, *Letters Sent*, Department of Utah; C. F. Smith to A. Cumming, April 23, 1860.

NOTES TO CHAPTER 13

1. *Journal History*, September 1, 1858.

2. Luke Gallup, "Diary," December 30, 1860, Utah State Historical Society.

3. Ibid.

4. Burton, *City of Saints*, p. 249.

5. *Deseret News*, December 21, 1859.

6. *Journal History*, September 11, 1858.

7. George Albert Smith to T. B. H. Stenhouse, Historian's Office "Letter Book," XIV, p. 51.

8. *Journal History*, September 16, 1858.

9. Ibid.

10. Gove, *The Utah Expedition*, p. 185.

11. *Deseret News*, October 13, 20, November 3, 1858; *Journal History*, October 30, 1858. Another version of the story was told by the *Deseret News*: "On Thursday week last, Oct. 21st, while Mr. Jones was on his return to the [*sic*] this city, they met on Black's Fork, and McDonald, swearing he would kill Jones, leveled his pistol at him, as he was dismounting, and the ball passed through the collar of

his overcoat to his left shoulder. Mr. Jones, to prevent the murderer's firing on him again, and to protect himself, returned the fire, when the ball passed through Cunningham's throat and neck, killing him on the spot."

12. Stenhouse, *Rocky Mountain Saints*, p. 417.

13. Ibid., p. 419.

14. *Deseret News*, July 11, 1860.

15. Ibid.

16. Albert Perry Rockwood, "History of Utah Penitentiary, 1855–1878," Bancroft Collection, University of California.

17. William A. Hickman, *Brigham's Destroying Angel: Being the Life and Confession and Startling Disclosures of the Notorious "Bill" Hickman and Danite Chief of Utah* (Salt Lake City: Shepard Publishing Co., 1904), p. 150.

18. Brigham Young to George Q. Cannon, December 24, 1858, *Brigham Young Papers*, Manuscript Section, C.H.O.

19. The details of the Bernard murder vary according to the partisan approach of Mormons and Gentiles. Nevertheless, I have attempted to approximate the events from available materials: Brigham Young to George Q. Cannon, December 24, 1858, *Brigham Young Papers*, Manuscript Section, C.H.O.; *Valley Tan*, December 10, 17, 22, 1858; *Deseret News*, October 13, November 3, 1858.

20. *Deseret News*, November 3, 1858.

21. Ibid.

22. *Journal History*, December 18–23, 1858.

23. Ibid. Loc. cit., note 19.

24. Juanita Brooks, ed., *On the Mormon Frontier: The Diary of Hosea Stout*, II (Salt Lake City: University of Utah Press, 1964), p. 672.

25. Wilford Woodruff, "Diary," January 3, 1859, Manuscript Section, C.H.O.

26. *Valley Tan*, December 22, 1858.

27. William A. Hickman, *Brigham's Destroying Angel*, passim.

28. In seven years of research this writer has found little to support Hickman's claim.

29. Stenhouse, *Rocky Mountain Saints*, p. 418.

30. *Valley Tan*, January 18, 1859.

31. Gove, *The Utah Expedition*, pp. 380–383; Cradlebaugh, *Utah and the Mormons*, p. 23; Wilford Woodruff, "Diary," September 27, 1858; Brooks, *Hosea Stout*, II, p. 700; *Valley Tan*, August 10, 17, 1859; *Deseret News*, August 10, 1859, January 10, 1860.

32. *Deseret News*, January 10, 1860.

33. Hickman, *Destroying Angel*, p. 141.

34. Ibid., pp. 25–26.

35. Ibid., pp. 35–76.

36. Justitia to Brigham Young, November 1859, *Brigham Young Papers*, Manuscript Section, C.H.O.

37. Hickman, *Destroying Angel*, pp. 144–145.

38. William A. Hickman to Brigham Young, January, 1859, *William A. Hickman Papers*, Manuscript Section, C.H.O.

39. Hickman, *Destroying Angel*, p. 146.

40. Ibid.; "Historian's Office *Journal*: December 26, 1859–February 19, 1861," January 19, 1860, Manuscript Section, C.H.O.

41. *The Mountaineer*, January 21, 1860.

42. "Brigham Young's Office Journal, August 8, 1858–January 31, 1862," April 3, 1860, Manuscript Section, C.H.O.

43. William A. Hickman to Brigham Young, no date, *Brigham Young Papers*, Manuscript Section, C.H.O.

44. Charles Walker, "Diary," I, Manuscript Section, Brigham Young University, p. 78.

45. Ibid.

46. Ibid.; Brooks, *Hosea Stout*, II, pp. 701–702; *Journal History*, August 27, 1859; *Valley Tan*, August 31, 1859; *Deseret News*, August 31, September 1, September 2, 1859.

47. Hickman, *Destroying Angel*, pp. 134–135.

48. Ibid., p. 211.

49. John Bennion, "Journal: 1855–1877," II, Utah State Historical Society, p. 79; Brooks, *Hosea Stout*, II, p. 668.

50. Affidavit signed by C. Drown, February 11, 1858, *Brigham Young Papers*, Manuscript Section, C.H.O.

51. Ibid.

52. Brooks, *Hosea Stout*, II, p. 703.

53. Hickman, *Destroying Angel*, p. 134.

54. Ivy B. Eddy to Wilford Woodruff, November 28, 1889, *Wilford Woodruff Papers*, Manuscript Section, C.H.O.

55. *Valley Tan*, September 12, 1859, November 2, 1859.

56. Charles Lowell Walker, "Diary," October 22, 1859.

57. Ibid.

58. Ibid.

59. Wilford Woodruff, "Journal," January 11, 1864, Manuscript Section, C.H.O.

NOTES TO CHAPTER 14

1. *Journal History*, January 12, 1859.

2. T. S. W., "Manuscript" (copy) Utah State Historical Society. Although the work is identified only by the three letters it was probably written by Thomas S. Williams shortly before his death in 1860.

3. *New York Times*, June 8, 1858.

4. T. S. W., "Manuscript," p. 38.

5. Ibid.

6. C. F. Smith to Adjutant General of the Army, July 11, 1859, *Letters Sent*, Department of Utah, Records of the War Department.

7. Myron Brewer to Brigham Young, December 23, 1857, *Myron Brewer Papers*, Manuscript Section, C.H.O.

8. Myron Brewer to General Wm. H. Kimball, *Myron Brewer Papers*, Manuscript Section, C.H.O.

9. T. S. W., "Manuscript," p. 38.

10. *Journal History*, December 12, 1858.

11. T. S. W., "Manuscript," p. 38.

12. *Deseret News*, July 20, 1859.

13. Ibid.

14. *Myron Brewer Papers*, Manuscript Section, C.H.O.; no other identification furnished.

15. Ibid.

16. John M. Wallace to General A. S. Johnston, June 17, 1859, *Myron Brewer Papers*, Manuscript Section, C.H.O.

17. Ibid., July 9, 1859.

18. Ibid.

19. *Journal History*, August 31, 1859, Manuscript Section, C.H.O.

20. Historian's Office *Journal:* June 11, 1859–December 25, 1859, August 22, 1859; Brooks, *Hosea Stout*, II, p. 699.

21. Brooks, *Hosea Stout*, II. p. 699.

22. F. J. Porter to Daniel Spencer, May 23, 1859, *Letters Sent*, Department of Utah, Records of the War Department.

23. Ibid.

24. Affidavit of Jeter Clinton (copy) (n.d.), *Jeter Clinton file*, Manuscript Section, C.H.O.

25. J. H. Marshall to A. S. Johnston, March 25, 1859, *Letters Sent*, Department of Utah, Records of the War Department.

26. Ibid.

27. Charles E. Brewer to General Johnston, March 24, 1859, *Albert Sidney Johnston Papers*, Barret Collection, Tulane University. Apparently the physicians at Camp Floyd were the first to introduce such drugs as potassium iodide, tincture of ferric chloride, and opiate. Dr. Seymour Bicknell Young recorded that these physicians were the first to use anesthesia in the territory "and from that time on anesthesia was brought across the plains by ox teams that hauled freight for the old Godbe Pitts Drug Company," Blanche E. Rose, "Early Utah Medical Practice," *Utah Historical Quarterly*, X (January, 1942): 22–24.

28. Historian's Office *Journal*, June 11, 1859–December 25, 1859, p. 159; *Valley Tan*, August 17, 1859.

29. *Valley Tan*, August 17, 1859.

30. Ibid.; Tracy, "The Utah War," p. 73.

31. Lorenzo Brown, "Journal," I, p. 347, Manuscript Section, C.H.O.

32. *Journal History*, August 11, 1859.

33. U. S. Senate Executive Document Number 2, 36th Congress, 1st Session, Serial No. 1024, p. 214.

34. Ibid.; Tracy, "The Utah War," p. 63.

35. U. S. Senate Executive Document Number 2, 36th Congress, 1st Session, Serial No. 1024, p. 214.

36. *Journal History*, August 16, 1859; *The Mountaineer*, September 17, 1859; this second Mormon newspaper made its appearance on August 27, and was published and edited by Seth Blair, James Ferguson, and Hosea Stout. Apparently, the official Church organ, the *Deseret News*, had spent so much of its energy answering the Gentile organ, the *Valley Tan*, that Brigham Young felt the need for a second publication. *The Mountaineer* disappeared from the stands in 1861. J. Cecil Alter, *Early Utah Journalism* (Salt Lake City: *Utah Historical Quarterly* (1938): 324.

37. Joel Terry to Brigham Young, August 30, 1859, *Brigham Young Papers*, Manuscript Section, C.H.O.; *Journal History*, August 30, 1859.

38. Joel Terry to Brigham Young, (no date), *Brigham Young Papers*, Manuscript Section, C.H.O. On October 1, 1888, Spencer was arrested and later tried for murder. However a predominantly Gentile jury brought in a verdict of not guilty. The presiding judge dismissed the panel with the following remarks: "Gentlemen of the jury. In the verdict that you have rendered you have doubtless done it honestly. But if this is not a case of murder speaking from a practice of over twenty-five years I have never seen one in a court of Justice. I am now of the opinion that Brother Young was exactly right in his opinion in argument to the jury, when he said that the law, in courts of justice in this county, was no protection, You may now be discharged." *The Salt Lake Sunday Herald*, May 12, 1889.

39. *Journal History*, August 16, 1859.

40. David Candland, "Documents," November [22], 1858, Manuscript Section, C.H.O.

41. Ibid.

42. *The Mountaineer*, June 9, 1860; *Deseret News*, June 6, 1860.

43. Farmer, *My Life with the Army*, p. 27.

44. Ibid.

45. Ibid.; *New York Times*, July 3, 1860.

46. Ibid. [*sic*]

47. Ibid. [*sic*]

NOTES TO CHAPTER 15

1. William Laud, "Diary," p. 6, Manuscript Section, C.H.O.

2. J. H. Beadle, *Life in Utah; or the Mysteries and Crimes of Mormonism Being an Expose of the Secret Rites and Ceremonies of the Latter-day Saints, with a Full and Authentic History of Polygamy and the Mormon Sect from Its Origin to the Present Time* (Philadelphia: National Printing Co., 1870), p. 198.

3. Leonard J. Arrington, *Great Basin Kingdom: Economic History of the Latter-day Saints, 1830–1900* (Lincoln: University of Nebraska Press, 1966), p. 81.

4. *Deseret News*, May 26, 1869.

5. *Journal History*, July 6 and July 8, 1858.

6. Ibid.

7. *New York Times*, October, 1858.

8. Beadle, *Life in Utah*, p. 199.

9. John Orton: "Diary" (typescript), Brigham Young University.

10. *New York Times*, August 13, 1858.

11. Arrington, *Great Basin Kingdom*, pp. 197–198.

12. Ibid.

13. Ibid.

14. Ibid.

15. Kate B. Carter, ed., *Heart Throbs of the West*, I (Salt Lake City: Daughters of the Utah Pioneers, 1951), p. 161.

16. *Journal History*, April 11, 1859.

17. Ibid., August 25, 1858.

18. Historian's Office *Journal:* December 13, 1858–May 31, 1859, Manuscript Section, C.H.O.

19. *Journal History*, April 11, 1859.

20. Ibid., October 26, 1858.

21. Brigham Young letter file, 1859, no other information available.

22. William Jennings, "Material Progress in Utah," p. 2, Bancroft Collection.

23. A brief history of the town of Wilson, Utah, pp. 2–3.

24. Edward W. Tullidge, *History of Salt Lake City and Its Founders* (Salt Lake City: Star Printing Company, 1886), p. 670.

25. *Valley Tan*, March 3 and 13, 1859.

26. Historian's Office *Journal*, June 1, 1859–December 25, 1859, July 1, 1859, Manuscript Section, C.H.O.

27. *Deseret News*, October 5, 1859.

28. Ibid., August 17, 1859.

29. R. L. Campbell to G. A. Smith, July 15, 1859, *Journal History*.

30. *Deseret News*, November 16, 1859.

31. Ibid.

32. Ibid., August 17, 1859.

33. *The Rocky Mountain News*, October 5, 1860.

34. Ibid.

35. Ibid., October 31, 1860.

36. *Journal History*, July 4, 1860.

37. Ibid.

38. Brigham Young to W. H. Hooper, March 8, 1860, *Brigham Young Papers*, Manuscript Section, C.H.O.

39. Arrington, *Great Basin Kingdom*, p. 208.

40. Brigham Young, *Addresses*, January 14, 1861, Manuscript Section, C.H.O.; "Elias Smith, Journal of a Pioneer Editor, March 6, 1859–September 23, 1863," edited by A. R. Mortensen, *Utah Historical Quarterly*, XXI (April, 1953): 154.

41. Ibid.

42. Brigham Young to Andrew Moffitt, July 18, 1861, *Brigham Young Papers*, Manuscript Section, C.H.O.; Brigham Young to George Q. Cannon, July 26, 1861, *Brigham Young Papers*, Manuscript Section, C.H.O.

43. Brigham Young to H. B. Clawson, July 24, 1861, *Brigham Young Papers*, Manuscript Section, C.H.O.

44. *Journal of Discourses*, XIII, p. 123.

NOTES TO CHAPTER 16

1. Phelps, "Diary," September 8, 1859.

2. *Returns of the Utah Expedition, 1857–1861*, Department of Utah, Records of the War Department.

3. S. Cooper to General A. S. Johnston, January 11, 1860, *Albert Sidney Johnston Papers*, Barret Collection, Tulane University.

4. A. S. Johnston to daughter, February 15, 1860, *Albert Sidney Johnston Papers*, Barret Collection.

5. Tracy, *The Utah War*, pp. 81–82.

6. Roland, *Albert Sidney Johnston*, p. 237.

7. Unidentified newspaper clipping, *Albert Sidney Johnston Papers*, Barret Collection, Tulane University.

8. Johnston to William Preston Johnston, November 3, 1858, *Albert Sidney Johnston Papers*, Barret Collection, Tulane University.

9. James Love to A. S. Johnston, June 11, 1860, *Albert Sidney Johnston Papers*, Barret Collection, Tulane University.

10. *Returns of the Utah Expedition, 1857–1861*, Department of Utah, Records of the War Department.

11. L. A. Williams to E. R. S. Canby, April 12, 1860, Department of Utah, Records of the War Department.

12. P. S. Geo. Cooke to L. Thomas, June 19, 1861, *Letters Sent*, Department of Utah, Records of the War Department.

13. Ibid.

14. Ibid.

15. General Order No. 13, *General Orders Book*, Department of Utah, Records of the War Department.

16. *War of the Rebellion*, Series 1, Volume 53, p. 492.

17. Smith, "Journal," p. 262.

18. Furniss, *Mormon Conflict*, p. 231.

19. Roland, *Albert Sidney Johnston*, p. 256.

20. Ibid., p. 260.

21. E. B. Long, ed., *Personal Memoirs of U. S. Grant* (New York: The World Publishing Company, 1952), p. 187.

22. Bruce Catton, *The Centennial History of the Civil War, Vol. 2: Terrible Swift Sword* (New York: Doubleday & Company, Inc., 1963), p. 225.

23. Roland, *Albert Sidney Johnston*, p. 336.

24. Ibid.

25. Catton, *Terrible Swift Sword*, p. 238.

26. Bruce Catton, *This Hallowed Ground* (New York: Doubleday & Company, Inc., 1955), p. 87.

27. Lynn I. Perrigo, *Our Spanish Southwest* (Dallas: Banks Upshaw and Company, 1960), p. 229.

28. Mark Mayo Boatner, *The Civil War Dictionary* (New York: David McKay Company, Inc., 1959), p. 97.

29. According to the figures compiled by Rodenbaugh, the Third, Sixth, Seventh, and Tenth Infantry suffered 448 deaths, while the Second Cavalry Second Dragoons listed 138 deaths.

30. House Document Number 5, 56th Congress, 2nd Session, Serial No. 4100, p. 153.

INDEX